CRACKNELL'S COMPANION

CASES &

Torts

Ninth Edition

D G CRACKNELL
LLB, Barrister, Middle Temple

OLD BAILEY PRESS

OLD BAILEY PRESS
200 Greyhound Road, London W14 9RY

First published 1961
Ninth edition 2000

ISBN 1 85836 060 9

British Library Cataloguing-in-Publication.

A CIP Catalogue record for this book is available from the British Library.

Printed and bound in Great Britain

Contents

Contents

Preface
to the Ninth Edition

The last edition was published four years ago and there have been many relevant developments since that time. Fifty case summaries have been added to the text and significant changes have been made to the statutes to take account of recent enactments, amendments and substitutions.

Statutes now covered include the Defamation Act 1996, the Damages Act 1996 and the Social Security (Recovery of Benefits) Act 1997.

As to cases, amongst those added to the text are *Director of Public Prosecutions v Jones* [1999] 2 All ER 257 (House of Lords: rights over public highways), *Roberts v Chief Constable of the Cheshire Constabulary* [1999] 2 All ER 326 (Court of Appeal: damages for false imprisonment) and *Platform Home Loans Ltd v Oyston Shipways Ltd* [1999] 1 All ER 833 (House of Lords: damages for negligent valuations).

Cases decided after the coming into force of the Supreme Court of Judicature Act 1873 are High Court decisions unless it is indicated otherwise.

Developments up to 1 July 1999 (including only statutory provisions in force on that date) have been taken into account.

D G CRACKNELL

November 1999

Preface
to the First Edition

This work is not intended to compete with other legal textbooks, but it is hoped that it will be of use as a companion to textbooks, lecture notes and correspondence courses. It is intended primarily for the student who does not have access to or time to take full advantage of a law library and finds it difficult to ascertain the facts of cases or the wording of Acts of Parliament to which he has been referred in the course of his studies. Other students are more fortunate in so far as they have the opportunity to make full use of a law library, but it is thought that even they might find it to be of assistance to have this work at hand, especially when revising for examinations.

An attempt has been made to include those cases and statutory provisions which are of importance to students. The statutes speak for themselves and the case notes contain an outline of the facts and a summary of those points in the judgment which are vital from a student's point of view. Cross-references have been made in order that the student who refers to one case will have little difficulty in finding others in which the same or a similar point arose. There is also a short glossary of Latin words and phrases that a student is likely to encounter during his reading.

D G CRACKNELL

July 1961

Cases

AB v South West Water Services Ltd [1993] 2 WLR 507
(Court of Appeal)

The plaintiffs suffered ill effects as a result of drinking the defendants' contaminated water. The defendants admitted liability for compensatory damages: could the plaintiffs also recover, inter alia, exemplary damages?

Held, they could not as public nuisance was not within the torts recognised in *Rookes* v *Barnard* as grounding a claim for exemplary damages.

Abbot v Refuge Assurance Co Ltd [1961] 3 All ER 1074

On the advice of an experienced counsel, to whom the facts had been put fully and fairly, the defendants preferred charges against the plaintiff and he was convicted of, inter alia, forgery, arising out of the payment to the plaintiff's secretary of the surrender value of a life insurance policy taken out by the plaintiff's wife with the defendants. The Court of Criminal Appeal held that the case against the plaintiff should not have been allowed to go to the jury and discharged him and he sought damages for malicious prosecution.

Held, taking into account all factors which should have been considered by the defendants when deciding whether to prosecute the plaintiff, and among them counsel's opinion which was a potent though not a conclusive factor, the plaintiff had not discharged the onus of proving that the defendants had not reasonable and probable cause to initiate the prosecution. The fact that the defendants were concerned to recover the money of which they had been defrauded did not constitute an improper motive or show malice on the part of the defendants in prosecuting because the law imposed a duty to prosecute for felony (ie forgery) before civil proceedings might be instituted. It followed that the plaintiff's action failed. (See also *Glinski* v *McIver*.)

Adams v Lancashire and Yorkshire Railway Co (1869) LR 4 CP 739

The plaintiff was a passenger on the defendants' railway on an afternoon in July. Owing to the defendants' negligence the door of the compartment would not stay shut and when the plaintiff was making yet another attempt to secure it he fell out of the train and received injuries in respect of which he claimed damages. There was room in the carriage for the defendant to sit away from the door and at the time of the accident the train was three minutes' journey from the next station.

Held, the plaintiff could not succeed as the inconvenience caused by the opening of the door was not so great as to make it reasonable for him to run the risk of attempting to shut it. (But see *Sayers v Harlow Urban District Council.*)

Adams v Ursell [1913] 1 Ch 269

Using 'the most approved appliances', the defendant established a fried fish shop in a working-class district but next to the plaintiff's house which was of a rather better character. The plaintiff brought an action to restrain the nuisance caused by odour and vapour from the defendant's premises and the defendant urged that an injunction should not be granted as it would cause great hardship to the poor people who bought food at his shop.

Held, the plaintiff would succeed as the defendant could carry on his business in a more suitable place somewhere in the neighbourhood. It did not follow 'that because a fried fish shop is a nuisance in one place it is a nuisance in another' (*per* SWINFEN EADY J).

Aitchison v Page Motors Ltd (1953) 154 LT 128

By arrangement with the plaintiff, the defendants, who were garage proprietors, sent her car to the manufacturers for repair. When the repairs were completed the defendants' service manager went to collect the car but, instead of driving straight to the defendants' garage, drove it elsewhere and in so doing negligently collided with a bus, wrecking the car in the process.

Held, the defendants were answerable to the plaintiff for the loss of her car. The service manager was acting within his authority and in the course of his employment when he fetched the car and the defendants were liable for the consequences of the negligent way in which he performed that service. (But see *Sanderson v Collins* and *Hilton v Thomas Burton (Rhodes) Ltd.*)

Al-Nakib Investments (Jersey) Ltd v Longcroft [1990] 3 All ER 321

The plaintiff shareholder subscribed for shares by way of a rights issue and some months later he bought more shares through the stock market. He subsequently alleged that he had subscribed for and bought the shares relying on a prospectus, issued by the defendant directors, containing misrepresentations.

Held, the defendants had owed the plaintiff a duty of care in respect of his subscription but not where he had used the prospectus for a different purpose, eg buying shares on the stock market. (Applied: *Smith v Eric S Bush* and *Caparo Industries plc v Dickman.*)

Al Saudi Banque v Clark Pixley [1989] 3 All ER 361

The plaintiff banks made loans or further loans to a company, allegedly in reliance on the company's accounts which had been audited by the defendants. After the company had been compulsorily wound up and the plaintiffs had lost their money, they claimed damages in negligence alleging that the accounts had not reflected a true and fair view of the company's affairs.

Held, their action would be dismissed as there was not a sufficiently close or direct relationship between the parties to give rise to the degree of proximity necessary to establish a duty of care on the part of the defendants. (Applied: *Smith v Eric S Bush*; approved in *Caparo Industries plc v Dickman.*)

Alcock v Chief Constable of the South Yorkshire Police
[1991] 4 All ER 907 (House of Lords)

In the Hillsborough Stadium disaster, 95 spectators were crushed to death and over 400 injured. Although suffering or dying recognisable individuals were not depicted, scenes from the ground were broadcast live on television and later as news items. Reports were also given on radio. The sixteen plaintiffs all had relatives (or, in one case, a fiance) in the area of the disaster; some of the plaintiffs had been in other parts of the ground. The relatives of thirteen plaintiffs were killed, two were injured and one escaped unhurt. The defendant (who was responsible for crowd control) admitted liability in negligence in respect of those who were killed or injured but, when the plaintiffs claimed damages for nervous shock resulting in psychiatric illness alleged to have been caused by seeing or hearing news of the disaster, he denied that he had owed them any duty of care.

Held, the plaintiffs' claims could not succeed as they had failed to satisfy both the tests of reasonable foreseeability and of proximity. 'What [is] in issue is whether the defendant owed any duty in tort to the plaintiffs to avoid causing the type of injury of which each plaintiff complains. In essence this involves answering the twin questions of (a) whether injury of this sort to each particular plaintiff was a reasonably foreseeable consequence of the acts or omissions constituting the breach of duty to the primary victim and (b) whether there existed between the defendant and each plaintiff that degree of directness or proximity necessary to establish liability' (*per* LORD OLIVER OF AYLMERTON). (Applied in *McFarlane v EE Caledonia Ltd* and *White v Chief Constable of the South Yorkshire Police*; but see *McLoughlin v O'Brian*.)

Alexander v North Eastern Railway Co (1865) 6 B & S 340

In a notice which was intended to act as a caution, the defendant railway company stated that the plaintiff had been fined £9 1s 10d, including costs, with an alternative of three weeks' imprisonment, for refusing to pay his fare. The actual alternative was two weeks' imprisonment. The plaintiff brought an action for libel and the defence relied upon the substantial and sufficient accuracy and truth of the notice.

Held, it was for the jury to decide whether the statement was substantially true and in this case they thought that it was. (See also Defamation Act 1952, s5.)

Alexandrou v Oxford [1993] 4 All ER 328 (Court of Appeal)

The plaintiff's shop was burgled, and an alarm was activated at both the shop and the local police station. Two police officers checked the premises but failed to inspect the rear of the shop where the burglars had forced entry. Some hours later a substantial amount of goods was removed from the shop. The plaintiff sued the chief constable alleging that the police had been negligent in failing to take adequate precautions to discover why the alarm had been activated and in assuming that it was a false alarm. The trial judge found as a fact that the theft would have been prevented had the police officers properly inspected the rear of the building and were thus in breach of the duty of care they owed to the plaintiff.

Held, the chief constable's appeal would be allowed. 'If there is a duty of care it is ... owed to all members of the public who give information of a suspected crime against themselves or their property ... on the facts of this case ... there was no such special relationship between the plaintiff and the police as was present in the *Dorset Yacht* case' (*per* GLIDEWELL LJ). (Applied: *Hill v Chief Constable of West Yorkshire*; distinguished: *Home Office v Dorset Yacht Co Ltd*; see also *Osman v Ferguson*.)

Allen v Gulf Oil Refining Ltd [1981] 1 All ER 353 (House of Lords)

A private Act of Parliament authorised Gulf Oil to carry out certain works and to acquire compulsorily certain land near Milford Haven in order that 'further facilities for the importation of crude oil and petroleum products and for their refinement should be made available.' After the refinery was in operation, a person living nearby alleged that it caused a nuisance by smell, noise and vibration.

Held, Gulf Oil were entitled to statutory immunity in respect of any nuisance which they were able to prove was an inevitable result of constructing and operating on the site a refinery which conformed with Parliament's intention. To the extent that any actual nuisance exceeded such inevitable nuisance, Gulf Oil would be liable. (Applied in *Gillingham Borough Council v Medway (Chatham) Dock Co Ltd.*)

Alliance and Leicester Building Society v Edgestop Ltd
[1994] 2 All ER 38

It was alleged that an employee of the defendant estate agents had fraudulently overvalued certain hotels in order to procure the plaintiffs to make substantial loans and that the defendants were vicariously liable in deceit. The defendants pleaded contributory negligence, pursuant to s1(1) of the Law Reform (Contributory Negligence) Act 1945.

Held, this defence had been correctly struck out as contributory negligence is not a defence to an action for deceit at common law and nothing in the 1945 Act has affected that position. (Distinguished: *Gran Gelato Ltd v Richcliff (Group) Ltd.*)

Ancell v McDermott [1993] 4 All ER 355 (Court of Appeal)

The first defendant drove over an obstruction in the road, rupturing his fuel tank. He continued to drive, leaving a trail of diesel fuel on the road. Some officers of Hertfordshire police noticed the diesel fuel and notified Bedfordshire police of the spillage. Some 20 minutes after the spillage commenced an officer of Bedfordshire police noticed the spillage and reported it to Bedfordshire highways department. Ten minutes later a car skidded on the diesel fuel and was involved in a collision. The passengers and husband of the driver who was killed as a result sued (inter alia) the Hertfordshire and Bedfordshire chief constables. The chief constables applied to strike out the claims against them, but this was refused.

Held, the chief constables' appeals would be allowed. The police were under no duty of care to protect road users from, or to warn them of, hazards discovered by the police on the highway and there was here no special relationship between the plaintiffs and the police giving rise to an exceptional duty to prevent harm from dangers created by another. (Approved: *Clough v Bussan.*)

Anderson v Gorrie [1895] 1 QB 668 (Court of Appeal)

The defendant, a judge of the Supreme Court of Trinidad and Tobago, was found to have acted oppressively and maliciously, to the prejudice of the plaintiff and to the perversion of justice, in so far as he committed the plaintiff for contempt of court and held him to excessive bail.

Held, the plaintiff was not entitled to damages as the defendant, a judge of a court of record, had acted in his judicial capacity

Anderson (W B) & Sons Ltd v Rhodes (Liverpool) Ltd [1967] 2 All ER 850

T bought potatoes from R, a wholesaler. T became heavily indebted to R who, due to bad book-keeping, did not know of the state of T's account. The plaintiffs sought a reference as to T's credit from R, who replied 'They are all right'. At this time, unknown to R, T owed him £2,500. After making several purchases from the plaintiffs on credit, T became insolvent. The plaintiffs sued R for damages for negligence in making the statement as to T's creditworthiness.

Held, the claim would succeed. R owed the plaintiffs a duty of care and was liable for the negligent statement. Section 6 of the Statute of Frauds Amendment Act 1828 did not constitute a defence to a claim based on negligence. (See also *Hedley Byrne & Co Ltd v Heller & Partners Ltd.*)

Andrews v Hopkinson [1956] 3 All ER 422

The plaintiff obtained a 1934 Standard saloon motor car from the defendant. A week later, the steering mechanism failed and, as a result, the plaintiff was seriously injured in a collision with a lorry.

Held, the plaintiff was entitled to damages for the negligence of the defendant in delivering to the plaintiff for use on the road a car which was in a dangerous condition, as the defect could have been discovered by reasonable diligence on the part of the defendant and he had failed either to have the car examined or to warn the plaintiff that it had not been examined.

Andrews v *Mockford* [1896] 1 QB 372 (Court of Appeal)

The defendants promoted the Sutherland Reef Co and issued a prospectus which contained a fraudulent statement as to the yield of certain gold-bearing reefs. The plaintiff kept this by him and after reading a paragraph in the *Financial News* concerning a rich discovery, news inspired by a telegram from the son of one of the defendants which, to the defendants' knowledge, contained false statements, he bought 50 shares in the market. It was found that the purpose of the prospectus and telegram was to persuade the plaintiff to buy shares in the market, not merely to induce him to apply for shares in the company which, in the event, was wound up within a year.

Held, the plaintiff was entitled to recover his losses as in these circumstances the function of the prospectus was not exhausted. (See also *Langridge* v *Levy*.)

Andrews v *Schooling* [1991] 3 All ER 723 (Court of Appeal)

Having acquired two adjacent semi-detached houses the defendants converted them into flats, although they only painted the walls of the cellar. The plaintiff having been granted a long lease of one of the flats, including the cellar, she discovered damp penetration arising from the fact that the cellar had an inadequate damp-proofing system. She claimed damages for, inter alia, breach of the duty imposed by s1 of the Defective Premises Act 1972.

Held, her claim would be successful as s1(1) of the 1972 Act imposes liability for non-feasance as well as misfeasance and, without proper damp-proofing, the flat was unfit for habitation for the purposes of that provision.

Anns v *Merton London Borough Council* [1977] 2 All ER 492 (House of Lords)

A group of seven long leaseholders (only two being original lessees) of residential properties in a two storey block sued the local authority and the builders of the block for negligence, on the basis that inadequate foundations had caused structural damage to their properties. Had the local authority owed the plaintiffs a duty of care?

Held, (1) local authorities are under a duty to give proper consideration to the question whether they should inspect foundations, on the basis of powers contained in the Public Health Act 1936. (2) When an inspection is carried out, it must be made with reasonable care. To found a negligence claim, a plaintiff must prove that the action taken was not within the limits of a discretion bona fide exercised. (3) The duty is owed to owners or occupiers of the house. (4) The duty is to take reasonable care to secure that the builders do not cover in foundations which do not comply with byelaw requirements. (5) Where damage is caused to the house, the cause of action arises, for the purpose of the Limitation Act, when the state of the building is such that there is present or imminent danger to the health or safety of persons occupying it. (See also *Dutton* v *Bognor Regis Urban District Council* and *East Suffolk Rivers Catchment Board* v *Kent*; but see *Murphy* v *Brentwood District Council*.)

Arsenson v Casson, Beckman, Rutley & Co [1975] 3 All ER 901 (House of Lords)

The plaintiff agreed to sell his shares in a company to the first defendant at a value to be determined by the company's auditors, the second defendants, whose valuation acting as experts and not as arbitrators should be final and binding on all parties. The plaintiff sought inter alia to claim in negligence against the second defendants on the ground that their valuation was erroneous. The second defendants argued that the statement of claim disclosed no reasonable cause of action.

Held, the functions of the second defendants as valuers were entirely different from the functions performed by a judge. Therefore, there were no grounds of public policy which could justify any immunity from suit. Quaere, whether the second defendants would have been immune had they been appointed to act as arbitrators. Per Lord Simon: the immunity of an arbitrator depends upon there being a formulated dispute between at least two parties which his decision is required to resolve. (See also *Sutcliffe v Thackrah*.)

Armagas Ltd v Mundogas SA, The Ocean Frost [1986] 2 All ER 385 (House of Lords)

In order to secure the sale of a ship to the plaintiffs, the defendants' vice-president (transportation) and chartering manager, one Magelssen, told them that he had express authority to charter the ship back for three years. This was not the case and the plaintiffs were aware that Magelssen had no general authority to enter into charters of this kind. When the defendants failed to honour a three-year charter the plaintiffs contended that they (the defendants) were vicariously liable for Magelssen's deceit.

Held, their claim would fail as the defendants had done nothing to represent that Magelssen had the necessary specific authority to enter into the charter. (Applied *Lloyd v Grace Smith & Co.*)

Armory v Delamirie (1721) 1 Stra 505

A chimney sweeper's boy found a jewel set in a socket. He took his find to a goldsmith who refused to return the jewel. The boy brought an action for trover.

Held, he would succeed as he had such a property in the jewel as would enable him to keep it against all but the rightful owner. By way of damages, he should recover the value of the best jewel that would fit the socket. (See also *Moffat v Kazana* and *Bridges v Hawksworth*.)

Ashby v White (1703) 2 Ld Raym 938

The vote of a man who was entitled to vote was wrongfully refused by a returning officer.

Held, he was entitled to damages. 'If a man gives another a cuff on the ear, though it cost him nothing … yet he shall have his action, for it is a personal injury' (*per* HOLT CJ). (See also *Constantine v Imperial London Hotels Ltd.*)

Ashton v Jennings (1675) 1 Freem KB 393

The defendant was a justice of the peace and an esquire; the plaintiff was a doctor of divinity. Their wives disagreed as to which of them should have precedence at a funeral and the defendant's wife gently laid hands upon the wife of the plaintiff to remove her.

Held, her action constituted a battery. (But see *Coward v Baddeley*.)

Ashton v Turner [1980] 3 All ER 870

After spending the evening together drinking heavily, the plaintiff persuaded his friend to join him in a burglary. They were disturbed and chased; their car crashed at high speed and the plaintiff – the passenger – sustained serious injuries. The friend was convicted of burglary, dangerous driving and driving with more than the permitted amount of alcohol in his blood and, inter alia, the plaintiff sued him in negligence.

Held, as a matter of public policy, the law would, in certain circumstances, refuse to recognise the existence of duty of care owed by one participant in a crime to another participant in the same crime in respect of an act done in connection with the commission of that crime and this was such a case. In any case, the maxim volenti non fit injuria applied and afforded the friend a complete defence. (See also *Pitts v Hunt*.)

Associated Newspapers plc v Insert Media Ltd [1991] 3 All ER 535 (Court of Appeal)

By arrangement with newspaper distributors and retailers, the defendants proposed to insert detached advertising leaflets and samples in the plaintiffs' newspapers. If necessary, the defendants were prepared to print a disclaimer on the inserts to the effect that they were not approved by the plaintiffs.

Held, the plaintiffs were entitled to an injunction restraining the proposed activity as, on the facts, a substantial body of the public at large would perceive or assume that the inserts were made by the plaintiffs or with their authority. The proposed disclaimer would be unlikely to come to readers' attention and, if it did, it was likely to confuse them. 'Since they have been purchased [the newspapers] are the property of the newsagents and there can be no limit on the uses which they make of their papers provided that there is no actionable passing off' (*per* SIR NICOLAS BROWNE-WILKINSON V-C). (See also *Erven Warnink BV v J Townend & Sons (Hull) Ltd.*)

Astaire v Campling [1965] 3 All ER 666

An article in *The People* named the plaintiff and stated that he was the 'man known in the fight game as "Mr X"'. In an action for libel the plaintiff pleaded eight innuendoes and in support of them relied on statements made in papers other than *The People* and in a BBC interview before or on the same day as the alleged libel. These statements contained disparaging references to a 'Mr X' and a syndicate in connection with British boxing.

Held, the relevant paragraphs of the plaintiff's statement of claim would be struck out as the innuendoes were not derived from the article published in *The People*. 'The plaintiff is not entitled by adopting the device of pleading innuendoes to recover from the defendants damages for defamatory statements made about him by other persons which are not either expressly or by implication approved, adopted or repeated in the statement by the defendants in respect of which the action is brought' (*per* DIPLOCK LJ). (See also *Tolley v J S Fry & Sons Ltd*.)

Atkinson v Newcastle and Gateshead Waterworks Co
(1877) 2 Ex D 441 (Court of Appeal)

Statute required the defendant water company to keep a certain pressure in their pipes and, in the event of their failure to do so, imposed a penalty of £10. Because the supply was not so maintained the plaintiff's timber-yard and saw mills were burnt down.

Held, the statute did not entitle the plaintiff to bring an action for damages. (But see *Groves v Lord Wimborne*.)

Attia v British Gas plc [1987] 3 All ER 455 (Court of Appeal)

Having engaged the defendants to install central heating in her house, the plaintiff returned home to see smoke pouring from the loft. The fire raged for over four hours and the house and contents were extensively damaged. The defendants admitted liability but disputed the plaintiff's claim for damages for nervous shock and psychological reaction.

Held, the plaintiff would be entitled to succeed if she could prove psychiatric damage (not merely grief, sorrow or emotional distress) and the psychiatric damage was a reasonably foreseeable consequence of the defendants' negligence. (But see *Alcock v Chief Constable of the South Yorkshire Police*.)

Attorney-General v Corke [1933] Ch 89

The owner of a disused brickfield permitted persons to bring caravans on to the field and to live in them there on payment of a weekly rent. There was evidence that the occupants of the caravans committed acts in the neighbourhood of, but not on, the brickfield which amounted to nuisance and a menace to health.

Held, applying the principle of *Rylands v Fletcher*, the owner of the brickfield would be restrained by injunction from permitting the camp inhabitants from engaging in the activities of which complaint was made. (See also *Shiffman v Order of St John* and *A-G v PYA Quarries Ltd*; but see *Smith v Scott*.)

Attorney-General (on the relation of Glamorgan County Council and Portardawe Rural District Council) v PYA Quarries Ltd
[1957] 1 All ER 894 (Court of Appeal)

Quarry owners so conducted their operations that neighbouring householders were discomfited by vibration from explosions and by the dust which emanated from the quarry in dry weather. There was evidence that nuisance from vibration and dust could be avoided by the exercise of proper care.

Held, the vibrations and the dust were a public nuisance and an injunction had been rightly granted to restrain the quarry owners from carrying on their business in such a manner as 'to occasion a nuisance to Her Majesty's subjects by dust or by vibration'. (See also *Attorney-General v Corke*; but see *Rose v Miles*.)

Atwell v Michael Perry & Co [1998] 4 All ER 65

The second defendant, a barrister, represented the plaintiff in civil proceedings which the plaintiff lost at that stage. In an action for damages, the plaintiff alleged that the second defendant had been negligent in failing to take a particular point (which, on appeal, was taken successfully by another barrister) and in advising that an appeal would have no reasonable prospect of success.

Held, the claim relating to the particular point would be struck out since the second defendant was there protected by an advocate's immunity. Although the advice relating to appeal prospects was not covered by immunity, on the facts as pleaded that claim would also be struck out. 'If it is right for public policy reasons to hold counsel immune for the manner in which he conducted the case in court, it is, on the pleaded facts of this case, right to hold counsel immune against the inadequacies in his pre-trial deliberations as to how he should conduct the case. ... In my opinion, there is no distinction of any legitimacy to be drawn between an advice on the prospects of an appeal, on the one hand, and an advice as to whether an action should be brought on the other hand. It is accepted, I think, that an advice that an action should not be brought which leads to the action not being brought and loss being suffered accordingly may be the subject of a negligence action brought against the incompetent professional who gave the advice' (*per* SIR RICHARD SCOTT V-C). (Applied: *Rondel v Worsley* and *Saif Ali v Sydney Mitchell & Co.*)

Baker v T E Hopkins & Son Ltd See Ward v T E Hopkins & Son Ltd

Baker v Willoughby [1969] 3 All ER 1528 (House of Lords)

The defendant negligently injured the plaintiff's left leg, causing stiffness, and some loss of amenity and earning capacity. Shortly before the trial, the plaintiff's left leg had to be amputated after a shooting by bank robbers. The defendant argued that the second injury obliterated the effects of the first.

Held, the injury sustained in the robbery should be ignored, because far from reducing the plaintiff's disability, the second injury merely became a concurrent cause of the disabilities caused by the defendant. 'A man is not compensated for the physical injury; he is compensated for the loss which he suffers as a result of that injury. His loss is not having a stiff leg, it is his inability to lead a full life' (*per* LORD REID). (But see *Jobling v Associated Dairies Ltd.*)

Balfour v *Barty-King* [1957] 1 All ER 156 (Court of Appeal)

Part of a large country house had been converted into separate dwelling-houses. The plaintiff owned one of these and the defendants occupied the adjoining premises which had also been converted. There was a severe frost and the pipes in the defendants' loft became frozen. At the request of the defendants, some builders undertook to thaw the pipes and their workmen, neither of whom was a plumber, set about their task with a blow-lamp which, in the circumstances, was a highly dangerous operation. Some felt lagging caught fire and the flames spread to the plaintiff's premises and caused a great amount of damage.

Held, the defendants were liable because the fire was caused by the negligence of the independent contractors who were invited by them to do the work and for this reason, the fire did not begin 'accidentally' within the meaning of s86 of the Fires Prevention (Metropolis) Act 1774, and it was not the act of a stranger. (See also *Sturge* v *Hackett*.)

Banque Financière de la Cité SA v *Westgate Insurance Co Ltd* [1990] 2 All ER 947 (House of Lords)

The appellant banks made substantial loans to one Ballestero who then disappeared. The appellants' brokers (through a dishonest servant) had deceived the banks into believing that they had insurance cover to protect them in the event of the non-payment of the loans and the respondents (through one of their employees) had become aware of this fraud. Were the respondents, the appellants' insurers, under a duty of care to disclose to the appellants the brokers' deception?

Held, they were not: failure to disclose did not amount to the breach of any legal duty. In any case, the appellants would not have been able to recover the amount of the loans under the insurance policies because they (the policies) contained a fraud exemption clause. The brokers' fraud was therefore the cause of the loans to Ballestero, but not the cause of their loss. (Distinguished in *South Australia Asset Management Corp* v *York Montague Ltd*.)

Barnes v *Hampshire County Council* [1969] 3 All ER 746

The plaintiff aged five was injured in a road accident while on her way home from a school maintained by the defendants. The school normally closed at 3.30, and the plaintiff's mother always waited for her at the gate. On the day of the accident the school closed at 3.25 and the plaintiff, finding no one to meet her, started for home alone.

Held, the defendants were under a duty not to release the children before 3.30. Although a premature release would very seldom cause an accident, it could, as on this occasion, foreseeably do so. The defendants were liable. (See also *Carmarthenshire County Council* v *Lewis*.)

Barnett v *Chelsea and Kensington Hospital Management Committee* [1968] 1 All ER 1068

A night watchman was taken to a hospital complaining of vomiting. The duty casualty officer refused to see him, and told him to go home and get his own doctor. A few hours later, he died of arsenical poisoning.

Held, the doctor was negligent in not seeing the man, but the death was not the result of that negligence. Even had the doctor seen him, he would have died. Accordingly, the hospital was not liable. (See also *Cassidy* v *Minister of Health*.)

Barrett v *Enfield London Borough Council* (1999) The Times 18 June; [1999] 3 All ER 193 (House of Lords)

The plaintiff had spent most of his childhood in local authority care and he alleged that, by virtue of the authority's negligence in failing, inter alia, to place him for adoption, to place him in suitable foster homes and to handle properly his reintroduction to his mother, he had suffered psychiatric injury in adult life. Should his action for damages have been struck out?

Held, it should not: the difficult questions of law to which the claim gave rise should be considered in the light of the actual (as opposed to hypothetical) facts. LORD SLYNN OF HADLEY said that in *X and Others (Minors)* v *Bedfordshire County Council* [1995] 3 All ER 353 the House of Lords had established that decisions by local authorities whether or not to take a child into care were not ones which the courts would review by way of a claim for damages in negligence. The question in the instant case was different, since the child had already been taken into care. The allegations were largely directed to the way in which the powers of the local authority had been exercised. It was arguable, and that was all that was now needed, that if some of the allegations were made out a duty of care had been owed and had been broken. Other allegations involved the exercise of a discretion which the court might consider to be not justiciable, eg, whether it was right to arrange adoption at all, although the question of whether adoption was ever considered and if not, why not, might be a matter for investigation in a claim of negligence. It did not follow that because the court should be slow to hold that a child could sue its parents for negligent decisions in its upbringing that the same should apply necessarily to all acts of a local authority. (But see *Phelps* v *Hillingdon London Borough Council*.)

Basébé v *Matthews* (1867) LR 2 CP 684

It was alleged that the defendant, falsely and maliciously, and without reasonable or probable cause, appeared before the magistrate and, by making false, scandalous, and malicious statements caused the justice wrongfully to convict the plaintiff of assaulting and beating her. The plaintiff claimed damages for malicious prosecution.

Held, the action would fail as the criminal proceeding had not been determined in favour of the accused. It made no difference that the plaintiff had no right of appeal against the conviction.

Batty v *Metropolitan Property Realizations Ltd* [1978] 2 All ER 445 (Court of Appeal)

Land consisting of a plateau and steep slope was sold to builders who in turn sold it to a development company. They agreed that the builders would construct houses on the land, financed by the company who would also find eventual purchasers. The plaintiffs bought one of the houses on a 999 year lease and the company sold the reversion to the builders. After three years a severe land slip damaged the plaintiffs' garden and, when the plaintiffs sued, inter alia, the builders and the company the trial judge found that the house itself had been doomed from the outset because the land on which it was built was unstable. Both claims were successful, but against the company only in contract.

Held, the plaintiffs were entitled to succeed against the company also in tort as the company had been in breach of its common law duty to examine the site with reasonable care to see whether a house fit for habitation could safely be built there. Similarly, although the builders did not own the land at the time, they had owed a duty to potential occupiers to act as a careful and competent builder would have acted in examining and investigating the land on which they proposed to build the house and they had been in breach of this duty. (Doubted in *D & F Estates Ltd v Church Commissioners for England*; see also *Murphy v Brentwood District Council*.)

Baume & Co Ltd v A H Moore Ltd [1958] 2 All ER 113 (Court of Appeal)

The plaintiffs, Baume & Co Ltd, had traded in England as sellers of watches for some 100 years and since 1878 the word 'Baume' had been their registered trade mark. The defendants, A H Moore Ltd, began to import and sell watches bearing the mark 'Baume & Mercier, Geneve' and the plaintiffs claimed, inter alia, that this use of the word 'Baume' was calculated to pass off the goods sold by the defendants as the plaintiffs' goods. The watches imported and sold by the defendants were made by a Swiss company known as Baume & Mercier SA, and it was established that the use by the defendants of the word 'Baume' was an honest use by them of the makers' own name.

Held, this use would be restrained by injunction as there was a real probability that watches marked 'Baume & Mercier, Geneve' would be associated with the plaintiffs' goods. (See also *Bollinger (J) v Costa Brava Wine Co Ltd (No 2)*.)

Baxter v Camden London Borough Council [1999] 1 All ER 237 (Court of Appeal)

The defendants converted a Victorian house into three flats, one on each floor. The only noise barriers were ceilings and wooden floors: sound insulation regulations did not then extend to London. The question arose: Where tenants of the same landlord are adjoining occupiers of flats can their landlord be liable in nuisance where one tenant's reasonable use and enjoyment of his flat is interfered with by noise from the ordinary use of the adjoining flat?

Held, the landlord could not be so liable. '... the authorities ... show that ordinary use of residential premises without more is not capable of amounting to a nuisance. Ordinary use may only give rise to a nuisance if it is unusual or unreasonable having regard to the purpose for which the premises were constructed ... the conversion in 1975 reduced the sound insulation between the floors but by how much one cannot tell. What is clear ... is that it did not change the purpose for which the house was used. There was nothing unusual or unreasonable about the conversion which was done in accordance with the building standards of the time' (*per* TUCKEY J). NB: This decision was affirmed by the House of Lords [1999] 4 All ER 449. (See also *Smith v Scott*.)

Bayley v Manchester, Sheffield and Lincolnshire Railway Co (1873) LR 8 CP 148

One of the defendants' porters mistakenly believed that a passenger, the plaintiff, was in the wrong train. As the train was moving off he violently pulled the plaintiff out of the carriage and caused him to fall down on the platform.

Held, the defendants were liable to the plaintiff in respect of his injuries as the porter had acted within the course of his employment. (See also *Dyer v Munday*.)

Beach v Freeson [1971] 2 All ER 854

The defendant, a Member of Parliament, wrote letters to the Law Society and to the Lord Chancellor saying that he had been requested by one of his constituents to refer a firm of solicitors, the plaintiffs, for investigation. The plaintiffs sued for libel.

Held, the letters were both published on occasions of qualified privilege. The defendant had a moral or social duty in passing his constituent's complaint on to the proper quarter. The Law Society had an interest in receiving it as the solicitors' disciplinary body. The Lord Chancellor had an interest in receiving it as affecting the administration of justice. 'The judge must ... do his best in the light of such evidence as he has, coupled with his own views as to what the defendant's duties, moral or social, were in the circumstances' (*per* GEOFFREY LANE J).

Bebee v Sales (1916) 32 TLR 413

A father gave his 15 year old son an airgun for a Christmas present. A neighbour complained that the boy had smashed a window with it but the father let him retain possession of the gun; he afterwards shot another boy in the eye.

Held, the father was liable for negligently allowing his son to keep and use a dangerous weapon. (But see *Gorely v Codd*.)

Benham v Gambling [1941] 1 All ER 7 (House of Lords)

A child of 2½ years of age was involved in a road accident and died on the same day. His father and administrator brought an action against the negligent driver claiming damages for loss of expectation of life and the question arose as to how these damages were to be assessed.

Held, actuarial assessment is normally irrelevant, as are future pecuniary prospects, wealth and social status, as the court must arrive at a reasonable figure for the loss of prospective happiness. Damages awarded on this ground should always be very moderate: in this case £200. (But see *Pickett v British Rail Engineering Ltd* and s1 of the Administration of Justice Act 1982.)

Beoco Ltd v Alfa Laval Co Ltd [1994] 4 All ER 464 (Court of Appeal)

The question arose, inter alia, whether the plaintiffs could recover damages which they would have incurred by way of loss of profit on lost production during the period necessary to repair the defect in a heat exchanger supplied by the defendants and caused by their breach of contract, where because of a supervening event (the negligence of the plaintiffs' engineers) those repairs were not carried out or were subsumed in other more extensive repairs.

Held, the same principles applied in contract as in tort and the answer was therefore in the negative. (See also *Jobling* v *Associated Dairies Ltd*.)

Berkoff v Burchill [1996] 4 All ER 1008 (Court of Appeal)

The plaintiff actor, director and writer was well known for his work on stage, screen and television. It was alleged that words used in articles written by the first defendant and published by the second defendant in the *Sunday Times* conveyed the meaning that the plaintiff was hideously ugly. Were these words capable of being defamatory?

Held, they were. '... it would, in my view, be open to a jury to conclude that in the context the remarks about Mr Berkoff gave the impression that he was not merely physically unattractive in appearance but actually repulsive. It seems to me that to say this of someone in the public eye who makes his living, in part at least, as an actor, is capable of lowering his standing in the estimation of the public and of making him an object of ridicule' (*per* NEILL LJ). (See also *Sim* v *Stretch*.)

Bernstein (Lord) v Skyviews and General Ltd [1977] 2 All ER 902

The defendant company used an aircraft to fly over the plaintiff's country house for the purpose of photographing it.

Held, the plaintiff's action for trespass failed, since the rights of a landowner in the air space above his land are restricted to such height as is necessary for the ordinary use and enjoyment of his land and the structures upon it, and the defendant's flight was hundreds of feet above the ground. Apart from common law, the defendant was protected by s40(1) of the Civil Aviation Act 1949, which exempted certain flights by aircraft from actions in trespass or nuisance. The taking of photographs cannot of itself make an act a trespass. (But see *Clifton* v *Viscount Bury*.)

Berry v British Transport Commission [1961] 3 All ER 65 (Court of Appeal)

The plaintiff was convicted of pulling the communication cord on a train without reasonable and sufficient cause but her appeal to quarter sessions against conviction was allowed and she was awarded 15 guineas costs. In an action for damages for malicious prosecution she alleged as special damage the difference between her actual costs and the amount awarded.

Held, the special damage alleged was sufficient in law to support an action for malicious prosecution as an award of costs in a case of this kind (ie in criminal as opposed to civil proceedings) is not intended necessarily to compensate a successful appellant.

Best v Samuel Fox & Co Ltd [1952] 2 All ER 394 (House of Lords)

As a result of an accident which occurred in the course of his employment due to the negligence of his employers, a married man became incapable of sexual intercourse. His wife claimed damages for loss of her husband's consortium.

Held, the wife was not entitled to bring an action of this kind.

Billings (A C) & Sons Ltd v Riden [1957] 3 All ER 1 (House of Lords)

The appellants, a firm of building contractors, were employed to remove a sloping ramp leading to the front door of a house and the appellants' workmen advised the caretaker's wife that while the work was in progress it was best to approach the house by a route across the forecourt of the neighbouring house. This route passed within a very few feet of a small sunken area on that property and one night, after dark, the respondent, a woman of 71 years of age who had visited the caretaker's wife, sought to use it to leave the premises, but she fell into the sunken area and was injured.

Held, the respondent was entitled to recover damages for negligence as the appellants were in breach of the ordinary duty to take reasonable care that all persons who might be expected to visit the premises at which they were working should not be exposed to danger by their acts.

Bird v Jones (1845) 7 QB 742

A part of Hammersmith Bridge, which was normally used as a public footpath, was wrongfully enclosed by the defendants for the benefit of spectators watching a boat race. The plaintiff wanted to cross the bridge and insisted on using the footpath which, on this occasion, had been closed to the public. He climbed the temporary fence, but two policemen said that he could not go any further and that if he wanted to cross the bridge he would have to do so on the other side. He remained in the enclosure for more than half an hour and claimed to be entitled to damages for false imprisonment.

Held, his action would not succeed as a way of escape had been open to him if he chose to use it.

Blagg v Sturt (1846) 10 QB 899

An inhabitant of St Albans wrote to the Home Secretary in such terms as to suggest that the clerk to the justices of the peace for that borough had acted improperly and dishonestly. The clerk to the justices sued for libel.

Held, he should succeed. The letter was not privileged as the Home Secretary had 'no direct authority in respect of the matter complained of, and was not a competent tribunal to receive the application' (*per* LORD DENMAN CJ). (But see *Beach v Freeson*.)

Blake v *Barnard* (1840) 9 C & P 626

In an action for an assault it was alleged that the defendant 'presented a certain pistol loaded with gunpowder, ball, and shot at the plaintiff, and threatened and offered therewith to shoot the plaintiff and blow out his brains'.

Held, this was an assault unless the plaintiff failed to prove that the pistol was in fact loaded or the defendant showed that he had added words indicating that he did not really intend to carry out his threat. (But see *R* v *St George* and *Stephens* v *Myers*.)

Bliss v *Hall* (1838) 4 Bing NC 183

The plaintiff objected to the business of a candle-maker being carried on by his neighbour, the defendant, as he found that the process involved resulted in the emission of noxious vapours and smells from the defendant's messuage. The defendant argued that the plaintiff's action in nuisance should fail as his business was being carried on by him on the same premises for three years before the plaintiff occupied those adjoining.

Held, this fact would not defeat the plaintiff's claim as he occupied his house with all the rights which the common law afforded, including a right to wholesome air. It would have been otherwise if the vapours and smells had been 'hallowed by prescription' (*per* VAUGHAN J). (But see *Sturges* v *Bridgman*.)

Bloodworth v *Gray* (1844) 7 Man & G 334

On several occasions the defendant suggested to others that his son-in-law, the plaintiff, was suffering from venereal disease. The plaintiff brought an action for defamation.

Held, notwithstanding the plaintiff's failure to prove special damage, he was entitled to succeed as the defendant's words were actionable per se.

Blyth v *Birmingham Waterworks Co* (1856) 11 Exch 781

A water company laid pipes in accordance with statutory provisions but during an extremely cold winter, such as no man could have foreseen, a plug burst and caused injury to the plaintiff.

Held, the plaintiff could not recover damages as the defendants had not been negligent, ie there had not been an 'omission to do something which a reasonable man, guided upon those considerations which ordinarily regulate the conduct of human affairs, would do, or something which a prudent and reasonable man would not do' (*per* ALDERSON B).

Boardman v *Sanderson* [1964] 1 WLR 1317 (Court of Appeal)

The defendant was negligent in backing his car out of a garage and, in consequence, caused injury to an eight year old boy. The boy's father heard him scream and ran to his assistance and suffered nervous shock when he saw his son with his leg injured. The defendant knew that the boy's father was within earshot and was bound to run out when he heard the scream.

Held, the father was entitled to damages in respect of the shock caused to him and it mattered not that he did not witness the accident. 'It seems to me that the case satisfies the relevant test, being that of reasonable foreseeability discussed by the House of Lords in *Hay (or Bourhill) v Young*, and by the Privy Council in *Overseas Tankship (UK) v Morts Dock & Engineering Co Ltd*' (*per* DANCKWERTS LJ). (See also *Hinz v Berry*.)

Bolam v Friern Hospital Management Committee [1957] 2 All ER 118

The plaintiff was suffering from mental illness and was advised by a consultant psychiatrist to undergo electro-convulsive therapy, but there were two bodies of competent medical opinion as to whether relaxant drugs should be used in this form of treatment. The plaintiff was admitted to the defendants' hospital, but was not warned of the risk of fracture involved. In the course of the treatment the plaintiff sustained severe physical injuries, including fractures of the pelvis, and it was admitted that the use of relaxant drugs would have excluded the risk of fracture.

Held, the plaintiff could not recover damages for negligence as a doctor is not negligent, if he acts in accordance with a practice approved by a responsible body of medical men, merely because there is a body of such opinion that takes a contrary view. To recover damages for failure to give warning the plaintiff was required to show not only that the failure was negligent, but also that if he had been warned he would not have consented to the treatment. (See also *Philips v William Whiteley Ltd*, *Knight v Home Office*, *Gold v Haringey Health Authority* and *Chatterton v Gerson*.)

Bollinger (J) v Costa Brava Wine Co Ltd (No 2) [1961] 1 All ER 561

The plaintiffs were 12 incorporated companies which produced wine in the Champagne district of France and supplied it in England and Wales. Their wine, which had a high reputation, was known and had been known for many years as 'Champagne'. The defendants were a company importing a wine produced in Spain, which they offered for sale under the name of 'Spanish Champagne'. The plaintiffs sought, inter alia, an injunction to restrain the defendants from passing-off as Champagne, or as wine produced in the Champagne district of France, wine not so produced.

Held, the injunction would be granted, because a considerable number of people were likely to be misled by the description 'Spanish Champagne', and because the description was an attempt to attract the goodwill connected with the reputation of Champagne. (See also *White Hudson & Co Ltd v Asian Organisation Ltd*.)

Bolton v Stone [1951] 1 All ER 1078 (House of Lords)

During a cricket match a batsman drove a ball out of the ground and it hit and injured the plaintiff. The ball travelled nearly 100 yds and cleared a protective fence which was, in effect, 17 ft above the cricket pitch and 78 yds from the striker. There was evidence that the ball had been hit out of the ground on some six occasions during the last 30 years.

Held, the plaintiff was not entitled to damages in negligence or nuisance as the probability of such an injury would not be anticipated by a reasonable man. (But see *Hilder v Associated Portland Cement Manufacturers Ltd* and *Reffell v Surrey County Council*; but see *Miller v Jackson*.)

Bonnington Castings Ltd v Wardlaw [1956] 1 All ER 615 (House of Lords)

The respondent who had worked for eight years in the appellants' foundry, contracted pneumoconiosis through inhaling air containing silica dust. The main source of this dust was from pneumatic hammers and there was no known protection against dust produced by this operation, but part of it came from swing grinders because the dust-extraction plant for these grinders had not been kept free from obstruction as required by statutory regulations.

Held, the respondent should recover damages for breach of statutory duty as he had shown that the dust from the swing grinders had contributed materially to his condition. (See also *Hudson v Ridge Manufacturing Co Ltd*; but see *Wilsher v Essex Area Health Authority* and *Hotson v East Berkshire Area Health Authority*.)

Bourhill v Young See *Hay (or Bourhill) v Young*

Bowater v Rowley Regis Corporation [1944] 1 All ER 465

The plaintiff was employed by the defendant corporation as a carter and on the material occasion he had been provided with a horse which was known to be restive and given to running away. After protesting, the plaintiff eventually took the animal out in deference to an order given by a superior, but the horse again ran away and the plaintiff was injured.

Held, he was entitled to damages as the defendant corporation had been negligent. They could not rely on the maxim volenti non fit injuria as the plaintiff was not employed to manage difficult horses and he could not be said to have undertaken the risk involved. (But see *Watt v Hertfordshire County Council*.)

Bower v Peate (1876) 1 QBD 321

The parties owned adjoining houses and the defendant employed a contractor to pull his down and rebuild it. Because the contractor did not provide sufficient support during the excavation of the foundations, the plaintiff's house was damaged.

Held, the defendant was liable as 'a man who orders a work to be executed, from which, in the natural course of things, injurious consequences to his neighbour must be expected to arise, unless means are adopted by which such consequences may be prevented, is bound to see to the doing of that which is necessary to prevent the mischief, and cannot relieve himself of his responsibility by employing someone else – whether it be the contractor employed to do the work from which the danger arises or some independent person – to do what is necessary to prevent the act he has ordered to be done from becoming wrongful' (*per* COCKBURN CJ).

Bradford Corporation v *Pickles* [1895] AC 587 (House of Lords)

The appellants owned a waterworks and the respondent owned land from which water flowed naturally on to ground from which the appellants enjoyed a valuable supply of water. The respondent commenced operations on his land which had the effect of discolouring and diminishing the appellants' water supply and they sought an injunction to restrain his harmful activities which, they alleged, were activated by malice and with a view to induce them to buy his land.

Held, the injunction would not be granted, as the respondent's action was lawful and no matter how ill his motive might be, he had a right to act as he did. (See also *Hollywood Silver Fox Farm Ltd* v *Emmett*.)

Brandon v *Osborne Garrett and Co Ltd* [1924] 1 KB 548

The plaintiffs, who were husband and wife, were shopping in certain premises when part of the skylight, which was under repair, due to the negligence of the contractors doing the work, fell and injured the husband, a man who was naturally of a nervous disposition. The wife was not struck by the falling glass but she immediately and instinctively clutched her husband's arm in an attempt to pull him to safety. The sudden effort brought on a recurrence of thrombosis and she claimed to be entitled to damages.

Held, she would succeed as, in the circumstances, her actions were natural and proper. (But see *Cutler* v *United Dairies (London) Ltd.*)

Brent Walker Group plc v *Time Out Ltd* [1991] 2 All ER 753 (Court of Appeal)

In an action for libel the plaintiffs alleged that an article in the defendants' magazine indicated, inter alia, that their chairman had a 'history of close association with violent mobsters and racketeers'. The defendants pleaded fair comment on a matter of public interest and in their defence relied, inter alia, on privileged but unproven evidence by a police officer during a criminal trial which led to the chairman's conviction of theft.

Held, this statement had properly been struck out of the defence as the defendants had failed to show that they had given a fair and accurate report of the earlier proceedings. 'The authorities establish beyond doubt that if a statement made by a witness in judicial proceedings is republished, the republisher is not entitled to privilege unless it is, or is part of, a fair and accurate report of such proceedings. In principle, therefore, it is in my judgment clear that someone wishing to republish *and* to comment must establish *both* that his republication is fair and accurate *and* that his comment is fair' (*per* PARKER LJ).

Bridges v *Hawkesworth* (1851) 21 LJ QB 75

A stranger, who could not afterwards be traced, accidentally dropped a bundle of bank notes to the value of £55 on the floor of the defendant's shop. A traveller, the plaintiff, handed them to the defendant with a view to their being restored to their rightful owner if he should return.

Held, as against everyone but the true owner, the plaintiff was entitled to the money. (But see *Elwes* v *Brigg Gas Co.*)

Bridlington Relay Ltd v Yorkshire Electricity Board
[1965] 1 All ER 264

The plaintiffs carried on a business of relaying sound and television broadcasts and they sought an injunction to restrain the defendants from so operating a newly-erected power line as to interfere with their transmissions.

Held, their claim in nuisance could not succeed as the use of their aerial for this particular business was use of a special kind unusually vulnerable to interference. 'It is … established by authority that an act which does not, or would not, interfere with the ordinary enjoyment of their property by neighbours in the ordinary modes of using such property cannot constitute a legal nuisance' (*per* BUCKLEY J). Indeed, his lordship suggested that it could not be said that the ability to receive television free from occasional, even if recurrent and severe, electrical interference is so important a part of an ordinary householder's enjoyment of his property that such interference should be regarded as an actionable nuisance. (Distinguished in *Hunter* v *Canary Wharf Ltd*; but see *Halsey* v *Esso Petroleum Co Ltd*.)

Brimelow v Casson [1924] 1 Ch 302

There was evidence that the plaintiff paid his chorus girls such a low wage that in order to make a living they had to resort to immorality. The defendants, who represented the interests of the different classes of person engaged in the theatre, induced theatre proprietors not to allow the plaintiff to use their theatres, either by breaking existing contracts to do so or by refraining from entering into new contracts with him.

Held, the defendants were justified in taking this course. (See also *Sorrell* v *Smith*.)

British Celanese Ltd v A H Hunt (Capacitors) Ltd [1969] 2 All ER 1252

The plaintiffs occupied a factory site on a trading estate. The defendants were manufacturers of electronic components and occupied a site on the estate 150 yards away. For business purposes, the defendants brought on to the site some strips of metal foil several feet in length. Some of the strips were blown by the wind on to an overhead electric power cable. A 'flash over' occurred and caused a power failure which resulted in the plaintiffs' machinery at their factory stopping, and material solidified in the machines. The machines had to be cleaned before production could restart, and the plaintiffs claimed loss of profits from the defendants.

Held, the defendants were liable in negligence and nuisance, but not under the rule in *Rylands* v *Fletcher*. They were not liable under *Rylands* v *Fletcher* because the use of their premises for storing metal foil did not by itself create special risks. They owed a duty of care to the plaintiffs because they ought to have had them in contemplation as neighbours likely to be closely or directly affected by their acts or omissions, and they were therefore liable in negligence and the damage suffered by the plaintiffs was not too remote. They were liable in private nuisance because the method of storing the metal strips resulted in interference with the beneficial enjoyment of the plaintiffs' factory whereby the plaintiffs suffered damage which was not too remote.

British Road Services Ltd v Slater [1964] 1 All ER 816

At a slight bend in the road there grew an oak tree of considerable age on the grass verge or bank adjoining the defendant's land. During the hours of darkness a lorry drew into the side of the road to allow another lorry to pass and the load of the first lorry, 16 ft 4 ins from the ground, struck a substantial branch of the tree and a packing case fell into the path of the other lorry and caused it to run off the road and suffer damage. The plaintiffs owned both lorries and sought to recover damages on the ground that the branch was a nuisance. Until this accident occurred neither the defendants nor the highway authority had cause to regard the branch as a hazard to traffic.

Held, although the branch constituted a nuisance because it prevented the convenient use of the highway, the plaintiffs' action should fail. While the source of the nuisance (ie the branch) was plain for all to see, the defendants, having inherited the nuisance, were not liable for the consequences of failing to remedy it until they were aware that it was a nuisance or, with ordinary and reasonable care, should have become so aware.

British Telecommunications plc v One In A Million Ltd
[1998] 4 All ER 476 (Court of Appeal)

The defendants registered and sold Internet domain names. Without obtaining the plaintiffs' consent, they registered 'bt.org' and offered to sell it to the plaintiffs. The plaintiffs contended that the defendants' activities amounted to, inter alia, passing off and they sought injunctive relief.

Held, the trial judge had been correct in granting a final injunction quia timet. 'The registrations were made with the purpose of appropriating the respondents' property, their goodwill, and with an intention of threatening dishonest use by them or another. The registrations were instruments of fraud and injunctive relief was appropriate just as much as it was in those cases where persons registered company names for a similar purpose' (*per* ALDOUS LJ*).* (See also *Reddaway (Frank) & Co Ltd* v *George Banham & Co Ltd.*)

British Transport Commission v Gourley [1955] 3 All ER 796
(House of Lords)

The respondent, an eminent civil engineer, was seriously injured in a railway accident for which the appellants admitted liability. The respondent claimed, inter alia, damages for loss of earnings and the trial judge awarded him £37,720.

Held, this sum should be reduced to £6,695 as the respondent was entitled to such amount as would compensate him for the loss of his taxed earnings, liability to income tax not being so remote that it should be disregarded in assessing damages under this head. (See also *Lewis* v *Daily Telegraph Ltd, Nabi* v *British Leyland (UK) Ltd* and *Parry* v *Cleaver.*)

Broadley v *Guy Clapham & Co* [1994] 4 All ER 439 (Court of Appeal)

The plaintiff underwent a knee operation. Within a month or so, she knew that she was suffering something other than the direct and inevitable consequence of the surgery. The underlying question was as to her date of knowledge for the purposes of ss11 and 14 of the Limitation Act 1980.

Held, she was fixed with a cause of action when she knew, or could have known with the help of medical advice reasonably obtainable, that her injury had been caused by damage resulting from something done or not done by the surgeon during the operation. On the facts, within the three year period she had both broad knowledge that the operation had caused an injury to her foot and specific knowledge that the operation had been carried out in such a way as to damage a nerve in her leg thereby causing foot drop. It followed that her cause of action was time-barred. (See also *Dobbie* v *Medway Health Authority*.)

Broadway Approvals Ltd v *Odhams Press Ltd* [1965] 2 All ER 523 (Court of Appeal)

A boy received some stamps 'on approval' from the plaintiff company and later solicitors wrote on their behalf demanding the return of the stamps or the amount that they were said to be worth. The boy's mother brought this to the notice of *The People*, a newspaper published by the defendants, and they published an article under the heading 'What a way to run a business … scaring kids with solicitors' letter. Stamp it out!' The plaintiffs sued the defendants for libel and the plaintiff company was awarded £5,000 and its managing director £10,000 by way of damages.

Held, there should be a new trial as the learned judge had misdirected the jury by saying that there was a punitive aspect in damages. 'It is now established that compensation is the normal basis for damages for defamation and that punitive or exemplary damages should only be awarded in the case of a defendant who profited from his own wrongdoing in publishing the defamation' (*per* SELLERS LJ). Further, although the defendants had failed to prove justification, they had succeeded in fair comment and their failure to apologise or retract and their persistence in a plea of justification were not in themselves evidence of malice. (See also *Cassell and Co Ltd* v *Broome*.)

Brooke v *Bool* [1928] 2 KB 578

Morris told Bool that he thought he could smell gas coming from the plaintiff's shop. They decided to investigate and Morris began to examine part of a gas pipe with a naked light. The plaintiff sued Bool in respect of the considerable damage which the resulting explosion did to her shop.

Held, the action would succeed as, inter alia, Morris and Bool were joint tortfeasors: 'the act which was the immediate cause of the explosion was their joint act done in pursuance of a concerted purpose' (*per* SALTER J).

Brown v *Rolls Royce Ltd* [1960] 1 All ER 577 (House of Lords)

The appellant contracted industrial dermatitis caused by contact with oil while he was in the employment of the respondents. It was found, inter alia, that the respondents did not provide barrier cream and that a type of barrier cream was commonly supplied by employers to men doing such work as the appellant was doing.

Held, the appellant was not entitled to damages as he had not proved that the respondents had been negligent, and the findings of the court had not raised a presumption of negligence which the respondents were required to rebut. (But see *Kimpton* v *Steel Company of Wales Ltd*.)

Brunsden v *Humphrey* (1884) 14 QBD 141 (Court of Appeal)

The plaintiff and the cab which he was driving both suffered as a result of the negligence of the defendant's servant. Damages were awarded to the plaintiff in the county court in respect of the damage to his cab and he afterwards brought an action in the High Court in respect of personal injury.

Held, the High Court action was not barred by the earlier proceedings in the county court. 'Two actions may be brought in respect of the same facts, where those facts give rise to two distinct causes of action' (*per* BRETT MR). (See also *Darley Main Colliery Co* v *Mitchell*; but see *O'Sullivan* v *Williams*.)

Bryanston Finance Ltd v *de Vries* [1975] 2 All ER 609 (Court of Appeal)

The defendant and C prepared circulars to be sent to the shareholders of B (a public company), accusing S, the chairman both of B and of B's banking subsidiary, of defalcation. The circulars were dictated to shorthand typists, but they were sent only to S, in order to induce him to settle a separate action. B, the subsidiary and S sued the defendant and C for libel. C submitted to a consent judgment. At the trial, the judge rejected the defence of privilege and awarded the plaintiffs £500 damages against the defendant.

Held, (1) *per* LORD DENNING MR: the actionable publication was on an occasion of qualified privilege, since it is in accord with the reasonable and usual course of business for a businessman to dictate letters to a typist; the former has an interest in dictating the letter, and the latter has a duty to take it down. *Per* LAWTON LJ: the judge misdirected himself on qualified privilege. Publication to typists attracts privilege only if such privilege would have protected publication to the intended recipients. The publication to the shareholders of B would have been privileged, but not the publication to S, since it involved threats and was not fairly warranted. (2) The damages were too high in any event. *Per* LAWTON LJ: nominal damages are appropriate where publication is only to clerks. (3) Where one of two joint tortfeasors has consented to judgment, judgment cannot be given against the other, if the first judgment has been satisfied. The plaintiffs had not told the judge whether the judgment against C had been satisfied, and therefore judgment should not have been entered against the defendant. (See also *Osborn* v *Thomas Boulter and Son* and *Jameson* v *Central Electricity Generating Board (Babcock Energy Ltd, third party)*.)

Bunker v *Charles Brand & Son Ltd* [1969] 2 All ER 59

The defendants were the main contractors responsible for the tunnel on the new extension of the London Underground. They used a digging machine owned by London Transport for this work. The machine needed modifying, and they engaged the plaintiff's employers to do the work at a time when no tunnelling was in progress. The plaintiff had an opportunity of seeing the machine in situ. To reach the front of the machine it was necessary to cross free-running rollers on either side, and it was found that the plaintiff must have appreciated the danger in crossing them. In attempting to do so, he fell and was injured.

Held, the defendants were 'occupiers' of the tunnel and responsible for the machine since, despite the employment of the plaintiff's employers as specialist contractors, they retained control of the tunnel and the machine. Accordingly, they owed a common duty of care to the plaintiff under s2 of the Occupiers' Liability Act 1957, and were not absolved by s2(4) and (5) from their liability, merely by reason of the plaintiff's knowledge of the danger.

Burmah Oil Company (Burma Trading) Ltd v *Lord Advocate* [1964] 2 All ER 348 (House of Lords)

When the Japanese invaded Burma the appellants' installations were destroyed by order of the British government. It was admitted that the installations were destroyed lawfully and that the military situation rendered their destruction expedient for the defence of His Majesty's other territories, ie to delay the enemy and allow the withdrawal of British troops from Burma; it was assumed that the installations were destroyed by an exercise of the royal prerogative. Did such an exercise of the royal prerogative give any legal right to compensation to the persons who had suffered loss thereby, ie the appellants?

Held, the appellants were entitled to compensation (not necessarily the full cost of reinstatement) out of the revenues of the Crown, but the opposite would have been the case if the destruction of the installations could properly have been called 'battle damage', ie accidental or deliberate damage done by either side in the course of fighting operations. 'When the motive of destruction is a deliberate long-term strategy then, unless it be shown by the Crown that the damage has also an impact and importance for the purpose of the battle and would have been done for that purpose in any event, the subject is entitled to compensation' (*per* LORD PEARCE). (See also *Saltpetre Case* and *Mulcahy* v *Ministry of Defence*.)

Burns v *Edman* [1970] 1 All ER 886

The plaintiff brought an action in respect of the death of her husband. The deceased was a criminal whose income was derived from the proceeds of criminal offences.

Held, (1) damages for loss of expectation of life under the Law Reform (Miscellaneous Provisions) Act 1934 were assessed at only £250, judicial notice being taken of the fact that 'the life of a criminal is an unhappy one'; (2) the claim under the Fatal Accidents Acts failed in relation to both the plaintiff and her children because of the maxim ex turpi causa non oritur actio: the support of which the defendants had been deprived flowed directly from criminal offences.

Buron v Denman (1848) 2 Exch 167

An officer of the Royal Navy was instructed to suppress the slave trade. The Governor of Sierra Leone requested him to free two British subjects held as slaves by a Spaniard at the Gillanas, and after he had obtained the release of the two slaves in question he concluded a treaty for the abolition of slavery with the king of that country. The officer then fired the Spaniard's barracoons and liberated his slaves. The Government and the Admiralty adopted and ratified these acts. The Spaniard sought damages for trespass.

Held, the action would fail as the officer's actions were an act of State in respect of which no action would lie against either him or the Crown.

Burton v Hughes (1824) 2 Bing 173

Kitchen, a furniture dealer, lent some furniture to the plaintiff and the plaintiff placed it in a house occupied by a third party, where it was wrongfully seized by the defendants.

Held, the plaintiff was entitled to maintain an action to recover the goods as 'a simple bailee has a sufficient interest to sue in trover' (*per* BEST CJ). (See also *Manders v Williams*.)

Burton v Islington Health Authority [1993] QB 204 (Court of Appeal)

The plaintiff alleged that she had been born with abnormalities because the defendants had negligently carried out an operation on her mother when she was an embryo in her mother's womb. The defendants applied to strike out the claim on the ground that, at the time of the alleged negligence, the plaintiff had no legal status.

Held, the claim would not be struck out as the plaintiff had a cause of action. (Followed: *Montreal Tramways v Leveille*.)

Burton v Winters [1993] 1 WLR 1077 (Court of Appeal)

In 1975 the defendants' predecessor in title built a garage which allegedly encroached 4½ inches on to the plaintiff's land. In 1986 the plaintiff was refused a mandatory injunction in trespass and nuisance requiring the removal of the offending part of the garage wall, but the judge ordered damages to be assessed. Could the plaintiff exercise her common law right of abatement of the nuisance?

Held, she could not. 'This never was an appropriate case for self-redress, even if the plaintiff had acted promptly. There was no emergency. There were difficult questions of law and fact to be considered and the remedy by way of self-redress, if it had resulted in the demolition of the garage wall, would have been out of all proportion to the damage suffered by the plaintiff. But even if there had ever been a right of self-redress, it ceased when [the judge] refused to grant a mandatory injunction' (per LLOYD LJ).

Butterfield v Forrester (1809) 11 East 60

In the course of repairing his house the defendant obstructed the highway by placing a pole across it. One evening while riding his horse violently the plaintiff came into collision with the pole, but there was evidence that, at the time of the accident, it could be seen at a distance of 100 yards.

Held, the plaintiff's action for damages would fail. 'If he had used ordinary care he must have seen the obstruction; so that the accident appeared to happen entirely from his own fault' (*per* BAYLEY J).

Byrne v *Boadle* (1863) 2 H & C 722

The plaintiff was passing the defendant's premises when he was struck by a falling barrel of flour.

Held, this fact in itself was prima facie evidence of negligence, and the burden of disproving the validity of this presumption rested on the defendant. (See also *Scott* v *London and St Katherine Docks Co.*)

Byrne v *Deane* [1937] 2 All ER 204 (Court of Appeal)

A typewritten lampoon which accused the plaintiff of informing the police of the illegal use of gambling machines was put on the wall of a club house. The defendants, the proprietors and secretary of the club, allowed the lampoon to remain on the wall and in so doing, the plaintiff contended, they published the alleged libel.

Held, the defendants had taken part in the publication of the words objected to but they were not liable in damages as the lampoon was not defamatory of the plaintiff.

Byrne v *Hall Pain & Foster* [1999] 2 All ER 400 (Court of Appeal)

The plaintiffs proposed to purchase a flat. On the instructions of their mortgagees, on 2 June 1988 the defendant surveyors inspected the property and prepared a written report. Relying on the report, the plaintiffs exchanged contracts to purchase the flat on 8 July 1988, completion taking place on 22 July 1988. Subsequently, defects in the property came to light. The plaintiffs alleged that the defendants' work had been carried out negligently and on 18 July 1994 they issued a writ claiming damages. Was their action statute-barred by virtue of s2 of the Limitation Act 1980?

Held, it was: for these purposes the decisive date was the date of exchange of contracts. '… the plaintiffs on exchange became irrevocably committed to acquiring the lease, a lease worth less than they reasonably believed, and one which they would not have committed themselves to acquire but for the defendants' negligent report. That, as it seems to me, plainly resulted in "actual (as opposed to potential or prospective) loss or damage of a kind recognised by the law", as SAVILLE LJ expressed it in *First National Commercial Bank plc* v *Humberts* [1995] 2 All ER 673' (*per* SIMON BROWN LJ).

Cadbury Schweppes Pty Ltd v *Pub Squash Co Pty Ltd* [1981] 1 All ER 213 (Privy Council)

In 1974 the appellants began marketing in Australia a soft drink called 'Solo': it was sold in cans of a distinctive colour and its sale was promoted by intensive advertising on radio and television. A year later the respondents launched a similar drink which they called 'Pub Squash'; the cans and advertising were similar to those of 'Solo', sales of which began to fall.

Held, although the tort of passing off was wide enough to encompass descriptive material such as slogans or visual images if it had become part of the goodwill of a plaintiff's product, here it had never become a distinguishing feature of 'Solo' or generally associated with it and the consuming public had not been deceived or misled. Accordingly, the judge had been entitled to conclude that the appellants had not established a cause of action in tort for passing off, even though the respondents had deliberately taken advantage of their advertising campaign. (See also *Exxon Corpn v Exxon Insurance Consultants International Ltd.*)

Cambridge Water Co Ltd v Eastern Counties Leather plc
[1994] 1 All ER 53 (House of Lords)

Regular but relatively small spillages of a solvent used in the defendants' tanning process seeped through the tannery floor and percolated underground a distance of 1.3 miles to the plaintiffs' borehole. The plaintiffs sought injunctive relief and damages in negligence and nuisance and under the rule in *Rylands v Fletcher*. The claims in negligence and nuisance failed for lack of reasonable foreseeability that such damage would occur.

Held, the action under *Rylands v Fletcher* would also fail as the defendants had not known, and could not reasonably have foreseen, that the seepage would cause the pollution. 'Having regard … in particular to the step which this House has already taken in *Read v J Lyons & Co Ltd* to contain the scope of liability under the rule in *Rylands v Fletcher*, it appears to me to be appropriate now to take the view that foreseeability of damage of the relevant type should be regarded as a prerequisite of liability in damages under the rule. Such a conclusion can … be derived from Blackburn J's original statement of the law; and I can see no good reason why this prerequisite should not be recognised under the rule, as it has been in the case of private nuisance … Classically, this would have been regarded as a case of nuisance; and it would seem strange if, by characterising the case as one falling under the rule in *Rylands v Fletcher*, the liability should thereby be rendered more strict in the circumstances of the present case … I would not hold that [the defendants] should be exempt from liability on the basis of the exception of natural use [of their land]' (*per* LORD GOFF OF CHIEVELEY).

Campbell v Paddington Corporation [1911] 1 KB 869

The plaintiff was in the habit of letting seats in rooms to persons who wished to view public processions passing down Edgware Road. On the occasion of the funeral of King Edward VII the defendants erected a stand which constituted a public nuisance and a serious obstruction to the view from the plaintiff's rooms.

Held, the plaintiff could recover by way of damages the profits which, but for the defendants' act, she would probably have made by the letting of seats. (See also *Rose v Miles.*)

Campbell v *Spottiswoode* (1863) 3 B & S 769

A dissenting minister, the plaintiff, was editor of the *British Ensign* and in his paper he advanced a scheme for the dissemination of religious truth among the Chinese. The defendant, the owner of another publication, suggested in its columns that in making these proposals the plaintiff was an imposter, and that his real purpose was to put money into his own pocket by increasing the circulation of the *British Ensign*. The plaintiff brought an action for libel.

Held, he was entitled to succeed. Although the defendant honestly believed that what he wrote was true, his serious allegations were completely without foundation.

Canadian Pacific Railway Co v *Lockhart* [1942] 2 All ER 464 (Privy Council)

The respondent was injured by one of the appellant's servants who was travelling in his own car on the appellant's business. The accident was caused by the servant's negligence and the car was uninsured. The appellant had previously prohibited the use by the employees of their own cars unless they were sufficiently insured. Alternative transport was available.

Held, the appellant was liable as, at the time of the accident, his servant was engaged on an authorised act although he was performing it in an improper manner. (See also *Smith* v *Stages*; but see *Twine* v *Bean's Express Ltd*.)

Caparo Industries plc v *Dickman* [1990] 1 All ER 568 (House of Lords)

The plaintiffs owned shares in Fidelity plc. After receipt of the accounts for 1984, which had been audited by the defendants, they purchased more shares and later made a successful take-over bid. The plaintiffs alleged that the accounts had been inaccurate and misleading, showing a profit of some £1.2m instead of a loss of over £400,000. The plaintiffs sought damages for negligence and the question arose whether the defendants had owed them a duty of care either as shareholders or potential investors.

Held, they had not. Auditors of public company accounts did not owe a duty of care to members of the public buying shares in the company because there was not a relationship of proximity between them and individual shareholders buying more shares were in no better position. '... in addition to the foreseeability of damage, necessary ingredients in any situation giving rise to a duty of care are that there should exist between the party owing the duty and the party to whom it is owed a relationship characterised by the law as one of "proximity" or "neighbourhood" and that the situation should be one in which the court considers it fair, just and reasonable that the law should impose a duty of a given scope on the one party for the benefit of the other. But it is implicit ... that the concepts of proximity and fairness embodied in these additional ingredients are not susceptible of any such precise definition as would be necessary to give them utility as practical tests, but amount in effect to little more than convenient labels to attach to the features of different specific situations which, on a detailed examination of all the circumstances, the law recognises pragmatically as giving rise to a duty of care of a given scope' (*per* LORD BRIDGE OF HARWICH). (Approved: *Al*

Saudi Banque v *Clark Pixley*; see also *McNaughton (James) Papers Group Ltd* v *Hicks Anderson & Co* and *Marc Rich & Co AG* v *Bishop Rock Marine Co Ltd, The Nicholas H.*)

Capital and Counties Bank Ltd **v** *George Henty & Sons*
(1882) 7 App Cas 741 (House of Lords)

The defendants, who had quarrelled with the manager of a branch of the plaintiff bank, sent a circular to many of their customers (who knew nothing of the squabble and showed the circular to strangers) informing them that they would not 'receive in payment cheques drawn on any of the branches of the' plaintiff bank. It was contended that the plaintiff bank was entitled to damages for libel on the ground that the circular imputed insolvency.

Held, their action would fail. There was no case fit to be left to the jury as in their natural meaning the words were not libellous and the imputation suggested by the plaintiff bank was not one which would be drawn by reasonable persons.

Capital and Counties plc **v** *Hampshire County Council; Digital Equipment Co Ltd* **v** *Hampshire County Council; John Munroe (Acrylics) Ltd* **v** *London Fire and Civil Defence Authority; Church of Jesus Christ of Latter Day Saints (Great Britain)* **v** *West Yorkshire Fire and Civil Defence Authority* [1997] 2 All ER 865 (Court of Appeal)

The Hampshire cases arose out of a fire at a modern commercial building of which Capital and Counties plc were the developers and head lessees and Digital Equipment Co Ltd were occupiers as underlessees. The building was equipped with a heat-activated sprinkler system. Twenty-seven minutes after the fire brigade's arrival the sprinkler system was shut down on their instructions. Almost immediately, the fire went out of control and the building became a total loss. The trial judge found that, in having the sprinklers turned off, the fire brigade had been negligent and that a total loss would have been averted had the fire brigade left the sprinklers on and fought the fire. He was unable to say what would have happened if the fire brigade had not turned up at all. The plaintiffs were awarded damages: see [1996] 4 All ER 336. Similar questions of law arose in the other two cases (see [1996] 4 All ER 318 and (1996) The Times 9 May) but there the claims failed.

Held, appeals against all of the decisions would be dismissed. 'Although the [Fire Services Act 1947] does not in express terms confer on the fire authority the power to fight fires, it is implicit in the powers conferred in s30(1), (2) and (3) and indeed the whole tenor of the 1947 Act that they do have such a power. The style of drafting adopted may be no more than the recognition that any citizen is entitled to fight fires, although in doing so he will not enjoy the immunity from suit for trespass afforded to fire officers and constables by s30(1). ... The question whether, in the absence of a statutory duty, a statutory power to act can be converted into a common law duty to exercise the power has been extensively considered by the House of Lords in *Stovin* v *Wise (Norfolk County Council, third party)* ... In our judgment the fire brigade are not under a common law duty to answer the call for help and are not under a duty to take care to do so. If therefore they fail to turn up or fail to turn up in time because they have carelessly misunderstood the message, got lost on the way or run into a tree, they are not liable. [See, eg, *Hill v Chief Constable of West Yorkshire.*] ... But where the rescue/protective service itself by negligence creates the danger which caused the plaintiff's injury there is no doubt in our judgment the plaintiff can recover. ... it seems to us that there is no difference in principle if, by some positive negligent act, the rescuer/protective service substantially increases the risk; he is thereby creating a fresh danger, albeit of the same kind or of the same nature, namely fire. [See, eg, *Knightley v Johns.*] ... In our judgment there is no doubt on which side of the line a case such as the *Hampshire* case falls. It is one where the defendants, by their action in turning off the sprinklers, created or increased the danger. There is no ground for giving immunity in such a case. ... Although the powers are very wide, there is nothing in s30 which permits them to be exercised negligently. If it had been intended to exclude liability for negligence express provision could readily have been made. None was ...' (*per* STUART SMITH LJ). (But see *East Suffolk Rivers Catchment Board v Kent* and *Phelps v Hillingdon London Borough Council*.)

Capps v *Miller* [1989] 2 All ER 333 (Court of Appeal)

The defendant in his car ran into the plaintiff on her moped and caused her severe brain damage: he admitted liability. However, as, contrary to statutory regulations, the chin strap of the plaintiff's crash helmet had been unfastened, he claimed that she had been contributorily negligent. The helmet had come off before her head hit the road and this had clearly contributed to the extent of her injuries.

Held, contributory negligence had been established and, making a distinction between wearing a helmet with its strap unfastened and not wearing a helmet at all, the plaintiff's damages would be reduced by 10 per cent. (See also *Froom v Butcher*.)

Carberry v *Davies* [1968] 2 All ER 817 (Court of Appeal)

A car owner asked one of his employees to drive the owner's son about in the evenings in the owner's car. One evening there was an accident, caused by the employee's negligence, and a motor-cyclist was injured.

Held, the owner was vicariously liable. (See also *Ormrod v Crosville Motor Services Ltd*.)

Carmarthenshire County Council v *Lewis* [1955] 1 All ER 565 (House of Lords)

A mistress in charge of the appellants' nursery school was about to take David, who was about three and three-quarter years of age, and a little girl out for a walk, but she left the classroom and during the time that she was away, about ten minutes, she visited the lavatory and attended to a child who had fallen down and cut himself. When she returned she found that David had left the classroom and made his way out of the school playground through an unlocked gate and down a lane into a busy highway where he caused a lorry to swerve so that it struck a telegraph pole. The driver of the lorry was killed and his widow, the respondent, brought an action for damages for negligence.

Held, although the mistress had not been negligent, the respondent should succeed as the appellants had failed to give any explanation that would discharge the presumption of negligence that arose from the escape of the child on to the road, and such an accident as happened should have been in the contemplation of any reasonable person. It was not necessary that the precise result should have been foreseen. (See also *Barnes v Hampshire County Council*.)

Carr-Glynn v Frearsons [1998] 4 All ER 225 (Court of Appeal)

Having prepared a testatrix's will, the defendant solicitors negligently failed to advise the testatrix to sever a joint tenancy so as to enable a property to pass to the plaintiff in accordance with the will's provisions.

Held, the plaintiff's action for damages would be successful. 'I am satisfied that in failing to advise that a notice of severance ought to be served immediately [the defendants] fell below the standard of care to be expected from a competent solicitor acting reasonably. The judge found that, if that advice had been given, the testatrix would have acted upon it. ... On a proper analysis, the service of a notice of severance was part of the will-making process. ... I am satisfied that, subject to the need to avoid the injustice of imposing double liability on the solicitors, it would be consistent with the approach of the majority of the House of Lords in *White v Jones* to recognise that the [plaintiff] is a person in a relation to whom the assumption of liability by the [defendants] towards their client, the testatrix, ought to be extended. It is essential, also, to have in mind that this is a case in which, prima facie, the [plaintiff] would receive no benefit from a successful claim by the estate against the solicitors. The proceeds would form part of the residuary estate in which she has no beneficial interest' (*per* CHADWICK LJ). (But see *Walker v Geo H Medlicott & Son*.)

Cassell and Co Ltd v Broome [1972] 1 All ER 801 (House of Lords)

In an action for libel the jury awarded £15,000 compensatory and £25,000 exemplary damages. The defendants appealed on the question of exemplary damages. The Court of Appeal upheld the award, but said that exemplary damages could be awarded outside the situations itemised in *Rookes v Barnard* (qv) and that decision was per incuriam and should not be followed.

Held, (1) *Rookes v Barnard* was not decided per incuriam, and it was improper for the Court of Appeal to advise judges not to follow a decision of the House. (2) Exemplary damages were properly awarded since there was evidence on which the jury could find that the defendants calculated that the profit made out of the wrongdoing would probably exceed the damages at risk. 'Calculated' means that the defendant directed his mind to the material advantages involved. (3) The damages were not so excessive that no jury of reasonable men could have awarded so large a sum. (See also *Drane v Evangelou* and *Rantzen v Mirror Group Newspapers (1986) Ltd*.)

Cassidy v Daily Mirror Newspapers Ltd [1929] 2 KB 331 (Court of Appeal)

Under the heading 'Today's gossip', the *Daily Mirror*, which was owned by the defendants, published a photograph of the plaintiff's husband and a certain Miss X 'whose engagement has been announced'. The defendants maintained that they had received the photograph and information in the ordinary course of business and published it in good faith. The plaintiff, who was living apart from her husband, brought an action for libel.

Held, the publication could be defamatory and as the jury had found that the photograph and caption conveyed to reasonably minded people an aspersion on the plaintiff's moral character, she was entitled to succeed. (See also *Tolley* v *J S Fry & Sons Ltd*; but see s4 of the Defamation Act 1952.)

Castle v St Augustine's Links Ltd (1922) 38 TLR 615

The plaintiff was driving his taxi cab from Deal to Ramsgate when a ball driven from the 13th tee of a golf course owned by the defendants struck his windscreen and caused him injury. There was evidence that balls driven from this particular tee frequently landed on or over the highway.

Held, the plaintiff would recover damages as the tee and the hole were, in these conditions and in the place where they were situated, a public nuisance. (See also *Dollman* v *A & S Hillman Ltd* and *Miller* v *Jackson*.)

Cavanagh v Ulster Weaving Co Ltd [1959] 2 All ER 745 (House of Lords)

While carrying cement on a roof a labourer slipped and fell off a ladder; an expert witness for his employers testified that the system adopted for the carrying of cement was 'perfectly in accord with good practice'. This evidence was not contradicted, but the jury found that the employers had been negligent.

Held, the jury's verdict should not be disturbed as the expert evidence establishing practice in the trade was not, in the circumstances of the case, conclusive of the issue of negligence in favour of the employers. 'I am quite unable to hold that there was no evidence on which the jury could hold, as they did, that the [employers] were negligent' (*per* LORD KEITH), ie had failed to use reasonable care for the labourer's safety. (See also *Ward* v *T E Hopkins & Son Ltd*; but see *Wright* v *Cheshire County Council*.)

Century Insurance Co Ltd v Northern Ireland Road Transport Board [1942] 1 All ER 491 (House of Lords)

One of the respondents' employees was delivering petrol to a garage. While the petrol was flowing from the lorry to the tank the employee, in lighting a cigarette, negligently threw away the lighted match. There followed a violent explosion.

Held, the respondents were liable for the resulting damage as at the time of the explosion the lorry driver was acting within the course of his employment.

Chadwick v *British Transport Commission* [1967] 2 All ER 945

In December 1957, near Chadwick's home, there was a severe railway crash in which 90 people were killed and many others were trapped or injured.. Risking the collapse of a wrecked carriage, Chadwick voluntarily took an active part throughout the night in rescue operations. As a result of the horror of this experience, Chadwick suffered a severe and disabling anxiety neurosis, necessitating hospital treatment. Before the accident, Chadwick had been a busy and successful man though, 16 years before, he had suffered some psycho-neurotic symptoms. In an action brought by Chadwick the defendants conceded that the accident was caused by their negligence but they denied liability in damages to the plaintiff.

Held, the plaintiff's claim should succeed. The defendants owed a duty of care to rescuers, and the plaintiff's illness was suffered as a result of breach of that duty. (Approved in *White* v *Chief Constable of the South Yorkshire Police*; see *Hay (or Bourhill)* v *Young* and *Ward* v *T E Hopkins & Son Ltd.*)

Chapronière v *Mason* (1905) 21 TLR 633 (Court of Appeal)

The defendant sold the plaintiff, a solicitor, a bath bun which contained a stone. The plaintiff claimed damages in respect of a broken tooth.

Held, the principle of res ipsa loquitur applied. The presence of the stone was prima facie evidence of negligence, and threw upon the defendant the onus of giving evidence to rebut it.

Chatterton v *Gerson* [1981] 1 All ER 257

The defendant specialist treated the plaintiff for a chronic and intractible pain. After two months the pain returned and the defendant repeated the treatment. Again the operation was unsuccessful; the plaintiff also found that her right leg was completely numb and this considerably impaired her mobility. She claimed damages for assault and/or negligence and/or breach of duty.

Held, her action would be dismissed. As she had been under no illusion as to the general nature of the operations performed by the defendant, there had been no lack of real consent on her part and her claim for trespass to the person therefore could not succeed. While a doctor is obliged to warn his patient of any real risk of misfortune, here the numbness was not a foreseeable risk of the operation so the defendant was not under a duty to warn the plaintiff of it. In any case, even if the defendant had failed in his duty to warn the plaintiff of the implications inherent in the second operation, she had not proved that if she had been properly informed she would have refused to proceed. (See also *Bolam* v *Friern Hospital Management Committee.*)

Chatterton v *Secretary of State for India in Council* [1895] 2 QB 189 (Court of Appeal)

In the course of his duty the defendant, the Secretary of State for India, told the Parliamentary Under-Secretary for India that the removal of the plaintiff, a captain in HM

Indian Staff Corps, from the effective to the half-pay list, had been recommended by the Commander-in-Chief in India and the Government of India.

Held, an action for libel could not lie as such a communication is absolutely privileged. (See also *Fayed v Al-Tajir.*)

Chaudhry v Prabhaker [1988] 3 All ER 718 (Court of Appeal)

The plaintiff, who knew nothing about cars, asked the defendant, a close friend who knew something about them although he was not a mechanic, to find her a suitable secondhand car, stipulating that it should not have been involved in an accident. He saw one being sold by a car sprayer and panel beater and, although he noticed that the bonnet had perhaps been replaced, he recommended its purchase and the plaintiff bought it for £4,500. Within months it became clear that the car had been involved in an accident and poorly repaired and that it was unroadworthy.

Held, the defendant was liable as he, a gratuitous agent, had been in breach of the duty of care which he owed to the plaintiff to exercise the degree of care and skill (measured objectively) reasonably to be expected of him in all the circumstances. (Applied: *Hedley Byrne & Co Ltd v Heller & Partners Ltd.*)

Christie v Davey [1893] 1 Ch 316

The parties lived in adjoining semi-detached houses. The plaintiff gave music lessons and held musical parties in his house which annoyed the defendant considerably. Maliciously and for the purpose of vexing and annoying the plaintiff, the defendant blew whistles, knocked on trays or boards, hammered, shrieked and shouted when lessons or parties were in progress in the plaintiff's house.

Held, this interference could be restrained by injunction, but it would have been otherwise if both parties had been perfectly innocent. (But see *Bradford Corporation v Pickles.*)

Church of Jesus Christ of Latter Day Saints (Great Britain) v West Yorkshire Fire and Civil Defence Authority See *Capital and Counties plc v Hampshire County Council*

Clark v Chambers (1878) 3 QBD 327

Acting wrongfully and without authority, the defendant erected a barrier armed with spikes which was capable of blocking up a private road. Without the defendant's knowledge a stranger removed some of these spikes and left them in an upright position on the footpath. On a dark night while the plaintiff was lawfully using the footpath he came into contact with this obstruction and received injuries.

Held, the plaintiff's action for damages would succeed although the immediate cause of his injury was the intervening act of a third party. (See also *Weld-Blundell v Stephens.*)

Clay v A J Crump & Sons Ltd [1963] 3 All ER 687 (Court of Appeal)

The plaintiff, a builders' labourer employed by building contractors, was injured by the collapse of a wall. Demolition contractors engaged in the project (the demolition of an existing building and the erection of a new one on the same site) and the architects had allowed the wall to remain in the belief that it was safe but an expert, looking at the wall with reasonable care, would have seen that it was dangerous. Neither the demolition contractors nor the architects examined the wall carefully and, when the building contractors entered upon the site, they examined it only cursorily because they assumed (as the demolition contractors and the architects would expect them to assume) that the demolition contractors and the architects had deliberately left it standing having satisfied themselves that the wall was safe.

Held, both the architects and the demolition contractors were liable to the plaintiff in negligence because the plaintiff was within that class of persons whom they should have had in contemplation as being affected by their acts or omissions and, on the facts, they were in breach of the duty of care which they therefore owed him. It was no defence for them to say that the building contractors had the last opportunity of examining the safety of the site and that for this reason the chain of causation was broken although the building contractors, who were not entitled to assume that the demolition contractors and the architects had completely fulfilled their duty, were also liable as the plaintiff's employers for breach of their duty to take reasonable care for his safety.

Cleghorn v Oldham (1927) 43 TLR 465

Miss Oldham, the defendant, was playing golf with the plaintiff's brother. The plaintiff, Miss Cleghorn, was carrying the defendant's clubs, but when her brother made a bad drive the defendant played at an imaginary ball to show him how the stroke should be played. Unfortunately, at the end of her 'follow through', the defendant struck the plaintiff and she claimed damages in respect of the resulting injuries.

Held, the plaintiff was entitled to judgment as she had not voluntarily undertaken the risk of being injured as a result of the defendant's negligence. (See also *Condon v Basi*; but see *Hall v Brooklands Auto Racing Club*.)

Clifton v Viscount Bury (1887) 4 TLR 8

The line of fire of the 12th Middlesex Volunteer Corps on their range on Wimbledon Common passed over the plaintiff's land. There was evidence that the bullets ordinarily passed over at 75 ft above the surface.

Held, although this was not technically a trespass, the plaintiff, by reason of the risk involved, had 'a legal grievance' which entitled him to an injunction. (But see *Bernstein (Lord) v Skyviews and General Ltd*.)

Close v *Steel Company of Wales Ltd* [1961] 2 All ER 953 (House of Lords)

The appellant, an employee of the respondents, was injured when the bit of a drill shattered. Bits occasionally shattered, but there was no evidence of any such accident having happened previously as the fragments were small and light and did not fly out with force. The respondents were under a statutory duty to fence 'dangerous' parts of machinery.

Held, the respondents were not in breach of this duty. The bit was not a 'dangerous' part of the machinery because danger from the use of the bit in the drill was not reasonably foreseeable. 'It seems clear that, in the ordinary course of human affairs, danger could not reasonably be anticipated from the use of the drill unfenced. It cannot, therefore, be classed as dangerous' (*per* LORD DENNING). (See also *Cummings (or McWilliams) v Sir William Arrol & Co Ltd.*)

Clough v *Bussan* [1990] 1 All ER 431

Two cars were involved in an accident and a passenger in one of them sued both drivers for damages in respect of her injuries. One of the drivers alleged that, if the accident had been caused by the malfunctioning of traffic lights, it had been caused or contributed to by the police because they had known about the lights for 35 minutes and had not put an officer on duty at the crossroads.

Held, this contention would be dismissed because, on the facts, nothing had occurred to give rise, on the part of the police, to a duty of care to this particular driver or, indeed, to motorists generally. (Applied: *Yuen Kun-yeu v Attorney-General of Hong Kong* and *Hill v Chief Constable of West Yorkshire*; approved in *Ancell v McDermott*.)

Clunis v *Camden and Islington Health Authority* [1998] 3 All ER 180 (Court of Appeal)

The plaintiff was discharged from a mental hospital and moved into the defendant's area: the defendant was under a statutory duty to provide after-care services for him. The plaintiff stabbed a Mr Zito to death and he pleaded guilty to manslaughter on grounds of diminished responsibility. When the plaintiff sued for damages, alleging negligence in the after-care provision, the defendant sought to have the claim struck out on the grounds: (i) that it was based on the plaintiff's own illegal act; and (ii) that the defendant's statutory duties did not give rise to a common law duty of care.

Held, the defendant's application should have succeeded on both grounds. '... we consider the defendant has made out its plea that the plaintiff's claim is essentially based on his illegal act of manslaughter, he must be taken to have known what he was doing and that it was wrong, notwithstanding that the degree of his culpability was reduced by reason of mental disorder. The court ought not to allow itself to be made an instrument to enforce obligations alleged to arise out of the plaintiff's own criminal act (doubted: *Meah v McCreamer* [1985] 1 All ER 367) ... Is it in the circumstances just and reasonable to superimpose such a common law duty of care on an authority in relation to the performance of its statutory duties to provide after-care? We do not think so. We find it difficult to suppose that Parliament intended to create such an extensive and wide-ranging liability for breaches of responsibility ...' (*per* BELDAM LJ). (Applied: *X and Others (Minors) v Bedfordshire County Council* [1995] 3 All ER 353; see also *Harris v Evans*.)

Colledge v Bass Mitchells & Butlers Ltd [1988] 1 All ER 536 (Court of Appeal)

Having sued his employers for damages for negligence, before the trial the plaintiff was offered and he accepted voluntary redundancy. Should the redundancy payment be deducted from the award of damages?

Held, it should. On the facts, it was unlikely that the plaintiff would have been made redundant, but for his injury, and the redundancy payment had therefore been received as a result of the accident. (But see *Smoker v London Fire and Civil Defence Authority*.)

Collingwood v Home and Colonial Stores Ltd [1936] 3 All ER 200 (Court of Appeal)

A fire began on the defendants' premises and spread to and damaged the plaintiff's shop. The fire was in some way connected with the electrical wiring, but it was impossible to say precisely how it began.

Held, the plaintiff was without a remedy as the fire began 'accidentally' and the defendants were protected by s86 of the Fires Prevention (Metropolis) Act 1774.

Collins v Renison (1754) Say 138

The plaintiff, who was trespassing in the defendant's garden, erected a ladder in that garden so that he could nail a board to his (the plaintiff's) house. The defendant forbade him to to this and when the plaintiff refused to come down the ladder he shook it and the plaintiff fell and was injured.

Held, the plaintiff was entitled to damages as 'such force, as was used in the present case, is not justifiable in defence of the possession of land' (*per* RYDER CJ). (See also *Revill v Newbery*.)

Coltman v Bibby Tankers Ltd, The Derbyshire [1987] 3 All ER 1068 (House of Lords)

The defendants' 90,000 ton bulk carrier sank with the loss of all hands. The plaintiffs, personal representatives of a crew member, claimed damages for negligence, arguing, inter alia, that the ship was 'equipment' within s1 of the Employers' Liability (Defective Equipment) Act 1969.

Held, this argument would be successful. '... the mere fact that ships and vessels were not expressly included in the definition [in s1(3) of the 1969 Act] cannot have been intended to have the effect of cutting down the ordinary meaning of the word "equipment" by excluding ships or vessels from that word' (*per* LORD GOFF OF CHIEVELEY). (See also *Knowles* v *Liverpool City Council.*)

Colvilles Ltd v Devine [1969] 2 All ER 53 (House of Lords)

The appellants owned a steelworks where steel was manufactured by the injection of oxygen into converters. The oxygen was supplied by a pipe from the premises of a third party, about a mile away, and was connected up to the main distribution centre in the appellants' factory. From there the oxygen was taken by hose, under the appellants' control, to a lance through which it was injected into the molten metal in the converters. The respondent, an employee of the appellants, was working on a platform 15 ft from the ground, when there was an explosion in the proximity of a converter, about 75 yds away. Scared by the explosion, the respondent jumped off the platform and was injured. He claimed damages from the appellants. The probable cause of the explosion was a fire caused by friction from foreign bodies in the oxygen system. The appellants had not been warned of this danger by the makers of the plant, which had been recently installed, nor had any comparable accident occurred previously.

Held, as the plant was under the management of the appellants and, since such an explosion would not have occurred in the ordinary course of things if they had taken proper care, the maxim res ipsa loquitur applied. Although it was not necessary for there to be positive proof of the existence of foreign bodies in the oxygen to establish the appellants' explanation, for it to be a defence, it must be consistent with no negligence on their part. As the appellants had not adduced evidence of any inspection of the filter system in the plant, they had not discharged the onus imposed on them by the maxim. (See also *Scott* v *London & St Katherine Docks Co.*)

Condon v Basi [1985] 2 All ER 453 (Court of Appeal)

The parties were playing for opposing sides in a local league football match. The defendant tackled the plaintiff in a manner which constituted, as the county court judge found, 'serious and dangerous foul play' and the plaintiff suffered a broken leg.

Held, the defendant's appeal against an award of damages for negligence would be dismissed. 'I do not think it makes the slightest difference in the end if it is found by the tribunal of fact that the defendant failed to exercise that degree of care which was appropriate in all the circumstances, or that he acted in a way to which the plaintiff cannot be expected to have consented. In either event, there is liability' (*per* SIR JOHN DONALDSON MR). (See also *Cleghorn* v *Oldham.*)

Connolly v Camden and Islington Area Health Authority
[1981] 3 All ER 250

When the plaintiff was about three weeks old, he was given a serious overdose of anaesthetic for which the defendants admitted liability. He would never be able to earn a living and his total expectation of life had been reduced to 27½ years. Damages were awarded for pain, suffering and loss of amenities, future care, loss of earnings and special damage: could they also be awarded for 'the lost years'?

Held, they could, but on the facts the child's claim under this head would be assessed at nil. 'I think a child qualifies as such under this head of damage dependent on the ability to prove. It is difficult enough in the case of a teenager or a middle-aged person to prove something for lost years. It is more difficult for a child, but I can envisage … far more examples than … that of a television star. I can envisage the only son of a father who owns a prosperous business' (*per* COMYN J). (See also *Pickett v British Rail Engineering Ltd*; but see s1 of the Administration of Justice Act 1982.)

Constantine v Imperial London Hotels Ltd [1944] 2 All ER 171

Without just cause the plaintiff, the famous West Indian cricketer, was refused accommodation at one of the defendant's hotels although he was received and lodged at another hotel owned by them. There was no evidence of special damage.

Held, the plaintiff was entitled to recover nominal damages of £5 5s. (See also *Ashby v White*.)

Conway v Wimpey (George) & Co Ltd [1951] 1 All ER 363
(Court of Appeal)

A driver employed by the defendants was under strict orders not to carry passengers and there was a notice in the cab of his lorry by way of confirmation of these instructions. Nevertheless, he gave a lift to the plaintiff who was injured as a result of the driver's negligence.

Held, the defendants were not liable for his injuries as the plaintiff was a trespasser. (But see *Young v Edward Box & Co Ltd.*)

Cook v Alexander [1973] 3 All ER 1037 (Court of Appeal)

The plaintiff, a teacher at an approved school, sued the *Daily Telegraph,* its editor and the writer of a 'parliamentary sketch' for libel in respect of a report of a debate in the House of Lords about the school in question.

Held, the report was protected by qualified privilege, since the sketch was an abbreviated but fair report of parliamentary proceedings. The writer may select those parts of a debate which are of special public interest and report them 'in a manner which fairly and faithfully gives an impression of the events'. (See also *Wason v Walter.*)

Cook v Lewis [1952] 1 DLR 1 (Supreme Court of Canada)

Cook and Akenhead were out bird-shooting. They fired their guns almost at the same moment but at different birds. It was found that, due to negligence, one Lewis had been struck by some of their bird-shot, but it was impossible to say whether it came from the gun of Cook or from that of Akenhead.

Held, although Cook and Akenhead were not joint tortfeasors, in the circumstances of the case they were both liable unless either of them could discharge the burden of exculpating himself. (See also s10 of the Partnership Act 1890.)

Cookson v Knowles [1978] 2 All ER 604 (House of Lords)

In an action under the Fatal Accidents Acts, questions arose as to the award of interest on the damages and the impact of inflation.

Held, awards in normal fatal accident cases should be divided into two parts. The first should be the pecuniary loss up to the date of trial ('the pre-trial loss'), upon which interest should run at half the short term interest rate current during that period. The second should be the pecuniary loss thereafter ('the future loss'), the dependency being calculated on the basis of the deceased's notional earnings at the date of trial, on which loss no interest should be payable. No allowance should be made for future inflation after the date of the trial. (See also *Pickett* v *British Rail Engineering Ltd* and *Stanley v Saddique.*)

Cope v Sharpe (No 2) [1912] 1 KB 496 (Court of Appeal)

One Chase was lessee of some sporting and shooting rights over land owned by the plaintiff, and the defendant was his gamekeeper. A serious fire broke out on the plaintiff's land to the south of Chase's shooting, on which there were some sitting pheasants; although at least 50 people were engaged in fighting the blaze the defendant set fire to some patches of heather between the main fire and the shooting in the hope of stopping the fire from spreading and harming the birds. The defendant said that he did this because he did not think that the beaters knew how to deal with the fire, but shortly afterwards they managed to put it out. The plaintiff brought an action for trespass.

Held, the defendant was entitled to judgment as in the circumstances his actions had been reasonably necessary.

Corbett v Barking Havering and Brentwood Health Authority [1991] 1 All ER 498 (Court of Appeal)

The plaintiff was born in October 1977: two weeks later his mother died as a result of medical negligence and he was cared for by his grandparents. A writ claiming damages under the Fatal Accidents Act 1976 was issued in August 1985 and the action came to trial in May 1989. The sole issue was the assessment of damages to be apportioned under s3(1) of the 1976 Act.

Held, the court would not interfere with the trial judge's estimate of the notional nanny's net in-hand wages of £100 a week at the date of trial as the basis for calculating damages for loss of dependency or with his decision not to include a figure for expenditure on additional cover. The judge should assess the multiplier as at the date of the mother's death, taking into account facts known at the date of trial (although the court could impose a sanction for any delay in bringing proceedings by withholding interest on pre-trial damages: see s35A of the Supreme Court Act 1981). Here, therefore, a multiplier of 12 was too low: 15 would be substituted, with 3½ for post-trial damages, the multiplier of 15 including a small addition to take account of the possibility that the plaintiff would proceed to tertiary education at the age of 18. (Applied: *Spittle v Bunney* and *Cookson v Knowles*.)

Cork v Kirby Maclean Ltd [1952] 2 All ER 402 (Court of Appeal)

A painter, who was subject to epileptic fits, had been forbidden by his doctor to work at heights. He did not tell this to his employer but while working on a platform, which was some 20 ft above the level of the ground and did not satisfy the requirements of the Building (Safety, Health and Welfare) Regulations 1948, he had a fit, fell and was killed. His widow claimed damages for breach of statutory duty.

Held, both the painter and his employers were at fault and they shared the responsibility for the accident. For this reason, under s1(1) of the Law Reform (Contributory Negligence) Act 1945, the plaintiff's widow could recover one-half of the damage resulting from her late husband's fall. (See also *Fitzgerald v Lane*.)

Coward v Baddeley (1859) 4 H & N 478

The plaintiff stopped to look at a house which was on fire and advised a fireman, the defendant, to play his hose on a neighbouring building. The defendant considered that he was being assaulted and gave the plaintiff into the custody of the police, but it was found that the plaintiff had touched the defendant merely with a view to attracting his attention.

Held, the defendant's action could not be justified. (But see *Ashton v Jennings*.)

Credit Lyonnais Bank Nederland NV v Exports Credits Guarantee Department [1999] 1 All ER 929 (House of Lords)

As a consequence of their activities, Mr Chong and Mr Pillai (an employee of the defendant) would have been liable to the plaintiff bank jointly and severally for deceit. However, only some of those activities were in the course of Mr Pillai's employment. Was the defendant vicariously liable for the plaintiff's loss?

Held, it was not. '... before there can be vicarious liability, all the features of the wrong which are necessary to make the employee liable have to have occurred in the course of the employment. Otherwise there is no liability. You cannot ... combine the actions of Mr Pillai in the course of his employment with actions of Mr Chong, which if done by Mr Pillai would be outside the course of Mr Pillai's employment, and say [the defendant] is vicariously liable for the consequence of Mr Pillai's and Mr Chong's combined conduct' (*per* LORD WOOLF MR).

Crofter Hand Woven Harris Tweed Co Ltd v Veitch [1942] 1 All ER 142 (House of Lords)

Crofters in the Isle of Lewis in the Outer Hebrides wove Harris tweed. Yarn for making this cloth was spun by five mill owners on the island but many of the crofters began to import yarn from the mainland as cloth made from this yarn could be sold at a much cheaper price.

The Transport and General Workers Union, of which 90 per cent of the workers in the mills were members, asked the mill owners to increase the wages of their employees. The employers replied that this was impossible because of the competition from the crofters who wove yarn imported from the mainland; in view of this, the union, whose members controlled the docks, imposed an embargo upon all Harris tweed woven from mainland yarn. The crofters, whose trade was destroyed by the embargo, claimed damages from officials of the union.

Held, as the real purpose of the embargo was to benefit members of the union, the fact that it resulted in damage to the crofters who had used mainland yarn did not make it an unlawful conspiracy which was actionable at law. (See also *Thomson (D C) & Co Ltd v Deakin*.)

Cross v Kirklees Metropolitan Borough Council [1998] 1 All ER 564 (Court of Appeal)

At 9.30 am the elderly plaintiff slipped and fell on an icy footway (pavement). The defendant highway authority had received a forecast warning of icy conditions and, in accordance with its policy and practice, the road in question (but not its footway) had received the 'full grit' treatment. Having suffered quite serious injuries as a result of her fall, the plaintiff alleged that the defendant had been in breach of s41 of the Highways Act 1980 and the trial judge shared this view. The defendant appealed.

Held, The appeal would be allowed: in all the circumstances it had not been unreasonable for the defendant not to have taken remedial or preventative measures before the plaintiff suffered her accident. (But see *Goodes v East Sussex County Council*.)

Crossley v Rawlinson [1981] 3 All ER 674

As a result of the defendant's negligence, a tarpaulin on his lorry caught fire; he stopped his lorry at the side of the road. Seeing the fire, the plaintiff AA patrolman grabbed a fire extinguisher and ran towards the lorry along the ordinary country footpath. His foot went down a pothole covered by grass and he suffered injury.

Held, his action would be dismissed as it was not reasonably foreseeable that he – a rescuer – would suffer any injury while running towards the scene of danger. (But see *Videan v British Transport Commission*.)

Crowhurst v Amersham Burial Board (1878) 4 Ex D 5

The defendants planted yew trees near to railings which formed part of the wall surrounding their cemetery. The trees grew through and beyond the railings and projected over an adjoining meadow on which the plaintiff pastured his horse. As a result of eating a portion of the yew tree which had grown over the meadow, the horse was poisoned and died.

Held, the plaintiff was entitled to damages. (But see *Ponting v Noakes*.)

Cummings v *Granger* [1977] 1 All ER 104 (Court of Appeal)

The plaintiff, in circumstances which rendered her a trespasser, entered the defendant's breakers' yard at night. She was attacked and injured by the defendant's untrained Alsatian guard dog. Expert evidence was that the dog's behaviour was normal for an untrained Alsatian with a territory to defend.

Held, (1) the requirements of the Animals Act 1971, s2(1), were satisfied. The likelihood of the damage was due to characteristics not normally found except in particular circumstances, namely the circumstances whereby the dog ran loose in the yard which it regarded as part of its territory. (2) The action failed, since in all the circumstances it was not unreasonable for the defendant to have kept the dog to protect his property (s5(3)(b)), and since the plaintiff, having known about the dog and seen a warning notice, voluntarily accepted the risk (s5(2)). (See also *Curtis* v *Betts* and the Guard Dogs Act 1975, s1.)

Cummings (or McWilliams) v *Sir William Arrol & Co Ltd* [1962] 1 All ER 623 (House of Lords)

An experienced steel erector fell 70 feet to his death and his widow sought damages for negligence against his employers and for breach of statutory duty under the Factories Act 1937 against the occupiers of the site. Safety belts, which would probably have saved the man had he used one, had been removed from the site two or three days before the accident, but he had never used a safety belt in the past when one was available and it was highly probable that he would not have worn a safety belt on the occasion in question if one had been provided. The defendant employers had not instructed or exhorted the deceased to use a safety belt and the practice of not wearing them, save in exceptional circumstances which did not obtain here, was widely established among steel erectors.

Held, assuming that the defendants were in breach of their respective duties in not providing a safety belt, nevertheless they were not liable in damages because their breach of duty was not the cause of the accident as the deceased would not have worn a safety belt if one had been provided and there was no duty on the employers to instruct or exhort the deceased to wear a safety belt.

Cunningham v *Whelan* (1917) 52 Ir LT 67

The plaintiff was driving an empty cart when he saw 24 bullocks and heifers (a 'mass' of cattle), the property of the defendant, on the highway in front of him. There was no one in charge of the animals and, although the plaintiff stopped his horse, they pressed in on the cart and upset it, causing injury to both the cart and the plaintiff.

Held, the plaintiff was entitled to damages as an owner is bound to use care and caution to prevent his animals from straying in such numbers as to render the highway positively unsafe or dangerous to those who use it.

Curran v Northern Ireland Co-ownership Housing Association Ltd
[1987] 2 All ER 13 (House of Lords)

The plaintiffs' predecessor in title extended the house with the aid of an improvement grant from the Northern Ireland Housing Executive: statute required the work to be 'executed to the satisfaction' of the executive. The plaintiffs discovered that the extension's construction was defective and they sued, inter alia, the executive for negligence.

Held, their action could not succeed as, in all the circumstances it would not be fair and reasonable to impose a duty of care on the executive in favour of the plaintiffs. The statute's purpose was to ensure that public money was properly spent, rather than to protect recipients of grant aid, and the executive had no control over building operations once grant aid had been approved. (See also *Murphy* v *Brentwood District Council*.)

Curtis v Betts [1990] 1 All ER 769 (Court of Appeal)

When the defendants' large bull mastiff was being loaded into the back of their Land Rover, the plaintiff, aged ten, who lived opposite and had known the dog since it was a puppy and was very friendly with it, approached it and was bitten on the face. The plaintiff sued for damages, relying on s2(2) of the Animals Act 1971.

Held, his action would be successful. The requirement of s2(2)(a) of the 1971 Act was satisfied (any damage which it caused was likely to be severe) as were the requirements of s2(2)(b), (c) (tendency to defend their own territory, here the back of the Land Rover, and the defendants were aware of that characteristic). (See also *Cummings* v *Granger*.)

Cutler v United Dairies (London) Ltd [1933] 2 KB 297
(Court of Appeal)

A horse drawing a milk cart owned by the defendants galloped away without its driver and ran into a field. The driver attempted to pacify the horse but as he did not meet with success he shouted 'Help, help!' and the plaintiff went to his aid. The plaintiff received injuries when the horse reared and knocked him down.

Held, the principle volenti non fit injuria applied and the plaintiff was not entitled to damages. (But see *Haynes* v *Harwood*.)

Cutler v Vauxhall Motors Ltd [1970] 2 All ER 56 (Court of Appeal)

The plaintiff's right ankle was grazed by the admitted negligence of the defendants. Prior to the accident the plaintiff had suffered from varicosity in the veins of both legs, and would have probably required an operation at some future date. The graze set off the varicose condition and the operation was carried out immediately. The defendants contended that damages were not recoverable in respect of the loss of wages suffered while the plaintiff was in hospital for the operation.

Held, the defendants' contention would be successful. The object of damages is to place the plaintiff in as good a position as he was in before the wrong, and thus the plaintiff cannot be recouped for a loss which, had there been no accident, he would in all probability have been obliged to bear himself. (See also *Salih* v *Enfield Health Authority*.)

D & F Estates Ltd v Church Commissioners for England
[1988] 2 All ER 992 (House of Lords)

Between 1963 and 1965 Wates Ltd, the third defendants, were employed by the second defendants (now in liquidation) to build a block of flats on the first defendants' land. In 1965 the first defendants granted the plaintiffs a 98 year lease of one of the flats and in 1980, while the plaintiffs were on holiday, it was discovered by decorators that some plaster was loose. Remedial work was necessary and when the plaintiffs sued to recover, inter alia, the cost of it the judge found that sub-contractors employed by Wates Ltd had carried out the plastering negligently.

Held, the third defendants were not liable because the cost of repairing the plaster, before the defect had caused personal injury or physical damage to other property, was not recoverable in tort as it was pure economic loss. They were not vicariously liable for their subcontractors' negligence: their only duty had been to employ competent plasterers and this they had done. (Doubted: *Batty* v *Metropolitan Property Realizations Ltd*; not followed: *Anns* v *Merton London Borough* and *Junior Books Ltd* v *Veitchi Co Ltd*; see also *Murphy* v *Brentwood District Council*.)

Daily Mirror Newspapers Ltd v Gardner [1968] 2 All ER 163
(Court of Appeal)

The defendant, who was President of the National Federation of Newsagents, sent a letter to all members on the Federation's behalf, calling for a boycott of the *Daily Mirror*. It was expected that the newsagents would tell their wholesalers to discontinue supplies of the newspaper for a week. This would result in the wholesalers having to break their continuing contracts for supplies with the plaintiffs, but the defendant had no knowledge of the nature of this contract. The plaintiffs sought an injunction restraining the defendant from interfering with their contractual relationship with the wholesalers.

Held, allowing the plaintiffs' claim, the defendant had induced a breach of contract without lawful justification. It was immaterial that he did not know the details of the contract between the plaintiffs and the wholesalers, as he had acted recklessly not caring whether he caused a breach of contract or not. Furthermore the plaintiffs had made out a prima facie case that the defendants had used unlawful means to injure their trade. The boycott recommendation amounted to unlawful means because it was to be regarded as contrary to the public interest by virtue of the Restrictive Trade Practices Act 1956. (See also *Greig* v *Insole*.)

Dale v Wood (1822) 7 Moore CP 33

The plaintiff, who alleged that he had been beaten, bruised, wounded and ill treated by the defendant, claimed damages for assault. The defendant proved that he made his attack after the plaintiff had approached him on horseback, dismounted, provoked and held up his stick at him.

Held, the defendant was justified in acting as he did and the plaintiff's action would fail. (But see *Lane* v *Holloway.*)

Daly v *General Steam Navigation Co Ltd* [1980] 3 All ER 696 (Court of Appeal)

As a result of the defendants' negligence, the plaintiff, wife and mother of two young children, suffered permanent disability in her right arm. Her claim for damages included a claim for 'partial loss of housekeeping capacity' in respect of both the pre-trial period and the future years. In the pre-trial period she had not in fact employed domestic help; for lack of means she had managed as best she could with such help as her family could give her.

Held, in regard to the pre-trial period, the court had to consider the plaintiff's actual loss and, as no domestic help had been employed, her loss of housekeeping ability fell to be assessed as part of her general damages for pain, suffering and loss of amenity. As to the future years, the proper measure of damages was the estimated cost of employing domestic help for eight hours a week during the plaintiff's life expectancy and it was immaterial that she might choose to spend those damages in other ways. (See also *Hay* v *Hughes.*)

Dann v *Hamilton* [1939] 1 All ER 59

The plaintiff was a voluntary and non-paying passenger in a car driven by one Hamilton who, to her knowledge, was under the influence of drink to such an extent as substantially to increase the chances of a collision arising from his negligence. The plaintiff had the opportunity of getting out of the car before the occurrence of the accident in which she was injured and Hamilton was killed. The plaintiff claimed damages against Hamilton's estate and the defence relied upon the maxim volenti non fit injuria.

Held, the plaintiff should succeed as she had not, by implication, consented to or agreed to absolve Hamilton from liability in respect of subsequent negligence on his part. (See also *Bowater* v *Rowley Regis Corporation* and the Law Reform (Contributory Negligence) Act 1945; but see *Morris* v *Murray.*)

Darbishire v *Warran* [1963] 2 All ER 310 (Court of Appeal)

The plaintiff's Lea Francis shooting brake was seriously damaged in a collision as a result of negligent driving by the defendant. The market value of the Lea Francis was £85 and the plaintiff's insurance company paid the plaintiff £80. Although the plaintiff was advised that the repair of the car was uneconomic, he had it repaired at a cost of £192 and sought to recover from the defendant by way of damages the difference between the cost of repairs and the amount received from the insurance company.

Held, the plaintiff should recover only £30, ie the difference between the market value of the car and the amount received from the insurance company plus £25 being the cost of hiring another car. The Lea Francis was not an irreplaceable article and, as it would be treated as a constructive total loss, the measure of damages was its value. By having the car repaired, the plaintiff had omitted to take all reasonable steps to mitigate his loss ie he had not tried to buy a similar car. (See also *Ironfield v Eastern Gas Board*.)

Davey v Harrow Corporation [1957] 2 All ER 305 (Court of Appeal)

The plaintiff brought an action claiming damages for nuisance and for an injunction on the ground that the roots of trees, the property of the defendant corporation, who were the adjoining owners, had penetrated into his land and caused subsidence so that his house was extensively damaged.

Held, he was entitled to succeed and it was immaterial whether the trees were planted or self-sown. (See also *Lemmon v Webb*.)

Davidson v Chief Constable of North Wales [1994] 2 All ER 597 (Court of Appeal)

Exercising their own judgment but acting on information received from a store detective, two police officers had arrested the plaintiff on suspicion of shoplifting and kept her at the police station for two hours. She was released when the police heard from the store that payment for the goods in question had in fact been made. The plaintiff sued, inter alia, the detective's employers for damages for false imprisonment.

Held, her action would fail as it could not be said that the detective's acts had 'amounted to some direction, or procuring, or direct request, or direct encouragement that [the police] should act by way of arresting [the plaintiff]' (*per* SIR THOMAS BINGHAM MR). 'Whether a request by itself is sufficient to make a person liable does not arise in this case. What is clear … is that merely giving information is not enough. That does not give rise to false imprisonment. [The detective] did no more than that. However much one may look at evidence and analyse what possible consequences might or would arise from the information which she gave, the fact is that all she did was give the information' (*per* STAUGHTON LJ).

Davies v Taylor [1972] 3 All ER 836 (House of Lords)

In an action by the plaintiff under the Fatal Accidents Acts in respect of the death of her husband, the defendant argued that since the plaintiff had deserted her husband five weeks before the accident, there was no 'dependency' for the purpose of the Act.

Held, a plaintiff under the Fatal Accidents Acts need only prove as a reasonable expectation, and not on the balance of probabilities, that pecuniary benefit would have been derived from the deceased. But the present plaintiff failed, having shown a mere speculative possibility as opposed to a reasonable expectation of a reconciliation with her husband. (See also s1 of the Fatal Accidents Act 1976.)

Davis v Radcliffe [1990] 2 All ER 536 (Privy Council)

By statute, the Isle of Man Treasurer, subject to directions from the Isle of Man Finance

Board, had power to grant and revoke banking licences. The plaintiffs had deposited money with a bank, but it collapsed shortly after the revocation of its licence. The plaintiffs alleged the Treasurer had owed depositors a duty of care to carry out his functions so that depositors' (funds would be safe and that his breach of that duty had caused them loss.

Held, the plaintiffs' claim had rightly been struck out as disclosing no reasonable cause of action either in negligence or breach of statutory duty. (Applied: *Yuen Kun-yeu v A-G of Hong Kong.*)

De Keyser's Royal Hotel Ltd v Spicer Brothers Ltd (1914) 30 TLR 257

The defendants used a steam pile-driving machine during the night on a building site in the vicinity of the plaintiffs' hotel. There was evidence that, because of the considerable noise caused by this operation, the guests at the hotel were unable to sleep and after-dinner speakers were unable to make themselves heard.

Held, by pile-driving at night the defendants were not conducting their building operations in a reasonable and proper manner, and an injunction would be granted to restrain the driving of piles between 10 pm and 6.30 am. (See also *Leeman v Montagu.*)

Delacroix v Thevenet (1817) 2 Stark 63

The defendant posted a letter to the plaintiff which contained matter which was defamatory of him. As the defendant was believed to have known, the plaintiff's clerk was in the habit of opening all letters addressed to the plaintiff which were not marked 'private'.

Held, there was sufficient evidence for the jury to consider whether the defendant intended the defamatory statement to be published. In the event, the plaintiff was awarded damages of £100. (But see *Bryanston Finance Ltd v de Vries.*)

Denny v Supplies & Transport Co Ltd [1950] 2 KB 374
(Court of Appeal)

A dock labourer noticed that a cargo of timber which he was required to unload had been badly and negligently stacked by stevedores and suggested to his employers that it was a case for the payment of danger money. The man was injured in the course of this work as a result of the shifting of the timber and he claimed damages from the stevedores.

Held, the labourer would succeed. Although he was aware of the danger, there was no practical alternative to proceeding with the work. (See also *Targett v Torfaen Borough Council.*)

Department of the Environment v Thomas Bates & Son
[1990] 2 All ER 943 (House of Lords)

The defendant builders constructed an office block in 1970/71 and the plaintiffs were underlessees of the upper nine storeys. In 1981/82 it was discovered that low-strength concrete had been used in pillars and that, although capable of supporting the existing load, they were unable to support the design load safely. Seeking to recover the cost of strengthening the pillars, the plaintiffs maintained that the defendants had owed them a duty of care in the construction of the building. The judge found that there had been no cracking of the building or imminent danger to the health or safety of the plaintiffs' employees or the public.

Held, the plaintiffs' claim could not succeed as they had suffered purely economic loss. 'It has been held by this House in *Murphy* v *Brentwood District Council* that *Anns* v *Merton London Borough Council* was wrongly decided and should be departed from, by reason of the erroneous views there expressed as to the scope of any duty of care owed to purchasers of houses by local authorities when exercising the powers conferred on them for the purpose of securing compliance with building regulations. The process of reasoning by which the House reached its conclusion necessarily included close examination of the position of the builder who was primarily responsible, through lack of care in the construction process, for the presence of defects in the building. It was the unanimous view that, while the builder would be liable under the principle of *Donoghue* v *Stevenson* in the event of the defect, before it had been discovered, causing physical injury to persons or damage to property other than the building itself, there was no sound basis in principle for holding him liable for the pure economic loss suffered by a purchaser who discovered the defect, however such discovery might come about, and who was required to expend money in order to make the building safe and suitable for its intended purpose' (*per* LORD KEITH OF KINKEL). (Applied: *Murphy* v *Brentwood District Council*; see also *Nitrigin Eireann Teoranta* v *Inco Alloys Ltd.*)

Derbyshire County Council v *Times Newspapers Ltd* [1993] AC 534 (House of Lords)

Could a local authority sue for defamation?

Held, it could not: it would be contrary to the public interest for organs of government, central or local, to have that right. 'There are ... features of a local authority which may be regarded as distinguishing it from other types of corporation, whether trading or non-trading. The most important of these features is that it is a governmental body. Further, it is a democratically elected body ... It is of the highest public importance that a democratically elected governmental body, or indeed any governmental body, should be open to uninhibited public criticism. The threat of a civil action for defamation must inevitably have an inhibiting effect on freedom of speech ... I can only add that I find it satisfactory to be able to conclude that the common law of England is consistent with the obligations assumed by the Crown under the [convention for the Protection of Human Rights and Fundamental Freedoms]' (*per* LORD KEITH OF KINKEL). (But see *South Hetton Coal Co Ltd* v *North-Eastern News Association Ltd.*)

Derry v *Peek* (1889) 14 App Cas 337 (House of Lords)

The plaintiff brought an action for deceit against company directors. The plaintiff had purchased shares in the company, relying upon a prospectus issued by the defendants. The prospectus contained a false statement.

Held, the defendants were not liable because they made the statement in the honest belief that it was true. 'Fraud is proved when it is shown that a false representation has been made (1) knowingly, or (2) without belief in its truth, or (3) recklessly, careless whether it be true or false' (*per* LORD HERSCHELL).

Dews v *National Coal Board* [1987] 2 All ER 545 (House of Lords)

The plaintiff miner belonged to a compulsory pension scheme to which he paid weekly contributions. He was injured at work, for which the defendant employers were liable, and for the latter part of his sick leave he received no pay and therefore made no pension contributions, although this did not affect his pension rights. In his claim for loss of earnings he included the contributions which he would have made to the pension scheme during this latter period.

Held, his claim could not succeed as it would amount to double recovery, but he would have been entitled to compensation if he had lost pension rights. (Applied: *Parry* v *Cleaver*.)

Digital Equipment Ltd v *Hampshire County Council* See *Capital and Counties plc* v *Hampshire County Council*

Dimond v *Lovell* [1999] 3 All ER 1 (Court of Appeal)

The defendant drove his car into the back of the plaintiff's: her car was damaged. While her car was in a garage for repair, the plaintiff hired a car, the agreement providing that payment could be postponed until her claim against the defendant had been concluded and that the owner could conduct any litigation necessary to recover the damages. The agreement did not satisfy the formal requirements of the Consumer Credit Act 1974, but the owner sought, in the plaintiff's name, to recover as damages the hire charges.

Held, the claim could not succeed. Since the agreement had not satisfied the relevant statutory requirements, it was not enforceable against the plaintiff. She had therefore received a benefit (the use of the hire car) from a third party (the owner) at no cost to herself, offsetting the loss caused by the defendant's negligence, and she could not recover damages to recompense the third party unless a trust could be imposed on those damages for the third party's benefit. Here, such a trust would not be imposed. '... the 1974 Act has enacted than an agreement not "properly executed" is unenforceable. It is not, in my judgment, the function of the courts to remedy that unenforceability by creating a trust in favour of [the owner] over damages payable to [the plaintiff]' (*per* SIR RICHARD SCOTT V-C). (Applied: *Hunt* v *Severs*; *McCall* v *Brooks* [1984] RTR 99 disapproved.)

Director of Public Prosecutions v *Jones* [1999] 2 All ER 257 (House of Lords)

Having been part of a peaceful protest group which had formed on the roadside verge adjacent to the perimeter fence of Stonehenge, the defendants were convicted of taking part in a trespassory assembly, contrary to s14B(2) of the Public Order Act 1986.

Held, the defendants had not committed this offence. 'The question to which this appeal gives rise is whether the law today should recognise that the public highway is a public place, on which all manner of reasonable activities may go on ... in my judgment it should. Provided these activities are reasonable, do not involve the commission of a public or private nuisance, and do not amount to an obstruction of the highway unreasonably impeding the primary right of the general public to pass and repass, they should not constitute a trespass. Subject to these qualifications, therefore, there would be a public right of peaceful assembly on the public highway. ... Further, there can be no basis for distinguishing highways on publicly owned land and privately owned land. The nature of the public's right of use of the highway cannot depend upon whether the owner of the sub-soil is a private landowner or a public authority. Any fear, however, that the rights of private landowners might be prejudiced by the right as defined, are unfounded. The law of trespass will continue to protect private landowners against unreasonably large, unreasonably prolonged or unreasonably obstructive assemblies upon these highways. ... If ... the common law of trespass is not as clear as I have held it to be, then at least it is uncertain and developing, so that regard should be had to the European Convention in resolving the uncertainty and in determining how it should develop: *Derbyshire CC v Times Newspapers Ltd* ... I would invoke article 11 to clarify or develop the common law in the terms which I have held it to be; but ... I do not find it necessary to do so' (*per* LORD IRVINE OF LAIRG LC). (But see *Harrison v Duke of Rutland.*)

Dobbie v *Medway Health Authority* [1994] 4 All ER 450 (Court of Appeal)

In 1973 the plaintiff underwent a mastectomy, but it subsequently appeared that the growth had been benign. In 1988 she heard of a similar case in which a surgeon had been found to be guilty of negligence and she appreciated, for the first time, that her breast need not have been removed. She instituted proceedings.

Held, her claim was time-barred under s11 of the Limitation Act 1980: time had started to run against her for the purposes of s14(1) of the 1980 Act when she knew that her injury was capable of being attributed to the defendants' act or omission irrespective of whether, at that point, she knew that the act or mission was actionable or tortious. In view of the long delay, it would be inequitable to the defendants to exercise discretion under s33 of the 1980 Act and disapply the limitation period. (But see *Halford v Brooks* and *Hartley v Birmingham City District Council.*)

Dodd Properties (Kent) Ltd v *Canterbury City Council* [1980] 1 All ER 928 (Court of Appeal)

In 1968 the plaintiffs' building was damaged by the defendants' pile-driving operations on an adjoining site. Shortly before the hearing in 1978 the defendants admitted liability and the question arose as to the date at which damages should be assessed.

Held, the cost of repairs was to be assessed at the earliest date when, having regard to all the circumstances, they could reasonably be undertaken. Taking due account of, inter alia, the plaintiffs' financial stringency in 1970 (the earliest date when it would have been physically possible to put the work in hand), the fact that it made commercial sense to postpone the repairs until the outcome of the action and the defendants' wrongful denial of liability, the cost of the repairs should be assessed at the date of the action, ie 1978. (See also *Perry v Sidney Phillips & Son*.)

Dodds v Dodds [1978] 2 All ER 539

A man suffered fatal injuries as a result of his wife's negligent driving. His administrators claimed damages under the Fatal Accidents Acts on behalf of the couple's young son, as a dependant.

Held, the validity of the son's claim under this head was not affected by the wife's negligence. (See also *Hay v Hughes*.)

Dollman v A & S Hillman Ltd [1941] 1 All ER 355 (Court of Appeal)

The plaintiff was walking along the pavement in front of the defendants' butchers' shop when she slipped on a piece of fat and received injuries. It was established that the fat came from the defendants' shop, but there was no conclusive evidence as to how the fat reached the pavement.

Held, the defendants were liable in nuisance as well as in negligence.

Donaldson v McNiven [1952] 1 All ER 1213 (Court of Appeal)

The defendant's 13-year-old son promised his father that he would only use his air-gun in the cellar for firing matchsticks. He obtained some pellets surreptitiously and fired them in an alley-way, thereby causing injury to the plaintiff.

Held, in these circumstances, the defendant had not been negligent and the plaintiff's action would fail. (But see *Newton v Edgerley*.)

Donoghue v Stevenson See *M'Alister (or Donoghue) v Stevenson*

Donovan v Gwentoys Ltd [1990] 1 All ER 1018 (House of Lords)

When aged 16 and an employee of the defendants, the plaintiff had slipped and fallen at work. Shortly before the expiration of the limitation period, she consulted solicitors: they applied for legal aid but failed to serve a writ until some 5½ months after the limitation period had expired. Nearly a further three years passed before the defendants became fully aware of the nature of the claim and the date of the accident: they maintained that the action was statute barred by virtue of s11 of the Limitation Act 1980 and the plaintiff sought relief under s33(1) of that Act.

Held, the action was statute barred. While the judge's discretion under s33(1) of the 1980 Act was unfettered (and it was not fettered by s33(3) of that Act), he had to consider the fairness of the situation and the degree of prejudice to the respective parties. Here, the defendants would have great difficulty in defending so long after the event and the plaintiff's prejudice would be slight as she had a strong claim against her solicitors for failing to institute proceedings in due time. (But see *Shapland* v *Palmer, Stubbings* v *Webb* and *Hartley* v *Birmingham City District Council.*)

Doughty v Turner Manufacturing Co Ltd [1964] 1 All ER 98 (Court of Appeal)

A workman at the defendants' factory inadvertently knocked a loose asbestos cement cover into molten liquid at 800° Centigrade. After a minute or so the liquid erupted and injured bystanders, one of whom was the plaintiff. The defendants did not appreciate that the immersion of the cover would produce an explosion and they were not to blame for not appreciating it, but tests subsequently showed that such an explosion was inevitable. The plaintiff sought damages in negligence.

Held, his action should fail as in the state of knowledge at the time of the explosion the accident was not foreseeable. The damage here suffered was of an entirely different kind to that which might have resulted from the foreseeable splash when the cover became immersed in the molten liquid and for this reason it could not be said that the plaintiff's injuries were a result of a 'magnified splash' for which the defendants were liable. (But see *Boardman* v *Sanderson* and *Hughes* v *Lord Advocate.*)

Doyle v Olby (Ironmongers) Ltd [1969] 2 All ER 119 (Court of Appeal)

The plaintiff was induced by fraudulent misrepresentations to buy the defendants' ironmongers' business. The business was so bad that the plaintiff was forced to sell it. He brought an action for deceit against the defendant.

Held, the proper measure of damages for deceit, as distinct from damages for breach of contract, was all the damage directly flowing from the tort. The plaintiff recovered his overall loss up to his final disposal of the business less any benefits he had received. Per curiam, foreseeability is not the appropriate test of remoteness of damage in deceit. (Applied in *Smith New Court Securities Ltd* v *Scrimgeour Vickers (Assed Management) Ltd*); see *East* v *Maurer* and *Smith Kline & French Laboratories Ltd* v *Long.*)

Drane v Evangelou [1978] 2 All ER 437 (Court of Appeal)

Associates of the defendant landlord invaded the maisonette when the plaintiff protected tenant was out and put his belongings in the back yard. The landlord had 'behaved atrociously': the judge said that the facts were sufficient to found a claim in trespass and he awarded the plaintiff £1,000 by way of damages.

Held, the defendant's appeal would be dismissed as the award was appropriate as exemplary damages or aggravated damages. 'Such conduct ... can ... be punished by the civil law by an award for exemplary damages' (*per* LORD DENNING MR). (See also *Rookes* v *Barnard.*)

Dunlop v *Woollahara Municipal Council* [1981] 1 All ER 1202 (Privy Council)

Dr Dunlop purchased some land on which he hoped to erect eight-storey flats. Acting on the advice of their solicitors, and without acting mala fide, the council passed two resolutions restricting development, inter alia, to three storeys. Dr Dunlop obtained declarations that both resolutions were invalid and void. As Dr Dunlop had lost financially as a result of the delay in reselling the land, he claimed damages, inter alia, for negligence and abuse of public office.

Held, the court had correctly dismissed Dr Dunlop's claim. Even if the council owed Dr Dunlop a duty of care to ascertain whether they had power to pass the resolutions, no breach of that duty had been proved as they had received advice, albeit wrong advice, from their solicitors. As to 'the well-established tort of misfeasance by a public officer in the discharge of his public duties' (*per* LORD DIPLOCK), the council were here an 'officer' but there had been no 'misfeasance' as their decision had not been actuated by malice. (See also *F* v *Wirral Metropolitan Borough Council* and *Jones* v *Swansea City Council.*)

Dyer v *Munday* [1895] 1 QB 742 (Court of Appeal)

The manager of the defendant's furniture business assaulted the plaintiff in the course of removing a bedstead from her house. He was summoned and convicted and fined and the fine was paid. In an action for trespass and assault the defendant relied on s45 of the Offences Against the Person Act 1861 (which provides that where a person had been convicted of assault and battery and the fine paid that person 'shall be released from all further or other proceedings, civil or criminal, for the same cause').

Held, the plaintiff would be awarded damages. Although this statutory provision released the defendant's manager from further liability it did nothing to release the defendant from liability for the tortious act of a servant committed in the course of his employment. (See also *Lloyd* v *Grace, Smith & Co.*)

Dymond v *Pearce* [1972] I All ER 1142 (Court of Appeal)

A lorry driver for his own convenience parked his lorry for the night at the side of a well lit road. The plaintiff was a pillion passenger on a motor bicycle which collided with the back of the lorry. The plaintiff was injured.

Held, leaving a lorry on the highway for a considerable period for the driver's convenience constitutes a nuisance by obstruction, actionable if it causes damage to a member of the public. But the sole cause of the accident was the negligence of the motor cyclist, and therefore the plaintiff was not entitled to damages for nuisance from the lorry owners. There was no evidence of negligence by the lorry driver. (See also *Rouse* v *Squires.*)

East v *Maurer* [1991] 2 All ER 733 (Court of Appeal)

The defendant owned two hair salons in Bournemouth: he sold one of them to the plaintiffs who, in making the purchase, were partly induced by his representation that he had no intention of working in the other, save in emergencies. He continued working full-time in the other salon and, such was his reputation, the plaintiffs' business was never profitable and they were forced to sell it at a loss. The plaintiffs sued for damages: the judge found that the defendant's representations were false and awarded the plaintiffs, inter alia, £15,000 for loss of profits, based on the profits the defendant would have made, less 25% for the plaintiffs' lesser experience.

Held, while damages for loss of profits may properly be recovered in an action for deceit, here the judge had assessed them on the wrong basis. The correct approach was to assess the profit the plaintiffs might have made if the false representation had not been made (ie, the profit they might have made in another salon bought for a similar sum) and on that basis the appropriate sum was £10,000. (See also *Doyle* v *Olby (Ironmongers) Ltd.*)

East Suffolk Rivers Catchment Board v *Kent* [1940] 4 All ER 527 (House of Lords)

A wall of a river collapsed and flooded the respondents' land. The appellants, the catchment board for the area, in exercise of a statutory power, attempted to repair the wall, adopting a method which was impracticable and using an insufficient number of men.

Held, the appellants were not liable for the damage suffered by the respondents as they had exercised their discretion honestly and, in such circumstances, the only duty which they owed to the respondents was not to add to the damage which they would have suffered if they (the appellants) had decided to do nothing.

Egger v *Viscount Chelmsford* [1964] 3 All ER 406 (Court of Appeal)

The plaintiff was a judge of Alsatian dogs and her name appeared on the list of judges kept by the Kennel Club. The assistant secretary of the Kennel Club wrote to inform the secretary of another dog club that the Kennel Club's Committee was unable to approve the appointment of the plaintiff as judge at a dog show and it was found that his words were defamatory of the plaintiff. It was also found that the occasion was privileged and that five of the Committee of the Kennel Club were actuated by malice, but that three members and the assistant secretary were not.

Held, those who were not actuated by malice were not liable to the plaintiff in damages for libel. 'All I would say is that the defence of qualified privilege is a defence for the *individual* who is sued, and not a defence for the publication. Speaking generally, I cannot believe that an agent should be made answerable for the malice of his principal. It is very different when it is sought to make an innocent principal answerable for the malice of his agent. Then you come into a different realm altogether. You come into the law of agency. An innocent principal is liable for the fraud, or, I would add, the malice of his agent, acting within the scope of his authority, whether the agent is acting for his principal's benefit or not. Even in a joint tort, the tort is the separate act of each individual. Each is severally answerable for it: and, being severally answerable, each is entitled to his own defence. If he is himself innocent of malice, he is entitled to the benefit of it. He is not to be dragged down with the guilty' (*per* LORD DENNING MR).

Electrochrome Ltd v Welsh Plastics Ltd [1968] 2 All ER 205

The defendants' employee negligently drove a lorry so as to damage a fire hydrant on an industrial estate where the plaintiffs' factory was sited. As a result of the damage to the hydrant, it was necessary to cut off the supply of water for several hours while repairs were being made. The plaintiffs' factory was unable to work without the water supply, and they sued to recover the amount of their loss from the defendants.

Held, the claim must fail as the duty of care owed by the defendant was owed to the owner of the hydrant and not to the plaintiff: damnum sine injuria. (See also *Margarine Union GmbH v Cambay Prince Steamship Co Ltd* and *SCM (United Kingdom) Ltd v W J Whittal & Son Ltd*.)

Elguzouli-Daf v Commissioner of Police of the Metropolis See *Olotu v Home Office*

Elias v Pasmore [1934] 2 KB 164

Two police inspectors entered the offices of the National Unemployed Workers movement and arrested one Hannington, for whose arrest a warrant had been issued. While they were there, they unlawfully seized a number of documents.

Held, this fact did not render the police officers trespassers ab initio as to the premises, but only as to the documents. (See also *Six Carpenters' Case, The*.)

Ellis v Loftus Iron Co (1874) LR 10 CP 10

The defendants' land was separated from that of the plaintiff by wire fencing. The defendants' horse and one of the plaintiff's mares got close together on either side of the fence and the horse injured the mare by biting and kicking the animal through the fence.

Held, the plaintiff was entitled to damages in trespass as the horse's mouth and feet protruded through the fence and over his land. (But see *Wandsworth District Board of Works v United Telephone Co Ltd*; see also s4 of the Animals Act 1971.)

Elvin & Powell Ltd v Plummer Roddis Ltd (1933) 50 TLR 158

A man, who said he was a buyer, entered the plaintiffs' warehouse and ordered coats to the value of about £350. He said he wanted them sent at once to the defendants' Brighton branch. The goods were dispatched and the man then telegraphed the defendants saying: 'Goods dispatched to your branch in error. Sending van to collect.– Elvin and Powell'. A man later presented himself at the defendants' premises and said he was employed by the plaintiffs; after some inquiries had been made, the coats were handed to him. Neither the coats nor the man were seen again. The plaintiffs claimed damages for wrongful conversion and negligence while acting as bailees.

Held, judgment would be entered in favour of the defendants as they were involuntary bailees and had acted reasonably and without negligence. (But see *Perry (Howard E) & Co Ltd* v *British Railways Board*.)

Elwes v *Brigg Gas Co* (1886) 33 ChD 562

A gas company took a 99-year lease of certain land for the purpose of erecting a gasholder. In the course of excavations they discovered a prehistoric boat 6 ft below the surface.

Held, the boat was the property of the lessor. (See also *South Staffordshire Water Co* v *Sharman*.)

Emanuel (H and N) Ltd v *Greater London Council* [1971] 2 All ER 835 (Court of Appeal)

An arrangement was made whereby a firm of independent contractors, engaged by the Ministry of Works, would remove two war-time bungalows and all materials and rubbish from a site owned by the defendant council. The contractors started a fire to burn unwanted materials. Sparks blew on to the plaintiffs' property and the resulting fire caused damage.

Held, the council as occupier was liable for the escape of fire caused by the negligence of anyone other than a stranger. The contractors were on the land with the council's leave, and although the contractors were forbidden by the terms of their contract from starting fires on the land, the council could reasonably have anticipated that they might start a fire.

Emeh v *Kensington and Chelsea and Westminster Area Health Authority* [1984] 3 All ER 1044 (Court of Appeal)

The plaintiff mother of three normal children had an abortion and at the same time sterilisation which was performed negligently: some months later she again became pregnant. Not wanting a further operation, she allowed the pregnancy to continue but when born her child was congenitally abnormal. She claimed damages for negligence.

Held, her action would succeed as her decision not to have an abortion was neither a novus actus interveniens nor a failure to mitigate damage. There was no rule of public policy which prevented the plaintiff from recovering in full the financial damage sustained by her as the result of the negligent failure to perform the sterilisation operation properly, regardless of whether the child was healthy or abnormal. Accordingly the plaintiff was entitled to damages for loss of future earnings, maintenance of the child up to trial, maintenance of the child in the future, the plaintiff's pain and suffering up to the time of the trial and future loss of amenity and pain and suffering, including the extra care that the child would require. (See also *Thake* v *Maurice*.)

Erven Warnink B V v *J Townend & Sons (Hull) Ltd* [1979] 2 All ER 927 (House of Lords)

The plaintiffs manufactured and distributed 'advocaat', a distinct and recognisable alcoholic drink made almost exclusively in the Netherlands which had been sold in England for over

50 years. In 1974 the defendants began to market 'Old English Advocaat', a drink similar in many ways to 'advocaat', although it was unlikely that purchasers would confuse the two products. However, as 'Old English Advocaat' was wine rather than spirit-based, excise duty was less and it could be sold at a lower price.

Held, the plaintiffs were entitled to an injunction restraining the defendants from selling or distributing under the name 'advocaat' any similar drink which was not spirit-based. 'Where the falsehood is a misrepresentation that the competitor's goods are goods of definite class with a valuable reputation, and where the misrepresentation is likely to cause damage to established traders who own goodwill in relation to that class of goods, business morality seems to require that they should be entitled to protect their goodwill. The name of the tort committed by the party making the misrepresentation is not important, but in my opinion the tort is the same in kind as that which has hitherto been known as passing off' (*per* LORD FRASER OF TULLYBELTON). (Applied in *Taittinger* v *Allber Ltd*; see also *Cadbury Schweppes Pty Ltd* v *Pub Squash Co Pty Ltd* and *Associated Newspapers plc* v *Insert Media Ltd*.)

Esso Petroleum Co Ltd v *Mardon* [1976] 2 All ER 5 (Court of Appeal)

The plaintiff company interviewed the defendant as a prospective tenant of a new filling station. The defendant was told that the plaintiff estimated that the annual petrol consumption of the station in its third year of operation would amount to 200,000 gallons. In reliance upon the said statement the defendant entered into a three-year tenancy of the station. In fact, as the plaintiff should have known, the site was not good enough to have a consumption of more than 70,000 gallons per year. The defendant incurred substantial losses, including loss of a capital sum provided by a family company controlled by him. The plaintiff claimed possession of the station. The defendant counterclaimed for damages under, inter alia, the principle in *Hedley Byrne & Co Ltd* v *Heller & Partners Ltd*.

Held, (1) the statement was a negligent representation made by a party holding himself out as having special expertise, in circumstances which gave rise to a duty to take reasonable care to see that the representation was correct. (2) The duty of care existed during the pre-contractual negotiations and survived the making of the tenancy agreement. (3) The defendant was entitled to damages for the negligent misstatement, the damages being the same in contract and in tort, namely the amount the defendant had lost by being induced to enter the contract. (4) The capital sum was recoverable notwithstanding that it had not been provided by the defendant, since the contrary would be a denial of justice. (See also *Midland Bank Trust Co Ltd* v *Hett, Stubbs and Kemp*.)

Evans v *London Hospital Medical College* [1981] 1 All ER 715

The defendants, a pathologist and two toxicologists, carried out a post-mortem on the plaintiff's infant son and, in their report to the police which was submitted to the Director of Public Prosecutions, they stated that they had found morphine in certain of the child's organs. The plaintiff was charged with her son's murder but, after a pathologist engaged by the plaintiff had reported that he could find no traces of morphine in other organs, the prosecution offered no evidence against her and she was acquitted. The plaintiff claimed damages for negligence or malicious prosecution.

Held, the plaintiff had no claim for malicious prosecution as the law had been set in motion, not by the defendants but either by the police when they requested the original report or by the Director of Public Prosecutions when, on the strength of the report, the decision to prosecute was made. Both claims should also be dismissed because they were covered by the absolute immunity from any form of civil action conferred on a witness in criminal proceedings in respect of his evidence, such immunity extending to cover statements made prior to the commencement of proceedings if it could fairly be said to be part of the investigation of a crime or possible crime. (See also *Taylor* v *Serious Fraud Office*.)

Exxon Corpn v Exxon Insurance Consultants International Ltd
[1981] 2 All ER 495

After much time and effort, the plaintiff company decided to use the word 'Exxon' as part of its corporate name and as its main trade mark. Without the plaintiff's licence or consent, the defendant company adopted the same word as part of its corporate name.

Held, the plaintiff company was entitled to an injunction restraining passing off by the defendant by its continued use of the word 'Exxon' and from allowing its name incorporating the word 'Exxon' to remain on the companies' register. (See also *Reddaway* v *Banham*.)

F v Wirral Metropolitan Borough Council [1991] 2 All ER 648
(Court of Appeal)

Suffering from depression, the plaintiff mother agreed that her two children be taken into voluntary short-term care by a local authority pursuant to s1 of the Children Act 1948. Subsequently, acting under powers conferred by the same statute, the authority assumed parental control over the children and later resolved that the children should remain in care for the foreseeable future. The plaintiff claimed damages for, inter alia, loss of parental rights.

Held, the claim had properly been struck out. There was not, and the court would not create, a tort of interference with parental rights and, even if there had been a breach by the authority of the statutory code, it would give rise only to public law remedies to protect the welfare of the children and the remedy of damages for the tort of misfeasance in a public office. (See also *Dunlop* v *Woollahara Municipal Council*.)

Fardon v Harcourt-Rivington (1932) 146 LT 391 (House of Lords)

The defendant left his dog, which had no vicious propensities, in his parked car. When the plaintiff walked past the car the dog jumped at the rear window and a splinter of glass flew into his eye. The plaintiff claimed damages in respect of this injury.

Held, he could not succeed as 'people must guard against reasonable probabilities, but they are not bound to guard against fantastic possibilities' (*per* LORD DUNEDIN). (See also *Bolton v Stone.*)

Farrugia v Great Western Railway Co [1947] 2 All ER 565 (Court of Appeal)

The defendants' lorry driver attempted to drive a lorry carrying a large container under a bridge, but the load was so big that it was impossible to clear it. The container hit the bridge and fell off on to the plaintiff, a boy, and injured his leg. At the time of the accident the plaintiff was running behind the lorry, but shortly before he had been on the lorry as a trespasser and it was assumed that when the accident occurred he was a trespasser on the highway.

Held, the plaintiff was entitled to damages as the defendants had been negligent and had committed a breach of duty towards any person who was in the area where a person was liable to be injured as a result of the danger created by their negligence. (But see *Hay (or Bourhill) v Young.*)

Fay v Prentice (1845) 1 CB 828

The defendant erected a cornice at the side of his house projecting over the plaintiff's garden. Rain water flowed from the cornice into the garden.

Held, the erection of the cornice was a nuisance from which the law would infer injury to the plaintiff. (See also *Smith v Ciddy.*)

Fayed v Al-Tajir [1987] 2 All ER 396 (Court of Appeal)

The plaintiff, a United Arab Emirates national, claimed damages for libel in respect of a memorandum published by the defendant, that country's acting ambassador in London, to a counsellor in that country's London embassy.

Held, the action could not succeed as the memorandum was protected by absolute privilege. (See also *Chatterton v Secretary of State for India in Council.*)

Fels v Hedley & Co Ltd (1903) 21 RPC 91 (Court of Appeal)

The plaintiffs manufactured soap containing naphtha and sold it under the name 'Fels-Naptha'. Some two years later the defendants marketed 'Ladybird Naptha Soap'.

Held, they were entitled to do so as 'Naptha' was a descriptive word which merely denoted an ingredient contained in the soap. (But see *Baume & Co Ltd v A H Moore Ltd.*)

Ferguson v Welsh [1987] 3 All ER 777 (House of Lords)

A district council wished to demolish a building and they invited tenders for the work, the invitation stipulating that subcontractors were not to be used without the council's consent. Mr Spence's tender was accepted but, without consent, he arranged for the Welsh brothers to carry out the work. They employed an unsafe system of work as a result of which the plaintiff, their employee, sustained serious injury. The Welsh brothers and Mr Spence were not covered by insurance: were the council, as occupiers of the premises, liable in respect of the plaintiff's injuries?

Held, they were not as there had not been any 'use' of the premises by the plaintiff within s2(2) of the Occupiers' Liability Act 1957. '... if I ask myself, in relation to the facts of the present case, whether it can be said that Mr Ferguson's injury arose from a failure by the council to take reasonable care to see that persons in his position would be reasonably safe in using the premises for the relevant purposes, the answer must, I think, be No. There is no question, as I see it, of Mr Ferguson's injury arising from any such failure; for it arose not from his use of the premises but from the manner in which he carried out his work on the premises. For this simple reason, I do not consider that the 1957 Act has anything to do with the present case' (*per* LORD GOFF OF CHIEVELEY).

Fetter v Beale (1701) 1 Ld Raym 339, 692

It appeared that the plaintiff sued the defendant for battery and recovered £11 'and that after that recovery part of his skull by reason of the said battery came out of his head'. Eight years later he brought another action in respect of this consequence of the battery.

Held, this second action could not be maintained.

First National Commercial Bank plc v Humberts See Byrne v Hall Pain & Foster

Fish v Kapur [1948] 2 All ER 176

Mrs Fish claimed damages for negligence from her dentist, the defendant, because, in extracting a wisdom tooth, he left part of the root of the tooth in her jaw which he also fractured. There was evidence that a dentist could leave part of the root of a tooth or fracture a jaw without any blame attaching to him.

Held, Mrs Fish could not maintain a successful action as the doctrine of res ipsa loquitur did not apply and she had not proved that the defendant had been guilty of negligence. (But see *Cook v Lewis*.)

Fisher v CHT Ltd [1966] 1 All ER 88 (Court of Appeal)

The first defendants were proprietors of a club with a restaurant, the restaurant being managed and run under licence by the second defendants. The latter decided to redecorate the restaurant and employed X Ltd to do all the new plaster work but doing the electrical work themselves. The first defendants were not engaged on the work, but their maintenance man took a considerable interest in it. The plaintiff, a plasterer employed by X Ltd, was injured when the second defendants' electrician switched on the current, when he should not have done so. The plaintiff sued, inter alia, for breach of the Occupiers' Liability Act 1957.

Held, the first defendants as well as the second defendants were occupiers under the 1957 Act because, though the second defendants had the use of the restaurant, the first defendants still had the right to go through it and controlled the door to the whole premises. Therefore, they were under the common duty of care to all the visitors, including the plaintiff. (See also *Wheat v E Lacon & Co Ltd*.)

Fitzgerald v Lane [1988] 2 All ER 961 (House of Lords)

The plaintiff walked onto a pelican crossing while the lights were against him: he was hit first by the first defendant's car and then by the second defendant's car. In an action for personal injury against both defendants, the Court of Appeal said that if each of the three parties was at fault the plaintiff was only entitled to recover half (not two-thirds) of the damages awarded. The plaintiff appealed.

Held, his appeal would be dismissed as his conduct had to be contrasted with the totality of the defendants' tortious conduct. On the facts, the plaintiff's share of responsibility for his injuries was at least as great as that of the defendants jointly. (See also *Cork v Kirby McLean Ltd*.)

Forster v Outred & Co [1982] 2 All ER 753 (Court of Appeal)

In February 1973 the plaintiff, the freehold owner of a farm, executed a mortgage deed charging the property as continuing security for the liabilities to a certain company of her improvident son. In January 1975 the company demanded payment and in August that year the mother paid it almost £70,000. In January 1977 she issued a writ claiming damages for negligence against the defendant solicitors alleging that they had been in breach of their duty to explain the contents of the mortgage to her before she signed it. The plaintiff took no further step until December 1979 when she gave notice of intention to proceed and in February 1980 the defendants applied to strike out the action for want of prosecution. In March 1980 the plaintiff issued a second writ against the defendants claiming damages for negligent advice in relation to the mortgage.

Held, the judge had been right to dismiss the first action for want of prosecution in the light of inordinate and inexcusable delay. As to the second, the plaintiff's cause of action was complete when, in reliance on the allegedly negligent advice, she had acted to her detriment by incurring a contingent liability which was capable of monetary assessment, ie, in February 1973 when she executed the mortgage. It followed that the second writ had been issued outside the six years' limitation period. (Applied in *Moore (DW) & Co Ltd v Ferrier*; but see *Midland Bank Trust Co Ltd v Hett, Stubbs and Kemp*.)

Fouldes v Willoughby (1841) 8 M & W 540

The plaintiff and his two horses embarked on the defendant's ferry boat. The defendant told the plaintiff that, because of his misconduct, he must remove the horses, but when the plaintiff refused to do so the defendant took the horses from him and put them on the landing slip. The plaintiff remained on the ferry and the horses, which were turned loose on the road, were sold by the person who took possession of them. The plaintiff brought an action for trover.

Held, he was without a remedy as a mere wrongful asportation of a chattel does not, as a general rule, amount to a conversion.

Fowler v *Lanning* [1959] 1 All ER 290

In his statement of claim in an action for damages for trespass to the person the plaintiff alleged that '… the defendant shot the plaintiff. By reason of the premises the plaintiff sustained personal injuries and has suffered loss and damage'.

Held, the statement of claim disclosed no cause of action, as the onus of proof of the defendant's intention or negligence lay on the plaintiff. The plaintiff should either have alleged that the shooting was intentional or that the defendant was negligent, stating the facts alleged to constitute such negligence. (See also *Letang* v *Cooper*.)

Froom v *Butcher* [1975] 3 All ER 520 (Court of Appeal)

The plaintiff was injured when the car he was driving was in collision with the defendant's car. Although the accident was caused by the defendant's negligence, the plaintiff would not have suffered head and chest injuries had he been wearing a seat belt.

Held, the plaintiff was guilty of contributory negligence in not wearing a seat belt. Normally damages should be reduced by 25 per cent where injury would have been prevented by the wearing of a seat belt. (See also *Capps* v *Miller*.)

GWK Ltd v *Dunlop Rubber Co Ltd* (1926) 42 TLR 376

GWK Ltd agreed with the manufacturers of 'Bal-lon-ette' tyres that their tyres should be used on all new GWK cars. Two GWK cars were sent to the Glasgow Exhibition but, on the night before the exhibition opened, the defendants removed the 'Bal-lon-ette' tyres and substituted their own.

Held, they were liable in damages to GWK Ltd, for trespass to goods and to the manufacturers of 'Bal-lon-ette' tyres for a wrongful and malicious interference with their contractual rights. (But see *Thomson (D C) & Co Ltd* v *Deakin*.)

Galoo Ltd v *Bright Grahame Murray* [1995] 1 All ER 16 (Court of Appeal)

It was contended, inter alia, that the defendant auditors had owed the plaintiff purchaser of shares in another company a duty of care when preparing accounts which, to their (the defendants') knowledge, were to be relied on by the plaintiffs in calculating the purchase price of the shares and were to be prepared for that specific purpose.

Held, the judge had been correct in refusing to strike out this part of the plaintiffs' claim. 'The distinction between the set of facts which it was held in *Morgan Crucible Co plc* v *Hill Samuel Bank Ltd* would suffice to establish a duty of care owed by auditors from those facts which it was held in *Caparo Industries plc v Dickman* would not have this effect is inevitably a fine one. In my judgment that distinction may be expressed as follows. Mere foreseeability that a potential bidder may rely on the audited accounts does not impose on the auditor a duty of care to the bidder, but if the auditor is expressly made aware that a particular identified bidder will rely on the audited accounts or other statements approved by the auditor, and intends that the bidder should so rely, the auditor will be under a duty of care to the bidder for the breach of which he may be liable' (*per* GLIDEWELL LJ).

Gammell v Wilson [1981] 1 All ER 578 (House of Lords)

A 15-year old boy was killed in a road accident caused by the defendants' negligence. The plaintiff, his father, claimed damages as administrator of his son's estate under s1 of the Law Reform (Miscellaneous Provisions) Act 1934 and under the Fatal Accidents Act 1976 for loss of his and his wife's dependencies consequent on the son's death.

Held, where a person died in consequence of a defendant's negligence before he himself could bring a claim for damages or prosecute it to judgment, his estate was entitled to recover damages under s1 of the 1934 Act for his lost earnings in the lost years and such recovery was not excluded by s1(2)(c) of that Act. In this case the judge had correctly awarded estimated earnings less living expenses and applied a multiplier of 16 years. As to loss of expectation of life, although the figure did not remain immutable and had to take due account of inflation, £1,250 was here an appropriate figure. No award was made under the 1976 Act as, in view of the son's intestacy, the plaintiff and his wife had received more under the 1934 Act than the value of their dependencies. (Applied: *Rose v Ford*; see also *White v London Transport Executive*; but see s1 of the Administration of Justice Act 1982.)

Garnham, Harris & Elton Ltd v Alfred W Ellis (Transport) Ltd [1967] 2 All ER 940

The plaintiffs employed the defendant carriers to carry copper wire from London to Glasgow, on terms which provided that no claims would be allowed for loss unless notified within a short time. The defendants sub-contracted the work without the plaintiffs' permission and without making proper inquiries about the sub-contractor. In fact, the sub-contractor was a fraud, and the wire disappeared without trace. The question arose as to whether the defendants were liable in conversion.

Held, the sub-contracting was a deliberate interference with the plaintiffs' rights amounting to conversion of the goods, to which the exemption clause afforded no defence, and the plaintiffs were entitled to damages. (Sub-contracting without the plaintiffs' consent was not permitted by the contract.) (See also *Morris v C W Martin & Sons Ltd*.)

General Cleaning Contractors Ltd v Christmas [1952] 2 All ER 1110 (House of Lords)

The plaintiff was an experienced window cleaner in the employ of the defendants. While he was cleaning a window at the Caledonian Club the sash closed on his finger and he lost his balance, fell and was injured. The defendants had made safety belts available, but the plaintiff had not used one because there were no hooks to which it could have been attached.

Held, the plaintiff was entitled to damages as the defendants had failed to provide wedges to prevent sashes closing and to instruct the plaintiff to test sashes for looseness and were therefore in breach of their duty to 'take reasonable care to lay down a reasonably safe system of work' (*per* LORD OAKSEY). (See also *Page* v *Cumbria County Council*; but see *Marshall* v *Gotham Co Ltd*.)

General Engineering Services Ltd v Kingston and St Andrew Corp
[1988] 3 All ER 867 (Privy Council)

At a time when the respondents' firemen were 'going slow' in support of a pay claim, they took 17 minutes (instead of the normal 3½) to reach the appellants' premises and, as a result, those premises were completely destroyed by fire.

Held, the respondents were not vicariously liable for the appellants' loss. 'Here the unauthorised and wrongful act by the firemen was a wrongful repudiation of an essential obligation of their contract of employment, namely the decision and its implementation not to arrive at the scene of the fire in time to save the building and its contents. This decision was not in furtherance of their employers' business. It was in furtherance of their industrial dispute ... Such conduct was the very negation of carrying out some act authorised by the employer, albeit in a wrongful and unauthorised mode. Indeed in preventing the provision of an essential service, members of the fire brigade were ... guilty of a criminal offence' (*per* LORD ACKNER). (But see *United Africa Co Ltd* v *Saka Owoade*.)

George and Richard, The (1871) 24 LT 717

Due to the improper navigation of the *George and Richard,* the ship collided with the *Eleutheria*. The carpenter on board the *Eleutheria* was killed and it was contended that his child who, at the time of the accident, was en ventre sa mere, was entitled to damages under the Fatal Accidents Act 1846.

Held, this argument would be upheld.

Gilbert v Stone (1647) 82 ER 902

In an action for trespass, the defendant maintained that he was not liable as 12 men had forced him to go into the plaintiff's house by threatening to kill him (the defendant) if he refused to comply with their wishes.

Held, this plea would not succeed as fear cannot justify a trespass upon another.

Gillingham Borough Council v Medway (Chatham) Dock Co Ltd
[1992] 3 All ER 923

The plaintiff council granted planning permission for the development of a former dockyard by the defendants as a commercial port, knowing that it would be used 24 hours a day. Access to the port was through a residential area. The plaintiffs sought to restrain the passage of heavy goods vehicles to and from the port between 7 pm and 7 am on grounds of public nuisance: the defendants conceded that such traffic constituted a substantial interference with the residents' enjoyment of their properties.

Held, the action would be dismissed. 'I note … that it is only a nuisance inevitably resulting from the authorised works on which immunity is conferred … where planning consent is given for a development or change of use, the question of nuisance will thereafter fall to be decided by reference to a neighbourhood with that development or use and not as it was previously.' (*per* BUCKLEY J). (Applied: *Allen v Gulf Oil Refining Ltd.*)

Glasgow Corporation v Muir [1943] 2 All ER 44 (House of Lords)

On a wet day the appellants allowed a church picnic party to have their tea in their (the appellants') tea room. It was necessary for members of the picnic party to carry the tea urn through a passage where some children were buying ices and sweets and, for some unexplained reason, they dropped it and some of the children were scalded by the tea.

Held, the appellants were not liable in negligence in respect of the children's injuries as 'there was no reasonably foreseeable danger to the children from the use of the premises which the appellants permitted to be made' (*per* LORD WRIGHT). (But see *Hill v James Crowe (Cases) Ltd.*)

Glasgow Corporation v Taylor [1922] 1 AC 44 (House of Lords)

A seven-year-old boy died as a result of eating the berries of a poisonous shrub growing in a public park which was under the management and control of Glasgow Corporation, and his father sought damages in respect of the death of his son. It was alleged, inter alia, that the berries presented a tempting appearance to children and that the corporation knew that the berries were poisonous but had taken no precautions to warn children of the danger of picking them or to prevent them from doing so.

Held, these facts disclosed a good cause of action.

Glinski v McIver [1962] 1 All ER 696 (House of Lords)

The plaintiff having been acquitted of a charge of conspiracy to defraud sought damages for malicious prosecution against the defendant police officer who laid the information and the trial judge asked the jury (i) Has it been proved that the police officer in starting the prosecution of the plaintiff was actuated by malice? and (ii) Did the defendant honestly believe that the plaintiff was guilty of the offence? The jury answered 'Yes' to the first question, 'No' to the second and the trial judge (influenced by the jury's answer to the second question) held that there was no reasonable and probable cause for the prosecution and gave judgment for the plaintiff. Before laying the information the defendant had consulted with a solicitor of the legal department of New Scotland Yard and with counsel and (it seems) acted in accordance with their advice.

Held, the essentials to a successful action for malicious prosecution were that the plaintiff was prosecuted by the defendant and was acquitted, that the prosecution was without reasonable and probable cause and that the prosecution was malicious. While the trial judge had been correct in leaving the first question to the jury, on the facts there was no evidence that the defendant did not conspire to defraud and no question should have been put to the jury on this issue. Instead, the trial judge should have considered independently whether there was reasonable and probable cause for the prosecution and it was their lordships' view that there was. In view of this, the plaintiff's action failed. Malice is for the jury and cause is for the judge. Malice, provided that there is some evidence of it, must be left to the jury as a question whole and entire; but the whole question of cause is for the judge and he leaves to the jury only those disputed questions in relation to it on which he needs their help. If the only evidence of lack of actual belief is lack of reasonable belief, he does not need their help at all, for lack of reasonable belief is a matter for him' (*per* LORD DEVLIN). (See also *Malz* v *Rosen.*)

Gold v Haringey Health Authority [1987] 2 All ER 888 (Court of Appeal)

A consultant obstetrician at the defendants' hospital told the plaintiff that sterilisation would be 'irreversible' but he did not warn her that there was a risk of failure. After having the operation, the plaintiff again became pregnant and she claimed damages for negligent misrepresentation and negligence.

Held, her action could not succeed. The statement that the operation was 'irreversible' could not reasonably be construed as a representation that the operation was bound to achieve its objective and at the material time (1979) there was a substantial body of responsible doctors who would not have warned of the risk of failure. (See also *Bolam* v *Friern Hospital Management Committee* and *Sidaway* v *Bethlem Royal Hospital Governors.*)

Goldman v Hargrave [1966] 2 All ER 989 (Privy Council)

The appellant was the owner and occupier of land adjacent to that of the respondents. A tree on the appellants' land was struck by lightning and caught fire. Initially, the appellant took steps to deal with the burning tree, but subsequently he left the fire to burn itself out and took no steps to prevent the fire spreading. This brought a fresh risk, the risk of revival of the fire, which, it was found, was a foreseeable risk by a man in the appellant's position. Some days later, the wind having freshened, the fire revived and spread on to the respondent's property and caused extensive damage.

Held, the appellant was liable in negligence because, although he did not initially cause the fire and had taken the right steps initially, he was guilty of negligence by not taking the prudent step of putting the fire out. Further, as the fire which caused the damage was that revived as a result of the appellant's negligence, it did not 'accidentally begin' within the meaning of the Fires Prevention (Metropolis) Act 1774, which accordingly afforded no defence. (See also *Musgrove* v *Pandelis* and *Leakey* v *National Trust.*)

Goodes v East Sussex County Council (1999) The Times 7 January (Court of Appeal)

At about 7.10 am, when overtaking vehicles on the A267, the plaintiff's car skidded on ice on the road surface, left the road and he suffered severe injuries. A forecast of frost had been received by the defendant at 11.45 pm the previous evening. Pre-salting had been arranged, starting at 5.30 am, and the stretch of road where the accident occurred would have been treated within 15 minutes after its occurrence. Had the defendant highway authority been in breach of its duty, imposed by s41 of the Highways Act 1980, to maintain the road?

Held, it had. Once the defendant had decided that the forecast conditions were such as to necessitate pre-salting, logic and the proper performance of its duty dictated that the gritting vehicles should be ordered out at such a time that they would be able to complete their rounds by the time the frost was sufficient to give rise to a real risk of dangerous icy patches on the roads. There was a likelihood of ice forming from about 6 am and, since the object of the exercise was to prevent this happening, the defendant's decision should have been to send out the vehicles not later than 4 am. (But see *Cross v Kirklees Metropolitan Borough Council*.)

Gordon v Harper (1796) 7 Term Rep 9

The plaintiff let his mansion-house and furniture to one Biscoe. The sheriff, the defendant, wrongfully took the furniture in execution and the plaintiff sued him in trover.

Held, the action would fail as the plaintiff had parted with his right of possession: he had let the goods to Biscoe. (But see *Burton v Hughes*.)

Gorely v Codd [1966] 3 All ER 891

The defendant allowed his 17-year-old son to have an air rifle while not supervised by an adult. The boy was mentally retarded academically, but was otherwise normal. The defendant gave the son adequate instruction and forbade him to use the gun on the highway. While larking about with three other boys in a field, bounded by hedges and in a sparsely populated country district, the son negligently discharged the gun and injured the plaintiff.

Held, as the defendant had given proper and adequate instruction to his son in the use of the air rifle and as, to all intents and purposes, the son was a normal boy, the defendant was not negligent. (But see *Bebee v Sales*.)

Gorris v Scott (1874) LR 9 Exch 125

A shipowner, the defendant, agreed to take the plaintiffs' sheep from Hamburg to Newcastle, but some of them were washed overboard because in breach of a statutory duty, no pens had been provided on the ship.

Held, the plaintiffs could not recover damages for breach of statutory duty as the object of the statute was to protect the animals from contagious disease, not the perils of the sea. (See also *Atkinson v Newcastle and Gateshead Waterworks Co.*)

Gough v *Thorne* [1966] 3 All ER 398 (Court of Appeal)

The plaintiff, a thirteen-and-a-half-year-old girl, crossed the road at the signal of a halted lorry driver, without pausing to see whether in fact the road was clear. She was struck by a vehicle which was being driven at excessive speed, and wrongly overtaking the lorry on its far side.

Held, an ordinary child of that age (unlike an adult) could not be reasonably expected to pause to see for herself whether it was safe to cross, and hence the plaintiff was not contributorily negligent.

Gran Gelato Ltd v *Richcliff (Group) Ltd* [1992] 1 All ER 865

The first defendants granted the plaintiffs an underlease of shop premises for almost ten years, the plaintiffs paying a premium of £30,000 and subsequently spending almost £100,000 on alterations and fittings. In answer to 'inquiries before lease' from the plaintiffs' solicitors, the second defendants (the first defendants' solicitors) had said that they were not aware of any rights inhibiting the tenants' enjoyment of the property. When the underlease had about 4½ years to run, the head lessor exercised a break clause option. The plaintiffs claimed damages for negligence against both defendants and damages against the first defendants under s2(1) of the Misrepresentation Act 1967.

Held, the claim against the second defendants would be dismissed as in a normal conveyancing transaction the sellers' solicitors do not in general owe the buyers a duty of care when answering their enquiries. On the other hand, there had been a misrepresentation and the plaintiffs were entitled to damages from the first defendants. In such circumstances the defence of contributory negligence, under s1 of the Law Reform (Contributory Negligence) Act 1945, was available to the first defendants in relation to the claim under s2(1) of the 1967 Act but, on the facts, the plaintiffs had not been contributorily negligent. By way of damages the plaintiffs were entitled to rent paid after discovery of the break clause, 50% of the premium and costs of acquisition and all the costs of abortive attempts at disposal of the property. However, they could not recover loss which flowed solely from the commercial failure of their business before the break clause came to light. (Distinguished in *Alliance and Leicester Building Society* v *Edgestop Ltd.*)

Grant v *Australian Knitting Mills Ltd* [1936] AC 85 (Privy Council)

Grant brought some 'Golden Fleece' woollen underwear and contracted dermatitis because the garment contained excess sulphites which, it was found, had been negligently left in it in the process of manufacture. The defect could not have been detected by reasonable examination.

Held, he could recover damages in contract from the retailers for breach of an implied warranty or condition under the Australian equivalent to s14 of the Sale of Goods Act 1893, and the manufacturers were liable in tort as they were in breach of their duty of care. (See also *Wilsons & Clyde Coal Co Ltd* v *English.*)

Grappelli v Derek Block (Holdings) Ltd [1981] 2 All ER 272
(Court of Appeal)

The defendants, managers or agents of the plaintiff, a professional musician with an international reputation, had to cancel certain concert bookings as they had been made without the plaintiff's authority. When telling the concert hall managers, the defendants' representative falsely stated that the plaintiff was seriously ill and that it was doubtful whether he would ever tour again. This false information was passed to members of the public who inquired about the cancelled concerts, but shortly afterwards notices appeared in newspapers giving dates of concerts by the plaintiff during a tour of England, including some on the same dates (although in different towns) as the cancelled concerts. The plaintiff brought an action for libel and slander alleging, inter alia, that the false statement and the newspaper notices gave rise to the innuendo that the plaintiff had given a reason for cancelling the original concerts which he knew to be false.

Held, there was no cause of action in defamation as it arose as soon as the words complained of were published and any extrinsic facts which were relied on to support a legal innuendo had to be known at the time of publication by the person to whom the words were published. Further, where there was publication to a limited number of persons a plaintiff pleading a legal innuendo is required to identify in his pleading the person or persons who knew of the special facts which enabled them to understand the innuendo. However, the court added that the plaintiff should rely on his allegation of injurious falsehood. (But see *Hayward v Thompson*.)

Greater Nottingham Co-operative Society Ltd v Cementation Piling and Foundations Ltd [1988] 2 All ER 971 (Court of Appeal)

The plaintiffs contracted for the extension of their office premises and the defendant subcontractors were to provide the piles. The defendants also entered into a collateral contact with the plaintiffs requiring the exercise of reasonable care and skill without defining the way in which the work was to be carried out. Due to the defendants' negligence, an adjoining building was damaged, but the plaintiffs claimed, inter alia, damages for their economic loss caused by delayed completion of the work.

Held, their claim could not succeed as it was to be assumed that the parties had defined their relationship in the collateral contract and this did not make the defendants responsible for any economic loss suffered by the plaintiffs. (See also *Simaan General Contracting Co v Pilkington Glass Ltd (No 2)*.)

Greenhalgh v British Railways Board [1969] 2 All ER 114
(Court of Appeal)

The plaintiff was injured by tripping over a pot-hole on an accommodation bridge over the railway. The bridge was built about 1870 'for the accommodation of the owners and occupiers of land adjoining the railway'. The public began to use the bridge as a footpath, and it was shown as such on the definitive map prepared by the local authority. The plaintiff did not live on land adjoining the railway, and although the local authority had built an estate on either side of the line and approach roads to the bridge, it had left the bridge out of repair. The plaintiff sued the Board claiming that they were responsible for her injuries.

Held, inter alia, the Board owed the plaintiff no duty under the Occupiers' Liability Act 1957 as a visitor, for a 'visitor' did not include a person using the land in pursuance of a public or private right of way. (See also *Holden* v *White.*)

Greenock Corporation v Caledonian Railway Co [1917] AC 556 (House of Lords)

The appellants built a concrete children's paddling pool in the bed of a stream, the course and natural flow of which they thereby altered and obstructed. As a result of this, during extraordinary rainfall, the stream overflowed and damaged the respondent's property.

Held, the appellants were liable as the rainfall, although extraordinary, was not unprecedented in Scotland and was not, therefore, a damnum fatale (act of God). (But see *Nichols* v *Marsland.*)

Greers Ltd v Pearman & Corder Ltd (1922) 39 RPC 406

The defendants were the registered proprietors of a trade mark comprising the words 'Banquet Brand' but they had expressly disclaimed the right to exclusive use of those words. In spite of this, they wrote to the plaintiffs and alleged that, by using the word 'Banquet' in connection with their own goods, they had infringed their trade mark.

Held, in the circumstances, this allegation was in itself evidence of malice. (But see *Balden* v *Shorter.*)

Gregory v Piper (1829) 9 B & C 591

A master told his servant to put some rubbish near to, but not touching, a neighbour's wall. The servant used ordinary care but some of the rubbish naturally ran against the wall.

Held, the master was answerable in trespass as the running against the wall was the necessary or natural consequence of the act which he had ordered to be done.

Greig v Insole [1978] 3 All ER 449

Certain professional cricketers who had played for English county clubs entered into contracts with World Series Cricket, an Australian company, to play in 'test matches' to be organised by the company in Australia and possibly elsewhere. The International Cricket Conference effectively banned the players from test matches under their jurisdiction and it seemed that the Test and County Cricket Board for the United Kingdom would ban the players from competitive county cricket.

Held, World Series Cricket was entitled to declarations that the move and the anticipated move were an unlawful inducement to the players contracted to them to break their contracts. 'At common law, it constitutes a tort for a third person deliberately to interfere in the execution of a valid contract which has been concluded between two or more other parties, if five conditions are fulfilled: First, there must be either (a) "direct" interference or (b) "indirect" interference coupled with the use of unlawful means ... Secondly, the defendant must be shown to have had knowledge of the relevant contract. Thirdly, he must be shown to have had the intent to interfere with it. Fourthly, in bringing an action, other than a quia timet action, the plaintiff must show that he has suffered special damage, that is, more than nominal damage. In any quia timet action, the plaintiff must show the likelihood of damage to him resulting if the act of interference is successful . ... Fifthly, so far as is necessary, the plaintiff must successfully rebut any defence based on justification which the defendant may put forward ... One point, however, requires to be emphasised. If these five conditions are fulfilled and the defendant is shown to have had that intention to interfere with the relevant contract which is necessary to constitute the tort, it is quite irrelevant that he may have acted in good faith and without malice or under a mistaken understanding as to his legal rights; good faith, as such, provides no defence whatever to a claim based on this tort' (*per* SLADE J). The ICC and TCCB were not entitled to statutory immunity as they were not employers' associations within s28(2) of the Trade Union and Labour Relations Act 1974.

Griffiths v Liverpool Corporation [1966] 2 All ER 1015 (Court of Appeal)

A pedestrian slipped and suffered injury when walking on a flagstone which protruded half an inch above the rest of the pavement. It was found as a fact that the flagstone was dangerous. On the evidence a regular system of inspection was desirable, and labourers could have been found to make such an inspection, but if dangers had been discovered there were insufficient workmen to make them safe. The particular flagstone could not have been made safe.

Held, the plaintiff's claim should succeed. The highway authority had not proved that they had taken such care as was in all the circumstances reasonably required to make sure the highway was safe. Liability for breach of statutory duty for non-repair of the highway under s1 of the Highways (Miscellaneous Provisions) Act 1961 is absolute, subject to the statutory defences made available by the Act. (See now s58 of the Highways Act 1980.)

Groves v Lord Wimborne [1898] 2 QB 402 (Court of Appeal)

An employer was required by statute to fence certain dangerous machinery. The statute provided that in the event of a breach of this duty a fine not in excess of £100 could be imposed and, at the discretion of the Secretary of State, the whole or any part of this could be applied for the benefit of the injured person or his family. In breach of this statutory duty some machinery was left unfenced and, as a result, an employee received serious injuries.

Held, he would be awarded £150 by way of damages for breach by his employer of the statutory duty. (See also *Monk* v *Warbey*.)

Gulf Oil (GB) Ltd v Page [1987] 3 All ER 14 (Court of Appeal)

Following litigation between the parties, the defendants flew a light aircraft over the

Cheltenham race meeting, where the plaintiffs were entertaining customers, towing a sign 'Gulf exposed in fundamental breach'. The plaintiffs sought an interlocutory injunction to restrain further display of the sign; the judge refused this relief on the ground that it is never granted – where, as here, the defendant intended to plead justification.

Held, the injunction would be granted as, on the facts, there was a prima facie case that publication was being made as part of a concerted plan to inflict damage on the plaintiffs and it followed that the general rule did not apply. (But see *Harakas* v *Baltic Mercantile and Shipping Exchange Ltd.*)

H v *Ministry of Defence* [1991] 2 All ER 834 (Court of Appeal)

The plaintiff soldier having suffered most unusual and very distressing injuries as a result of the defendants' admitted negligence, he applied for trial by jury.

Held, such a trial would not be appropriate in this or, as a general rule, any other personal injury action as damages were best assessed by the judge in the light of the conventional scale of awards. 'If ... personal injuries resulted from conduct on the part of those who were deliberately abusing their authority, there might well be a claim for exemplary damages and this could place the case in an exceptional category ... within the general judicial discretion with its bias against a trial by jury ... That is not this case' (*per* LORD DONALDSON OF LYMINGTON MR).

Hadmor Productions Ltd v *Hamilton* [1982] 1 All ER 1042 (House of Lords)

A company made a series of 15 programmes for television using freelance performers and technicians. The first two programmes were transmitted by a television station and the company had reasonable expectations that the station would purchase and transmit the remaining 13 programmes. However, the local branch of a union blacked the programmes on the ground that their members could be threatened with redundancy if ready-made programmes were brought in from outside. Faced with the likelihood of disruption, the station decided not to transmit any more of the programmes and the company sought an injunction to restrain the union from preventing the programmes' transmission.

Held, the judge had been right to refuse the relief sought. Even if the company had been able to establish that the union's acts amounted to the tort of interfering with its business by unlawful means or intimidation, the union would probably have been entitled to immunity under s13(1) of the Trade Union and Labour Relations Act 1974 as they had been acting in contemplation or furtherance of a trade dispute as defined in s29(1) of that Act. (But see *Universe Tankships Inc of Monrovia* v *International Transport Workers' Federation* and s224 of the Trade Union and Labour Relations (Consolidation) Act 1992.)

Hague v *Deputy Governor of Parkhurst Prison; Weldon* v *Home Office* [1991] 3 All ER 733 (House of Lords)

The question arose whether a convicted prisoner who, while serving his sentence, had been restrained in a way not permitted by the Prison Rules 1964 had a cause of action in private law for breach of statutory duty or false imprisonment.

Held, he did not have a claim for breach of statutory duty if the prescribed procedure had not been followed, provided the power (eg of segregation) had been exercised in good faith. A claim for false imprisonment could not succeed as he had already been deprived of his liberty. 'I … agree … that no action of damages for false imprisonment lies … on the ground of subjection to intolerable conditions; though I accept that … an action for damages for negligence may be available to the prisoner …' (*per* LORD GOFF OF CHIEVELEY). (But see *R v Governor of Brockhill Prison, ex parte Evans (No 2)*, *Meering v Grahame-White Aviation Co Ltd* and *Racz v Home Office*.)

Hale v Jennings Brothers [1938] 1 All ER 579 (Court of Appeal)

As a result of 'fooling about' by a passenger, a chair, with its occupant, broke away from the defendants' chair-o'-plane and injured the plaintiff who was the owner of a shooting gallery on adjoining ground.

Held, although there had been no negligence on the part of the defendants, they were liable to the plaintiff as the principle of *Rylands v Fletcher* applied to this situation. (But see *Sochacki v Sas* and *Read v J Lyons & Co Ltd*.)

Haley v London Electricity Board [1964] 3 All ER 185 (House of Lords)

The appellant, a blind man, lived in south-east London and one morning on his way to work tripped over a long-handled hammer which the respondents had leaned against a railing to protect pedestrians from an excavation which they (the respondents) had made in the pavement before the usual protective fences had arrived at the site. The appellant had approached the excavation in the proper way, waving his white stick in front of him, but it had passed over the lower end of the hammer handle. It was found that the respondents had given adequate warning to ordinary people with good sight.

Held, it was reasonably foreseeable that a blind person may have passed along this particular pavement and the respondents had failed to discharge their duty to take reasonable care not to act in a way likely to endanger any person who may reasonably be expected to walk along it. It followed that the appellant was entitled to recover damages at common law for negligence. 'There is no authority which would compel one to take the view that the obligations of those responsible for the safety of foot pavements is restricted to those persons who have normal sight … they must have regard to all road users, which include the blind and other persons' (*per* LORD GUEST).

Halford v Brookes [1991] 3 All ER 559 (Court of Appeal)

In April 1978 the plaintiff's daughter was strangled and stabbed to death while in the company of the second defendant, a 15-year-old boy. Six months later the boy said that his stepfather, the first defendant, had carried out the killing. At his trial in November 1978 the boy was acquitted of murder, but the plaintiff strongly suspected that both defendants had been involved: her solicitor advised her that any further prosecution rested with the Director of Public Prosecutions. The plaintiff consulted new solicitors in 1985 and they advised her that civil proceedings for trespass to the person were feasible. She immediately applied for legal aid: it was granted in 1987 and she then issued a writ. Denying liability, the defendants maintained that the claim was time-barred.

Held, the primary limitation period had expired as the plaintiff had had sufficient 'knowledge of the facts', for the purposes of s14 of the Limitation Act 1980, at the conclusion of the second defendant's trial for murder. However, discretion would be exercised under s33 of the 1980 Act to allow the action to proceed as, in all the circumstances, the plaintiff could not be criticised for the delay, a fair trial would not be jeopardised by it and the inability of the defendants to satisfy any judgment was not a good reason for preventing the plaintiff from pursuing her civil claim. (See also *Stubbings* v *Webb* and *Nash* v *Eli Lilly & Co.*)

Hall v Brooklands Auto Racing Club [1933] 1 KB 205 (Court of Appeal)

Two cars collided during a motor race and one of them crashed through iron railings some 4 ft 5 in from the edge of the track and injured the plaintiff. This was the first accident of its kind in 23 years.

Held, the owners of the track were not liable to the plaintiff in respect of the injuries which he received as, while they were under a duty to see that the course was as free from danger as reasonable care and skill could make it, they were not liable for accidents which could not reasonably have been foreseen, nor were they required to guard against dangers inherent in the sport which could have been foreseen by a spectator and of which he would be held to have agreed to take the risk.

Halsey v Esso Petroleum Co Ltd [1961] 2 All ER 145

The plaintiff's house was in Fulham in a road zoned for residential purposes and the defendants had an oil depot on the opposite side of the road in an area zoned for industrial purposes. Acid smuts emitted from the defendants' chimneys damaged the paintwork of the plaintiff's car while standing in the road outside his house and also clothing hung out to dry in the plaintiff's garden. There also came from the depot a pungent and nauseating smell, but this had not affected the plaintiff's health. Although the defendants had attempted to soundproof their boilerhouse, at night noise from the boilers caused the plaintiff's windows and doors to vibrate and prevented him from sleeping. In addition, there was noise from enormous tankers arriving at and leaving the depot between 10 pm and 6 am.

Held, the defendants were liable under the rule in *Rylands* v *Fletcher* in respect of damage to the plaintiff's car and clothing (ie for damage caused by the escape of a harmful substance from the defendants' premises); for a private nuisance in respect of damage to his clothing (ie for causing material injury to the plaintiff's property resulting from the trade carried on by the defendants in neighbouring property); for a public nuisance in respect of damage to his car (ie such damage was special damage suffered by the plaintiff); for a private nuisance in respect of the smell (it was unnecessary to show injury to the plaintiff's health); for a private nuisance in respect of noise from the boilers and tankers in the depot (ie the noise interfered with the ordinary physical comfort of ordinary people living in this part of Fulham); and for both a private and a public nuisance in respect of noise caused by tankers on the highway (ie for a public nuisance because it was an unreasonable user of the highway which caused special damage to the plaintiff and for a private nuisance because it materially interfered with the plaintiff's enjoyment of his house). (See also *Rose v Miles*; but see *Heath v Brighton Corporation*.)

Hannah v Peel [1945] 2 All ER 288

The plaintiff, a lance-corporal in the Royal Artillery, was stationed in a house which was owned by, but had never been actually occupied by, the defendant. During his stay the plaintiff accidentally discovered a valuable brooch in a wall crevice in an upstairs room. The real owner of the brooch could not be traced and the parties disagreed as to which of them should have it.

Held, the plaintiff was entitled to the brooch as the defendant had never been in physical possession of the house and had no knowledge of the existence of the brooch until it was found by the plaintiff.

Harakas v Baltic Mercantile and Shipping Exchange Ltd [1982] 2 All ER 701 (Court of Appeal)

A bureau established by the International Chamber of Commerce to combat maritime fraud issued a notice in the Baltic Exchange stating that it had information which would be made available to persons contemplating business with a certain company. On the company's application, a judge granted an interlocutory injunction restraining the bureau and the exchange from further publishing information alleging that the company had been engaged in fraudulent dealings.

Held, this injunction would be discharged. 'This court never grants an injunction in respect of libel when it is said by the defendant that the words are true and that he is going to justify them. So also, when an occasion is protected by qualified privilege, this court never grants an injunction to restrain a slander or libel, to prevent a person from exercising that privilege, unless it is shown that what the defendant proposes to say is known by him to be untrue so that it is clearly malicious. So long as he proposes to say what he honestly believes to be true, no injunction should be granted against him' (*per* LORD DENNING MR). (But see *Gulf Oil (GB) Ltd v Page*.)

Harris v Birkenhead Corporation [1976] 1 All ER 341 (Court of Appeal)

The defendant corporation, as part of a slum clearance programme, made a compulsory purchase order for, inter alia, a house owned by the second defendant and occupied by a tenant. In July, 1967, the corporation served a notice of entry. From December, 1967, the house was empty and derelict. In 1968 the four-year-old plaintiff trespassed in the house, and was injured by falling from an open (or broken) window. The plaintiff brought an action under the Occupiers' Liability Act 1957.

Held, (1) on the facts of the case the defendant corporation was the occupier of the house. Although it had not taken possession, it had by the notice of entry asserted its right to control the property, and the property had ceased to be physically occupied. (2) The corporation was liable, for the property was near a public street; a child might easily pass through the door and suffer grave risk of injury; the corporation on the facts knew of the ruinous condition of the property; as a humane person it should have taken reasonable steps to prevent children from trespassing. (See also *Wheat v E Lacon & Co Ltd*.)

Harris v Evans [1998] 3 All ER 522 (Court of Appeal)

Advice given by a health and safety inspector led to certain local authorities serving notices under the Health and Safety at Work etc Act 1974 on the plaintiff in respect of his mobile bungee-jumping business and effectively caused the discontinuance of the business. It subsequently appeared that the inspector's advice had not been in line with Health and Safety Executive (HSE) policy. The plaintiff sued the inspector and the HSE claiming damages for negligence.

Held, his actions could not succeed. '... the question for us, left open in *Welton v North Cornwall District Council* [1997] 1 WLR 570, is whether an enforcing authority, in giving advice that leads to the issue of improvement or prohibition notices, owes a duty of care to the owner of the business enterprise in question. In my judgment, subject to one qualification not relevant to the present case, it does not. ... The 1974 Act itself provides remedies against errors or excesses on the part of inspectors and enforcing authorities. I would decline to add the possibility of an action in negligence to the statutory remedies. The one qualification I have in mind is this. It could be that a particular requirement imposed by an inspector, whether expressed in an improvement notice or prohibition notice or expressed in advance advice, might introduce a new risk or danger not present in the business activity as previously conducted. ... I would not be prepared to rule out the possibility that damage thus caused could be recovered by means of a negligence action' (*per* SIR RICHARD SCOTT V-C). (Applied: *X and Others (Minors) v Bedfordshire County Council* [1995] 3 All ER 353; see also *Clunis v Camden and Islington Health Authority*.)

Harris v James (1876) 45 LJQB 545

Senhouse let a field to James for the purpose of being worked as a lime quarry. The ordinary way of getting limestone was by blasting and Senhouse authorised the erection of lime kilns. The blasting and smoke from the kilns was a nuisance to the plaintiff who occupied adjoining land and he brought an action against Senhouse and James.

Held, Senhouse as well as James was liable as he had authorised the commission of the nuisance.

Harris v Wyre Forest District Council See Smith v Eric S Bush

Harrison v British Railways Board [1981] 3 All ER 679

The plaintiff was a guard on a train which the second defendant attempted to board as it was moving out of Weybridge station. Railway rules required the plaintiff, in the event of an emergency, to signal the driver to stop or to apply the brakes himself – or both. The train continued to accelerate: the plaintiff then tried to grab hold of the second defendant who fell off the train, pulling the plaintiff with him.

Held, the second defendant was liable in negligence to the plaintiff, but as the plaintiff had failed to apply the brakes he had been contributorily negligent and the damages payable were reduced by 20 per cent. 'Why should the defendant, who, by lack of reasonable care for his own safety, creates a dangerous situation which invites rescue, be in a better position than he who creates a similar situation by lack of reasonable care for another's safety? I can think of no reason, nor has any been suggested to me. In each case, of course, liability will attach only if the defendant ought, as a reasonable man, to have foreseen the likelihood of intervention by a rescuer' (*per* BOREHAM J). (But see *Crossley* v *Rawlinson*.)

Harrison v Duke of Rutland [1893] 1 QB 142 (Court of Appeal)

The Duke of Rutland, the defendant, owned a grouse moor which was crossed by a highway, the soil of which he also owned. The plaintiff went on to this highway, not for the purposes of using it as a highway, but merely, by waving his umbrella and handkerchief, to prevent the birds from flying towards the shooting butts. The defendant had the plaintiff forcibly restrained from such activity until the drive was over and the plaintiff brought an action for assault.

Held, he could not succeed as, by using the highway in an unreasonable and unusual manner, he was a trespasser. (See also *Hickman* v *Maisey*.)

Hartley v Birmingham City District Council [1992] 2 All ER 213 (Court of Appeal)

The plaintiff was injured while visiting the defendants' school premises. Although her husband had promptly notified the defendants of her intention to make a claim and the defendants' insurers had made two offers of settlement which the plaintiff deemed to be unacceptable, her solicitors did not issue a writ until one day after the expiration of the limitation period. Should relief be granted under s33(1) of the Limitation Act 1980?

Held, it should as the test was whether it would be fair and just so to do. The delay had not affected the defendants' ability to defend the proceedings and the fact that the plaintiff would have had a cast-iron action against her solicitors would not, in all the circumstances, defeat her claim to relief. 'If in this case the discretion is not to be exercised in favour of the plaintiff I find it difficult to envisage circumstances in which it could ever be so exercised' (*per* PARKER LJ). (But see *Dobbie* v *Medway Health Authority*.)

Harvey v R G O'Dell Ltd [1958] 1 All ER 657

The plaintiff and one Galway were employed by the defendants and they travelled to Hurley in Galway's motor-cycle combination to do some repair work. They were authorised by the defendants to use this form of transport and after they had worked for some hours they went to Maidenhead to get some more tools and materials and to obtain refreshments. On the return journey, due partly to Galway's negligence, they were involved in an accident and the plaintiff was injured and Galway was killed. In May 1952, letters of administration of Galway's estate were granted to his widow and in April 1954, the plaintiff sued the defendants alleging that they were vicariously liable for Galway's negligence. In March, 1955, the defendants claimed contribution against Galway's estate under s6(1)(c) of the Law Reform (Married Women and Tortfeasors) Act 1935, and, alternatively, damages against Galway's estate for breach of an implied term of Galway's contract of service that he would indemnify them against any liability resulting from his negligence.

Held, the defendants were vicariously liable to the plaintiff for Galway's negligence as the journey from Maidenhead was within the scope of Galway's employment, but as Galway was employed as a storekeeper at the defendants' yard there was no implied term in his contract of service that he would indemnify them for failure on his part to drive with care. However, the defendants, as joint tortfeasors with Galway, were entitled to 100 per cent contribution from Galway's estate as their claim for contribution was, by reason of s1(4) of the Law Reform (Miscellaneous Provisions) Act 1934, subsisting within the meaning of s1(1) of that Act at the date of Galway's death and a right to contribution under s6(1)(c) of the 1935 Act is not a cause of action in tort and therefore the defendants' claim was not barred under s1(3) of the 1934 Act. (See *also Jones v Manchester Corporation*; but see *Hilton v Thomas Burton (Rhodes) Ltd* and s1 of the Civil Liability (Contribution) Act 1978.)

Hay v Hughes [1975] 1 All ER 257 (Court of Appeal)

Two children aged four and two were orphaned when their parents were killed in an accident for which the defendant was liable. The maternal grandmother took the children into her house, and cared for them as an unpaid mother-substitute. An action was brought on behalf of the children under the Fatal Accidents Acts.

Held, (1) in calculating the annual dependency in respect of the mother's services, no deduction should be made for the grandmother's voluntary services, since the children obtained this benefit not as a result of their mother's death, but simply because the grandmother had taken it upon herself to render them services. (2) The judge's application of a multiplier of 9 and the total award of £16,400 were correct. (See also *Daly v General Steam Navigation Co Ltd, Hayden v Hayden* and *Dodds v Dodds.*)

Hay (or Bourhill) v Young [1942] 2 All ER 396 (House of Lords)

The appellant, a fish-wife, who was eight months pregnant, was standing 45 ft from the place where a negligent motor cyclist collided with a motor car and received fatal injuries. She did not see the accident as it happened on the other side of a stationary tramcar, but she heard the impact and afterwards saw blood on the road. This caused her to wrench and injure her back and also caused her severe nervous shock which resulted in her being off work for some time and in her child being stillborn.

Held, the appellant was unable to succeed in her claim for damages against the deceased motor cyclist's personal representatives. The deceased owed no duty to the appellant as she was not at the time of the collision within the area of potential danger caused by his negligence. (But see *Boardman v Sanderson*.)

Hayden v Hayden [1992] 4 All ER 681 (Court of Appeal)

An infant plaintiff's mother was killed when a car driven by the defendant father overturned. The father admitted liability and he replaced the mother's lost services by caring for the plaintiff himself.

Held, s4 of the Fatal Accidents Act 1976 did not apply (the father's services were not a benefit which had accrued as a result of the death) and the value of the father's services should be taken into account in assessing the plaintiff's damages. As to whether the gratuitous services of a relative did or did not result from the death of the mother, *Hay v Hughes* would be followed rather than *Stanley v Saddique*.

Haynes v Harwood [1935] 1 KB 146 (Court of Appeal)

The defendants negligently left their two-horse van unattended in a crowded street in which there were many children. Possibly because a boy threw a stone at them, the horses bolted and a police constable, the plaintiff, who was on duty in a police station, dashed out and stopped them, but was injured in the process. He sued for damages and the defendants relied on the maxim volenti non fit injuria.

Held, the maxim did not afford any defence and the plaintiff was entitled to recover as his actions and his injuries were the natural and probable consequence of the negligence of the defendants. 'If what is relied upon as a novus actus interveniens is the very kind of thing which is likely to happen if the want of care which is alleged takes place, the principle embodied in the maxim is no defence' (*per* GREER LJ). (But see *Knightley v Johns*.)

Hayward v Thompson [1981] 3 All ER 450 (Court of Appeal)

Between 1970 and 1975 the plaintiff contributed over £200,000 to the Liberal Party. On 9 April 1978 an article appeared in the Sunday Telegraph stating that the names of two more people 'connected with' an alleged murder plot had been given to the police and that one of them was 'a wealthy benefactor of the Liberal Party'. The following Sunday the newspaper published a second article, naming the plaintiff, recalling his generosity to the Liberal Party and recording his statement that the police wanted to interview him about the alleged plot. In an action for libel the plaintiff contended that the words in the articles meant and were understood to mean that he was guilty or reasonably suspected of participating in or condoning the alleged plot and that the second article identified him as the person referred to in the first article: he did not identify any particular persons who understood the articles to refer to him, but the defendant raised no objection on that account. The jury found in the plaintiff's favour and awarded him £50,000 by way of damages.

Held, the defendants' appeal would be dismissed. The words used in the first article were clearly capable of bearing the meaning attributed to them by the plaintiff and, as the only question was one of identification, the judge had correctly directed the jury that they were entitled to look at the second article in order to identify the person referred to in the first. As the defendants had not objected to the plaintiff's omission to specify particular persons to whom the words had been published and the special circumstances known to those persons, the jury were entitled to take into account all the evidence and to give it such weight as they thought fit; they might well have inferred that many people on reading the first article understood it to refer to the plaintiff. 'If the defendant intended to refer to the plaintiff, he cannot escape liability simply by not giving his name ... Even if he did not aim at the plaintiff or intend to refer to him, nevertheless if he names the plaintiff in such a way that other persons will read it as intended to refer to the plaintiff, then the defendant is liable ... the meaning of the words in a libel case is not a matter of construction as a lawyer construes a contract. It is a matter of impression as an ordinary person gets on a first reading, not on a later analysis' (*per* LORD DENNING MR). (See also *Hulton (E) & Co v Jones* and *Lewis v Daily Telegraph Ltd*; but see *Grappelli v Derek Block (Holdings) Ltd*.)

Heath v Brighton Corporation (1908) 98 LT 718

The incumbent and trustees of a church, the plaintiffs, sought an injunction to restrain the alleged nuisance caused by the defendants' electricity works which were in the immediate vicinity of the church. It was not alleged that the low hum or note of the machinery had led to a diminution of the congregation; the only person who was personally annoyed was the incumbent, but he was not prevented from preaching or conducting the accustomed services.

Held, the plaintiffs had not shown a sufficiently serious annoyance to entitle them to the injunction which they claimed.

Hedley Byrne & Co Ltd v Heller & Partners Ltd [1963] 2 All ER 575 (House of Lords)

The appellants, becoming doubtful about the financial position of Easipower Ltd, asked their bank to communicate with Easipower's bankers, the respondents. This they did by telephone asking the respondents 'in confidence, and without liability on [the respondents'] part', whether Easipower would be good for a contract of £8,000 to £9,000. The respondents replied that they believed Easipower 'to be respectably constituted and considered good for its normal business engagements'. Six months later the appellants' bank wrote to the respondents to ask whether they considered Easipower trustworthy, in the way of business, to the extent of a £100,000 per annum contract and the respondents replied: 'Respectably constituted company, considered good for its ordinary business engagements'. The appellants relied upon the respondents' statements and as a result lost over £17,000 when Easipower Ltd went into liquidation. The appellants sought to recover this loss from the respondents as damages on the ground that the respondents' replies were given negligently and in breach of the respondents' duty to exercise care in giving them.

Held, while bankers are under a duty to give honest answers and, perhaps, owe enquirers (such as the appellants) a duty of care, in this case the respondents never undertook any duty to exercise care in giving their replies and it followed that there was no liability on their part. 'The appellants' bank, who were their agents in making the enquiry, began by saying "they wanted to know in confidence and without responsibility on our part", ie on the part of the respondents. So I cannot see how the appellants can now be entitled to disregard that and maintain that the respondents did incur a responsibility to them' (*per* LORD REID). (Applied in *Henderson* v *Merrett Syndicates Ltd* and *Spring* v *Guardian Assurance plc*; see also *White* v *Jones*, *Esso Petroleum Co Ltd* v *Mardon* and *Chaudhry* v *Prabhaker*.)

Hellwig v *Mitchell* [1910] 1 KB 609

The defendant, the manager of a hotel, in the presence of others, said to the plaintiff: 'I cannot have you in here; you were on the premises last night with a crowd, and you behaved yourself in a disorderly manner and you had to be turned out.' The defendant threatened the plaintiff that he would 'call in the police, and have you turned out'.

Held, the plaintiff's action for damages would not succeed as the defendant's words did not impute the commission of a criminal offence punishable with imprisonment in the first instance and, for this reason, were not actionable without proof of special damage.

Hemmens v *Wilson Browne* [1993] 4 All ER 826

P instructed a solicitor to draft a document giving the plaintiff the right to call on P at any time in the future to pay her £110,000. The document as drafted did not confer any enforceable rights on the plaintiff. Some weeks later the plaintiff called upon P to fulfil his promise and he refused. The plaintiff sued the solicitor claiming (inter alia) that he owed her a duty of care and was in breach of that duty.

Held, her action would fail. Although the solicitor had been negligent, damage to the plaintiff was reasonably foreseeable and there was a sufficient degree of proximity between the parties, it would not be fair, just or reasonable for a duty of care to be imposed because P was still alive and could rectify the situation and could also sue the solicitor. It was not necessary for the law to give the plaintiff a remedy, as it was in *Ross* v *Caunters*.

Hemmings v *Stoke Poges Golf Club Ltd* [1920] 1 KB 720 (Court of Appeal)

The plaintiffs, husband and wife, were employed by the defendant golf club, and to enable them to perform their duties properly they were required to live in a cottage owned by the defendants. The plaintiffs left the service of the defendants and the defendants gave them notice to quit. The plaintiffs refused to go so the defendants broke into the cottage and ejected them. The plaintiffs sued for trespass, assault and battery.

Held, the action would fail as it was found that the defendants had used no more force than was necessary.

Henderson v Henry E Jenkins and Sons [1969] 3 All ER 756 (House of Lords)

A fatal accident was caused when the brakes on the defendants' lorry failed because of a sudden escape of brake fluid from a corroded pipe. The pipe could not be seen on visual inspection, and the manufacturers did not advise its removal for inspection. The defence of latent defect was raised.

Held, to rely upon the defence of latent defect, the defendants must show that they had taken all reasonable care. To do so they must lead evidence as to the history of the lorry, because corrosion had been caused by a chemical agent, and the defendants' standard of care could only be measured in relation to the previous user of the lorry. No such evidence was called and the defence failed.

Henderson v Merrett Syndicates Ltd [1994] 3 All ER 506 (House of Lords)

The plaintiff underwriting members of Lloyd's ('names') contended that the defendant underwriting agents who managed the plaintiffs' syndicates, either directly or through sub-agency agreements with other managing agents, had been negligent in the conduct of their affairs.

Held, the relationship between the parties was in itself sufficient to give rise to a duty on the part of the defendants to exercise reasonable skill and care in performing their services and this duty was the same in contract as in tort. Unless a contract precluded him from so doing, a plaintiff with concurrent remedies in tort or contract could choose whichever remedy seemed to him to be the more advantageous, not least (as here) for limitation purposes. 'In the present case liability can, and in my opinion should, be founded squarely on the principle established in *Hedley Byrne & Co Ltd v Heller and Partners Ltd* itself, from which it follows that an assumption of responsibility coupled with the concomitant reliance may give rise to a tortious duty of care irrespective of whether there is a contractual relationship between the parties, and in consequence, unless his contract precludes him from doing so, the plaintiff, who has available to him concurrent remedies in contract and tort, may choose that remedy which appears to him to be the most advantageous' (*per* LORD GOFF OF CHIEVELEY). (Approved: *Midland Bank Trust Co Ltd v Hett, Stubbs & Kemp*; applied in *Williams v Natural Life Health Foods Ltd*; see also *Joyce v Sengupta* and *Marc Rich & Co AG v Bishop Rock Marine Co Ltd, The Nicholas H.*)

Henderson v Temple Pier Co Ltd [1998] 3 All ER 324 (Court of Appeal)

On 28 January 1993 the plaintiff allegedly slipped and fell while boarding the defendant's ship moored on the Victoria Embankment. The plaintiff instructed solicitors to act for her on or about 22 February 1993. Between April and July 1994 the solicitors made unsuccessful attempts to identify the owner of the ship: their attempts were unsuccessful because they misspelt the ship's name. They discovered the owner's name later in July and on 25 July wrote to the defendant giving notice of the plaintiff's intention to claim damages. The action was commenced on 30 April 1997. The judge found that the solicitors had not provided a competent service. He identified the correct issue to be determined, ie whether the plaintiff was fixed with the deficiencies of her solicitors. He concluded that she did not have constructive knowledge and so dismissed the defendant's application for the striking-out of the claim on the ground that it was statute-barred pursuant to s11 of the Limitation Act 1980.

Held, the defendant's appeal would be allowed. 'Even if the solicitor is to be regarded as an appropriate expert, the facts were ascertainable by him without the use of legal expertise. The proviso [to s14(3)(b) of the 1980 Act] is not intended to give an extended period of limitation to a person whose solicitor acts dilatorily in acquiring information which is obtainable without particular expertise. ... It was not a complex inquiry, a site visit would have clarified the name of the ship and enabled speedy inquiries to be made to reveal the occupier. Instead the inquiries drifted as well as being misdirected. I am satisfied that on the proper construction of s14(3) of the [1980 Act] the plaintiff is fixed with constructive knowledge which her solicitors ought to have acquired ...' (*per* BRACEWELL J). (See also *Nash* v *Eli Lilly & Co.*)

Herd v Weardale Steel, Coal & Coke Co Ltd [1915] AC 67 (House of Lords)

A dispute arose in a coal mine and the appellant, one of the miners, in breach of his contract of service, refused to do certain work and asked to be taken to the surface before the end of his shift. The respondents, his employers, at first denied him the use of the lift and in consequence he was detained against his will for 20 minutes. The appellant brought an action for false imprisonment.

Held, the principle volenti non fit injuria applied, because he was only entitled to use the lift on the terms of the contract under which he entered the mine, and his claim would fail. (But see *Meering* v *Grahame-White Aviation Co Ltd.*)

Herniman v Smith [1938] 1 All ER 1 (House of Lords)

A timber-merchant, the plaintiff, was convicted of unlawfully and knowingly conspiring with another to cheat and defraud a builder, the defendant, who had preferred the charge. However, the conviction was quashed by the Court of Criminal Appeal and the plaintiff claimed damages for malicious prosecution.

Held, the plaintiff's action would not succeed as, in the circumstances, there was reasonable and probable cause for his prosecution. The question of the presence of reasonable and probable cause should be determined by the judge. (See also *Abbot* v *Refuge Assurance Co Ltd.*)

Herring v Boyle (1834) 1 CrM & R 377

A schoolmaster refused to let a ten-year-old boy go home for the Christmas holiday because his mother had not paid his fees. The scholar brought an action for false imprisonment but it was not shown that he was aware at the time that he was being restrained in any way.

Held, for this reason his action must fail. (Doubted in *Murray* v *Ministry of Defence*; see also *Bird* v *Jones*.)

Hewitt v Bonvin [1940] 1 KB 188 (Court of Appeal)

John, who lived in London, sought and obtained permission from his mother to borrow his father's car to take two girls home to Wisbech. Charles went with them and on the return journey, due to John's negligent driving, Charles was killed.

Held, Charles' administrator had no right of action against John's father as John was not driving his car as his servant or agent or for his purposes. (But see *Ormrod* v *Crosville Motor Services Ltd*.)

Hickman v Maisey [1900] 1 QB 752 (Court of Appeal)

For about an hour and a half the defendant, a 'racing tout', walked backwards and forwards along a highway, the soil of which, in addition to the land on either side, was owned by the plaintiff. Race-horses were trained on the plaintiff's land adjoining the highway and the defendant was on the highway for the purpose of taking notes of their performances.

Held, the defendant was a trespasser as he had exceeded the ordinary and reasonable user of the highway. (But see *Director of Public Prosecutions* v *Jones*.)

Hicks v Chief Constable of the South Yorkshire Police
[1992] 2 All ER 65 (House of Lords)

The plaintiffs, parents of two girls who were crushed to death in the Hillsborough football stadium disaster, as joint administrators of the girls' estates claimed damages for the benefit of each estate under s1(1) of the Law Reform (Miscellaneous Provisions) Act 1943 and s(1)(b) of the Administration of Justice Act 1982. The trial judge dismissed the action on the ground that the plaintiffs had failed to prove that the girls had suffered any recoverable damage for pre-death pain and suffering and the Court of Appeal adopted a similar approach.

Held, the plaintiffs' further appeal would be dismissed as it was impossible to say that the courts below had been clearly wrong to conclude that no physical injury had been suffered by the girls prior to the fatal crushing injuries.

Hilder v Associated Portland Cement Manufacturers Ltd
[1961] 3 All ER 709

The defendants were the owners and occupiers of land adjoining a public highway and they allowed children to play on the land and knew that they regularly played with a football. The only barrier between one of the 'goals' and the highway was a wall three feet two inches high and the ball went over the wall from time to time and had to be retrieved from the road. On one occasion the ball caused a passing motor cyclist to have an accident as a result of which he died.

Held, the defendants had failed to take reasonable care in all the circumstances and they were therefore liable in negligence in respect of the motor cyclist's death. A reasonable man would have concluded that there was a risk of damage to persons using the road and that such risk was not so small that he could safely disregard it. (See also *Castle* v *St Augustine's Links Ltd.*)

Hill v *Chief Constable of West Yorkshire* [1988] 2 All ER 238 (House of Lords)

Over some 11 years one Sutcliffe murdered 13 young women and attempted to murder eight more: in each case the modus operandi was the same. The mother of the last murder victim sued the police for negligence.

Held, her action could not succeed. The police do not normally owe a general duty of care to individual members of the public to identify and apprehend an unknown criminal and, even if they did, public policy required that they should not be liable in such circumstances. (Applied: *Rondel* v *Worsley*; distinguished: *Home Office* v *Dorset Yacht Co Ltd*; see also *Clough* v *Bussan* and *Alexandrou* v *Oxford*; but see *Capital and Counties plc* v *Hampshire County Council.*)

Hill v *James Crowe (Cases) Ltd* [1978] 1 All ER 812

In the course of his work the plaintiff lorry driver stood on a wooden case in the back of his lorry, waiting to receive some cartons. The case had been made by the defendants and it caved in because it had been badly nailed: the plaintiff fell to the ground and suffered injuries.

Held, the defendants' liability had been established under *Donoghue* v *Stevenson*. They were vicariously liable for the negligence of their workmen in the course of their employment and the plaintiff's injuries were a reasonably foreseeable consequence of such negligence. (See also *M'Alister (or Donoghue)* v *Stevenson.*)

Hill (Edwin) & Partners v *First National Finance Corp plc* [1988] 3 All ER 801 (Court of Appeal)

The defendant finance company granted a Mr Pulver a loan to purchase and develop a property and Mr Pulver engaged the plaintiffs as architects for the project. However, the property market collapsed and new restrictions were imposed on office developments; as a result, projects of this kind could not proceed at that stage. In the end, with a view to recouping their investment and the substantial amount of accumulated interest, the defendants agreed to finance the work out of their cash flow, but only if the plaintiffs were replaced as architects. Mr Pulver terminated the plaintiffs' contract and the plaintiffs alleged that the defendants had unlawfully procured Mr Pulver to breach his contract with them.

Held, this was not the case as the defendants' right to receive payment of principal and interest on their loan to Mr Pulver was a superior right which justified such interference with the plaintiffs' contract. (See also *Mogul Steamship Co Ltd* v *McGregor, Gow & Co.*)

Hilton v Thomas Burton (Rhodes) Ltd [1961] 1 All ER 74

Mid-way through the afternoon some employees of the defendant demolition contractors drove to a cafe in the defendants' van and on the return journey, as a result of the negligent driving of the van by one of the employees who was not the usual driver but was authorised to drive it, the foreman of the gang was killed. The defendants were quite willing for their van to be used to enable their employees to obtain refreshment when working away from the defendants' premises (as they were on the occasion in question) and the court was required to decide whether the defendants were liable in respect of the driver's negligence.

Held, they were not as, in driving to and from the cafe, the driver was not doing something that he was employed to do. 'This seems to me to be a plain case of what, in the old cases, was sometimes called going out on a frolic of their own' (per DIPLOCK J). (But see *Aitchison* v *Page Motors Ltd*.)

Hinz v Berry [1970] 1 All ER 1074 (Court of Appeal)

The plaintiff suffered 'nervous shock' in the form of a morbid depression amounting to a recognisable psychiatric illness after witnessing a family accident. The judge awarded £4,000 damages.

Held, although the award was high, it was not a wholly erroneous estimate. 'Somehow or other the court has to draw a line between sorrow and grief for which damages are not recoverable and psychiatric illness for which damages are recoverable' (LORD DENNING MR). (See also *Janvier* v *Sweeney*.)

Hiort v Bott (1874) LR 9 Exch 86

The plaintiffs, who were corn merchants, employed one Grimmett as their broker. In response to a telegram from Grimmett they sent some barley, together with an invoice and delivery order, to the defendant, a licensed victualler in Birmingham. The defendant had not ordered the barley and he had had no previous dealings with either the plaintiffs or Grimmett. At Grimmett's request, the defendant indorsed the delivery order in his favour. Grimmett thus obtained delivery of the barley, disposed of it and absconded. The plaintiffs sued the defendant for conversion.

Held, their action would succeed as the indorsement of the order by the defendant was unauthorised and in excess of what was required to secure the safe return of the barley to the plaintiffs. (But see *Elvin & Powell Ltd* v *Plummer Roddis Ltd*.)

Hoare & Co v McAlpine [1923] Ch 167

The vibration caused by the driving of piles by the defendants in preparation of a building site damaged an ancient hotel belonging to the plaintiffs on the other side of the road.

Held, on the principle of *Rylands* v *Fletcher,* the plaintiffs were entitled to damages. (But see *Noble* v *Harrison.*)

Hodgson v Trapp [1988] 3 All ER 870 (House of Lords)

The plaintiff suffered catastrophic injuries in a road accident for which the defendant admitted liability.

Held, in assessing damages, statutory attendance and mobility allowances were deductible but no account should be taken of the fact that investment income from the amount awarded could attract a higher rate of tax. (See also *McCamley* v *Cammell Laird Shipbuilders Ltd*; but see *Wadey* v *Surrey County Council* and *Wells* v *Wells.*)

Holden v White [1982] 2 All ER 328 (Court of Appeal)

A house-owner had a right of way 'for all purposes' over a pathway owned by the defendant and when the plaintiff milkman was delivering milk to the house he trod on a manhole cover in the pathway. The cover disintegrated and the plaintiff suffered injuries; he claimed damages for breach of the duty of care allegedly owed to him by the defendant by virtue of s1(2) of the Occupiers' Liability Act 1957.

Held, his claim would fail as he was not the defendant's 'visitor'. In order to be a 'visitor' a person had to be regarded at common law as an invitee or licensee or to be treated as such and, because at common law a person who crossed land in pursuance of a public or private right of way was not an invitee or licensee or treated as such, the plaintiff was not a 'visitor' vis-à-vis the defendant. (See also *McGeown* v *Northern Ireland Housing Executive.*)

Holley v Smyth [1998] 1 All ER 853 (Court of Appeal)

Believing that the plaintiff had been guilty of disreputable conduct in a financial transaction, the defendant sent the plaintiff's solicitors two draft press releases containing this allegation. The plaintiff sought an interlocutory injunction to restrain publication of the releases and the defendant made clear that he intended to justify his assertions if he was allowed to publish the releases and was subsequently sued for defamation. The injunction was granted: the defendant appealed.

Held, the injunction would be discharged since, on the material before the court, it could not be concluded that the threatened publication was plainly untrue.

Holliday v National Telephone Co [1899] 2 QB 392 (Court of Appeal)

The defendants were laying telephone wires and they contracted with a plumber to solder the joints. Owing to the negligence of the plumber, the plaintiff, a passer-by, was splashed with molten solder.

Held, the defendants were liable for the plaintiff's injuries as they and the plumber were jointly engaged on the work. Further, although the plumber was an independent contractor, the defendants were liable for the consequences of his negligence as, in circumstances such as this, they were under a duty to take care that those who do work on their behalf do not negligently cause injury to persons using the highway. (But see *Padbury v Holliday and Greenwood Ltd* and *Salsbury v Woodland*.)

Hollywood Silver Fox Farm Ltd v Emmett [1936] 1 All ER 825

The defendant owned a farm near to the plaintiffs' fox farm and following a dispute between them he caused guns to be fired on his own land, but as near as possible to the plaintiffs' breeding pens, during the breeding season. Such noises were likely to prevent a vixen from mating or to cause her to kill and devour her young.

Held, the plaintiffs were entitled to damages and an injunction to restrain the defendant from firing guns or making other noises in the vicinity of the plaintiff's fox farm during the breeding season. (See also *Christie v Davey*; but see *Bradford Corporation v Pickles*.)

Holmes v Mather (1875) LR 10 Exch 261

When the defendant was out for a drive in his carriage the horses, on being startled by a dog, ran away and became unmanageable. In the course of their flight they injured the plaintiff.

Held, her action for damages in trespass could not succeed.

Home Office v Dorset Yacht Co Ltd [1970] 2 All ER 294 (House of Lords)

Some Borstal boys, who were working on an island under the control and supervision of three officers, servants of the Home Office, left the island at night and damaged the plaintiff's yacht. A preliminary point of law was argued as to whether any duty of care was owed by the Home Office to the plaintiff.

Held, a duty of care was owed. There were no reasons of policy to grant the Home Office a general immunity from liability in relation to its reformative prison work. Such a duty did not automatically make the Home Office liable for the acts of the Borstal boys, for the duty was to take reasonable care in the exercise of powers of control so as to prevent loss and damage, and whether the duty had been broken and, if so, whether the damage was too remote were questions for the trial. Re LORD ATKIN'S statement of principle in *Donoghue v Stevenson:* 'I think that the time has come when we can and should say that it ought to apply unless there is some justification or valid explanation for its exclusion' (*per* LORD REID). (Distinguished in *Hill v Chief Constable of West Yorkshire* and *Alexandrou v Oxford*.)

Honeywill and Stein Ltd v Larkin Brothers (London's Commercial Photographers) Ltd [1934] 1 KB 191 (Court of Appeal)

The plaintiffs employed the defendants to take photographs of the interior of a cinema in which they (the plaintiffs) had installed sound reproduction apparatus. The defendants negligently used a magnesium flashlight and set light to the curtains. The plaintiffs sought to recover from the defendants the amount of compensation which they paid to the owners of the cinema.

Held, they were entitled to succeed for breach of contract or in negligence as they were themselves liable to the owners of the cinema for the defendant's negligence.

Horrocks v *Lowe* [1974] 1 All ER 662 (House of Lords)

The plaintiff sued the defendant, a local alderman, for slander in respect of statements made in a speech at an open council meeting. The defendant relied on qualified privilege as a defence. The judge held that the occasion was privileged, that the defendant had honestly believed the statements to be true, but that, since he had been actuated by 'gross and unreasoning prejudice', the defence was defeated by malice.

Held, the defence should have succeeded. A privilege will be lost if the occasion is used exclusively for a purpose, eg spite, or the obtaining of a personal advantage, other than that for which the privilege is accorded by the law. But courts should be slow to infer 'malice' where the defendant believed his statement to be true, and where, as here, the only evidence of malice is drawn from the contents of the speech and the circumstances in which it was made, such an inference cannot be drawn.

Horsfall v *Haywards* (1999) The Times 11 March (Court of Appeal)

The testator had intended to leave his house and contents in trust for his wife with remainder to the plaintiffs. The defendant solicitors negligently prepared the will so that the property passed to the widow absolutely. The trial judge awarded the plaintiffs damages based on the net value of the house, subject to the widow's interest, but the defendants appealed, contending that the plaintiffs were precluded from claiming against them by their failure to mitigate their loss, in particular by failing to bring a claim to vary the provisions of the trust by rectification under s20 of the Administration of Justice Act 1982.

Held, the appeal would be dismissed: intended beneficiaries under a negligently drafted will are not obliged to issue rectification proceedings under s20 of the 1982 Act to mitigate their loss, and to exhaust that remedy before suing the solicitor for negligence, if there is no prospect of the rectification proceedings resulting in any material recovery of the funds lost. Here, on the facts, there was no such prospect. Without fault on their part, by the time that the plaintiffs became concerned that all may not be well the time for bringing rectification proceedings had expired. (Distinguished: *Walker* v *Geo H Medlicott & Son.*)

Horsley v *MacLaren, The Ogopogo* [1971] 2 Lloyd's Rep 410 (Canada Supreme Court)

An action was brought under the Ontario Fatal Accidents Act in respect of the deaths of H and M, who were both guests on board the defendant's pleasure cruiser on a trip across a lake. Without negligence on the defendant's part, M fell overboard. The defendant's rescue attempts proving abortive, H dived into the lake to attempt a rescue. M and H died. At the trial, M's dependants failed, and did not appeal.

Held, the action in respect of the death of H failed, because there was no evidence of negligence on the part of the defendant during the rescue attempt placing M in a situation of peril. Semble, a duty of care is owed to one's guests to render assistance if they are injured accidentally at a time when the host should take reasonable care for their safety. (But see *East Suffolk Rivers Catchment Board* v *Kent* and *Harrison* v *British Railways Board*.)

Hotson v *East Berkshire Area Health Authority* [1987] 2 All ER 909 (House of Lords)

The plaintiff boy fell and injured his hip and was taken to the defendants' hospital. At first, the injury was incorrectly diagnosed (an admitted breach of duty) but after five days' severe pain he returned to the hospital and received appropriate treatment. A disability having developed, the plaintiff sued for negligence and the trial judge found that, on the balance of probabilities, even correct initial diagnosis and treatment would not have prevented the development of the disability.

Held, in the light of this finding, the plaintiff's action could not succeed as he had failed on the issue of causation. (See also *Kay* v *Ayrshire and Arran Health Board*; but see *Bonnington Castings Ltd* v *Wardlaw*.)

Hudson v *Ridge Manufacturing Co Ltd* [1957] 2 All ER 229

The plaintiff fractured his right wrist at work through a foolish prank played on him by one Chadwick, a fellow workman, and he claimed damages against his employers, the defendants, for breach by the defendants of their common law duty to take care for the safety of their workmen. The defendants knew that Chadwick had repeatedly made a nuisance of himself, but they had done nothing more than reprimand him.

Held, the plaintiff was entitled to succeed as the defendants had failed to take proper steps to put an end to Chadwick's conduct or to dismiss him if he persisted in it. (But see *Wilson* v *Tyneside Window Cleaning Co*.)

Hughes v *Lord Advocate* [1963] 1 All ER 705 (House of Lords)

In November some Post Office employees opened a manhole in order to gain access to a telephone cable and when, at about 5 pm, they left the site for a tea break, the manhole was covered by a shelter tent and a tarpaulin was pulled over the shelter so as to leave about two feet between the bottom of the tarpaulin and the ground. Paraffin warning lamps were left burning at the corners of the tent and two boys, aged eight and ten, took one of these and entered the tent to explore. The eight-year-old boy tripped over the lamp which fell into the manhole and caused an explosion as a result of which the boy suffered severe burns. It was found that the Post Office employees were negligent in leaving the manhole unattended as the presence of children in the immediate vicinity of the shelter was reasonably to be anticipated but that the explosion (as opposed to a fire) was not reasonably foreseeable.

Held, the boy was entitled to recover damages for negligence. 'This accident was caused by a known source of danger, but caused in a way which could not have been foreseen, and in my judgment that affords no defence' (*per* LORD REID). (Applied in *Jolley v Sutton London Borough Council*; but see *Doughty v Turner Manufacturing Co Ltd* and *Tremain v Pike*.)

Hughes v *National Union of Mineworkers* [1991] 4 All ER 278

The plaintiff police officer was injured while seeking to maintain peace between striking and working miners and, amongst others, he sued the Chief Constable, pursuant to s48(1) of the Police Act 1964, alleging that the officer in charge of operations at the colliery had deployed his forces negligently.

Held, his claim would be struck out because, as a matter of public policy, senior police officers charged with the task of controlling serious public disorder are not generally liable if officers under their command are injured by rioters. 'In my view s48 is concerned with the fact of vicarious liability and does not bear on the extent or definition of the torts for which the chief officer of police is to be vicariously liable' (*per* MAY J). (See also *Mulcahy v Ministry of Defence*; but see *Knightley v Johns*.)

Hulton (E) & Co v *Jones* [1910] AC 20 (House of Lords)

The Sunday Chronicle, which was owned by the appellants, published an article in which appeared statements defamatory of a person described as 'Artemus Jones', a churchwarden at Peckham. The writer of the article and the editor of the paper both believed 'Artemus Jones' to be a purely fictitious personage. A barrister, the respondent, who was not a churchwarden and did not live in Peckham, happened to have the same name as the imaginary churchwarden and brought an action for libel. He admitted that neither the author, the editor nor the appellants intended to defame him, but succeeded in showing that some of his friends thought that he was the subject of the article.

Held, the respondent was entitled to damages as it was no defence for the appellants to contend that the defamation was unintentional. (See also *Newstead v London Express Newspapers Ltd*.)

Hunt v *Severs* [1994] 2 All ER 385 (House of Lords)

In 1985, the plaintiff, riding on the pillion of a motor cycle driven by the defendant, suffered severe injuries in a road accident. The defendant's liability in negligence was never in dispute. After the plaintiff's discharge from hospital in 1987 the parties lived together; they married in 1990. As a result of her injuries, the plaintiff had no chance of being employed and future complications were a possibility: she had a life expectancy of 25 years. In arriving at his award for future cost of care and future loss of earnings, the judge took a multiplier of 14, discounting £1 pa at 4.5%. The damages included amounts for services rendered and to be rendered by the defendant in caring for the plaintiff and his travelling expenses in visiting the plaintiff in hospital.

Held, the judge's decision as to the multiplier would not be disturbed as the multiplier of 15, as substituted by the Court of Appeal, could not be seen as demonstrably giving a more accurate assessment. However, the award in respect of the defendant's travelling expenses and past and future care could not be allowed. 'The law now ensures that an injured plaintiff may recover the reasonable value of gratuitous services rendered to him by way of voluntary care by a member of his family ... But it is nevertheless important to recognise that the underlying rationale ... is to enable the voluntary carer to receive proper recompense for his or her services and I would think it appropriate for the House to take the opportunity [to say] that ... the injured plaintiff who recovers damages under this head should hold them on trust for the voluntary carer ... Once this is recognised it becomes evident that there can be no ground in public policy or otherwise for requiring the tortfeasor to pay to the plaintiff, in respect of the services which he himself has rendered, a sum of money which the plaintiff must then repay to him' (*per* LORD BRIDGE OF HARWICH). (Applied in *Dimond* v *Lovell*.)

Hunter v *British Coal Corp* [1998] 2 All ER 97 (Court of Appeal)

A vehicle driven by the plaintiff in the defendant's mine struck a hydrant and water began to escape: a fellow employee (Tommy) tried with him to turn off the hydrant, without success. The plaintiff went to look for a hose. When he was 20 to 30 metres away he heard a bang and, looking back, he saw a cloud of dust. He hurried to a stop valve 307 metres from the scene of the accident and, after some ten minutes, shut the water off. He then heard over the tannoy that a man had been injured: on his way back to the accident scene he was told that it seemed Tommy was dead. He replied: 'I killed him.' As a result of this experience the plaintiff suffered nervous shock and depression. He claimed damages for psychiatric injury and, although the judge found that negligence had been established, he dismissed the action. The plaintiff appealed.

Held, the appeal would fail. 'Where the plaintiff learns of an accident caused by the negligence of his employer and without negligence on his part for which he feels some responsibility as an actor who played some part in the events leading to it and who learns of the accident after it has happened, psychiatric injury suffered by him by reason of his feelings of guilt or otherwise is too remote to found an action for damages' (*per* SIR JOHN VINELOTT). (See also *White* v *Chief Constable of the South Yorkshire Police*.)

Hunter v *Canary Wharf Ltd; Hunter* v *London Docklands Development Corp* [1997] 2 All ER 426 (House of Lords)

In the first action, the plaintiffs sought redress for interference with television reception by Canary Wharf Tower, a building 250 metres high and over 50 metres square, erected on land developed by the defendants. In the second, the plaintiffs claimed damages in respect of damage caused by what they alleged were excessive amounts of dust created by the construction by the defendants of the 1,800 metres long Limehouse Link Road. The plaintiffs lived in areas affected by the interference or dust. Preliminary issues of law to reach the House of Lords in the first action were: (1) whether interference with television reception is capable of constituting an actionable nuisance, and (2) whether it is necessary to have an interest in property to claim in private nuisance and, if so, what interest in property will satisfy this requirement. In the second action, at this stage only question (2) arose.

Held, the answers were: (1) in the absence of an easement, more was required than the mere presence of a neighbouring building, and (2) a right to the land, greater than that of a mere licensee, was an essential element. (Distinguished: *Bridlington Relay Ltd v Yorkshire Electricity Board*; overruled: *Khorasandjian v Bush* [1993] 3 All ER 669.)

Hussain v *New Taplow Paper Mills Ltd* [1988] 1 All ER 541 (House of Lords)

The plaintiff's contract of employment stipulated that, if he was injured at work, he would receive full pay for 13 weeks and thereafter 50% of his pre-accident earnings by way of long-term sickness benefit. The defendant employers had insured against their sickness benefit liability and the contract of employment made it clear that this benefit was a continuation of earnings and taxable. The plaintiff sustained injury at work and the defendants were two-thirds to blame for the accident.

Held, both benefits should be deducted from the awards of damages for pre-trial and future loss of earnings. 'Looking at the payments made under the scheme by the defendants in the first weeks after the expiry of the period of 13 weeks of continuous incapacity, they seem to me indistinguishable in character from the sick pay which the employee receives during the first 13 weeks. They are payable under a term of the employee's contract by the defendants to the employee qua employee as a partial substitute for earnings and are the very antithesis of a pension, which is payable only after employment ceases. The fact that the defendants happen to have insured their liability to meet these contractual commitments as they arise cannot affect the issue in any way' (*per* LORD BRIDGE OF HARWICH). (Distinguished in *McCamley v Cammell Laird Shipbuilders Ltd.*)

Huth v *Huth* [1915] 3 KB 32 (Court of Appeal)

In an unsealed envelope the defendant posted a statement to the plaintiffs which they alleged was defamatory of them. In breach of his duty and out of curiosity the statement was taken out of the envelope and read by a butler and the plaintiffs maintained that this constituted a publication of the libel for which the defendant was responsible.

Held, the statement had not been published and the plaintiffs' action for damages would fail. (But see *Theaker v Richardson*.)

Hyett v *Great Western Railway Co* [1947] 2 All ER 264 (Court of Appeal)

The plaintiff noticed a fire in one of the defendants' railway wagons which contained drums of paraffin oil and while he was trying to unload the drums to avert the danger one exploded and he was injured. It was found that the fire could be attributed to the defendants' negligence.

Held, in the circumstances, the plaintiff's actions were reasonable and he was entitled to damages as his actions were of the kind which the defendants might reasonably have anticipated as likely to follow from their negligent act. (See also *Ward v T E Hopkins & Son Ltd*; but see *Thorogood v Van Den Berghs and Jurgens Ltd*.)

IBL Ltd v *Coussens* [1991] 2 All ER 133 (Court of Appeal)

Following his dismissal, the plaintiffs' former chairman failed to return the company's Rolls Royce and Aston Martin or to purchase the cars at prices offered by the company. The judge made an order under s3(2)(b) of the Torts (Interference with Goods) Act 1977 and the question arose as to how damages awarded for conversion under s3 of the 1977 Act, as an alternative to the return of the goods, were to be assessed.

Held, they should not be assessed arbitrarily as at either the date of the conversion or the date of judgment but ought to be such as, in all the circumstances, fairly compensated the owner for the loss of the goods. (See also *Munro v Willmott*.)

I M Properties plc v *Cape & Dalgleish* [1998] 3 All ER 203 (Court of Appeal)

As a result of the defendant auditors' negligence, a fraud was perpetrated against the plaintiffs and their total loss was £704,568.29. However, before these proceedings had been commenced, the plaintiffs entered into a settlement agreement with the perpetrator of the fraud whereby the plaintiffs received shares to the value of £430,000. Judgment was therefore entered for £274,568.29 and the judges awarded interest on £704,568.29 up to the date of the settlement and £274,568.29 thereafter.

Held, this approach had not been correct. By virtue of s35A(1) of the Supreme Court Act 1981, the judge was entitled to award interest only on the sum for which he gave judgment, ie, £274,568.29. (See also *Metal Box Ltd v Currys Ltd*.)

Ilkiw v *Samuels* [1963] 2 All ER 879 (Court of Appeal)

A lorry driver employed by the defendants had strict instructions from them that he was not in any circumstances to allow anyone else to drive his lorry. When it became necessary to move the lorry away from a conveyor belt from which it had been loaded the driver allowed another, who was obviously quite incompetent to drive the vehicle, to drive it away. He succeeded in moving the vehicle a few yards forward, found he could not stop it and the plaintiff received injuries as a result.

Held, the defendants were liable because the lorry driver had been negligent in allowing the other to drive it and the lorry driver's negligence arose in the course of his employment. The mere fact that the plaintiff's injuries resulted from an act done in disobedience to express instructions was of no necessary materiality in deciding whether or not the act was within the course of the lorry driver's employment. (See also *Limpus v London General Omnibus Co*.)

Imperial Chemical Industries Ltd v *Shatwell* [1964] 2 All ER 999 (House of Lords)

George and James Shatwell were qualified shotfirers employed by the appellants and, because they disregarded both the appellants' instructions and certain statutory regulations which imposed a duty on shotfirers personally (ie not on employers) and could not be bothered to await the arrival of longer wires, both were injured by an explosion in the course of their work for the appellants. Both George and James were aware of the appellants' instructions and the statutory regulations and fully appreciated the risk that they had taken, but George sued the appellants on the ground that he and his brother were equally to blame for the accident, and that the appellants were vicariously liable for James's conduct.

Held, although James's acts were a contributing cause of the injuries suffered by George, the appellants were not liable because the principle volenti non fit injuria afforded them a complete defence. (But see *Quarman* v *Burnett*.)

Innes v *Wylie* (1884) 1 C & K 257

The Caledonian Society of London was holding a meeting and dinner in Radley's Hotel. The plaintiff was a member of the Society, but a policeman was instructed by the Society, the defendants, to prevent him from entering the room where the meeting was to be held. The plaintiff brought an action for assault.

Held, the plaintiff would succeed as the defendants had failed to prove that the policeman was 'entirely passive like a door or a wall put to prevent the plaintiff from entering the room' (*per* LORD DENMAN CJ). (See also *Ashton* v *Jennings*.)

Ironfield v *Eastern Gas Board* [1964] 1 All ER 544

A car ran into a lorry which had its rear lights obscured by its tailboard. The owners of the lorry were guilty of negligence and the question arose whether the owner of the car was entitled to recover by way of special damages £10 for the insurance excess and £15 10s 7d for the loss of his 'no claims' bonus.

Held, he was as they were part of the damage which resulted from the accident. (See also *Scott* v *Shepherd*.)

Jameson v *Central Electricity Generating Board (Babcock Energy Ltd, third party)* [1999] 1 All ER 193 (House of Lords)

Jameson was employed by the third party and in the course of his employment he worked at two of the defendants' power stations. As a result of his exposure there to asbestos dust, he contracted a malignant disease. He sued his employers and the agreed value of his claim was £130,00. On 19 April 1988 he accepted £80,000 in 'full and final settlement and satisfaction' of his cause of action. On 24 April, before the agreed sum was paid, he died. After payment had been made to his estate, his executors sued the defendants on behalf of Jameson's widow claiming damages for loss of dependency under s1 of the Fatal Accidents Act 1976. Were the plaintiffs entitled to maintain these proceedings?

Held, they were not. '... as the settlement which the deceased entered into before his death was implemented in full by [his employers], nothing which [they] had agreed to pay having been left unpaid, its effect was to discharge the claim of damages against the other concurrent tortfeasors with effect from the date of the settlement. The plaintiffs cannot therefore satisfy the requirements of s1(1) of the 1976 Act, because [the defendants] would not have been liable, if death had not ensued, to an action of damages brought by the deceased in respect of the same tort' (*per* LORD HOPE OF CRAIGHEAD). (See also *Bryanston Finance Ltd* v *de Vries*.)

Janvier v *Sweeney* [1919] 2 KB 316 (Court of Appeal)

The plaintiff, a Frenchwoman, was engaged to a German who was interned on the Isle of Man. One of the defendants called at her house and falsely told her that he was representing the military authorities and that she was the woman they wanted as she had been corresponding with a German spy. In consequence the plaintiff suffered severe nervous shock.

Held, she was entitled to damages. (See also *McLoughlin* v *O'Brian*.)

JEB Fasteners Ltd v *Marks, Bloom & Co* [1983] 1 All ER 583 (Court of Appeal)

When preparing a company's accounts, the defendant auditors negligently included stock at a value of some £13,000 over the discounted cost without appending a note in the accounts to that effect. They knew that the company faced liquidity problems and was seeking outside financial support from, inter alia, the plaintiffs. After the accounts had been made available to them, the plaintiffs took over the company for a nominal amount. The plaintiffs claimed damages for negligence.

Held, as the defendants knew at the time the accounts were prepared that the company needed outside financial support and ought reasonably to have foreseen that a take-over was a possible means of obtaining finance and that a person effecting a take-over might rely on those accounts, it followed that they owed the plaintiffs a duty of care in the preparation of the accounts. The defendants had been in breach of that duty, but as they would not have acted differently had they known the true position the defendants' negligence was not a cause of any loss suffered by the plaintiffs and their action would therefore be dismissed. (See also *Yianni* v *Edwin Evans & Sons*.)

Jobling v *Associated Dairies Ltd* [1981] 2 All ER 752 (House of Lords)

In 1973, in the course of his employment and as a result of his employers' negligence, a man suffered a slipped disc; his earning capacity was reduced by 50 per cent. Nearly four years later he was found to be suffering from a spinal disease, unrelated to his accident, and by the time (1979) that his claim came to trial this disease had rendered him totally incapable of work.

Held, the employers' liability was limited to loss of earnings up to the time when the disease resulted in total incapacity. (See also *Beoco Ltd v Alfa Laval Co Ltd*; but see *Baker v Willoughby*.)

Jolley v Sutton London Borough Council [1998] 3 All ER 559 (Court of Appeal)

The defendants left lying (for at least two years) a boat on their land outside some flats. The 14-year-old plaintiff and his friend decided to repair it. They jacked it up but, while they were at work, the boat fell on the plaintiff and caused him serious injuries. The defendants accepted that they had been negligent in failing to remove the boat but contended that the accident was not one that they could have reasonably foreseen.

Held, the defendants' contention would be accepted and the plaintiff's action would therefore fail. 'The question which has to be asked is, was this accident in the words of Lord Pearce [in *Hughes v Lord Advocate*] "of a different type and kind from anything that a defender could have foreseen"? In answering this question it is necessary to have well in mind that the council should have appreciated that it is difficult to anticipate what children will do when playing with a boat of this sort. Boats, like cars, if they are left "abandoned" in an area where children have access, will certainly attract children to play with them. But what the plaintiff was engaged on was an activity very different from normal play. Even making full allowance for the unpredictability of children's behaviour, I am driven to conclude that it was not reasonably foreseeable that an accident could occur as a result of the boys deciding to work under a propped up boat. Nor could any reasonably similar accident have been foreseen' (*per* LORD WOOLF MR). (See also *Mullin v Richards*.)

Jones v Boyce (1816) 1 Stark 493

The plaintiff was a passenger on the defendant's coach. Shortly after leaving an inn, a coupling rein broke and, realising the danger, the plaintiff decided to jump from the coach and in consequence suffered a broken leg. In the event, the coachman avoided disaster by driving the coach to the side of the road.

Held, the plaintiff's action for damages would succeed. The defendant had placed him in such a situation that he was compelled to adopt a perilous alternative and the plaintiff's action was that of a reasonable and prudent man.

Jones v Manchester Corporation [1952] 2 All ER 125 (Court of Appeal)

A hospital board employed a recently qualified physician, Dr Wilkes, and a senior surgeon, Dr Sejrup. Due to negligence in the administration of an anaesthetic by Dr Wilkes during an operation which was being performed by Dr Sejrup, the patient died and his widow claimed damages against Dr Wilkes and the hospital board.

Held, she would succeed, but the hospital board was not entitled to an indemnity from Dr Wilkes as they were negligent in allowing him to act without adequate supervision and their employee, Dr Sejrup, was also guilty of negligence. (See also *Roe v Ministry of Health*.)

Jones v *Swansea City Council* [1990] 3 All ER 737 (House of Lords)

When the plaintiff's husband was a majority Ratepayers Party member of the council, she was granted permission by the council (as landlord and planning authority) to change the use of certain premises. The leader of the Labour group said that if he was returned at the forthcoming elections he would seek the reversal of the decision. The Labour group came to power and the decision was duly reversed. The plaintiff maintained that the council had been guilty of the tort of misfeasance in public office.

Held, while she would have had a good cause of action if she had alleged and proved that councillors had voted for the resolution with the object of damaging her, as she had not proved that councillors so voting had been infected by their leader's alleged malice her case was bound to fail. (See also *Dunlop* v *Wollahara Municipal Council*.)

Joyce v *Sengupta* [1993] 1 WLR 337 (Court of Appeal)

Arising out of false newspaper allegations that she had, inter alia, stolen some of the Princess Royal's letters, the plaintiff claimed damages for malicious falsehood (for which action she obtained legal aid) rather than defamation (for which legal aid was not available).

Held, she had been entitled so to choose her cause of action, even though the damages recoverable for malicious falsehood could be insignificant compared with the costs involved. 'Falsity is an essential ingredient of [malicious falsehood]. The plaintiff must establish the untruth of the statement of which he complains. Malice is another essential ingredient. A genuine dispute about the ownership of goods or land should not of itself be actionable. So a person who acted in good faith is not liable. Further, since the object of this cause of action is to provide a person with a remedy for a false statement made maliciously which has caused him damage, at common law proof of financial loss was another essential ingredient. The rigour of this requirement was relaxed by ... [s3 of the] the Defamation Act 1952 ... The false statement may also be defamatory, or it may not' (*per* SIR DONALD NICHOLLS V-C). (See also *Henderson* v *Merrett Syndicates Ltd*.)

Junior Books Ltd v *Veitchi Co Ltd* [1982] 3 All ER 201 (House of Lords)

Specialist sub-contractors, the appellants, laid composition flooring in the respondents' new factory. The appellants were nominated by the respondents' architect and the appellants had entered into a contract for the work with the main contractors. Two years after the floor was laid it developed cracks.

Held, although the relationship between the parties fell short (but only just) of a contractual relationship, the proximity between them was sufficiently close for the appellants to owe a duty of care to the respondents not to lay a defective floor which would cause the respondents' financial loss. 'I therefore ask first whether there was the requisite degree of proximity so as to give rise to the relevant duty of care relied on by the respondents. I regard the following facts as of crucial importance in requiring an affirmative answer to that question: (1) the appellants were nominated sub-contractors; (2) the appellants were specialists in flooring; (3) the appellants knew what products were required by the respondents and their main contractors and specialised in the production of those products;

(4) the appellants alone were responsible for the composition and construction of the flooring; (5) the respondents relied on the appellants' skill and experience; (6) the appellants as nominated sub-contractors must have known that the respondents relied on their skill and experience; (7) the relationship between the parties was as close as it could be short of actual privity of contract; (8) the appellants must be taken to have known that if they did the work negligently (as it must be assumed that they did) the resulting defects would at some time require remedying by the respondents expending money on the remedial measures as a consequence of which the respondents would suffer financial or economic loss' (*per* LORD ROSKILL). (Not followed in *D & F Estates Ltd v Church Commissioners for England*; see also *Esso Petroleum Co Ltd v Mardon*; but see *Nitrigin Eireann Teoranta v Inco Alloys Ltd* and *Lawton v BOC Transhield Ltd*.)

Kay v Ayrshire and Arran Health Board [1987] 2 All ER 417 (House of Lords)

The appellant's son was admitted to the defendants' hospital suffering from meningitis. While there, he was negligently given an overdose of penicillin. After recovering from the meningitis the boy was found to be deaf. He sued for damages and medical evidence indicated that, although deafness often followed meningitis, it had never been caused by an overdose of penicillin.

Held, the boy's claim could not succeed as, in the light of the expert evidence, his deafness had to be regarded as resulting solely from the meningitis. (See also *Hotson v East Berkshire Area Health Authority*.)

Kay v ITW Ltd [1967] 3 All ER 22 (Court of Appeal)

The plaintiff was injured when the assistant manager of the defendants' warehouse backed a diesel truck belonging to another firm. The manager was employed to drive cars on the premises and backed the truck in order to make space for a van which he wished to take into the warehouse.

Held, this act was within the scope of the manager's employment and the defendants were vicariously liable. (See also *Century Insurance Co Ltd v Northern Ireland Road Transport Board*.)

Kelsen v Imperial Tobacco Co (of Great Britain and Ireland) Ltd [1957] 2 All ER 343

The plaintiff was lessee of a ground floor room in Islington which he used as a tobacconist's shop. The premises had a flat roof and the plaintiff's landlords gave to the owners of the adjoining building consent to the defendants, who were wholesale tobacconists, erecting a large 'Players Please' sign which projected into the air space above the plaintiff's shop a distance of some 8 in.

Held, the invasion of the plaintiff's air space by the sign amounted to a trespass on the part of the defendants and not merely a nuisance, and he was entitled to a mandatory injunction requiring the defendants to remove such portion of the sign as projected over his premises. (See also *Woollerton & Wilson Ltd v Richard Costain Ltd*.)

Kemsley v Foot [1952] 1 All ER 501 (House of Lords)

Under the title 'Lower than Kemsley', *Tribune* published an article by Michael Foot which, without making any other direct reference to Lord Kemsley, suggested that he was a newspaper proprietor who prostituted his position by conducting his newspapers or permitting them to be conducted in an undesirable manner.

Held, the defence of fair comment was available as the article contained sufficient facts to form the basis of comment. (See also *London Artists Ltd v Littler*.)

Kennaway v Thompson [1980] 3 All ER 329 (Court of Appeal)

The plaintiff lived near a lake which was a centre for motor boat races and water skiing. Noise from these activities amounted to a nuisance but, instead of the injunction which the plaintiff had sought, the trial judge awarded her £1,000 for nuisance already suffered and £15,000 for the damage likely to be suffered in the future.

Held, in lieu of the £15,000 award, an injunction would be granted restricting the number and extent of racing activities in each year and the noise level of boats using the lake at other times. 'Intervention by injunction is only justified when the irritating noise causes inconvenience beyond what other occupiers in the neighbourhood can be expected to bear' (*per* LAWTON LJ). (But see *Miller v Jackson* and *Tetley v Chitty*.)

Kerr v Kennedy [1942] 1 All ER 412

The defendant told a common acquaintance that the plaintiff was a 'lesbian'.

Held, such a statement was an imputation of unchastity within s1 of the Slander of Women Act 1891, and was therefore actionable without proof of special damage.

Khorasandjian v Bush See Hunter v Canary Wharf Ltd

Kimpton v Steel Company of Wales Ltd [1960] 2 All ER 274 (Court of Appeal)

The plaintiff was employed as a maintenance electrician in the defendants' factory and while descending a set of three steel steps in the factory he slipped and injured himself. There was no handrail on either side of the steps, but s25 of the Factories Act 1937 required that: 'For every staircase ... a substantial handrail shall be provided and maintained'.

Held, the defendants were not in breach of this statutory duty as the steps were not a 'staircase', but the plaintiff could recover damages at common law for breach by the defendants of their duty to take reasonable care not to expose their servants to unnecessary risk. (See also *Close v Steel Company of Wales Ltd*.)

King v *Liverpool City Council* [1986] 3 All ER 544 (Court of Appeal)

The council flat above the plaintiff's flat became vacant; vandals entered, stole parts of the water system and caused the plaintiff's flat to be flooded on three occasions. The plaintiff sued the council for negligence.

Held, her action would fail: the council had not owed her a duty of care as, on the facts, it was impossible for them to take effective steps to defeat the actions of trespassing vandals. (Applied: *P Perl (Exporters) Ltd* v *Camden London Borough Council*; see also *Smith* v *Littlewoods Organisation Ltd*.)

Kirk v *Gregory* (1876) 1 ExD 55

The master of the house died in a state of delirium tremens and much feasting and drinking took place in the same building. In view of this, for safety's sake, the deceased's sister-in-law deemed it wise to remove some of his jewellery from the room where he lay and to put it in another place. Some of the jewellery disappeared from this place of 'safety'.

Held, the sister-in-law had acted in good faith but she was nevertheless liable in trespass as she had been unable to prove that her interference with the deceased's goods was reasonably necessary. (But see *Cope* v *Sharpe (No 2)*.)

Kirkham v *Chief Constable of the Greater Manchester Police* [1990] 3 All ER 246 (Court of Appeal)

The deceased, the plaintiff's husband, while suffering from clinical depression had been arrested and charged with an offence. The plaintiff told the police that he was a suicide risk but, after he had been remanded in custody, the police failed to follow the procedure for notifying the prison authorities that he had suicidal tendencies. At the remand centre the deceased was treated like a normal prisoner and he committed suicide there. The plaintiff claimed damages for negligence.

Held, her action would be successful as the police, by failing to pass on relevant information, had been in breach of their duty of care. The defence of volenti non fit injuria failed because, in the light of the deceased's mental condition, his suicide had not been a truly voluntary act. The maxim ex turpi causa non oritur actio did not apply as suicide is no longer an affront to the public conscience. (Applied in *Welsh* v *Chief Constable of the Metropolitan Police*, but see *Knight* v *Home Office*.)

Knight v *Home Office* [1990] 3 All ER 237

A man known to have suicidal tendencies was ordered to be detained in a remand prison pending his admission to hospital. Prison officers observed him at not less than 15 minute intervals but between these inspections, he hanged himself. His personal representatives claimed damages for negligence.

Held, their action could not succeed as the decision to observe the deceased at 15 minute intervals was a decision which could have been made by ordinary skilled medical staff in the position of the prison's medical staff. (See also *Bolam* v *Friern Hospital Management Committee*; but see *Kirkham* v *Chief Constable of the Greater Manchester Police*.)

Knightley v Johns [1982] 1 All ER 851 (Court of Appeal)

The defendant's car somersaulted and came to rest upside down near to the exit of a one-way tunnel in Birmingham. Police were quickly on the scene and, as he had not closed the tunnel to traffic, the inspector in charge ordered the plaintiff police officer to ride back on his motor cycle, against oncoming traffic, to do so. Both the ordering and making of this manoeuvre were in breach of police force standing orders. Near the entrance to the tunnel the plaintiff collided with an oncoming vehicle and was injured. The defendant conceded that he had been negligent and the trial judge found that he was wholly liable for the plaintiff's injuries.

Held, the inspector too had been negligent and his negligence had been the real cause – and a new cause – of the plaintiff's injuries and he and his employer were liable. As the inspector's negligence made the plaintiff's injuries too remote from the defendant's wrongdoing to be a consequence of it, the appeal would be allowed. 'In the long run the question is one of remoteness of damage, to be answered not by the logic of philosophers but by the common sense of plain men ... too much happened here, too much went wrong, the chapter of accidents and mistakes was too long and varied, to impose on [the defendant] liability for what happened to the plaintiff ... although it would not have happened had not [the defendant] negligently overturned his car' (*per* STEPHENSON LJ). (See also *Capital and Counties plc* v *Hampshire County Council* and *Pritchard* v *J H Cobden Ltd*; but see *Haynes* v *Harwood* and *Hughes* v *National Union of Mineworkers*.)

Knowles v Liverpool City Council [1993] 4 All ER 321 (House of Lords)

The respondent flagger, who was employed by the appellants, was manhandling a flagstone. The flagstone broke and the respondent dropped it and suffered injury. The manufacturers (who were not the appellants) were responsible for the flagstone's defect, but this defect could not reasonably have been discovered before the accident.

Held, the respondent was entitled to damages against the appellants as the flagstone was 'equipment' for the purposes of s1(1) of the Employers' Liability (Defective Equipment) Act 1969. 'The requirement of the subsection is that the equipment is provided "for the purposes of the employer's business" and not merely for the use of the employee' (per LORD JAUNCEY OF TULLICHETTLE). (See also *Coltman* v *Bibby Tankers Ltd, the Derbyshire*.)

Knupffer v London Express Newspaper Ltd [1944] 1 All ER 495 (House of Lords)

The respondent newspaper published an article referring to an association of political refugees which, it was admitted, would have been defamatory if it had been written about a named individual. The appellant was the head of the United Kingdom branch of the association which consisted of some 24 members.

Held, the appellant was not entitled to damages as the words were written of a class and he had failed to show that they were pointed at him as an individual.

Koursk, The [1924] P 140 (Court of Appeal)

Five vessels were in convoy in the Mediterranean in line abreast. The centre ship was the *Itria* and on her port hand were the *Clan Chisholm* and the *Koursk*. The *Koursk* got out of position and collided with the *Clan Chisholm* and a minute later the *Clan* Chisholm collided with and sank the *Itria*. It was found that the *Koursk* was two-thirds to blame for the collision with the *Clan Chisholm* which was itself one-third to blame. The owners of the *Itria* recovered judgment against the owners of the *Clan Chisholm* and then proceeded to sue the owners of the Koursk who maintained that this action should fail as, having recovered against one joint tortfeasor (the *Clan Chisholm*) they could not subsequently recover against the other, the *Koursk*.

Held, this plea would fail as the owners of the *Clan Chisholm* and the *Koursk* were not joint tortfeasors as they had no community of design. (But see *Brooke v Bool*.)

Lamb v London Borough of Camden [1981] 2 All ER 408 (Court of Appeal)

The owner of a house of quality near Hampstead Heath went to New York. She let her house and while she was away the local authority decided to replace the sewer in the road. In the course of this work a water main was broken; as a result the foundations of the house cracked and it became unsafe to live in. While the necessary repairs were in hand, the lady's furniture was put into store. Squatters invaded the empty house, were evicted and, although some precautions were taken, they moved in again: this time they caused extensive damage which would cost nearly £30,000 to repair. The lady said the expense of repairing the house was due to the council's negligence or to a nuisance created by them in the course of their work on the sewer and the council admitted liability for nuisance. Was she entitled to recover the cost of repairing the damage caused by the squatters?

Held, she was not as this damage was too remote. In all the circumstances the incursion of squatters was unlikely and the damage in question was not such as could have been foreseen when the water main was fractured. (See also *Home Office v Dorset Yacht Co Ltd* and *Smith v Littlewood Organisation Ltd*.)

Lane v Holloway [1967] 3 All ER 129 (Court of Appeal)

The plaintiff and the defendant lived in the same yard. At 11 pm one evening the plaintiff, after returning from a public house, was talking to a friend in the yard. Hearing this the defendant's wife called out 'You bloody lot'. The plaintiff replied: 'Shut up, you monkey-faced tart'. The defendant, hearing this, came outside and shouted 'What did you say to my wife?', to which the plaintiff replied by challenging the defendant to fight. The defendant then punched the plaintiff very hard: he was in hospital for a month.

Held, although self-defence is permissible, it must be reasonably commensurable with the attack which it presupposes. The blow given by the defendant was out of proportion to the occasion, and he was liable in damages. (But see *Dale* v *Wood*.)

Langlands (J) (Swanley) Ltd v British Transport Commission
[1956] 2 All ER 702

Part of the plaintiffs' wheat crop was damaged by two fires which were caused by sparks from engines on the defendants' railway. In respect of these two fires the defendants paid in compensation to the plaintiffs the sum of £127 18s 9d, which represented the market price of the probable yield of the damaged crop, but the plaintiffs claimed a further £49 lls, which was the amount of the statutory deficiency payment which they would have received if they had sold and delivered the wheat.

Held, they were entitled to succeed as the purpose of s1 of the Railway Fires Act 1905 was to put the plaintiffs in the position in which they would have been if the defendants had not been acting under statutory powers, and the loss of the deficiency payment was not too remote to be recoverable as damages for nuisance.

Langridge v Levy (1837) 2 M & W 519; affd (1838) 4 M & W 337

Langridge bargained with the defendant for the purchase of a gun. In the course of negotiations it was made known that Langridge wanted the gun for his own use and that of his sons and the defendant said that it had been made by Nock and that it was good, safe and secure. The plaintiff, one of Langridge's sons, knowing what had been said by the defendant in the course of bargaining, used the instrument, but it burst and injured him. It afterwards appeared that the gun had been badly made by a gunmaker who was very inferior to Nock.

Held, the plaintiff was entitled to damages as the defendant was responsible for the consequences of his fraud whilst the gun was in the possession of a person to whom his representation was either directly or indirectly communicated, and for whose use he knew it was purchased. (But see *Peek* v *Gurney*.)

Larmer v British Steel plc [1993] 4 All ER 102 (Court of Appeal)

The plaintiff was injured at his workplace when a heavy roller fell on his leg. He sued his employers for, inter alia, breach of duty under s29(1) of the Factories Act 1961, alleging that they had failed so far as was reasonably practicable to ensure that his workplace was 'made and kept safe'. The defendants denied liability, but did not specifically plead that it had not been practicable to make the workplace safe. The judge dismissed the claim. On appeal, the plaintiff contended that lack of reasonable practicability could only be relied on if it was pleaded and proved: for their part, the defendants argued that, in order to succeed, the plaintiff had to prove that the danger had been reasonably foreseeable by the defendants.

Held, the appeal would be allowed. If they were to escape liability, the defendants had to specifically plead and prove that it had not been reasonably practicable to keep the premises safe and this they failed to do. Reasonable foreseeability did not arise when considering a claim under s29(1) of the 1961 Act. 'To imply words in the section so as to introduce a test of reasonable foreseeability is to reduce the protection afforded by the 1961 Act for the workman' (per PETER GIBSON J).

Laws v Florinplace Ltd [1981] 1 All ER 659

The defendants opened a 'sex centre and cinema club' which showed 'explicit sex acts' and the plaintiffs, residents in a nearby street, sought an injunction and damages.

Held, as nuisance could extend to cases where the use made by a defendant of his property was such an affront to the reasonable susceptibilities of ordinary men and women as to constitute an interference with the reasonable domestic enjoyment of their property, there was here a triable issue and the balance of convenience was in favour of granting an interlocutory injunction.

Lawton v BOC Transhield Ltd [1987] 2 All ER 608

The plaintiff sued his former employers for negligence on the ground that a character reference given by them to his new employer had been inaccurate and/or unfair.

Held, while there was sufficient proximity between the parties for the defendants to owe the plaintiff a duty of care as to the contents of the reference and while it was reasonably foreseeable that a breach of that duty would lead to the plaintiff's financial loss, the plaintiff's action would fail as, on the facts, the reference was honest and accurate and not negligently written. (Applied *Junior Books Ltd v Veitchi Co Ltd.*)

League Against Cruel Sports Ltd v Scott [1985] 2 All ER 489

The plaintiffs having provided a wild deer sanctuary on Exmoor and, after being refused entry, the defendants' hunt having entered there on seven occasions, the plaintiffs sought damages and an injunction.

Held, their action would be successful. Trespass to land could be established if either the master of the hunt actually intended the hounds to enter the prohibited land or if by his negligence in controlling the hounds he failed to prevent them from entering the land. (See also *Westripp v Baldock.*)

Leakey v National Trust for Places of Historic Interest or Natural Beauty [1980] 1 All ER 17 (Court of Appeal)

The defendants owned and occupied a hill which was peculiarly liable to crack and slip as a result of weathering; the plaintiffs owned houses at the foot of it. After a large fall, the plaintiffs asked the defendants to remove the earth and debris from their land, but they refused, saying they were not responsible for what had occurred. The judge held that the defendants were liable in nuisance.

Held, their appeal would be dismissed. 'The duty is a duty to do that which is reasonable in all the circumstances, and no more than what, if anything, is reasonable, to prevent or minimise the known risks of damage or injury to one's neighbour or to his property. The criteria of reasonableness include the factor of what the particular man, not the average man, can be expected to do, having regard, amongst other things, where a serious expenditure of money is required to eliminate or reduce the danger, to his means' (*per* MEGAW LJ). (See also *Coldman v Hargrove* and *Sedleigh-Denfield v O'Callagan*.)

Lee Kar Choo v Lee Lian Choon [1966] 3 All ER 1000 (Privy Council)

The appellant had for many years sold tea in packets of an intriguing design, incorporating a prominent scroll of flowers surrounding a gold fish, and which was registered as a trade mark. The respondent began to sell tea in similar packets and with a similar design, though not an infringement of the trade mark. The labels did not cause actual confusion, but were calculated to enable the respondents' goods to be passed off to customers as those of the appellant, so it was found. The customers were mostly illiterate and ordered tea by reference to the prominent feature on the label.

Held, although there was no infringement of the trade mark, relief would be granted on grounds of passing off. The emphasis in the respondent's labels was on an essential part of the appellant's trade mark. (See also *Cadbury Schweppes Pty Ltd v Pub Squash Co Pty Ltd*.)

Leeman v Montagu [1936] 2 All ER 1677

The plaintiff bought a house in an area which was partly rural, but largely residential. In an orchard which was about 100 yds from this house the defendant kept some 750 cockerels which were in the habit of crowing from 2 am until 7 or 8 am. This noise made it impossible for the plaintiff to sleep.

Held, a nuisance had been proved and the plaintiff was entitled to an injunction to restrain the defendant from carrying on the business of poultry breeder in this manner.

Leigh and Sillivan Ltd v Aliakmon Shipping Co Ltd, The Aliakmon [1986] 2 All ER 145 (House of Lords)

The appellants had agreed to buy steel coils and they were to be shipped from Korea to the United Kingdom in the respondents' vessel. The goods were badly stowed and they suffered damage in the course of the voyage; at that time the risk, but not the legal property in the goods, had passed to the appellants. Had the respondents owed a duty of care in tort to the appellants in respect of the carriage of the goods?

Held, they had not because a person cannot claim in negligence for loss caused unless he had either legal ownership of, or a possessory title to, the goods at the time when the damage occurred.

Lemmon v Webb [1895] AC 1 (House of Lords)

Without giving notice to the appellant and without trespassing on his land, the respondent cut off some branches of the appellant's trees which were overhanging his soil.

Held, the respondent was entitled to do this. (See also *Smith v Giddy*.)

Letang v *Cooper* [1964] 2 All ER 929 (Court of Appeal)

In July 1957 the defendant drove his Jaguar over the plaintiff's legs while she was sunbathing. In February 1961 the plaintiff brought an action for damages for personal injuries for negligence and/or trespass to the person. Was her action statute barred under the proviso added to s2(1) of the Limitation Act 1939 by s2(1) of the Law Reform (Limitation of Actions, etc) Act 1954?

Held, it was; the injury was inflicted unintentionally and for this reason the plaintiff's only cause of action lay in negligence. 'The truth is that the distinction between trespass and case is obsolete ... Instead of dividing actions for personal injuries into *trespass* (direct damage) or *case* (consequential damage), we divide the causes of action now according as the defendant did the injury intentionally or unintentionally. If one man intentionally applies force directly to another, the plaintiff has a cause of action in assault and battery, or, if you so please to describe it, in trespass to the person. If he does not inflict injury intentionally, but only unintentionally, the plaintiff has no cause of action today in trespass. His only cause of action is in negligence, and then only on proof of want of reasonable care' (*per* LORD DENNING MR). (See also *Stanley* v *Powell* and *Wilson* v *Pringle*; but see *Stubbings* v *Webb*; see now s11 of the Limitation Act 1980.)

Lewis v *Daily Telegraph Ltd* [1963] 2 All ER 151 (House of Lords)

The defendants stated in their newspaper that 'Officers of the City of London Fraud Squad are inquiring into the affairs of Rubber Improvement Ltd and its subsidiary companies ... The Chairman of the Company ... is Mr John Lewis'. Both Mr Lewis and Rubber Improvement Ltd claimed damages for libel and maintained that the passage in question was capable of meaning that they were guilty of fraud. The defendants admitted that the words were libellous but pleaded justification in that the fraud squad were at the time of publication making such enquiries. Nevertheless, the plaintiffs were awarded damages and the defendants contended that the jury should have been directed that the words were not capable of the extended meaning which the plaintiffs attributed to them, ie that the plaintiffs were guilty of fraud.

Held, there should be a new trial as the judge had not ruled whether the words in question were capable of imputing guilt of fraud as distinct from suspicion and his failure to do so amounted to a misdirection. 'Whether the words are capable of defamatory meaning is for the judge, and where the words, whether on the face of them they are or are not innocent in themselves, bear a defamatory or more defamatory meaning because of extraneous facts known to those to whom the libel has been published, it is the duty of the judge to rule whether there is evidence of such extraneous facts fit to be left to the jury' (*per* LORD HODSON). Further, when awarding damages for loss of income or loss of profit the jury should take into account a plaintiff's income tax (or surtax) liability. (See also *Grappelli* v *Derek Block (Holdings) Ltd* and *British Transport Commission* v *Gourley*.)

Liesbosch (Dredgers) v *Edison (Steamships)* [1933] AC 449 (House of Lords)

While the *Liesbosch* was moored in harbour, due to negligent navigation the Edison fouled her moorings and carried her out to sea where she sank. The owners of the *Edison* admitted liability for the loss of the *Liesbosch* and the only question to be decided was the amount of damages which they should pay. The owners of the *Liesbosch* were engaged in contract work, subject to a time limit, and as the state of their funds did not enable them to purchase another dredger, they hired the Adria, which was much more expensive to work.

Held, the owners of the *Liesbosch* were entitled to the market price of a dredger comparable to the *Liesbosch*, the cost of adapting a new vessel and transporting it to the port in question and insuring it for the voyage, and compensation for their loss in respect of their inability to carry out their contract between the sinking of the *Liesbosch* and the date on which the new dredger could reasonably have been available. Interest on this sum would run from the date of the loss. No account would be taken of any special loss due to the financial position of the owners of the *Liesbosch* as their inpecuniosity was not traceable to the acts of the owners of the *Edison*. (But see *Hyett* v *Great Western Railway Co*.)

Lim Poh Choo v *Camden and Islington Area Health Authority* [1979] 2 All ER 910 (House of Lords)

The defendants admitted liability for irreparable brain damage suffered by the plaintiff senior psychiatric registrar following a minor operation. At the time she was 36 and her expectation of life was 37 years; if she had not suffered these injuries she would almost certainly have become a consultant.

Held, the judge had correctly awarded £20,000 plus interest for pain, suffering and loss of amenities. Again, the judge's award of £84,000 (£6,000 per annum x 14) for loss of future earnings and £8,000 for loss of pension rights would not be disturbed. In a case such as this future living expenses should be deducted from the cost of future care and damages under this head would be assessed using a multiplier of 12 giving an award of £76,800. It was only in exceptional cases that awards of damages could take into account the risk of future inflation. (But see *Wells* v *Wells*.)

Limpus v *London General Omnibus Co* (1862) 1 H & C 526

The driver of one of the defendants' omnibuses obstructed one of the plaintiff's omnibuses to prevent it passing. His action caused injury to one of the plaintiff's horses and severe damage to his omnibus. The defendants' driver had been instructed that 'he must not on any account race with or obstruct another omnibus, or hinder or annoy the driver or conductor thereof'.

Held, nevertheless, the defendants should make good the plaintiff's loss as they were liable for such of their driver's reckless and improper conduct as could be said to have occurred within the course of his employment. (See also *Whatman* v *Pearson*.)

Lincoln v *Hayman* [1982] 2 All ER 819 (Court of Appeal)

Two lorries collided and the plaintiff, the driver of one of them, was awarded a substantial sum by way of damages. The trial judge refused to deduct from the special damages awarded the amount of supplementary benefit received by the plaintiff pending trial.

Held, the deduction should have been made. 'The payments [of supplementary benefit] were made to the plaintiff because he was in need as a direct consequence of the injuries he suffered in the accident. They were made as of right, and if they are not deductible from his damages the plaintiff will pro tanto achieve double recovery, which is contrary to the basic principle of damages as compensation for loss actually suffered' (*per* DUNN LJ). (See also *British Transport Commission* v *Gourley*.)

Lister v *Romford Ice & Cold Storage Co Ltd* [1957] 1 All ER 125 (House of Lords)

The appellant was a lorry driver employed by the respondents and while he was backing his lorry in the yard of a slaughterhouse to which he had been sent to collect waste he negligently ran into and injured his father, who was also employed by the respondents on the same work. The father obtained judgment for damages against the respondents on the ground that they were vicariously liable for the appellant's negligence.

Held, the appellant had been in breach of his duty to the respondents to take due care and they were entitled to recover in damages from the appellant the amount for which they had been made liable to his father. (But see *Harvey* v *R G O'Dell Ltd*.)

Lloyd v *Grace, Smith & Co* [1912] AC 716 (House of Lords)

The appellant, a widow, sought advice from the respondents, a firm of solicitors of high repute, and in fact saw one Sandles, a managing clerk who conducted their conveyancing work without supervision. Sandles advised the appellant to sell two cottages and induced her to sign two documents which he said would enable the properties to be sold. The documents were in fact conveyances to Sandles and he dishonestly proceeded to dispose of the cottages to his advantage.

Held, although the fraud was not committed for the benefit of the respondents, they were liable as Sandles had acted in the course of his employment. (See also *Williams* v *Curzon Syndicate Ltd*; but see *Armagas Ltd* v *Mundogas SA, The Ocean Frost*.)

London Artists Ltd v *Littler* [1969] 2 All ER 193 (Court of Appeal)

Four actors gave notice to terminate their engagements in a play which was being staged by the defendant. Annoyed by this 'coincidence', the defendant wrote each of them a letter deploring their conduct, alleging a plot to end the run of the play. He informed the press of the contents of the letters, thus giving them wide publicity. When sued for defamation, the defendant pleaded fair comment.

Held, for the defence to succeed, there must be a substratum of fact upon which the comment is based. If, as in this case, the 'facts', ie the allegation of a plot to ruin the play, were untrue, the comment could hardly be said to be fair and the plea should fail. (See also *Kemsley v Foot*.)

Lonrho plc v Fayed [1991] 3 All ER 303 (House of Lords)

The plaintiffs alleged that certain of the defendants had, by false and fraudulent misrepresentations, induced the Secretary of State not to refer to the Monopolies and Mergers Commission the take-over of a company which they (the plaintiffs) had been anxious to acquire and that they had therefore lost the opportunity to acquire that company. They sued for the torts of wrongful interference with their trade or business and conspiracy to injure. The judge struck out both claims and the Court of Appeal accepted the claim of unlawful interference but upheld the judge's decision in relation to conspiracy as it had not been alleged that the predominant purpose of the conspiracy was to injure the plaintiffs.

Held, the unlawful interference decision would not be disturbed and the conspiracy claim would also be allowed to proceed to trial. As to the latter, where conspirators intentionally injured the plaintiff and used unlawful means to do so, it was no defence for them to show that their primary or predominant purpose had been to further or protect some legitimate interest of their own: it was sufficient to make their action tortious that they had used unlawful means. (See also *Lonrho v Fayed (No 5)*; but see *Mogul Steamship Co Ltd v McGregor, Gow & Co.*)

Lonrho plc v Fayed (No 5) [1994] 1 All ER 188 (Court of Appeal)

The question arose, inter alia, as to the essential ingredients of the tort of conspiracy to injure by lawful means.

Held, those ingredients 'are an agreement by two or more persons to do acts, lawful in themselves, for the sole or predominant purpose of causing injury to the plaintiff and which causes pecuniary loss to the plaintiff: see *Lonrho Ltd v Shell Petroleum Co Ltd* [1981] 2 All ER 456 and *Lonrho plc v Fayed*. It is not an action for defamation or malicious falsehood; nor is it a conspiracy to injure by unlawful means ... [counsel for the plaintiffs] contends that the defendants commit a tort if two or more agree to tell the truth about the plaintiffs, with the sole or predominant purpose of injuring them and in fact causing them pecuniary loss. [Counsel for the defendants] accepts that in this court that is the law' (*per* STUART-SMITH LJ).

Lonrho plc v Tebbitt [1992] 4 All ER 280 (Court of Appeal)

The plaintiffs brought an action against the Secretary of State and the Department of Trade claiming damages for breach of duty of care in failing to release the plaintiffs from an undertaking in time to allow them to bid for another company, so causing the plaintiffs economic loss.

Held, the plaintiffs had an arguable case. 'It does not ... appal me that it should be suggested that, if the Secretary of State imposes the restrictions of the undertaking on [the plaintiffs] in the public interest, the Secretary of State should thereby assume a private law duty to [the plaintiffs] to release the undertaking when it is no longer needed and the restriction on [the plaintiffs'] freedom to conduct its business no longer has a rationale' (*per* DILLON LJ). (But see *Murphy* v *Brentwood District Council*.)

Lord v Pacific Steam Navigation Co Ltd, The Oropesa
[1943] 1 All ER 211 (Court of Appeal)

A collision occurred between the *Manchester Regiment* and the *Oropesa* for which the *Manchester Regiment* was principally to blame. The master of the *Manchester Regiment* decided to discuss with the master of the *Oropesa* ways of salving his ship. He launched a lifeboat and, with several members of his crew, including the sixth engineer, set out across rough seas to meet his opposite number on the *Oropesa*. The lifeboat capsized and the sixth engineer was drowned. His parents sued the owners of the *Oropesa* for damages for loss of life which, they maintained, was the direct consequence of the negligence of the *Oropesa*.

Held, they would succeed as the death was directly caused by the collision. After the accident the master of the *Manchester Regiment* had acted reasonably and the crossing to see the master of the *Oropesa* did not constitute a novus actus interveniens.

Lowery v Walker [1911] AC 10 (House of Lords)

The defendant did not prevent members of the public from crossing his field on the way to the railway station, but he put a horse which, to his knowledge, was savage, in that field and it attacked and injured the plaintiff as he was making his way across it.

Held, the plaintiff, who was not a trespasser, was entitled to damages.

Lumley v Gye (1853) 2 E & B 216

Johanna Wagner had contracted to sing at the Queen's Theatre, of which the plaintiff was lessee and manager, for a certain period. The defendant was alleged to have maliciously 'enticed and procured' her to refuse to perform at that theatre and thereby to break her contract with the plaintiff.

Held, the plaintiff was entitled to damages. (See also *GWK Ltd* v *Dunlop Rubber Co Ltd*.)

Luxmore-May v Messenger May Baverstock [1990] 1 All ER 1067 (Court of Appeal)

The defendants, provincial auctioneers who claimed to be experts in the valuation of paintings, valued the plaintiffs' two paintings at £30 to £50. They sold at auction for £840 and five months later at a London auction for £88,000. The plaintiffs sought the difference between the two prices.

Held, their action would fail as the defendants had carried out their work competently and with due diligence and a competent valuer could have failed to spot the paintings' potential. (Applied: *Maynard* v *West Midlands Regional Health Authority*.)

Lyon v *Daily Telegraph Ltd* [1943] 2 All ER 316 (Court of Appeal)

The *Daily Telegraph,* which was owned by the defendants, published a letter which was highly critical of a radio entertainment called 'Hi Gang' in which the plaintiffs were the principal artistes. The letter bore the address of a vicarage and was signed 'A. Winslow'. The address was a false one and there was no clergyman of that name. In an action for libel the defendants pleaded fair comment.

Held, this defence would be upheld and the fact that the name and address of the correspondent were fictitious was not evidence of malice on the part of the defendants.

M'Alister (or Donoghue) v *Stevenson* [1932] AC 562 (House of Lords)

A shop assistant, the appellant, drank some ginger-beer which had been manufactured by the respondents. The ginger-beer, which was in a dark opaque glass bottle, had been sold by the respondents to a retailer who in turn sold the drink for consumption by the appellant. As a second glassful was being poured out for her the appellant noticed a decomposed snail float out of the bottle. She became seriously ill and claimed damages for negligence.

Held, the respondents owed the appellant a legal duty to take care that the bottle did not contain noxious matter and they would be liable to her if that legal duty was broken as the manufacturer of an article of food, medicine or the like, sold by him to a distributor in circumstances which prevent the distributor or the ultimate purchaser or consumer from discovering by inspection any defect, is under a legal duty to the ultimate purchaser or consumer to take reasonable care that the article is free from defect likely to cause injury to health. 'You must take reasonable care to avoid acts or omissions which you can reasonably foresee would be likely to injure your neighbour. Who, then, in law is my neighbour? The answer seems to be – persons who are so closely and directly affected by my act that I ought reasonably to have them in contemplation as being so affected when I am directing my mind to the acts or omissions which are called in question' (*per* LORD ATKIN). (See also *Chaproniere* v *Mason*; and *Department of the Environment* v *Thomas Bates & Son*; but see *Glasgow Corporation* v *Muir*.)

McAuley v *Bristol City Council* [1992] 1 All ER 749 (Court of Appeal)

Under the terms of a weekly tenancy the defendant landlords undertook to maintain the structure and exterior of the property while the plaintiff tenant was required to keep the premises, including the garden, in a clean and orderly condition and to give the defendants access 'for any purpose which may from time to time be required'. An unstable garden step caused the plaintiff to fall and break her ankle.

Held, the defendants were liable. On the facts, they had an implied right to repair the step and, by virtue of s4(4) of the Defective Premises Act 1972, they owed the plaintiff the duty of care imposed by s4(1) of that Act. (Applied: *Mint* v *Good*.)

McCall v Brooks See *Dimond v Lovell*

McCamley v Cammell Laird Shipbuilders Ltd [1990] 1 All ER 854 (Court of Appeal)

The plaintiff sustained very serious injuries at work and his employers admitted liability. Unknown to him at the time, the defendant employers' holding company had taken out a personal accident group insurance policy for the benefit of employees and under it payments were made independently of any fault and such payments were calculated by reference to an employee's annual wage. The plaintiff received £45,630 under the policy and the judge decided that this sum – and attendance and mobility allowances – should be disregarded in assessing damages.

Held, his decision in relation to the policy moneys had been correct but the two statutory allowances were deductible. (Followed *Hodgson v Trapp*; distinguished *Hussain v New Taplow Paper Mills Ltd*.)

McDermid v Nash Dredging and Reclamation Co Ltd [1987] 2 All ER 878 (House of Lords)

The defendants and their parent company were engaged in dredging operations and the plaintiff, a deckhand employed by the defendants, was injured while working on the parent company's tug which was under the control of a tug-master employed by the parent company. The plaintiff sued for damages and the trial judge found that the accident had been caused by the tug-master's negligence.

Held, the defendants were liable as they had failed to operate a safe system of work for the plaintiff. 'The plaintiff's claim in the proceedings was based on the allegation inter alia, of a "non-delegable" duty resting on his employers to take reasonable care to provide a "safe system of work" ... The defendants did not, and could not, dispute the existence of such a duty of care, nor that it was "non-delegable" in the special sense in which the phrase is used in this connection. This special sense does not involve the proposition that the duty cannot be delegated in the sense that it is incapable of being the subject of delegation, but only that the employer cannot escape liability if the duty has been delegated and then not properly performed' (*per* LORD HAILSHAM OF ST MARYLEBONE). (See also *Wilsons & Clyde Coal Co Ltd v English*.)

McFarlane v EE Caledonia Ltd [1994] 2 All ER 1 (Court of Appeal)

When the plaintiff painter on the defendants' Piper Alpha North Sea oil rig was off duty on a support ship 550 metres from this rig, there was a series of explosions on the rig which resulted in the death of 164 men. The plaintiff witnessed the tragedy, but the support ship went no nearer to the rig than 100 metres in its rescue attempts. He claimed damages for psychiatric illness suffered because of the things he had seen.

Held, his action could not succeed. 'In my judgment both as a matter of principle and policy the court should not extend the duty to those who are mere bystanders or witnesses of horrific events unless there is a sufficient degree of proximity, which requires both nearness in time and place and a close relationship of love and affection between plaintiff and victim. Even if I am wrong in this view, I think the plaintiff faces insuperable difficulty in this case. Not only is there no finding that it was reasonably foreseeable that a man of ordinary fortitude and phlegm would be so affected by what he saw, a finding which I would certainly decline to make on the evidence, but there is the finding that the plaintiff was probably not such a person. I think this is fatal to this submission' (*per* STUART-SMITH LJ). (Applied: *Alcock* v *Chief Constable of the South Yorkshire Police.*)

McGeown v Northern Ireland Housing Executive [1994] 3 All ER 53 (House of Lords)

The appellant tenant of the respondents tripped in a hole on a footpath crossing the respondents' estate and broke her leg. The public had a right of way over the footpath and the respondents had failed to keep its surface in good repair.

Held, the appellant was not entitled to damages. *Gautret* v *Egerton* (1867) LR 2CP 371 (owner of land over which a public right of way passes not liable for negligent nonfeasance) remained good law and no duty was owed under the Northern Ireland equivalent of s2 of the Occupiers' Liability Act 1957 as those who used a public right of way did so as of right, not with permission. (See also *Greenhalgh* v *British Railways Board.*)

McKay v Essex Area Health Authority [1982] 2 All ER 771 (Court of Appeal)

Early in her pregnancy a woman contracted German measles. Although her doctor took blood samples which were tested by the local health authority, the infection was not diagnosed and the child was born severely disabled. Did this child have a reasonable cause of action for being allowed to enter life damaged?

Held, she did not as such a claim would be contrary to public policy as a violation of the sanctity of human life. 'I cannot accept that the common law duty of care to a person can involve … the legal obligation to that person, whether or not in utero, to terminate his existence' (*per* ACKNER LJ). (See also the Congenital Disabilities (Civil Liability) Act 1976.)

McKew v Holland and Hannen and Cubitts (Scotland) Ltd [1969] 3 All ER 1621 (House of Lords)

The plaintiff suffered an injury caused by the defendants' fault. As a result he occasionally and unexpectedly lost control of his left leg which gave way beneath him. On one such occasion he was injured while attempting to descend some stairs.

Held, the defendants had not caused the second accident, since the chain of causation had been broken, because the plaintiff's conduct was unreasonable in that he knew his leg was liable to give way, and in that the stair was steep and without a handrail. 'I do not think that foreseeability comes into this' (*per* LORD REID). (But see *Wieland* v *Cyril Lord Carpets* Ltd.)

McLoughlin v *O'Brian* [1982] 2 All ER 298 (House of Lords)

When a mother, a person of reasonable fortitude, was at home, two miles away her husband and three of their children were involved in a serious road accident. One daughter died almost immediately and, an hour or so after the accident, the mother saw the other members of her family in hospital, an experience which caused her extreme distress. As a result of hearing of the accident from a following motorist and seeing its results for herself, the mother suffered severe and persisting nervous shock. Responsibility for the accident was admitted by others and the question arose as to the mother's entitlement to damages.

Held, her nervous shock was a reasonably foreseeable consequence of the negligence which caused the accident and it followed that she was entitled to damages, even though she was not at or near the scene when it happened or shortly afterwards. 'Space, time, distance, the nature of the injuries sustained and the relationship of the plaintiff to the immediate victim of the accident are factors to be weighed, but not legal limitations, when the test of reasonable foreseeability is to be applied' (*per* LORD SCARMAN). (See also *Page* v *Smith*; but see *Alcock* v *Chief Constable of the South Yorkshire Police*.)

McNaughton (James) Papers Group Ltd v *Hicks Anderson & Co* [1991] 1 All ER 134 (Court of Appeal)

While the plaintiffs were negotiating an agreed take-over of their rival MK Papers Group, who were in financial trouble, MK's chairman asked their accountants, the defendants, to prepare draft accounts for use in the negotiations. These accounts were shown to the plaintiffs but, after the take-over had been completed, they discovered that they contained certain discrepancies. The plaintiffs sued for damages in negligence.

Held, their action could not succeed as the defendants had not owed them a duty of care. 'To hold that in the circumstances of the present case [the defendants] owed a duty of care to [the plaintiffs] would require us to distinguish the facts of the present case from those of the *Caparo Industries* case when, in my judgment, no such valid distinction exists' (*per* BALCOMBE LJ).

McWilliams v *Sir William Arrol & Co Ltd* See *Cummings (or McWilliams)* v *Sir William Arrol & Co Ltd*

Malcolm v *Broadhurst* [1970] 3 All ER 508

The plaintiffs, husband and wife, suffered personal injuries as a result of the defendant's negligence. The husband's head injuries caused a personality change and intellectual deterioration. The wife, who already suffered from 'nervous disturbance', was so affected by her husband's condition that she was forced to abandon her full-time employment for six months. She also lost income as her husband's part-time secretary, because his illness prevented him from continuing as a self-employed man.

Held, the wife was entitled to loss of earnings from her full-time job: the defendant must take his victim as he finds her, ie with an 'eggshell personality'. But the loss of her part-time job was too remote. (See also *Meah v McCreamer (No 2)*.)

Malz v Rosen [1966] 2 All ER 10

The defendant preferred a charge of using behaviour likely to cause a breach of the peace against the plaintiff. The prosecution failed. The plaintiff sued for malicious prosecution.

Held, his action would fail. The fact that at the police station before the original charge was preferred a police sergeant had told the defendant that the plaintiff had committed an offence, constituted reasonable and probable cause for the prosecution. (See also *Glinski v McIver*.)

Manders v Williams (1849) 4 Exch 339

A firm of porter merchants in Dublin, the plaintiffs, supplied a customer in Wales, one David, with porter in casks on the terms that the empty casks were to be returned to Dublin, at David's expense and risk, or paid for by him at a certain price, at the option of the plaintiffs. The sheriff, the defendant, wrongfully seized 300 casks which were lying empty in David's cellar and the plaintiffs brought an action for trover.

Held, they would succeed, for as soon as the casks were empty, the right of property and the right of immediate possession in them reverted to the plaintiffs.

Marc Rich & Co AG v Bishop Rock Marine Co Ltd, The Nicholas H [1995] 3 All ER 307 (House of Lords)

A cargo vessel developed a cracked hull. A surveyor acting for the vessel's classification society (a non-profit-making body promoting safety at sea in the public interest) agreed that the vessel could continue its journey provided certain temporary repairs were carried out. The repairs failed, the ship sank and the cargo owners sued the classification society.

Held, even if carelessness on the surveyor's part had caused the loss, the action could not succeed. 'I am willing to assume (without deciding) that there was a sufficient degree of proximity in this case to fulfil [the] requirement for the existence of a duty of care. The critical question is therefore whether it would be fair, just and reasonable to impose such a duty [see, eg, *Caparo Industries plc v Dickman*]. ... In my judgment the lesser injustice is done by not recognising a duty of care. ... Given that the cargo owners were not even aware of [the surveyor's] examination of the ship, and that the cargo owners simply relied on the undertakings of the shipowners, it is in my view impossible to force the present set of facts into even the most expansive view of the doctrine of voluntary assumption of responsibility' (*per* LORD STEYN). (But see *Henderson v Merrett Syndicates Ltd*.)

Margarine Union GmbH v Cambay Prince Steamship Co Ltd [1967] 3 All ER 775

The plaintiffs were buyers of copra carried in the defendants' ship from Indonesia to

Hamburg. The plaintiffs' claim to the copra rested upon cif contracts in peculiar form under which property in the copra did not pass before delivery at Hamburg. Before leaving Indonesia the defendant carriers failed to fumigate the hold as a careful carrier should. The copra arrived in Hamburg badly damaged by cockroaches.

Held, the plaintiffs' claim in negligence would fail as at the time of the wrong they had no property in the copra. (See also *Simpson v Thomson* and *Electrochrome Ltd v Welsh Plastics Ltd*.)

Mason v Levy Auto Parts of England Ltd [1967] 2 All ER 62

The defendants' yard contained machinery, which was greased and stacked in wooden cases pending sale. There was also other inflammable material there. The defendants had installed fire-fighting equipment on the advice of the local fire brigade because of the considerable fire-risk. After a period of very dry weather, fire broke out in the yard; despite immediate steps taken to put the blaze out, it spread to the plaintiff's adjoining property where it destroyed trees and plants in his garden. The cause of the fire was unknown, but was probably caused by a workman's cigarette. The defendants disclaimed liability, inter alia, on the ground that the fire had 'accidentally begun' within s86 of the Fires Prevention (Metropolis) Act 1774.

Held, the defendants were liable under the principle in *Rylands v Fletcher,* because their use of the yard was non-natural user of the land, having regard to the material they had brought on to it, the manner in which it was stored and the character of the neighbourhood. As far as the statutory protection went, the defendants were not under any burden of disproving negligence when seeking its protection. (See also *Musgrove v Pandelis* and *Rylands v Fletcher.*)

Maynard v West Midlands Regional Health Authority
[1985] 1 All ER 635 (House of Lords)

Uncertain whether the plaintiff was suffering from tuberculosis or Hodgkin's disease, before obtaining test results which would have determined whether it was the former the defendants' consultants operated to see whether it was the latter. The plaintiff (who turned out to have tuberculosis) suffered damage to her vocal cords, an inherent risk of the operation. She maintained that the consultants had been negligent in operating before the test results were available.

Held, the plaintiff's claim would fail. Although there was a body of competent opinion which said that the consultants' decision was wrong there was an equally competent body which supported their approach. 'Differences of opinion and practice exist, and will always exist, in the medical as in other professions. There is seldom any one answer exclusive of all others to problems of professional judgment. A court may prefer one body of opinion to the other, but that is no basis for a conclusion of negligence' (*per* LORD SCARMAN). (Applied: *Luxmore-May v Messenger May Baverstock.*)

Meah v McCreamer See *Clunis v Camden and Islington Health Authority*

Meah v McCreamer (No 2) [1986] 1 All ER 943

The plaintiff having suffered brain damage in a road accident caused by the defendant's negligent driving, the plaintiff had sexually assaulted two women and they had been awarded damages against him. The plaintiff sought to recover the amount of these damages from the defendant.

Held, his action would be dismissed on grounds of remoteness and public policy. (See also *Malcolm v Broadhurst* and *Pritchard v J H Cobden Ltd.*)

Meering v Grahame-White Aviation Co Ltd (1919) 122 LT 44 (Court of Appeal)

In an action for false imprisonment it appeared that an infant, the plaintiff, who was employed in an aviation works, was suspected of stealing a keg of varnish. He complied with a request to go to the offices of his employers, the defendants, and to remain in the waiting room. Two of the company's police, who had accompanied him to the offices, stayed in the neighbourhood, and the plaintiff agreed to wait there on being told that he was wanted to give evidence in connection with certain thefts. The defendants argued that the plaintiff had not been detained in the waiting room as he was free to go when and where he liked.

Held, this plea would fail and the plaintiff was entitled to judgment as from the moment that he came under the influence of the police he was no longer a free man. A person can be imprisoned in law without actually knowing that he is being imprisoned. (See also *Murray v Ministry of Defence*; but see *Hague v Deputy Governor of Parkhurst Prison.*)

Merricks v Nott-Bower [1964] 1 All ER 717 (Court of Appeal)

The plaintiffs were two serving police officers and an investigation was carried out regarding the activities of street bookmakers within their area. As a result of this, the Assistant Commissioner of Police was said to have submitted a written report to the Commissioner of Police which was said to have stated that one of the plaintiffs 'had neither the determination nor the experience to deal with this type of problem' and that the other 'has not shown much drive in dealing with the same problem'. The plaintiffs claimed, inter alia, damages for libel.

Held, their statement of claim should not be struck out as the Assistant Commissioner's report was not clearly the subject of absolute privilege. (But see *Trapp v Mackie.*)

Mersey Docks and Harbour Board v Coggins & Griffith (Liverpool) Ltd [1946] 2 All ER 345 (House of Lords)

The question arose as to who was liable for the negligent act of a crane driver. The harbour authority, who let the crane to a firm of stevedores, employed, paid and had the power to dismiss him, but the conditions of hire stated that the crane driver should be regarded as a servant of the hirers (the stevedores). The stevedores were entitled to control the moving of the cargo but had no power to tell the driver how to work his crane.

Held, the harbour authority were liable for the crane driver's negligence as they were entitled to give the orders as to how the work should be done.

Metal Box Ltd v Currys Ltd [1988] 1 All ER 341

Goods stored in the plaintiffs' warehouse were lost in a fire resulting from the defendants' negligence. Judgment was entered for the value of the goods: were the plaintiffs entitled to interest on the judgment sum, from the date of the fire to the date of judgment, pursuant to s35A of the Supreme Court Act 1981?

Held, they were, even though the goods were not income-producing or any interest awarded might go to the plaintiffs' insurers. (See also *I M Properties plc v Cape & Dalgleish*.)

Metall und Rohstoff AG v Donaldson Lufkin Jenrette Inc [1989] 3 All ER 14 (Court of Appeal)

It was alleged, inter alia, that the defendants had adduced false evidence and submitted a false case for the primary purpose of defeating the plaintiffs' claims for the return of their metal.

Held, this would not give rise to the tort of abuse of the process of the court. 'If the use of court process is to expose a party to liability under this principle, the process must ... have been used for a predominant purpose "outside the ambit of the legal claim upon which the court is asked to adjudicate" ' (*per* SLADE LJ).

Midland Bank Trust Co Ltd v Green (No 3) [1981] 3 All ER 744 (Court of Appeal)

It was alleged, inter alia, that a farm was conveyed by a father to his wife pursuant to an agreement or arrangement between them whereby they conspired together by means of the conveyance to defraud and injure their son by depriving him of the benefit of an option to buy it.

Held, a husband and wife could be liable in damages for the tort of conspiracy even though they were the only parties to the conspiracy.

Midland Bank Trust Co Ltd v Hett, Stubbs & Kemp [1978] 3 All ER 571

By a formal agreement dated 24 March 1961 a father gave his son a 10 year option to purchase the freehold reversion of his farm. The solicitors who acted for both parties failed to register the option as an estate contract. In August 1967 the father conveyed the farm to his wife and in October 1967 the son attempted to exercise the option. As this was no longer possible, in July 1972 the son issued a writ against the solicitors claiming damages for breach of professional duty.

Held, the solicitors were liable in tort as they had been in breach of their duty to exercise reasonable care and skill. The cause of action arose when the damage occurred and as this was in August 1967 – when the farm was conveyed to the wife – the action was not statute barred. 'The instant case is one in which there was clearly between the defendants and [the son] a relationship of the sort which gave rise to a duty of care under the *Hedley Byrne* principle ... the interpretation of that principle ... in the *Esso* case leads to the conclusion that there was here a liability in tort when the damage occurred [in] August 1967' (*per* OLIVER J). Even if the solicitors' duty was only in contract, they had been under a continuing duty to register the option before a third party acquired an interest in the land and the contract was broken by the sale in August 1967. On this ground too the claim was not statute barred. (Approved in *Henderson* v *Merrett Syndicates Ltd*; see also *Junior Books Ltd* v *Veitchi Co Ltd* and *Ross* v *Caunters*; but see *Forster* v *Outred & Co*.)

Miller v Jackson [1977] 3 All ER 338 (Court of Appeal)

Cricket was played on a village ground since 1905. In 1970 houses were built in such a place that cricket balls would inevitably be hit into their gardens. The plaintiff, who bought one of the houses in 1972, sued the members of the cricket club for damages for negligence and nuisance, on the basis of incidents causing physical damage to the house and apprehension of personal injury.

Held, (1) The defendants were guilty of negligence, since the risk of injury was both foreseeable and foreseen. (2) The playing of cricket in the circumstances constituted an unreasonable interference with the plaintiff's enjoyment of land, and therefore a nuisance, since there was a real risk of serious injury. It is no defence that the plaintiff brought trouble on his own head by coming to live in the house; *Sturges* v *Bridgman* (qv) applied. (3) By reason of special circumstances, namely the plaintiff's knowledge when he bought his house that cricket was played nearby, and the interest of the village as a whole in the existence of a cricket ground, no injunction should be granted to restrain the playing of cricket, and the plaintiff's only remedy was in damages. (But see *Bolton* v *Stone* and *Kennaway* v *Thompson*.)

Mills v Brooker [1919] 1 KB 555

Some branches of the plaintiff's Bramley seedling apple trees overhung the defendant's land. The defendant picked the apples and sold them.

Held, the plaintiff was entitled to damages in conversion as the defendant's right to lop branches for the purpose of abating the nuisance did not carry with it a right to appropriate the severed branches or the fruit growing on them.

Ministry of Housing and Local Government v Sharp
[1970] 1 All ER 1009 (Court of Appeal)

The plaintiff ministry registered against land owned by N a land charge in the register maintained by the local authority. N sold the land. The purchaser requisitioned a local land charges search. The search was negligently made, and the certificate signed by the Registrar omitted the plaintiffs' charge. Since a certificate is conclusive in favour of a purchaser, the plaintiffs sued the Registrar for breach of an absolute duty to make a proper search under s17(2) of the Land Charges Act 1925, and the local authority as being vicariously liable for the negligent search made by the clerk.

Held, (1) the Registrar was not liable, since his statutory duty is not absolute. *Quaere*: whether he owes a duty of care under the statute. (2) The clerk (and, it was conceded, the local authority) was liable for the negligent search and misstatements. Although the search was requisitioned by the purchaser, the searcher should have foreseen that loss might be suffered by an incumbrancer. 'Voluntary assumption of liability' is not a necessary element in every case of the principle in *Hedley Byrne & Co Ltd* v *Heller & Partners Ltd*. (See also *Midland Bank Trust Co Ltd* v *Hett, Stubbs & Kemp*.)

Mint v *Good* [1950] 2 All ER 1159 (Court of Appeal)

A wall in front of two houses which were let to weekly tenants collapsed on the public footpath and injured the plaintiff. The danger could have been ascertained by inspection. No express agreement existed between the landlord and his tenants as to liability to repair and no right of entry to carry out repairs had been reserved to him.

Held, the landlord was liable for the plaintiff's injuries as there was an implied term that he would keep the premises in a reasonable and habitable condition. (See also *McAuley* v *Bristol City Council*.)

Minter v *Priest* [1930] AC 558 (House of Lords)

A solicitor, the defendant, was consulted by a person who wished to raise the necessary money to buy a house from the plaintiff. During their discussion the defendant advanced a scheme whereby he might share in the profits of the transaction, and took the opportunity of slandering the plaintiff. In an action for damages, the defendant relied upon the defence of privilege. The jury found that at the time when the slander was uttered the relationship of solicitor and client did not exist between the defendant and the person to whom he was speaking. They also found that the defendant was actuated by malice.

Held, the plaintiff was entitled to damages as the defendant's words were not protected by privilege. (But see *More* v *Weaver*.)

Moffatt v *Kazana* [1968] 3 All ER 271

The plaintiff's husband hid some bank-notes in a tin box, which he kept hidden in the roof of his house. The house was later sold to the defendant, one of whose employees found the money. Meanwhile, the husband had died; his wife, the plaintiff, brought an action to recover the money.

Held, the sale of the house to the defendant did not include the sale of the tin box with the money. The husband had never surrendered the ownership of the notes, by sale, abandonment or otherwise, and the plaintiff's claim succeeded. (But see *Armory* v *Delamirie*.)

Mogul Steamship Co Ltd v McGregor, Gow & Co [1892] AC 25 (House of Lords)

An associated body of traders, the defendants, tried to get the whole of the limited China tea-carrying trade into their own hands by offering exceptional and very favourable terms to customers who agreed to deal with them exclusively. The plaintiffs, whose own trade had been ruined by this arrangement, argued that the defendants were liable to them in damages as they had conspired to injure them.

Held, the action would fail as the defendants had sought merely to fulfil the lawful object of protecting and extending their trade with a view to increasing their profits, and the means employed with a view to achieving that end had not been unlawful. (See also *Hill (Edwin) & Partners v First National Finance Corp plc*; but see *Lonrho plc v Fayed.*)

Monk v Warbey [1935] 1 KB 75 (Court of Appeal)

In breach of a statutory duty the defendant allowed his car to be driven by a person who was not insured against third-party risks. That person, who was without means, drove negligently and injured the plaintiff.

Held, the plaintiff could maintain an action against the defendant for breach of statutory duty and need not first sue the actual driver of the car. (But see *Wentworth v Wiltshire County Council.*)

Monson v Tussauds Ltd [1894] 1 QB 671 (Court of Appeal)

At a trial of the plaintiff in Scotland upon a charge of murder, the jury returned a verdict of 'Not proven'. The prosecution had alleged that he had used a gun to commit the crime, but his successful defence was that the gun had been discharged accidentally. The defendants placed a model of the plaintiff and his gun in their exhibition of wax figures, and in the 'Chamber of Horrors', which contained models of many murderers and malefactors and was down a few steps from the model of the plaintiff, there was a representation of the place where the killing, in respect of which the plaintiff was tried and acquitted, took place. The plaintiff sued for libel and an interlocutory injunction to restrain the exhibition of the model of himself.

Held, he was not entitled to an interlocutory injunction but the court did not deny that the matter might be defamatory. (See also *Cassidy v Daily Mirror Newspapers Ltd.*)

Montreal Tramways v Leveille [1933] 4 DLR 337 (Supreme Court of Canada)

The appellants negligently caused injury to the respondent's wife who, at that time, was seven months pregnant. Two months later her daughter was born with club feet.

Held, the child was entitled to damages in tort. (Followed in *Burton v Islington Health Authority*; see also the Congenital Disabilities (Civil Liability) Act 1976.)

Moore (D W) & Co Ltd v Ferrier [1988] 1 All ER 400 (Court of Appeal)

In 1971 and 1975 the defendant solicitors prepared employment contracts containing restrictive covenants, but in 1980 it was found that these covenants did not serve the purpose intended by the plaintiff employers. In 1985 the plaintiffs brought an action for negligence and the defendants pleaded that the claim was barred by s2 of the Limitation Act 1980.

Held, this plea would be upheld as the plaintiffs would have suffered damage (because the contracts were of less commercial value than if properly drafted) when the agreements were executed, not when the alleged defects were discovered. (Applied *Forster* v *Outred & Co.*)

More v Weaver [1928] 2 KB 520 (Court of Appeal)

In writing to her solicitors, the defendant made certain uncomplimentary statements about the business capacity, character and financial position of the plaintiff, from whom the defendant had borrowed a large sum of money. The plaintiff claimed damages for libel.

Held, her action must fail as the communication was absolutely privileged. (But see *Minter* v *Priest.*)

Morgan Crucible Co plc v Hill Samuel Bank Ltd [1991] 1 All ER 148 (Court of Appeal)

After the plaintiffs had announced a take-over bid for First Castle Electronics plc and the formal offer document had been sent, the target company issued various defence documents which included a forecast of a 38% increase in profits, a forecast supported by the defendant bank and accountants. The plaintiffs increased their bid and the take-over was successful but it subsequently appeared, the plaintiffs maintained, that the forecast had been misleading and that, at the time of the bid, the target company had been worthless. In an action for negligence the plaintiffs contended that there was the necessary relationship of proximity giving rise to a duty of care.

Held, this was the case as, on the assumed facts, the defendants had intended the plaintiffs to rely on the profits forecast and related financial information and they had done so. (Distinguished: *Caparo Industries plc* v *Dickman*; see also *Galoo Ltd* v *Bright Grahame Murray.*)

Morgan v Odhams Press Ltd [1971] 2 All ER 1156 (House of Lords)

An article appeared on 8 November in a newspaper published by the defendants. It said that a named woman who was a key witness in the prosecution of a dog doping gang 'was kidnapped last week by members of the gang' and 'kept in a house in Finchley'. The plaintiff sued for libel alleging special facts by reason of which the words referred to him: the woman had stayed at his flat in Willesden from 26 October to 1 November and had been seen with him in public by several persons during that period. These persons gave evidence to the effect that they thought the words referred to the plaintiff. The jury awarded £4,750 damages.

Held, the matter was properly left to the jury since a reader with knowledge of the special facts could reasonably understand the words as referring to the plaintiff. It was not necessary for the words to contain 'a pointer or peg' for the identification of the plaintiff. Nor were the discrepancies as to time and place between the article and the special facts relevant, because 'the average reader does not read a sensational article with cautious and critical analytical care'. But a new trial was ordered since the judge had failed to direct the jury that damages would be affected by the small number of persons who could have understood any reference to the plaintiff.

Morris v C W Martin & Sons Ltd [1965] 2 All ER 725 (Court of Appeal)

The plaintiff sent her long white mink stole to a Mr Beder, a furrier, to be cleaned. Mr Beder did not do cleaning himself and the plaintiff agreed to his suggestion that the work be entrusted to the defendants who only worked for the trade and not for private individuals, although they knew that the fur belonged to one of Mr Beder's customers. The fur was stolen from the defendants' premises by one Morrissey whose duty it was to clean it, who had been employed by the defendants for about two months and whose honesty they had no reason to suspect. It was found that the defendants took all proper steps to safeguard goods in their possession and that they had not been negligent in employing Morrissey. Were the defendants liable for the loss of the fur?

Held, they were vicariously liable in conversion or negligence because the fur was stolen by Morrissey, the servant through whom the defendants, as bailees for reward towards the plaintiff, had chosen to discharge their duty to take reasonable care of the plaintiff's fur. It should be noted that the fact that the relationship between the parties was created by a sub-bailment might have been relevant to a claim in detinue and that 'a theft by any servant who is not employed to do anything in relation to the goods bailed is entirely outside the scope of his employment and cannot make the master liable' (*per* SALMON LJ). (See also *Bayley* v *Manchester, Sheffield and Lincolnshire Railway Co.*)

Morris v Murray [1990] 3 All ER 801 (Court of Appeal)

After drinking with the deceased for some hours, the plaintiff accepted the deceased's invitation to a joy ride in his light aircraft. They took off in adverse weather conditions, at a time when other flying had been suspended, and crashed shortly after take-off. The plaintiff survived and it was found that the deceased's blood-alcohol level had been more than three times the legal limit for motoring purposes. The plaintiff claimed damages from the deceased's estate.

Held, his claim was barred by the defence of volenti non fit injuria. Although the plaintiff too had been drunk, he had been aware of the risk he was taking in flying with the deceased on that occasion. (But see *Dann* v *Hamilton*.)

Morriss v Marsden [1952] 1 All ER 925

The plaintiff, a hotel manager, was violently attacked by one of his guests, the defendant. When later approached by the police the defendant gave a false name, address and reference.

On a charge of criminal assault, the defendant was found unfit to plead, but the plaintiff claimed damages for personal injuries.

Held, he would succeed as the defendant knew the nature and quality of his act. The fact that he did not know that it was wrong was immaterial.

Mouse's Case (1609) 12 Co Rep 63

The plaintiff and the defendant were sailing in a barge from Gravesend to London. A 'great tempest happened' and, in order to save the lives of those on board, the defendant threw overboard some of the plaintiff's goods.

Held, in these circumstances, he was entitled to do so.

Mulcahy v Ministry of Defence [1996] 2 All ER 758 (Court of Appeal)

While sharing in the firing of a howitzer during the Gulf War, the plaintiff suffered injury as a result, allegedly, of the gun commander's negligence.

Held, his action against the defendants, the gun commander's employers, would be struck out as disclosing no cause of action. 'If during the course of hostilities no duty of care is owed by a member of the armed forces to civilians or their property, it must be even more apparent that no such duty is owed to another member of the armed forces. This conclusion is wholly consistent with, and supported by, the decision of the House of Lords in *Burmah Oil Co (Burmah Trading) v Lord Advocate* and depends upon similar reasoning to that adopted by May J in relation to police officers in *Hughes v National Union of Mineworkers*. In my judgment, therefore, at common law, one soldier does not owe to another a duty of care when engaging the enemy in the course of hostilities' (*per* SIR IAIN GLIDEWELL).

Mullin v Richards [1998] 1 All ER 920 (Court of Appeal)

Two 15-year-old schoolgirls, Teresa and Heidi, while sitting at their desk had a 'sword fight' with their plastic rulers. One of the rulers snapped and a fragment of plastic entered Teresa's right eye, causing loss of its useful sight. Teresa sued Heidi and the local education authority. The claim against the latter was dismissed (on the facts, the class teacher had not been guilty of negligence) but the judge concluded that both girls had been negligent, that Teresa's injury was the foreseeable result and that her claim against Heidi would succeed subject to a 50 per cent reduction for contributory negligence. Heidi appealed, contending, inter alia, that the judge had erred when considering foreseeability by failing to take account of the fact that she was not an adult.

Held, the appeal would be allowed. There was insufficient evidence that the accident had been foreseeable: what had taken place was simply a schoolgirl's game. (See also *Jolley v Sutton London Borough Council*.)

Munro v Willmott [1948] 2 All ER 983

The defendant, the licensee of the Bell Inn, agreed to allow the plaintiff's car to remain in his yard without charge. After three years, because the vehicle was in the way, the defendant desired to have it removed, but the plaintiff could not be traced. The defendant spent some £85 on having the car repaired, put it up for auction and received £100 from the auctioneer as a result of the sale. Five months later the plaintiff re-appeared and, when she discovered that her car had been sold, brought a successful action in detinue and conversion. At the date of the judgment the car was worth £120 and the court had to decide the measure of damages to which she was entitled.

Held, the plaintiff would be awarded £35, ie the value of the car at the date of judgment less the increase in value attributable to the expenditure of money on it by the defendant. (See also the Torts (Interference with Goods) Act 1977, s6(1), and *IBL Ltd v Cousson*.)

Munroe (John) (Acrylics) Ltd v London Fire and Civil Defence Authority See Capital and Counties plc v Hampshire County Council

Munster v Lamb (1883) 11 QBD 588 (Court of Appeal)

On a charge relating to the burglary of the Brighton home of a barrister-at-law, the plaintiff, it was suggested by the defending solicitor, the defendant, that the plaintiff kept drugs in the house for a criminal and immoral purpose.

Held, the plaintiff was not entitled to damages for defamation as the defendant's statement was within the bounds of the privilege extended to advocates. (But see *Royal Aquarium etc Society Ltd v Parkinson*.)

Murphy v Brentwood District Council [1990] 2 All ER 908 (House of Lords)

In 1970 the plaintiff purchased from a construction company a house built on an in-filled site on a concrete raft foundation. Before giving building regulation approval, the defendant council had sought the advice of independent consulting engineers and they had recommended approval. In 1981 the plaintiff noticed serious cracks in the house and it was discovered that the raft foundation was defective. He sold the house for £35,000 less than its value in sound condition and sued the defendants for breach of statutory duty and/or negligence.

Held, his action could not succeed. He had suffered purely economic loss and the defendants had not owed him a duty of care when approving the plans. 'I have reached the clear conclusion that the proper exercise of the judicial function requires this House now to depart from *Anns v Merton London Borough Council* in so far as it affirmed a private law duty of care to avoid damage to property which causes present or imminent danger to the health and safety of owners, or occupiers, resting on local authorities in relation to their function of supervising compliance with building byelaws or regulations, that *Dutton v Bognor Regis United Building Co Ltd* should be overruled and that all decisions subsequent to *Anns* which purported to follow it should be overruled ... I should make it clear that I express no opinion on the question whether, if personal injury were suffered by an occupier of defective premises as a result of a latent defect in those premises, liability in respect of that personal injury would attach to a local authority which had been charged with the public law duty of supervising compliance with the relevant building byelaws or regulations in respect of a failure properly to carry out such duty' (*per* LORD MACKAY OF CLASHFERN LC). (Followed: *Sutherland Shire Council v Heyman*; applied: *Department of the Environment v Thomas Bates & Son*.)

Murray v Harringay Arena Ltd [1951] 2 All ER 320 (Court of Appeal)

A six-year-old boy was a spectator at an ice-hockey match. He was occupying a seat in the front row and during the match was hit in the eye by the puck. There was no evidence of a previous serious accident of this kind.

Held, the owners of the rink were not liable for the boy's injuries as it had not been shown that they had been negligent or in breach of their duty of care. This was a danger which was incidental to the game, could have been reasonably foreseen by any spectator and of which he would have been held to have taken the risk. The infancy of the spectator was immaterial. (See also *Wooldridge v Sumner.*)

Murray v Ministry of Defence [1988] 2 All ER 521 (House of Lords)

Suspecting the plaintiff of having committed the statutory offence of collecting funds for the IRA, Cpl Davies and five armed soldiers entered her Andersonstown house at 7am. Cpl Davies remained with the plaintiff while the other soldiers searched the house and at 7.30 am Cpl Davies formally arrested the plaintiff. The plaintiff claimed damages for false imprisonment in respect of the period 7-7.30 am.

Held, her claim would fail as she must have realised that she was under restraint amounting to an arrest throughout that period, even though no formal words of arrest had been spoken. 'Although on the facts of this case I am sure that the plaintiff was aware of the restraint on her liberty from 7 am, I cannot agree with the Court of Appeal that it is an essential element of the tort of false imprisonment that the victim should be aware of the fact of denial of liberty' (*per* LORD GRIFFITHS). (See also *Meering v Grahame-White Aviation Co Ltd* and *Roberts v Chief Constable of the Cheshire Constabulary*; doubted: *Herring v Boyle*.)

Musgrove v Pandelis [1919] 2 KB 43 (Court of Appeal)

The defendant's servant started the engine of the defendant's car while it was in a garage, but the petrol in the carburettor caught fire. The servant was negligent in not promptly turning off the petrol tap and in consequence the fire spread and burnt the car, the garage and the rooms over the garage which were occupied by the plaintiff.

Held, applying the principle of *Rylands v Fletcher,* the defendant was liable to make good the plaintiff's loss; s86 of the Fires Prevention (Metropolis) Act 1774 afforded him no protection as the fire which caused the damage was the fire which resulted from the negligent omission to turn off the petrol tap and therefore it did not begin 'accidentally'. (See also *Hoare & Co* v *McAlpine* and *Goldman* v *Hargrave*; but see *Collingwood* v *Home and Colonial Stores Ltd.*)

Nash v Eli Lilly & Co [1993] 4 All ER 383 (Court of Appeal)

The plaintiff group of patients alleged that they had suffered serious side effects as a result of using the defendants' arthritis drug. The question was, inter alia, when, in the light of ss11(4)(b) and 14 of the Limitation Act 1980, an action was time-barred and, if it was, when the court should exercise its discretion under s33 of that Act to disapply the limitation period.

Held, 'if the plaintiff held a firm belief [that his injury was attributable to the act or omission of the defendant] which was of sufficient certainty to justify the taking of the preliminary steps for proceedings by obtaining advice about making a claim for compensation, then such belief is knowledge and the limitation period would begin to run.' (*per* PURCHAS LJ). In deciding whether to exercise its discretion under s33, the court should consider all the circumstances of the case and the balance of prejudice to the respective parties. (See also *Broadley* v *Guy Clapham & Co* and *Henderson* v *Temple Pier Co Ltd.*)

National Coal Board v England [1954] 1 All ER 546 (House of Lords)

A shot-firer negligently acted in breach of the Explosives in Coal Mines Order 1934, and in so doing caused injury to a fellow miner.

Held, the injured miner was entitled to recover damages against their mutual employer. (See also *Ilkiw* v *Samuels*; but see *Lister* v *Romford Ice & Cold Storage Co Ltd.*)

National Coal Board v J E Evans & Co (Cardiff) Ltd [1951] 2 All ER 310 (Court of Appeal)

While digging a trench on land owned by a county council, the defendants damaged an underground electric cable belonging to the plaintiffs. Neither the county council nor the defendants knew of the existence of the cable.

Held, the defendants were not liable in trespass as the main cause of the accident was the placing of the cable by the plaintiffs' predecessors in title in the land of the county council without their knowledge or consent. (See also *Fowler* v *Lanning.*)

Navarro v Moregrand Ltd [1951] 2 TLR 674 (Court of Appeal)

The defendants' agent let a flat to the plaintiff but in the course of negotiations the agent asked for and was paid £225. It was illegal to make such a payment and the plaintiff sought to recover this sum from the defendants.

Held, he should succeed as when asking for the premium the agent had been acting in the course of his employment although in excess of his actual or ostensible authority. (See also *United Africa Co Ltd* v *Saka Owoade.*)

Newstead v *London Express Newspaper Ltd* [1939] 4 All ER 319 (Court of Appeal)

A 30-year-old unmarried hairdresser living in Camberwell, one Harold Newstead, brought an action for libel in respect of a statement published by the defendants in their newspaper to the effect that Harold Newstead, a 30-year-old Camberwell man, had been convicted of bigamy. The plaintiff contended that this statement was understood to refer to him although it actually referred to another man, a barman, of the same name who also lived in Camberwell.

Held, the plaintiff would succeed as the fact that the words were true of the barman did not in law make it impossible for them to be defamatory of the plaintiff. (See also *Hayward* v *Thompson* and the Defamation Act 1952, s4.)

Newton v *Edgerley* [1959] 3 All ER 337

The defendant allowed his 12-year-old son to buy a .410 gun and showed him how to use it. The boy's father told him that he was not to take the gun off the farm or use it when other children were present, and for this reason he did not instruct him how to handle the gun when in the presence of others. The boy disobeyed his father's instructions and when another boy made as if to take the gun that boy got his hand on the trigger and shot and injured the infant plaintiff who was about two yards away.

Held, the defendant was liable in negligence as he ought to have prevented his son from having the gun at all or, if he had the gun, he should have realised that his son would sooner or later go out with others and, accordingly, he should have given him very careful instructions as to the use of the weapon if others were present.

Nichols v *Marsland* (1876) 2 ExD 1 (Court of Appeal)

On land owned by the defendant there were three artificial lakes which had been formed by damming up a natural stream. A thunderstorm accompanied by heavy rain which continued for 10 hours, the like of which could not be remembered, caused the artificial banks to be carried away and the water rushed down the course of the stream and destroyed four bridges on land owned by the plaintiff. The jury found that the defendant had not been guilty of negligence.

Held, the flooding was caused by an Act of God and the defendant was not liable for the damage which resulted. (But see *Greenock Corporation* v *Caledonian Railway Co* and *Rylands* v *Fletcher*.)

Nitrigin Eireann Teoranta v *Inco Alloys Ltd* [1992] 1 All ER 854

In June 1981 the defendant manufacturers supplied alloy tubing for the plaintiffs' chemical production plant. In July 1983 the plaintiffs discovered cracks in the tube: despite reasonable investigation they failed to establish the cause of the trouble but they tried to repair it. On 27 June 1984 the tube ruptured and caused an explosion which caused the plant to shut down. On 21 June 1990 the plaintiffs sued for negligence, alleging that the tube was defective in both 1983 and 1984. The defendants maintained that their action was statute barred as any negligence had occurred in July 1983.

Held, this was not the case as the cracking then of the tube was simply damage to the tube itself, a defect in quality resulting in economic loss which was irrecoverable in negligence. However, the physical damage in 1984 gave rise to a cause of action in negligence and this was not statute barred. (Distinguished: *Pirelli General Cable Works Ltd* v *Oscar Faber & Partners*; not followed: *Junior Books Ltd* v *Veitchi Co Ltd*.)

Noble v Harrison [1926] 2 KB 332

A beech tree, which was at least 80 years old, was growing on the defendant's estate. One of its branches overhung the highway and suddenly, in fine weather, it broke off and fell on and damaged the plaintiff's motor coach which was passing underneath. The fracture was due to a latent defect not discoverable by any reasonably careful inspection and neither the defendant nor his servants knew that the branch was dangerous.

Held, the plaintiff could not recover damages in respect of his loss. The rule in *Rylands* v *Fletcher* did not apply as the tree was not in itself a dangerous thing and the growing of trees was a natural user of the soil and the plaintiff could not succeed in nuisance as the defendant had no knowledge, actual or imputed, of the danger. (See also *St Anne's Well Brewery Co* v *Roberts*.)

Nottingham v Aldridge [1971] 2 All ER 751

The second defendants (PO) employed the plaintiff (N) and the first defendant (A) as apprentices, both of whom were required by contract to attend at a residential training centre for a week beginning on a Monday. A borrowed a van and agreed to drive N to the centre. A could claim under his contract an allowance for his and N's travelling expenses. As a result of A's negligent driving to the centre on the Sunday night, N was injured.

Held, PO were not vicariously liable for A's negligence. A was not acting in the course of his employment since he was under no contractual duty to PO to drive or carry passengers to the centre. Although he was bound to attend at the centre, the mode of travel was at his discretion. Furthermore A was not acting as PO's agent because PO did not own the van and had never delegated to A the task or duty of driving himself or others to the centre. (See also *Ormrod* v *Crosville Motor Services Ltd*.)

Nykredit Mortgage Bank plc v Edward Erdman Group Ltd See South Australia Asset Management Corp v York Montague Ltd

Nykredit Mortgage Bank plc v Edward Erdman Group Ltd (No 2) [1998] 1 All ER 305 (House of Lords)

On 2 March 1990, in response to instructions from the plaintiff bank, the defendants negligently valued certain property at £3.5 million. Ten days later the plaintiffs advanced £2.45 million on the security of the property: the borrower defaulted immediately. Had the plaintiffs known the property's true value, they would not have lent the money: a fall in the property market after the valuation date greatly increased their loss. The property was sold in February 1993 for £345,000. The House of Lords decided (see *South Australia Asset Management Corp v York Montague Ltd*) that damages were limited to the amount of the overvaluation at the valuation date (agreed by the parties to be £1.4 million) and that no account should be taken of the property market's fall. The question now arose as to what interest should be awarded upon the damages in the light of s35A(1) of the Supreme Court Act 1981.

Held, interest was payable from the date on which the cause of action arose, ie the date on which the plaintiffs actually suffered the loss attributable to the defendants' breach of duty.

Ogwo v Taylor [1987] 3 All ER 961 (House of Lords)

Using a blowlamp to burn off paint from the facia boards of his house, the defendant negligently set fire to the premises. Although he was wearing standard protective clothing, the plaintiff fireman was injured while tackling the blaze in the roof space and he claimed damages for negligence.

Held, his action would succeed as the defendant had owed the plaintiff a duty of care and the plaintiff's injuries were a reasonably foreseeable consequence of the defendant's breach of that duty. It was immaterial whether the fire was 'ordinary' or 'exceptional'. (See also *Salmon v Seafarer Restaurants Ltd*.)

Olotu v Home Office [1997] 1 All ER 385 (Court of Appeal)

After being committed in custody for trial in the Crown Court, the plaintiff, inter alia, sued the Crown Prosecution Service (CPS) claiming damages for breach of its statutory duty (under reg 6(1) of the Prosecution of Offences Act (Custody Time Limits) Regulations 1987) to bring her before the court before the expiry of the custody time limit so that she might be granted bail.

Held, the claim would be struck out. 'It is a question of available remedies. The plaintiff was undoubtedly entitled to remedies in the criminal proceedings (bail) and in judicial review proceedings. The issue is whether she is entitled to an additional remedy against the CPS by way of a civil law claim for damages. It is common ground that it is not enough for the plaintiff simply to show that she has suffered damage in consequence of a breach of duty imposed by statute. The court must be satisfied that, on the true construction of the relevant statutory provisions, a right of action for damages has been created by Parliament. … I am … unable to accept [counsel for the plaintiff's] submission that a claim for damages lies against the CPS for breach of statutory duty. The statute and the regulations are silent on damages. There are strong indicators against the implied creation of a statutory tort of strict liability in a case such as this …' (*per* MUMMERY LJ). (Applied: *Elguzouli-Daf v Commissioner of Police of the Metropolis* [1995] 1 All ER 833.)

Ormrod v *Crosville Motor Services Ltd* [1953] 2 All ER 753

The owner of a car asked a friend to drive the vehicle from Birkenhead to Monte Carlo. During the journey, due to the friend's negligent driving, the car was involved in an accident.

Held, as the trip was being undertaken for the owner's purposes and with his consent, the friend was his agent and the owner was vicariously liable for his negligence. (See also *Scarsbrook* v *Mason* and *Carberry* v *Davies*.)

Oropesa, The See *Lord* v *Pacific Steam Navigation Co Ltd*

Osborn v *Boulter (Thomas) and Son* [1930] 2 KB 226 (Court of Appeal)

A firm of brewers, the defendants, wrote to one of their tenants, the plaintiff, who had complained to them about the poor quality of their beer, and falsely suggested that it was inferior because he had added water to it. The letter was dictated to a typist and the plaintiff maintained that this constituted publication of a libel.

Held, his action would fail. The communication and the occasion of its publication, the reasonable and ordinary course of business, were privileged. (See *Bryanston Finance Ltd* v *de Vries*.)

O'Sullivan v *Williams* [1992] 3 All ER 385 (Court of Appeal)

John allowed his girlfriend Linda the use of his car while he was away on holiday. During this time the car was severely damaged as a result of the defendant's negligence. John's claim was settled without prejudice to Linda's: was Linda now entitled to damages for loss of use of the car?

Held, she was not. 'There cannot be separate claims by the bailor and the bailee arising from loss or damage to the chattel. If the bailor recovers damages and the bailee has some interest in the property enforceable against the bailor, then the bailor must account appropriately to the bailee' (*per* FOX LJ). (Applied: *The Winkfield*; but see *Brunsden* v *Humphrey*)

Osman v *Ferguson* [1993] 4 All ER 344 (Court of Appeal)

P, a schoolteacher, formed an unhealthy attachment to a 15-year-old male pupil and harasssed him. In May 1987 he damaged property belonging to the boy's father. In mid-1987 P was dismissed from the school but continued the harassment. The police were aware of these facts and in late 1987 P told a police officer that the loss of his job was distressing and he feared he would do something criminally insane. In December 1987 P deliberately rammed a vehicle in which the boy was a passenger. The police laid an information against P in January 1988 alleging driving without due care and attention but it was not served. In March 1988 P shot and severely injured the boy and killed his father. The mother, as administratrix of the father's estate, and the boy sued the police alleging negligence in that, although the police had been aware of P's activities since May 1987, they had failed to apprehend or interview him, search his home or charge him with a more serious offence before March 1988. The police's application to strike out the statement of claim was dismissed.

Held, the police's appeal against this decision would be allowed. The general duty of the police to suppress crime does not carry with it liability to individuals for damage caused to them by criminals the police have failed to apprehend when it was possible to do so. Applying *Hill* v *Chief Constable of West Yorkshire* and *Alexandrou* v *Oxford*, it would be against public policy to impose such a duty. (See also *Ancell* v *McDermott*.)

Overseas Tankship (UK) Ltd v Miller Steamship Co Pty Ltd, The Wagon Mound (No 2) [1966] 2 All ER 709 (Privy Council)

The engineer of the appellants' ship carelessly allowed bunkering oil to overflow from their vessel *Wagon Mound* while she was in Sydney Harbour. This oil drifted to a wharf where two of the respondents' ships were undergoing repairs and welding was being done. The oil caught fire and the fire damaged the respondents' ships. They claimed in negligence. The evidence was that the risk of bunkering oil igniting on water was a possibility 'which could become an actuality only in very exceptional circumstances'.

Held, a reasonable man in the position of the engineer ought to have been aware of the nature of the risk and he was not justified in disregarding it, for it was a real risk which could not be brushed aside as far fetched; negligence had been established and the damages were not too remote. Semble, when the word 'direct' is used in determining whether damage caused to a member of the public was different from that caused to the rest of the public, so as to constitute special damage entitling the particular member of the public to sue in tort for public nuisance, the meaning of the word is narrower than when it is used in determining whether damage is too remote. (But see *The Wagon Mound (No 1)*, below.)

Overseas Tankship (UK) Ltd v Morts Dock & Engineering Co Ltd, The Wagon Mound (No 1) [1961] 1 All ER 404 (Privy Council)

Through the carelessness of the appellants' servants, a large quantity of bunkering oil was spilt into a bay while a vessel was discharging gasoline products and taking in oil. It was found as a fact that the appellants did not know, and could not reasonably have been expected to know, that the oil was capable of being set alight when spread on water. Molten metal falling from the respondents' wharf set fire to some cotton waste floating in the oil, which it turn ignited the oil itself and caused a serious fire. Considerable damage was done to the respondents' wharf and equipment.

Held, the appellants were not liable in negligence for the damage because they could not reasonably have foreseen it. 'The authority of *Polemis* has been severely shaken, though lip service has from time to time been paid to it. In their lordships' opinion, it should no longer be regarded as good law … It is a principle of civil liability, subject only to qualifications which have no present relevance, that a man must be considered to be responsible for the probable consequences of his act. To demand more of him is too harsh a rule … Thus foreseeability becomes the effective test. In reasserting this principle, their lordships conceive that they do not depart from, but follow and develop, the law of negligence as laid down by ALDERSON B in *Blyth* v *Birmingham Waterworks Co'* (*per* VISCOUNT SIMONDS). (But see *Smith* v *Leech Brain & Co Ltd* and *The Wagon Mound (No 2)*, above.)

Padbury v *Holliday and Greenwood Ltd* (1912) 28 TLR 494 (Court of Appeal)

Sub-contractors were employed to put metallic casements into the windows of a building being erected by the defendants. While one such casement was being put into position, the wind blew and an iron tool, which had been negligently placed by one of the sub-contractors' workmen on the window-sill, fell and injured the plaintiff.

Held, the plaintiff could not recover damages from the defendants as the injuries were caused by an act of collateral negligence on the part of the sub-contractors' employee. (But see *Honeywill and Stein Ltd* v *Larkin Brothers etc Ltd*.)

Page v *Sheerness Steel Co plc* See *Wells* v *Wells*

Page v *Smith* [1995] 2 All ER 736 (House of Lords)

The plaintiff's car was involved in a collision with the defendant's car in which the plaintiff suffered no physical injury. For 20 years prior to the accident the plaintiff had suffered from ME (myalgic encephalomyelitis) which had manifested itself from time to time with different degrees of severity but was then in remission. The plaintiff claimed damages for his injuries, alleging that as a result of the accident his ME condition had become chronic and permanent. At first instance the High Court found for the plaintiff, and the Court of Appeal allowed the defendant's appeal on the grounds, inter alia, that the plaintiff's injury was not foreseeable. The plaintiff appealed to the House of Lords.

Held, the appeal would be allowed. 'I am ... of opinion that any driver of a car should reasonably foresee that, if he drives carelessly, he will be liable to cause injury, either physical or psychiatric or both, to other users of the highway who become involved in an accident. Therefore he owes to such persons a duty of care to avoid such injury. In the present case the defendant could not foresee the exact type of psychiatric damage in fact suffered by the plaintiff who, due to his ME, was "an eggshell personality". But that is of no significance since the defendant did owe a duty of care to prevent foreseeable damage, including psychiatric damage. Once such duty of care is established, the defendant must take the plaintiff as he finds him' (*per* LORD BROWNE WILKINSON). (But see *White* v *Chief Constable of the South Yorkshire Police*.) NB The Court of Appeal had left open the contention that the trial judge's finding on causation was against the weight of evidence. The matter having returned to the Court of Appeal, the judge's finding was upheld. (See *Page* v *Smith (No 2)* [1996] 3 All ER 272.)

Page v *Smith (No 2)* See *Page* v *Smith*

Pannett v P McGuinness and Co Ltd [1972] 3 All ER 137
(Court of Appeal)

The defendant contractors had almost finished demolishing a warehouse on a site adjoining a public park. Three workmen were burning rubbish on the site and keeping a look-out for children who frequently trespassed on the land. The plaintiff, aged five, who had been chased off the site on several previous occasions, trespassed on the land and fell into the fire.

Held, the defendants were liable because, realising the extreme likelihood of infant trespassers coming on to the land, they had failed to do what common sense and humanity dictated to keep children off the site. Semble, it is nowadays immaterial whether the defendants are treated as occupiers or as independent contractors. (See also *Harris v Birkenhead Corporation.*)

Pape v Cumbria County Council [1992] 3 All ER 211

The plaintiff aged 57 was employed as a part-time cleaner by the defendants and was required to use various detergents and chemical cleaning products in the course of her employment. The defendants supplied the plaintiff with gloves, which she used occasionally, but they did not warn her of the danger of irritant dermatitis from sustained exposure of skin to cleaning products or instruct her to wear the gloves. The plaintiff later began to suffer from irritated skin on her hands and wrists, which developed into acute dermatitis affecting her entire skin, and she claimed damages for personal injuries.

Held, her action would be successful. The defendants had been under a duty to warn her of the dangers and to give the necessary instructions. As no attempt had been made to do these things, they had been in breach of their duty of care. (See also *General Cleaning Contractors Ltd v Christmas.*)

Parker v British Airways Board [1982] 1 All ER 834 (Court of Appeal)

The plaintiff passenger found a gold bracelet lying on the floor in the international executive lounge at Heathrow Airport. He handed it to a British Airways official and asked that the bracelet be returned to him if it was not claimed by its owner. The bracelet was never claimed: the airline sold it and kept the proceeds.

Held, the plaintiff was entitled to damages for conversion of and/or wrongful interference with the bracelet. 'It was suggested in argument that in some circumstances the intention of the occupier to assert control over articles lost on his premises speaks for itself. I think that this is right. If a bank manager saw fit to show me round a vault containing safe deposit boxes and I found a gold bracelet on the floor, I should have no doubt that the bank had a better title than I, and the reason is the manifest intention to exercise a very high degree of control. At the other extreme is the park to which the public has unrestricted access during daylight hours. During those hours there is no manifest intention to exercise any such control. In between these extremes are the forecourts of petrol filling stations, unfenced front gardens of private houses, the public parts of shops and supermarkets as part of an almost infinite variety of land, premises and circumstances. This lounge is in the middle band and in my judgment, on the evidence available, there was no sufficient manifestation of any intention to exercise control over lost property before it was found such as would give British Airways a right superior to that of Mr Parker or indeed any right over the bracelet. As the true owner has never come forward, it is a case of "finders keepers" ' (*per* DONALDSON LJ). (See also *Armory v Delamirie*.)

Parry v Cleaver [1969] 1 All ER 555 (House of Lords)

The plaintiff was knocked down by a motor car and was so injured that he had to retire from the police force. He was entitled to an ill-health award of £3 18s 6d per week for life. The defendant admitted liability for the accident, and the question was whether the award should be ignored in assessing damages.

Held, the award was akin to an insurance policy which should not enure for the benefit of the tortfeasor, and should therefore be ignored in assessing damages for loss of earnings, although it would be brought into account in respect of loss of retirement pension. (See also *British Transport Commission v Gourley, Smoker v London Fire and Civil Defence Authority* and *Dews v National Coal Board*.)

Peabody Donation Fund (Governors) v Sir Lindsay Parkinson & Co Ltd [1984] 3 All ER 529 (House of Lords)

The plaintiffs decided to build 245 houses on a hillside and, by statute, they were required to provide a suitable drainage system, to the satisfaction of the local authority. A drainage system using flexible pipes was approved by the local authority, but the plaintiffs (to the authority's knowledge) actually used rigid pipes which proved to be unsatisfactory. The plaintiffs maintained that the authority had been in breach of its duty to them to ensure that the drainage system was suitable and in accordance with approved plans.

Held, this contention would be rejected as the purpose of the statute was the protection of householders and the community generally, not the safeguarding of developers against economic loss resulting from their failure to comply with approved plans. (See also *Curran v Northern Ireland Co-ownership Housing Association Ltd*.)

Peek v Gurney (1873) LR 6 HL 377 (House of Lords)

A prospectus contained misrepresentations of fact and concealed the existence of a deed which, if known, would probably have prevented the formation of the company. A person who bought some of the shares from an allottee sought an indemnity against the loss which he suffered in consequence of his purchase.

Held, his claim would fail as when the allotment was completed the office of the prospectus was exhausted. (But see *Andrews v Mockford*.)

Percy v Hall [1996] 4 All ER 523 (Court of Appeal)

The plaintiff protesters at a military communications centre were arrested there over 150 times. The arrests were made under certain bye-laws and the plaintiffs, contending that those bye-laws were void for uncertainty, sought damages for false imprisonment and wrongful arrest.

Held, their claim could not succeed. The bye-laws were sufficiently certain to enable them to be upheld in circumstances such as these but, even if they had not been, the defence of lawful justification would have protected the arresting constables, provided they could show that they had acted in the reasonable belief that the plaintiffs had been committing a bye-law offence. (Distinguished in *R* v *Governor of Brockhill Prison, ex parte Evans (No 2).*)

Perl (P) (Exporters) Ltd v *Camden London Borough Council*
[1983] 3 All ER 161 (Court of Appeal)

The defendants owned a block of flats: one was occupied by the plaintiffs, an adjoining flat was vacant and unsecured. Thieves entered the vacant flat, knocked a hole in the common wall and stole 700 of the plaintiffs' garments. The plaintiffs sued the defendants in negligence.

Held, their action would fail as, in the absence of any special relationship between the defendants and the thieves, the defendants had not been negligent in failing to take steps to prevent the thieves from entering their premises for the purpose of breaking into those of the plaintiffs. (Applied in *King* v *Liverpool City Council*; see also *Topp* v *London Country Bus (South West) Ltd.*)

Perry v *Kendricks Transport Ltd* [1956] 1 All ER 154 (Court of Appeal)

The defendants parked one of their motor coaches on their vehicle park which was bordered by some waste land. The defendants removed the petrol from the coach, but, after removing the screw cap, a boy threw a lighted match into the petrol tank and there was an explosion. The infant plaintiff, who was crossing the waste land and approaching the boy who threw the match, was very severely burned and he brought an action for damages for personal injuries.

Held, the defendants were not liable under the rule in *Rylands* v *Fletcher* as the acts which caused the explosion were the acts of a stranger over whom they had no control and they were not liable in negligence as they had done all that could reasonably be expected of them to prevent children meddling with the disused motor coach.

Perry v *Sidney Phillips & Son* [1982] 3 All ER 705 (Court of Appeal)

Before buying a house, the plaintiff had it inspected by the defendant chartered surveyors. In the light of their satisfactory report, the plaintiff completed the purchase, but it afterwards appeared that, perhaps due to overwork, the defendants had failed to exercise the degree of care expected of a reasonably competent chartered surveyor and therefore that they were guilty of negligence.

Held, the correct measure of damages was the difference between the price actually paid and the market value at the date of purchase, together with interest until the payment of damages, regardless of whether the plaintiff intended to remain in the property or whether he had cut his losses by immediately reselling it. In the face of the defendants' denial of liability it had been reasonable for the plaintiff not to carry out the repairs immediately; he was therefore also entitled to damages for inconvenience, distress and discomfort. (See also *Darbishire v Warran* and *Swingcastle Ltd v Alastair Gibson*.)

Perry (Howard E) & Co Ltd v British Railways Board
[1980] 2 All ER 579

In support of striking steelworkers, a railway union refused to transport steel. Fearing an escalation of industrial disruption, the defendants refused to deliver to the plaintiff steel stockholders, or to allow the plaintiffs to collect 500 tons of the plaintiffs' steel lying in the defendants' depots. The plaintiffs sought an order under s4(2) of the Torts (Interference with Goods) Act 1977 that the defendants permit them to collect their steel.

Held, the order would be made as there was a wrongful interference with the plaintiffs' steel – a conversion within s1 of the 1977 Act – and the defendants' fears of an escalation of industrial action did not prevent their refusal to release the steel from being wrongful. As a result of the strike, steel was obtainable only with great difficulty, if at all, and, in all the circumstances, damages would not have been an adequate remedy. (See also *Hiort v Bott*.)

Pettersson v Royal Oak Hotel Ltd [1948] NZLR 136 (New Zealand Court of Appeal)

In view of his intoxicated condition, a customer was refused a drink and for this reason he threw a glass at the barman. The barman in turn threw a piece of the glass and it hit the customer on the back of the neck, but a splinter of glass entered the eye of the plaintiff who was standing nearby.

Held, his employer was liable as the barman's act, although an expression of personal resentment, was within the scope of his employment as it was an improper performance of his duty to keep order in the bar. (But see *Warren v Henleys Ltd*; see also *Keppel Bus Co Ltd v Ahmad*.)

Phelps v Hillingdon London Borough Council [1999] 1 All ER 421 (Court of Appeal)

With a history of 'lack of educational progress', assessment and help of various kinds dating back to 1980, in 1985 the plaintiff, then aged 11, was seen by Miss Melling, an educational psychologist employed by the defendants who were responsible for the plaintiff's education. Miss Melling failed to identify the plaintiff as dyslexic, but such a finding was made in 1990 by a clinical and educational psychologist to whom the plaintiff was referred by her parents. The plaintiff claimed that the defendants were vicariously liable for Miss Melling's alleged negligence in failing to identify her dyslexia.

Held, her action could not succeed since Miss Melling had not owed the plaintiff a duty of care. 'In my opinion the so-called rescue cases [see, eg, *Capital and Counties plc v*

Hampshire County Council] provide a valuable if not precise analogy. ... In the rescue cases there is undoubtedly a relationship between the victim and the rescue service and there may also be a foreseeability of deterioration in the safety of the plaintiff's person or property if care is not taken. But there is no proximity in the legal sense because there is no assumption of responsibility. ... in my opinion those same policy reasons dictate that it would not be fair, just or reasonable to impose ... a duty on an educational psychologist, such as Miss Melling, unless it is quite clear that in addition to performing her duty to her employers, she assumed personal responsibility to the plaintiff; and the burden is upon the plaintiff to show this' (*per* STUART-SMITH LJ). Here the plaintiff had not discharged that burden. (But see *Barrett* v *Enfield London Borough Council*.)

Philips v *William Whiteley Ltd* [1938] 1 All ER 566

A jeweller pierced a lady's ears to enable her to wear ear-rings. Some days later an abscess developed and the lady brought an action for damages.

Held, she would be unsuccessful as there was no evidence that the jeweller had departed from the standard of care to be expected of a man of his position and training. He was not expected to take all the precautions which would have been taken if a surgeon had performed the same minor operation. (See also Whitehouse v Jordan.)

Pickett v *British Rail Engineering Ltd* [1979] 1 All ER 774
(House of Lords)

As a result of inhaling asbestos dust while working in the defendant's workshop the plaintiff developed a lung disease. Symptoms first appeared in 1974 and in 1975 he sued for damages for personal injuries; the defendant admitted liability. At the date of the trial – 1976 – the plaintiff was aged 53 and, but for his injuries, he could have expected to work until he was 65. As it was, his life expectancy had been reduced to one year and, before his appeal as to quantum of damages was heard, he died, his widow being substituted as plaintiff.

Held, damages awarded to a plaintiff whose life expectancy had been diminished should include, as a separate head, damages for economic loss resulting from his diminished earnings capacity for the whole period of his pre-injury expectancy of earning life. Such damages should be assessed objectively, deducting the plaintiff's own living expenses which he would have incurred during the 'lost years'. As to interest on general damages for pain and suffering and loss of amenities, it should be added – in this case at 9 per cent – from the date of service of the writ to the date of the trial. (See also *Connolly* v *Camden and Islington Area Health Authority*; but see *Benham* v *Gambling,* and ss1 and 15 of the Administration of Justice Act 1982.)

Pickford v *Imperial Chemical Industries plc* [1998] 3 All ER 462
(House of Lords)

The plaintiff had worked as a secretary and typist since 1970, since 1983 with the defendants. In 1989 she sought medical advice concerning pain in her hands and in 1991 she sued the defendants, alleging that by their negligence they had caused her to sustain repetitive strain injury, subsequently amended to PDA4, a recognised prescribed disease. The trial judge dismissed her claim but, by a majority, the Court of Appeal allowed her appeal, reversing the judge's findings on causation, foreseeability and negligence. The defendants appealed against this decision.

Held, the appeal would be allowed: the Court of Appeal ought not to have disturbed the trial judge's findings. '... was ... the [plaintiff's] PDA4 ... caused by her work as opposed to being work related [?] Although she had failed to satisfy [the judge] that her cramp had an organic cause, it was still necessary for him to examine this issue in order to decide whether the disease might nevertheless have been caused by the prolonged typing work which the [plaintiff] said she had to do ... Taking the evidence as a whole, the judge was far better placed than the Court of Appeal was to assess to what extent, if at all, the [plaintiff] was exaggerating and which of the other witnesses who tended to contradict her were the more reliable. Here indeed were primary findings of fact on mundane matters, to adopt LORD BRIDGE's description in *Wilsher v Essex Area Health Authority*, with which the Court of Appeal were not entitled to interfere. ... The findings by the judge that the condition was not reasonably foreseeable in her case and that the [defendants] were not negligent in the respects alleged by her were, in my opinion, soundly based on the evidence. I do not think that the Court of Appeal should have interfered with his decision ...' (*per* LORD HOPE OF CRAIGHEAD).

Pidduck v Eastern Scottish Omnibuses Ltd [1990] 2 All ER 69 (Court of Appeal)

The plaintiff's husband, a retired bank employee, dependent (with his wife) on his bank pension, was killed in an accident for which the defendants admitted liability. Judgment was entered under s3(1) of the Fatal Accidents Act 1976 and the question arose whether allowances payable to the wife out of the deceased's pension fund were deductible from the damages to be awarded.

Held, they were not. Financial support received by the plaintiff before her husband's death could not correctly be described as a benefit she had received under the pension scheme. It followed that she had suffered loss of dependency on him and thus had suffered 'injury' within s3(1) of the 1976 Act. Her widow's allowances, payable under a different section of the pension scheme, were benefits which had accrued to her as a result of her husband's death for the purposes of s4 of the 1976 Act and therefore they would be disregarded. (See also *Smoker v London Fire and Civil Defence Authority*.)

Pigney v Pointers Transport Services Ltd [1957] 2 All ER 807

In July 1955 due to the negligence of his employers, Pigney was injured when, in the course of his employment, a jib fell on his head. The wound healed but, as a result of the accident, Pigney suffered from anxiety, neurosis and depression and these so sapped his powers of resistance that in January 1957, he hanged himself. Pigney's widow sued her late husband's employers for damages under the Law Reform (Miscellaneous Provisions) Act 1934 and the Fatal Accidents Acts 1846 to 1908.

Held, she was entitled to succeed as the damage sustained by her was damage due to Pigney's death and that was directly traceable to Pigney's injury in the accident for which his employers were responsible. It was not against public policy that the widow should recover damages as the damages awarded did not form part of Pigney's estate. (See also *Schneider* v *Eisovitch* and *Burns* v *Edman*.)

Pirelli General Cable Works Ltd v *Oscar Faber & Partners*
[1983] 1 All ER 65 (House of Lords)

In March 1969 the defendant consulting engineers negligently advised the plaintiffs on the design and erection of a chimney, about 160 ft high, at their works at Southampton. Cracks occurred and they were discovered by the plaintiffs in November 1977: the writ was issued in October 1978. The trial judge found that the cracks could not have developed later than April 1970 and that the plaintiffs could not with reasonable diligence have discovered them before October 1972.

Held, the plaintiffs' claim was time-barred as the cause of action accrued in April 1970, ie when the physical damage came into existence. (But see ss14A and 14B of the Limitation Act 1980 and *Nitrigin Eireann Teoranta* v *Inco Alloys Ltd*.)

Pitts v *Hunt* [1990] 3 All ER 344 (Court of Appeal)

The plaintiff, aged 18, and a friend (16) spent the evening drinking and then drove home on the friend's motor cycle, the plaintiff being aware that the friend was neither licensed nor insured. On the journey the friend, encouraged by the plaintiff, drove recklessly and, after an accident in which the friend was killed the plaintiff suffered severe injuries, it was found that the friend had been more than twice above the legal limit. The plaintiff claimed damages against the friend's personal representative.

Held, his action could not succeed on the grounds of the application of the maxim ex turpi causa non oritur actio, public policy and inability to find, in the circumstances, that the friend had owed the plaintiff any duty of care. (See also *Ashton* v *Turner*; but see *Revill* v *Newbery*.)

Platform Home Loans Ltd v *Oyston Shipways Ltd* [1999] 1 All ER 833 (House of Lords)

The defendant valuers valued a property at £1.5 million and the plaintiff lent the owner £1,050,195 (70 per cent) on the strength of these valuations. The owner having defaulted on his mortgage repayments, the plaintiff obtained possession and (the property market having collapsed) sold the property for £435,000. In the plaintiff's action for damages, the trial judge found that the defendants had been negligent, that the true value of the property at the date of valuation was £1 million and that the plaintiff's loss (loan less sale proceeds adjusted to take account of payments made, interest, etc) was £611,748.51. However, he also found that the plaintiff had been negligent in carrying out its loan procedures and, applying s1 of the Law Reform (Contributory Negligence) Act 1945, he reduced the defendants' liability by 20 per cent to £489,398.81. The Court of Appeal reduced this figure to £400,000, the extent of the over valuations (£0.5 million) less 20 per cent.

Held, the trial judge's award would be restored. 'The £500,000 is merely the amount of the overvaluation. The damage which the [plaintiff] suffered as a result of the transaction which they entered into in consequence of the overvaluation is not £500,000 but £611,748. This is the damage referred to in s1(1). This damage was due to the insufficiency of the security. The sufficiency of any security, however, depends on a combination of two factors: the value of the security and the amount of the advance. If the [defendants] had given a lower valuation, or if the [plaintiff] had lent a lower proportion of valuation, then in either case the [plaintiff's] loss would have been less. Accordingly, the loss of £611,748 which the [plaintiff] suffered was partly as a result of its own fault and partly of the fault of the [defendants] within the meaning of s1(1) of the Act. ... the [plaintiff] was found to be at fault in two respects. Neither of them caused or contributed to the overvaluation. The judge assessed the [plaintiff's] share in the responsibility for the overall damage at 20 per cent and reduced the damages to £489,398 accordingly. In my opinion this was the right approach. The amount of damages which the judge awarded properly reflected the 80 per cent overall loss for which the [defendants] have been found to be responsible and which, being less than the amount of the overvaluation, fell wholly within the scope of their duty of care' (*per* LORD MILLETT). (Applied: *South Australia Asset Management Corp v York Montague Ltd*.)

Poland v *John Parr and Sons* [1927] 1 KB 236 (Court of Appeal)

A servant of the defendants honestly but mistakenly believed that a boy, the plaintiff, was tampering with a bag of sugar on a waggon owned by the defendants. With a view to protecting the sugar and his masters' interests, the servant struck the plaintiff with his open hand. The plaintiff fell under the waggon and received injuries which led to the amputation of his right leg.

Held, the defendants were liable as their servant had acted within his implied authority to take reasonable steps to protect their property. (See also *Bayley* v *Manchester, Sheffield and Lincolnshire Railway Co* and *Keppel Bus Co Ltd* v *Ahmad*.)

Polemis & Furness, Withy & Co Ltd, Re [1921] 3 KB 560 (Court of Appeal)

By a term of a charterparty, both parties were excepted from liability for fire. On one voyage the ship carried petrol in leaky tins. At a port of call, due to the negligence of the charterers' servants, a plank fell into the hold and there immediately followed a rush of flames which resulted in the ship being totally destroyed.

Held, the exception clause did not protect the charterers where the loss was due to the negligence of their servants. They were therefore liable for the loss of the ship as they were liable for the direct consequences of their servants' negligence although those consequences could not have been reasonably anticipated. (But see *Liescbosch (Dredgers) v Edison (Steamships)* and *Overseas Tankship (UK) Ltd v Morts Dock & Engineering Co Ltd.*)

Ponting v *Noakes* [1894] 2 QB 281

The plaintiff's colt reached over the defendant's land and ate some branches of a yew tree growing there. The colt died and the plaintiff sued to recover its value.

Held, the action would not succeed as the animal's death was due to its wrongful intrusion.

Port Swettenham Authority v *T W Wu & Co (M) Sdn Bhd* [1978] 3 All ER 337 (Privy Council)

Cases of pharmaceutical goods were unloaded at a port in Malaysia and, while they were in the custody of the port authority, some of them disappeared and some of their contents were later found in the local chemist's shop. The port authority appealed against the decision that they were liable for the loss of the cases.

Held, their appeal would be dismissed. 'The undisputed facts … establish that the port authority were clearly bailees for reward. However this may be, in their Lordships' view the onus is always on the bailee, whether he be a bailee for reward or a gratuitous bailee, to prove that the loss of any goods bailed to him was not caused by any fault of his or of any of his servants or agents to whom he entrusted the goods for safe keeping. Accordingly the onus of proving that the loss of the goods deposited with the port authority for safe custody was not caused by the negligence or misconduct of their servants in the course of their employment, without any doubt lies on the authority' (*per* LORD SALMON). The port authority had been unable to discharge this onus. (See also *Morris* v *C W Martin & Sons Ltd.*)

Pritchard v *J H Cobden Ltd* [1987] 1 All ER 300 (Court of Appeal)

The plaintiff suffered permanent brain damage in a motor accident caused by the defendants' negligence. Subsequently, the plaintiff's marriage broke down and he claimed, inter alia, the extra expense he would incur as a result of the divorce.

Held, this claim would fail as, inter alia, the financial consequences of divorce in these circumstances are too remote to be recoverable. (See also *Knightley* v *Johns.*)

Pursell v *Horne* (1838) 3 N & P 564

Elizabeth 'cast and threw divers large quantities of boiling water' on the plaintiff.

Held, there was a battery as it 'includes all cases where a party is struck by any missile thrown by another' (*per* LORD DENMAN CJ). (See also *Innes* v *Wylie.*)

Quarman v *Burnett* (1840) 6 M & W 499

Two elderly ladies owned a carriage but hired a coachman and some horses from a certain job-mistress.

Held, they were not liable for the consequences of the coachman's negligence as he was not their servant.

R v Cotesworth (1704) 6 Mod Rep 172

A person spat in a doctor's face.

Held, this act was a battery. (See also *Pursell* v *Horne*.)

R v Governor of Brockhill Prison, ex parte Evans (No 2)
[1998] 4 All ER 993 (Court of Appeal)

Applying certain judicial decisions, the prison governor calculated that the appellant would be released from prison on 18 November 1996. On 15 November the Divisional Court ruled that those earlier decisions had been incorrect: the appellant should have been released on 17 September. Having been released on 15 November, the appellant claimed damages for false imprisonment during the period 17 September to 15 November.

Held, her action would be successful. 'Until the approach to the doctrine of precedent is changed, the practical consequence is that once the later decision has been given there is no right to rely on the earlier decision as correctly representing the law. ... From the governor's point of view, it is as though the earlier decision had not existed. However ... it is not open to this court to abandon the fairytale. If the sentence cannot provide the justification, what the governor is asking this court to do is to provide him with an immunity because of lack of fault, but this is a task beyond the proper role of this court. It is inconsistent with the nature of the tort [ie, that a person imprisoned without lawful authority is entitled to damages irrespective of any question of fault on the part of the person responsible for the imprisonment]' (*per* LORD WOOLF MR). (Distinguished: *Percy* v *Hall*; but see *Hague* v *Deputy Governor of Parkhurst Prison*.)

R v St George (1840) 9 C & P 483

On the trial of an indictment for feloniously attempting to discharge loaded arms, the court considered whether by pointing an unloaded pistol a common law assault had been committed.

Held, it had if the weapon had the appearance of being loaded, thus causing fear and alarm, and the range was such that it would have endangered life if it had been fired. (But see *Blake* v *Barnard*.)

Racz v Home Office [1993] 2 WLR 23 (House of Lords)

The plaintiff, a remand prisoner, alleged that he had been ill-treated by prison officers and he brought an action against the Home Office for damages for assault, misfeasance in public office and false imprisonment. The defendants sought to strike out the plaintiff's claim relating to misfeasance in public office in relation to which the plaintiff sought trial by jury.

Held, the claim would not be struck out as the defendants could be vicariously liable for this tort. However, the decision to refuse jury trial would not be disturbed as the courts below had properly exercised their discretion under s69 of the Supreme Court Act 1981. (But see *Hague* v *Deputy Governor of Parkhurst Prison*.)

Rance v Mid-Downs Health Authority [1991] 1 All ER 801

When the plaintiff was about 26 weeks pregnant, she had an ultrasound scan at the defendants' hospital. Although suspicions were aroused, the consultant radiologist decided that no further action should be taken. The baby was born with spina bifida. The plaintiff maintained that the defendants' alleged negligence had deprived her of the possibility of an abortion but the defendants contended that, even if the abnormality had been discovered, it would have been an offence under the Infant Life (Preservation) Act 1929 to terminate the pregnancy at that stage as the foetus was then 'a child capable of being born alive'.

Held, the plaintiff's claim would fail as, inter alia, in these circumstances an abortion would have been unlawful and it would be contrary to public policy to allow the plaintiff to recover.

Rantzen v Mirror Group Newspapers (1986) Ltd [1993] 4 All ER 975 (Court of Appeal)

The plaintiff was awarded £250,000 by way of damages for libel. The defendants appealed pursuant to s8 of the Courts and Legal Services Act 1990 on the ground, inter alia, that the award was excessive.

Held, in view of the court's powers under s8(2) of the 1990 Act and RSC Ord 59, r11(4) and in the light of article 10 of the Convention for the Protection of Human Rights and Fundamental Freedoms, the question was whether a reasonable jury could have thought the award necessary to compensate the plaintiff and re-establish her reputation. Here, the answer was in the negative and an award of £110,000 would be substituted. (See also *Sutcliffe v Pressdram Ltd*.)

Ratcliffe v Evans [1892] 2 QB 524 (Court of Appeal)

Under the name of Ratcliffe & Sons the plaintiff had for many years carried on the business of an engineer and a boiler-maker. An article in the *County Herald,* of which the defendant was proprietor, suggested that the plaintiff's business had ceased and that his firm no longer existed. It was found that the plaintiff's business suffered by reason of the publication of this statement.

Held, the plaintiff's action for damages for a false and malicious publication about his business would succeed. (But see *Greers Ltd v Pearman & Corder Ltd*.)

Reckitt & Colman Products Ltd v Borden Inc [1990] 1 All ER 873 (House of Lords)

Since 1955 the plaintiffs had marketed lemon juice in convenient plastic squeeze packs coloured and shaped like natural lemons. Thirty years later the defendants adopted a similar approach and the plaintiffs sought an injunction on grounds of passing-off. Granting the injunction, the trial judge said that, although the products were distinguished by their labels, the decisive factor for many shoppers was the lemon shape of the container.

Held, the defendants' appeal would be dismissed as their use of plastic lemon containers constituted a misrepresentation that their juice was the plaintiffs' juice. (But see *Cadbury Schweppes Pty Ltd* v *Pub Squash Co Pty Ltd*.)

Reddaway (Frank) & Co Ltd v George Banham & Co Ltd
[1896] AC 199 (House of Lords)

For some years the plaintiff had manufactured machine belting which was known throughout the trade as 'Camel Hair Belting'. Another manufacturer, the defendant, who was formerly employed by the plaintiff, began to stamp his goods 'Camel Hair Belting' and the plaintiff sought an injunction to restrain this user of the words 'camel hair' without clearly distinguishing his belting from that of the plaintiff.

Held, the plaintiff was entitled to the relief which he sought. (See also *Reckitt & Colman Products Ltd* v *Borden Inc* and *British Telecommunications plc* v *One In A Million Ltd*; but see *Fels* v *Hedley & Co Ltd*.)

Reffell v Surrey County Council [1964] 1 All ER 743

The plaintiff was a 12-year-old girl and a pupil at a school owned, controlled and maintained by the defendants. One afternoon she had cause to pass through a pair of double swing doors in the school corridor and, as she approached them, one door was swinging towards her. She put out her hand to stop it, but her hand went through a glass panel in the door and she suffered injuries. The glass panel was ⅙in thick and not toughened and, although there had been no previous accident at this door, the defendants appreciated the risk involved in the use of this kind of glass. Regulations made under the Education Act 1944 provided: 'In all parts of the buildings of every school … the properties of the materials shall be such that the … safety of the occupants … shall be reasonably assured'.

Held, the plaintiff was entitled to damages for breach of statutory duty as, on the facts, safety had not been reasonably assured. 'The duty to secure … that safety shall be reasonably assured … is an absolute duty and the test of breach or no breach is objective. Putting it another way, if safety is not reasonably assured in the premises in fact, then there is a breach' (*per* VEALE J). Further, on the facts, the defendants were liable at common law for negligence and also for breach of the common duty of care under s2(2) of the Occupiers' Liability Act 1957. (See also *Wheat* v *E Lacon & Co Ltd*; but see *Blyth* v *Birmingham Waterworks Co*.)

Reid v Rush & Tompkins Group plc [1989] 3 All ER 228
(Court of Appeal)

While working for the defendants in Ethiopia the plaintiff was injured when his Land Rover was involved in an accident driven by a person unknown. He was therefore without redress in Ethiopia, but he alleged that the defendants had been in breach of their duty of care as employers in failing either to insure him or to advise him to obtain cover himself.

Held, unless there was an express or implied term of the contract of employment to that effect (and here there was not), the defendants had not owed the plaintiff such a duty of care and his action had therefore properly been struck out. (See also *Van Oppen v Clerk to the Bedford Charity Trustees*.)

Revill v Newbery [1996] 1 All ER 291 (Court of Appeal)

At about 2am the plaintiff attempted to break into a brick shed on the defendant's allotment where he was sleeping to guard his property. The defendant loaded a shotgun, poked the barrel through a small hole in the door, and fired and hit the plaintiff at a range of around five feet. The plaintiff pleaded guilty to the relevant criminal offences, and claimed against the defendant under s1 Occupiers' Liability Act 1984 and for negligence. At first instance the plaintiff succeeded, the judge rejecting the defences of ex turpi causa non oritur actio, accident and self-defence but finding that the plaintiff was two-thirds to blame. The defendant appealed.

Held, the appeal would be dismissed. The duty of care owed to trespassers (by occupiers, under s1 of the 1984 Act, by other persons, at common law) applies even though the trespassers are engaged in criminal activity. Here, the defendant had used greater violence than was justified in self-defence and the finding as to contributory negligence would not be disturbed. (See also *Videan v British Transport Commission* and *Collins v Renison*; but see *Pitts v Hunt*.)

Reynolds v Kennedy (1748) 1 Wils 232

A judgment of condemnation by the sub-commissioners of excise in respect of the non-payment of duty on some brandy found on the plaintiff's ship was reversed by the commissioners of appeal. The plaintiff claimed damages for malicious prosecution.

Held, the action would fail as the fact that the sub-commissioners had given judgment in favour of the prosecutor showed that there was a foundation for the prosecution. (See also *Basébé v Matthews*.)

Reynolds v Times Newspapers Ltd [1998] 3 All ER 961 (Court of Appeal)

The defendants' newspaper, the *Sunday Times*, published an article about a political crisis in Ireland and the plaintiff's resignation from the office of Prime Minister. The plaintiff sued for libel and the defendants claimed, inter alia, qualified privilege.

Held, '... when applying the present English common law of qualified privilege, the following questions need to be answered in relation to any individual occasion. 1. Was the publisher under a legal, moral or social duty to those to whom the material was published (which in appropriate cases ... may be the general public) to publish the material in question? (We call this the duty test.) 2. Did those to whom the material was published (which again in appropriate cases may be the general public) have an interest to receive that material? (We call this the interest test.) 3. Were the nature, status and source of the material, and the circumstances of the publication, such that the publication should in the public interest be protected in the absence of proofs of express malice? (We call this the circumstantial test)' (*per* LORD BINGHAM CJ). On the facts, the first two tests had been satisfied but not the third. NB: This decision was affirmed by the House of Lords [1999] 4 All ER 609.

Rickards v Lothian [1913] AC 263 (Privy Council)

A tap in a lavatory on the top floor of a building leased to the defendants was turned on for a considerable time with the result that the water overflowed and damaged the plaintiff's stock in trade on the floor below. It was found that 'this was the malicious act of some person'.

Held, the plaintiff could not recover damages as the defendants had not been negligent and the rule in *Rylands* v *Fletcher* did not apply as having a reasonable and proper supply of water was an ordinary and proper user of a building. (But see *Northwestern Utilities Ltd* v *London Guarantee and Accident Co Ltd* and *Musgrove* v *Pandelis*.)

Roberts v Chief Constable of the Cheshire Constabulary [1999] 2 All ER 326 (Court of Appeal)

Roberts had been arrested for alleged conspiracy to burgle. Under Part IV of the Police and Criminal Evidence Act 1984 his detention should have been reviewed by 5.25 am: the review took place at 7.45 am when his further detention was authorised. He was awarded £500 compensatory damages for false imprisonment between 5.25 am and 7.45 am.

Held, the appeal against this decision would be dismissed. 'The question is whether the judge should have awarded only nominal damages on the basis that if the police had acted properly and carried out a review the respondent would have been detained anyway. ... All depends upon the circumstances. A person who was falsely imprisoned but who was unaware of his imprisonment and who suffered no harm would be entitled to only nominal damages. [Roberts] was not, however in that position here. He was no doubt aware of his imprisonment and, as I see it, he was entitled to be compensated for being unlawfully detained in a police cell for 2 hours 20 minutes when, in the absence of a review, he should have been released. ... I would only add this. A sum of £500 is substantially more that I would have awarded to compensate [Roberts] for false imprisonment for a period of 2 hours 20 minutes during which he was asleep, especially in circumstances in which if a review had been carried out at 5.25 am, his detention would have been lawful' (*per* CLARKE LJ). (See also *Meering* v *Grahame-White Aviation Co Ltd*.)

Roberts v Ramsbottom [1980] 1 All ER 7

A car driven by the defendant, a man of 73, collided with the plaintiff's parked car. Prima facie he had been negligent, but shortly before he left home he had suffered a stroke. Although he had experienced feelings of queerness, he had not been aware that he was unfit to drive.

Held, he could only escape liability if his actions had been wholly beyond his control, ie if the facts established automatism. As his condition did not amount to automatism, he was liable to the plaintiff. 'A defendant may be able to rebut a prima facie case of negligence by showing that a sudden affliction has rendered him unconscious or otherwise wholly incapable of controlling the vehicle' (*per* NEILL J).

Robertson v Ridley [1989] 2 All ER 474 (Court of Appeal)

The plaintiff member of an unincorporated members' club was riding his motor cycle on the club's driveway: he struck a pothole, fell off and suffered injury. Club rules provided that the chairman and secretary (the defendants) 'were responsible in Law ... for the conduct of the Club'.

Held, this rule had not qualified the common law rule that there is no liability between a club or its members on the one hand and individual members on the other and the plaintiff's action for damages would therefore fail.

Robinson v Balmain New Ferry Co Ltd [1910] AC 295 (Privy Council)

A barrister-at-law, the plaintiff, paid a penny to use the defendants' ferry but when he found that he would have to wait some 20 minutes, he changed his mind and tried to leave the wharf. In accordance with the defendants' regulations, a penny was also payable on leaving the wharf, but the plaintiff refused to pay this sum and for a time, after having attempted to force his way out, was forcibly detained by the defendants' officers. The plaintiff brought an action for false imprisonment.

Held, this action would fail as the toll was reasonable and the defendants were entitled to resist the plaintiff's forcible passage through their turnstile with the object of avoiding payment. (See also *Herd* v *Weardale Steel, Coal & Coke Ltd.*)

Robinson v Kilvert (1889) 41 ChD 88 (Court of Appeal)

The plaintiff occupied the ground floor of the defendants' premises for the purpose of storing brown paper. The defendants used a boiler in the basement in connection with their business as paper-box makers and it appeared that this had an adverse effect on the plaintiff's goods, although it would not have harmed any other kind of paper and did not inconvenience his employees. The plaintiff sought to restrain the use of the boiler.

Held, the plaintiff's case would fail as 'a man who carries on an exceptionally delicate trade cannot complain because it is injured by his neighbour doing something lawful on his property, if it is something which would not injure anything but an exceptionally delicate trade' (*per* LOPES LJ). (See also *Bridlington Relay Ltd* v *Yorkshire Electricity Board.*)

Robinson v Post Office [1974] 2 All ER 737 (Court of Appeal)

The plaintiff, while in the service of the defendant, slipped and fell because of oil negligently deposited on a ladder of the defendant, and sustained a wound on his shin. A doctor gave him an injection of anti-tetanus serum, as a result of which the plaintiff developed encephalitis which led to disability.

Held, every relevant matter was foreseeable, except the extent of the injury which was due to the plaintiff's allergy to the serum. But since the defendant must take the plaintiff as he found him, the defendant was liable for the resulting disability. 'The principle that a defendant must take the plaintiff as he finds him involves that if a wrongdoer ought reasonably to foresee that as a result of his wrongful act the victim may require medical treatment he is, subject to the principle of novus actus interveniens, liable for the consequences of the treatment applied although he could not reasonably foresee those consequences or that they could be serious.' (See also *Smith v Leech Brain & Co Ltd*; but see *Tremain v Pike*.)

Roe v Ministry of Health [1954] 2 All ER 131 (Court of Appeal)

Before an operation, a visiting specialist anaesthetist administered an injection of nupercaine. The injection became contaminated by phenol with the result that the patient was paralysed from the waist downwards, but by the standard of knowledge to be imputed to competent anaesthetists at the time of the accident, the anaesthetist had not been negligent.

Held, as no negligence had been proved, the hospital authorities were not liable, but they would have been responsible for the negligence of the anaesthetist as 'they are responsible for the whole of their staff, not only for the nurses and doctors but also for the anaesthetists and the surgeons. It does not matter whether they are permanent or temporary, resident or visiting, whole-time or part-time ... The only exception is the case of consultants or anaesthetists selected and employed by the patient himself' (*per* DENNING LJ). (See also *Bolam v Friern Hospital Management Committee*.)

Roles v Nathan [1963] 2 All ER 908 (Court of Appeal)

The flue of a coke-fired boiler was inefficient and an expert advised the sealing of a sweep hole. The expert warned the chimney sweeps who would carry out the work of the danger of gas and told them that they ought not in any case to stay too long in the alcove: he also told all concerned (including the sweeps) that the boiler ought not to be lit again until the sweep hole was sealed. The sweeps tried to seal the sweep hole while the boiler was alight and died in the attempt. Their widows brought actions for damages against the occupier of the premises.

Held, their actions should fail. The warnings given to the sweeps were enough to enable them to be reasonably safe and, for this reason, the occupier had discharged under s2(4)(a) of the Occupiers' Liability Act 1957 the common duty of care which he owed them. The court was divided as to whether the occupier was also protected by s2(3)(b) of the Act of 1957. (But see *Reffell v Surrey County Council*.)

Rondel v Worsley [1967] 3 All ER 993 (House of Lords)

The plaintiff was convicted of causing grievous bodily harm with intent to X, and nearly six years later issued a writ for negligence against the defendant, a barrister who had appeared for him, arguing that he would have been acquitted if the defendant had conducted his case properly. He argued that since *Hedley Byrne & Co Ltd v Heller & Partners Ltd* the position with regard to liability for professional negligence as between barrister and client had altered, so that there was liability.

Held, no action lay at the suit of a client against a barrister, for negligence in the conduct of a cause. The immunity of counsel from being sued for professional negligence in the conduct of a cause, civil or criminal, is based on public policy, not on his contractual incapacity to sue for fees, and it is in the public interest that the immunity should be retained. (Applied in *Atwell v Michael Perry & Co*; see also *Hill v Chief Constable of West Yorkshire*; but see *Saif Ali v Sidney Mitchell & Co*.)

Rookes v Barnard [1964] 1 All ER 367 (House of Lords)

The appellant was an employee of BOAC at London Airport and a member of his trade union, the Association of Engineering and Shipbuilding Draughtsmen. Being dissatisfied with the conduct of the AESD the appellant resigned from it and, as they were anxious to retain one hundred per cent union membership, the London Airport branch of the union resolved that BOAC should be informed that all members would withdraw their labour if the appellant were not removed from his post. BOAC eventually terminated the appellant's contract of service in accordance with its terms and the appellant sought a remedy against the respondents, two union members and an official of the union, all of whom had spoken in favour of the resolution, on the ground that they had wrongfully induced BOAC to act as they did. It was common ground that a trade dispute existed concerning the appellant's employment by BOAC and that all acts of the respondents were in furtherance of this trade dispute and the jury found that there was a conspiracy to threaten strike action by the members of AESD to secure the withdrawal of the appellant from his post, that the threat was made by the respondents and that the threats caused the appellant's dismissal by BOAC.

Held, the plaintiff should recover damages against the respondents as he had established a good cause of action at common law for the tort of intimidation. The respondents were not protected by s1 of the Trade Disputes Act 1906, as that section was not intended to give protection against an action for a conspiracy involving the use of unlawful means (eg the tort of intimidation) and s3 of the Act of 1906 did not provide immunity where, as here, there were threats to break contracts and tortious means (ie the tort of intimidation) were established. On the question of damages, their lordships held that exemplary damages should be awarded only in the case of oppressive, arbitrary or unconstitutional action by the servants of the government or where the defendant's conduct was calculated by him to make a profit for himself which could well exceed the compensation payable to the plaintiff. In the case which was then before them their lordships held that there was nothing to bring it within either of these categories and therefore that an award of exemplary damages was inappropriate. (See also *Cassell & Co Ltd v Broome* and *Sorrell v Smith*; but see the Trade Union and Labour Relations (Consolidation) Act 1992, s219(1)(b) and *AB v South West Water Services Ltd*.)

Rose v Ford [1937] 3 All ER 359 (House of Lords)

A young lady died as a result of injuries received in a motor accident four days before her death. The accident was caused by the negligent driving of the defendant; the plaintiff, the deceased's father and her personal representative, claimed and the court of first instance awarded damages of £300 for himself and his wife as dependants under the Fatal Accidents Acts 1846 to 1908. He also claimed damages for the benefit of his daughter's estate under the Law Reform (Miscellaneous Provisions) Act 1934, and under this second head the trial judge awarded £500 for pain and suffering and the loss of her right leg which was amputated two days before her death, but refused to make any award in respect of loss of expectation of life. The Court of Appeal awarded £20 for pain and suffering and £2 for loss of a leg. They refused to grant damages for loss of expectation of life as, in their view, they were not recoverable after the injured person had died. They said that if damages were allowable on this ground, £1,000 was a proper sum.

Held, this decision would be supported except that £1,000 damages for loss of expectation of life would be awarded as a right to such damages passed to the plaintiff under s1 of the Law Reform (Miscellaneous Provisions) Act 1934. (Applied in *Gammell* v *Wilson*; but see s1 of the Administration of Justice Act 1982.)

Rose v Miles (1815) 4 M & S 101

The defendant wrongfully moored a barge across a certain public navigable creek and in consequence the plaintiff was unable to navigate his barges, which were loaded with goods, along the waterway. The plaintiff proved that because of this, at a cost of £500, he was forced to unload the cargo and carry it over land.

Held, the plaintiff was entitled to damages. He had suffered special damage, in loss of time and money, because he was in the act of using the creek when the passage of his barges was obstructed. (But see *Attorney-General* v *PYA Quarries Ltd.*)

Ross v Caunters [1979] 3 All ER 580

A testator instructed the defendant solicitors to draw up his will which included a gift in favour of the plaintiff. The defendants sent the will to the testator with instructions as to its execution but they failed to warn him that attestation by a beneficiary's spouse would invalidate the gift to that beneficiary. The plaintiff's husband attested the will: when it was returned to the defendants they failed to notice that he had done so. After the testator's death, the defendants told the plaintiff that the gift to her was void and she sued them for damages in negligence.

Held, her action would succeed as a solicitor who was instructed by his client to carry out a transaction to confer a benefit on an identified third party owed a duty to that third party to use proper care in carrying out the instructions and the defendants had been in breach of that duty. The fact that the plaintiff's claim in negligence was for purely financial loss did not preclude it. (See also *White* v *Jones* and *JEB Fasteners Ltd* v *Marks, Bloom & Co*; but see *Hemmens* v *Wilson Browne.*)

Rouse v *Squires* [1973] 2 All ER 903 (Court of Appeal)

On a frosty December night an articulated lorry owned by third parties skidded on the M1 as a result of negligence and blocked the centre and nearside lanes. A car in the centre lane collided with the lorry. A second lorry stopped in the nearside lane. A third lorry driven too fast by the defendant, who did not maintain a proper look-out, failed to stop in time despite the fact that the accident was well illuminated. As a result, R, who was helping on the scene, was killed. R's widow brought an action against the defendant who claimed contribution from the third parties.

Held, if a driver negligently obstructs the highway, then his negligence may be held to have contributed to the causation of an accident of which the immediate cause was the negligent driving of a second vehicle which because of the presence of the obstruction collides with it or with some other vehicle or some other person. Since there was no breach in the chain of causation between the negligent driving of the third parties and the death of R, the third parties were 25 per cent to blame. (See also *Dymond* v *Pearce*; but see *Wright* v *Lodge*.)

Royal Aquarium and Summer and Winter Garden Society Ltd v *Parkinson* [1892] 1 QB 431 (Court of Appeal)

The plaintiffs, proprietors of the Royal Aquarium, applied to a meeting of the London County Council for renewal of their licence for music and dancing. In opposing the application, the defendant, a member of the council, said that a performance which he had seen at the Aquarium had been most indecent. The plaintiffs claimed damages for slander.

Held, they were entitled to succeed as the meeting of the council was not a court within the rule which would give the defendant's defamatory statement absolute privilege. (But see *Anderson* v *Gorrie*.)

Ruddiman & Co v *Smith* (1889) 60 LT 708

A lavatory was set apart for use by the defendants' clerks. One of them left a tap running and the plaintiffs, whose premises were below those of the defendants, suffered damage.

Held, the defendants were liable as use of the lavatory by the clerk was incidental to his employment.

Rylands v *Fletcher* (1868) LR 3 HL 330 (House of Lords)

The defendants wished to construct a reservoir on their land for use in conjunction with their mill and employed independent contractors, who were admittedly competent, to do the work. When the reservoir was filled, however, due to the negligence of the independent contractors, the water flowed through certain disused mine shafts on the defendants' land which appeared to have been filled with earth but were in fact connected with the mines owned by and underneath the land of the plaintiff, the defendants' neighbour. There was no negligence on the part of the defendants. The plaintiff brought an action in respect of the damage which he suffered as a result of the flooding of his mine.

Held, he would succeed. Their lordships approved the following statement made by BLACKBURN J when expressing the view of the Court of Exchequer Chamber: 'We think that the true rule of law is, that the person who, for his own purposes, brings on his land and collects and keeps there any thing likely to do mischief if it escapes, must keep it in at his peril; and if he does not do so, is prima facie answerable for all the damage which is the natural consequence of its escape. He can excuse himself by showing that the escape was owing to the plaintiff's default; or, perhaps, that the escape was the consequence of vis major, or the Act of God.' (See also *Crowhurst* v *Amersham Burial Board*; but see *Read* v *J Lyons Co Ltd* and *Nichols* v *Marsland*.)

SCM (United Kingdom) Ltd v W J Whittall and Son Ltd
[1970] 3 All ER 245 (Court of Appeal)

The defendants, building contractors, rebuilt a boundary wall. One of the workmen damaged an electric cable owned by the electricity board. The plaintiffs, factory owners, alleged that the defendants were negligent, that the accident caused a seven hour power failure at their factory, that physical damage to materials and machines and consequent loss of production was suffered, and that the damage was reasonably foreseeable.

Held, the defendants were prima facie liable. *Per* WINN and BUCKLEY LJJ: there is a general duty to guard against negligent infliction of any form of economic loss which is itself consequential on foreseeable physical injury or damage to property. *Per* LORD DENNING MR: the damage was not too remote. Although the law says as a matter of policy that pure economic loss often cannot be recovered, such loss is not too remote where it is consequential on material damage. (See also *Junior Books Ltd* v *Veitchi Co Ltd*.)

Saif Ali v Sydney Mitchell & Co [1978] 3 All ER 1033 (House Lords)

In an action by a client against his solicitor for negligence, the solicitor joined as third party the barrister who had advised in the matter. The barrister had settled proceedings in respect of a road accident against the husband of the driver of the car, on the basis that the wife was his agent. He did not join the wife as a defendant, and when it was sought to do so, any action against her was statute barred.

Held, although public policy required that a barrister should be immune from suit for negligence in respect of his acts or omissions in the conduct and management of litigation which caused damage to his client, such immunity was an exception to the principle that a professional person who held himself out as qualified to practise that profession was under a duty to use reasonable care and skill and was not to be given any wider application than was absolutely necessary in the interests of the administration of justice. Accordingly, a barrister's immunity from suit extended only to those matters of pre-trial work which were so intimately connected with the conduct of the case in court that they could fairly be said to be preliminary decisions affecting the way that case was conducted when it came to a hearing. Inasmuch as the barrister's advice and settling of the pleadings in fact prevented the plaintiff's case from coming to court as it should have done, it could not be said to have been intimately connected with the conduct of the plaintiff's case in court, and was therefore not within the sphere of a barrister's immunity from suit for negligence. A solicitor acting as an advocate in court enjoys the same immunity as a barrister. (Applied in *Welsh v Chief Constable of the Merseyside Police* and *Atwell v Michael Perry & Co*; but see *Rondel v Worsley* and *Somasundaram v M Julius Melchior & Co*.)

St Anne's Well Brewery Co v Roberts (1928) 140 LT 1 (Court of Appeal)

The plaintiffs owned the 'Custom House Inn', which was bounded on one side by a portion of the ancient wall of the city of Exeter, the property of the defendants. On either side of the fireplace in the kitchen of the inn recesses had been formed at some time unknown by means of excavations made in the wall. Much of the wall collapsed, completely demolishing the plaintiffs' inn, and they brought an action for damages.

Held, the plaintiffs' claim would fail as it had not been proved that the defendants had knowledge of the defect which caused the fall of the wall or that they could have discovered it by reasonable diligence. The doctrine of *Rylands v Fletcher* did not apply as the damage sustained by the inn did not arise from the abnormal or unnatural user of the defendants' property, and the defendants were not occupiers of the wall at the time of its collapse. (But see *Sedleigh-Denfield v O'Callagan* and *Attorney-General v Corke*.)

St Helen's Smelting Co v Tipping (1865) 11 HL Cas 642 (House of Lords)

The plaintiff bought an estate consisting of about 1,300 acres near to the defendants' copper smelting works. The vapour from the works proved injurious to the plaintiff's trees and crops and he claimed to be entitled to damages.

Held, he would succeed. The jury was correctly directed that an actionable injury was one producing sensible discomfort and that every man, unless enjoying rights obtained by prescription or agreement, was bound to use his property in such a way as not to injure that of his neighbour. The law was not concerned with trifling inconvenience and everything had to be considered from a reasonable point of view. In this case the jury was asked to consider whether the injury was such as visibly diminished the value of the property and the comfort and enjoyment of it. Time and locality were factors to be taken into account. (See also *Adams v Ursell*; but see *Robinson v Kilvert*.)

Salih v Enfield Health Authority [1991] 3 All ER 400 (Court of Appeal)

The defendant negligently failed to diagnose and warn the plaintiff mother that her child might be infected with rubella; as a result, she was unable to have the pregnancy terminated. The child when born was suffering from rubella and damages awarded included the basic cost of maintaining the boy. The plaintiff parents decided not to have any more children, but evidence suggested that they would have had at least one more child if they had not had to care for a son who was handicapped.

Held, the plaintiffs were not entitled to the basic cost of maintaining their son as, but for the defendants' negligence, they would probably have had another child and have incurred the cost of maintaining it. (Applied: *Cutler v Vauxhall Motors Ltd*.)

Salmon v *Seafarer Restaurants Ltd* [1983] 3 All ER 729

Due to the negligence of one of his employees in the course of his employment, fire broke out in the defendants' fish and chip shop. The plaintiff fireman was injured when a gas meter exploded in the heat.

Held, the defendants were liable as it was reasonably foreseeable that firemen would be required to attend the fire and that an explosion of the kind which occurred might result from it. (See also *Ogwo* v *Taylor*.)

Salsbury v *Woodland* [1969] 3 All ER 863 (Court of Appeal)

The first defendant (Dl) employed tree felling contractors (D2) to fell a tree which stood in Dl's front garden. D2 felled the tree negligently so that it broke telephone wires running across the garden. The wires fell into the road. The plaintiff, who was visiting a neighbouring house, went into the road to remove the wires. A car driven by D3 approached so swiftly that the plaintiff was injured when he threw himself on to the side of the road.

Held, (1) D1 was not liable for the negligence of D2, because D2 was an independent contractor and the work was neither of an inherently dangerous nature, nor was it carried out 'on' the highway. (2) The court would not interfere with the judge's finding that D3 ought to have seen the wires, because the judge had viewed the scene of the accident. (No arguments on causation were presented.)

Saltpetre Case (1606) 12 Co Rep 12

The question arose as to whether the King had a prerogative to dig and take saltpetre (which was used in the manufacture of gunpowder) on the ground that it was necessary for the defence of the realm. All the justices agreed that the King had this right and also that at common law every man may come upon his neighbour's land for the defence of the realm and may make bulwarks and trenches upon another's land with the same end in view. To save a city or town, a house next to one on fire may be pulled down, as may the suburbs of a city in time of war if such action should be required for the common safety. After excavations for saltpetre are completed, the King's servants must 'make the places in which they dig, so well and commodious to the owner as they were before' and when the threat of invasion, a public danger, is over 'the trenches and bulwarks ought to be removed, so that the owner shall not have prejudice in his inheritance'.

Samson v *Aitchison* [1912] AC 844 (Privy Council)

While the defendant's car was being driven by Albert, who was testing the vehicle on behalf of his mother, an intending purchaser of the car, due to Albert's negligence the car was involved in an accident in which the plaintiff received injuries. At the time of the accident the defendant was sitting at Albert's side.

Held, the defendant was liable in damages as he had not abandoned his right and duty to control the way in which the car was driven. (But see *Hewitt* v *Bonvin*.)

Sanderson v *Collins* [1904] 1 KB 628 (Court of Appeal)

The plaintiff lent a four-wheeled dog-cart to the defendant. Without the defendant's authority, his coachman took it out for his own purposes and negligently collided with a tramcar.

Held, the plaintiff could not recover the cost of repairing the vehicle from the defendant as, at the time of the accident, his coachman was not acting in the course of his employment. (But see *Aitchison* v *Page Motors Ltd.*)

Sayers v *Harlow Urban District Council* [1958] 2 All ER 342 (Court of Appeal)

The plaintiff put a penny in the slot and entered a cubicle in the defendants' public lavatory. As the handle was missing, she found that she was unable to re-open the door and after trying unsuccessfully for 15 minutes to attract attention she decided to climb over the door. In order to do this, she put her left foot on the lavatory seat and her right foot on the toilet roll and fixture, but the roll rotated and she fell to the ground and was injured.

Held, the plaintiff was entitled to damages as, in the circumstances, it was reasonable for her to attempt to climb out of the cubicle and the damage which she suffered was a natural and probable consequence of the defendants' negligence, but the amount of damages recoverable should be reduced by one-quarter as the plaintiff had been careless in depending on the toilet roll. (See also *Jones* v *Boyce.*)

Scally v *Southern Health and Social Services Board* [1991] 4 All ER 563 (House of Lords)

Statute required an employer to give his employees written particulars of the terms of their employment and made provision for recourse to an industrial tribunal by way of remedy for non-compliance.

Held, a breach by the employer of his statutory duty did not confer on the employee a civil right of action sounding in damages.

Scarsbrook v *Mason* [1961] 3 All ER 767

The plaintiffs were knocked down and injured as a result of the careless driving of a car in which the defendant was a passenger and one of a group who were jointly using the car for a trip to Southend. The defendant was not a guest, but an equal member of the party, having contributed 4s towards the cost of petrol.

Held, the members of the party were jointly and severally liable for the manner in which the car was driven (ie negligently) and the plaintiffs were entitled to damages against the defendant on the ground that the driver was acting as agent for each and all the members of the party. (See also *Samson* v *Aitchison.*)

Schneider v Eisovitch [1960] 1 All ER 169

The defendant was driving a car between Lyons and Paris when, due to his negligence, it left the road and crashed into a tree. The plaintiff who, together with her husband, was a passenger in the car, suffered physical injuries which made her unconscious, and her husband was killed instantly. On hearing of the accident, the plaintiff's brother-in-law and his wife at once flew from England to France to help the plaintiff and the plaintiff, believing that she was under a moral duty to do so, later undertook to pay their expenses out of any damages that she recovered. When the plaintiff had recovered consciousness she was told of her husband's death and suffered nervous shock which had 'quite serious consequences'. The plaintiff claimed, inter alia, damages for personal injuries.

Held, the amount awarded to her for special damage should include the expenses of her brother-in-law and his wife and damages for shock at her husband's death. (But see *Darbishire* v *Warran*.)

Scott v London and St Katherine Docks Co (1865) 3 H & C 596

A customs officer, the plaintiff, proved that when he was passing in front of the defendants' warehouse six bags of sugar fell upon him.

Held, 'where the thing is shewn to be under the management of the defendant or his servants, and the accident is such as in the ordinary course of things does not happen if those who have the management use proper care, it affords reasonable evidence, in the absence of explanation by the defendant, that the accident arose from want of care' (*per* ERLE CJ). (See also *Chaproniere* v *Mason*; but see *Stafford* v *Conti Commodity Services Ltd*.)

Scott v Shepherd (1773) 2 Wm Bl 892

The defendant threw a lighted squib from the street into a covered market which was crowded with people. The squib fell upon Yates' gingerbread stall and a bystander, one Willis, in order to protect himself and Yates' goods, seized the squib and threw it across the market on to the stall of Ryal who sold goods of a similar kind. With a view to protecting his goods Ryal threw the squib to another part of the building where it exploded in the plaintiff's face and put out one of his eyes.

Held, the plaintiff was entitled to damages as the natural and probable consequence of the defendant's unlawful act of throwing the squib was injury to somebody.

Sedleigh-Denfield v O'Callagan [1940] 3 All ER 349 (House of Lords)

The boundary between the appellant's premises and those of the respondents was a hedge and a ditch, both of which belonged to the respondents. Without informing the respondents, a trespasser laid a pipe in the ditch and some three years later this pipe, due to a misplaced protective grating or grid, became blocked and in consequence the appellant's garden was flooded. It appeared that one of the respondents' servants had cleared out the ditch twice yearly. The appellant claimed damages in nuisance.

Held, he would succeed because the respondents, who knew or ought to have known of the existence of the nuisance, permitted it to continue without taking reasonably prompt and efficient action to abate it. (See also *Leakey v National Trust.*)

Seligman v Docker [1948] 2 All ER 887

A landlord reserved exclusive rights of sporting and preserving game and due entirely to exceptional weather conditions there was an abnormal increase in the number of pheasants in the landlord's coverts. The tenant sought damages in respect of the injury which the birds did to his crops.

Held, as the landlord had not acted unreasonably, the tenant's action could not succeed. (But see *Davey v Harrow Corporation.*)

Shah v Standard Chartered Bank See Stern v Piper

Shapland v Palmer [1999] 3 All ER 50 (Court of Appeal)

The plaintiff suffered a whiplash injury when the defendant, driving a company car in the course of her employment, drove into the back of her car. Liability was never disputed, but on the last day of the three-year primary limitation period (under s11 of the Limitation Act 1980), the plaintiff issued a county court summons against the company, the defendant's employer. The summons was not served within the four-month period so these proceedings were struck out. The plaintiff now sued the defendant herself and asked the court to disapply the primary limitation period by exercising its discretion under s33 of the 1980 Act in her favour.

Held, it would do so; the action could proceed. 'I ... understand the *Walkley v Precision Forgings Ltd* [1979] 2 All ER 548 principle to exclude from s33 only actions which involve the same defendant and the same cause of action as was the subject of earlier, timeous proceedings. It follows that strictly it does not catch the plaintiff's second action here. That a cause of action against a personal defendant is not the same as one alleging vicarious liability on the part of a principal or employer is trite law. ... I ... rule that the s33 discretion arises in all cases save those which fall four-square within the *Walkley* principle. ... How ... should that discretion be exercised here? ... First and foremost it seems plain that the passage of time caused here by the abortive first proceedings occasioned this defendant no real prejudice whatever. ... Secondly ... when the summons was issued, there was no reason to doubt that a claim directed solely against the company was sufficient for the plaintiff's purpose. ... In short, having regard to all the various circumstances required by s33(3) to be brought into account in the exercise of our discretion, I conclude that it would be equitable, on the balance of prejudice which s33(1) requires to be struck, to disapply the limitation period' (*per* SIMON BROWN LJ). (See also *Hartley v Birmingham City District Council*; but see *Donovan v Gwentoys Ltd.*)

Sharpe v E T Sweeting & Son Ltd [1963] 2 All ER 455

The defendant building contractors contracted with the Corporation of Middlesbrough as independent contractors (ie, not as agents of the local authority) for the erection of some houses and in 1959 a concrete canopy over the front door of one of them fell upon and injured the plaintiff, the wife of the tenant. The canopy collapsed because of negligent construction by the defendants' servants and they (the defendants) could not reasonably have expected that there would be any intermediate examination likely to reveal the defect.

Held, the defendants were liable in respect of the plaintiff's injuries as the principles in *M'Alister (or Donoghue) v Stevenson* applied to this case. In other words, there was a sufficient proximity of relation between the plaintiff and the defendants for the defendants to owe her a duty of care and the fall of the canopy, and therefore the plaintiff's injuries, was due to the breach of this duty. (But see *Bottomley v Bannister* and *Dutton v Bognor Regis UDC*.)

Shiffman v Venerable Order of the Hospital of St John of Jerusalem [1936] 1 All ER 557

The defendants erected a casualty tent in Hyde Park at the request of the police and nearby a flagpole supported only by four guy ropes. While a sergeant, the only man on duty, who had been charged with the task of preventing interference with the flagpole was inside the tent assisting a casualty, the pole fell as a result of interference by children, and injured the plaintiff.

Held, the plaintiff was entitled to damages on the ground of negligence and the court could see no reason why the defendants should not also be liable under the rule in *Rylands v Fletcher*. (See also *Hale v Jennings Brothers*.)

Sidaway v Bethlem Royal Hospital Governors [1985] 1 All ER 643 (House of Lords)

The plaintiff agreed to have an operation on her spinal column in the defendant's hospital but the surgeon did not warn her of the risk (less than 1%) of damage to the spinal cord. The surgeon operated with due care and skill, but the spinal cord was damaged and the plaintiff was severely disabled. The plaintiff claimed that the surgeon's failure to warn her was a breach of duty.

Held, her claim would fail as the surgeon's non-disclosure of the risk accorded with a practice accepted as proper by a responsible body of neuro-surgical opinion. (See also *Gold v Haringey Health Authority*.)

Sim v Stretch [1936] 2 All ER 1237 (House of Lords)

The defendant sent this telegram to the plaintiff: 'Edith has resumed her service with us today. Please send her possessions and the money you borrowed, also her wages ...' In an action for libel the plaintiff argued that the words of the telegram were defamatory, that they suggested that, out of necessity, he had borrowed money from his housemaid and that he had failed to pay her her wages.

Held, the claim would fail as the words of the telegram were not reasonably capable of a defamatory meaning. The test to be applied is: 'Would the words tend to lower the plaintiff in the estimation of right-thinking members of society generally?' (*per* LORD ATKIN). (See also *Byrne* v *Deane* and *Berkoff* v *Burchill.*)

Simaan General Contracting Co v Pilkington Glass Ltd (No 2)
[1988] 1 All ER 791 (Court of Appeal)

The plaintiffs were main contractors for the erection of a building and the defendants' green glass was specified for the curtain walling. The plaintiffs subcontracted the erection of the curtain walling to another company which duly ordered the glass from the defendants. The glass supplied was defective and the building owner withheld payment from the plaintiffs until it was replaced: the plaintiffs sued for the resulting economic loss.

Held, their claim could not succeed as the defendants had not voluntarily assumed direct responsibility to the plaintiffs for the quality of the glass. Further, it would not be just and reasonable to impose on the defendants a duty of care not to make the plaintiffs' contract less profitable: the plaintiffs had a remedy against the subcontractor who in turn could claim against the defendants. (See also *Greater Nottingham Cooperative Society Ltd* v *Cementation Piling and Foundations Ltd.*)

Simpson v Thomson (1877) 3 App Cas 279 (House of Lords)

X insured two ships of Y's. The ships collided in the North Sea and, due to the negligence of the master of ship A, ship B was sunk. X paid Y under the insurance policy for the loss of B, but then sought to recover from Y as owner of the negligent ship A.

Held, the claim must fail. 'No precedent or authority has been found ... for an action against a wrongdoer ... except, on the part of one who had some property in, or possession of, the chattel injured' (*per* LORD PENZANCE). (See also *Electrochrome Ltd* v *Welsh Plastics Ltd.*)

Six Carpenters' Case, The (1610) 8 Rep 146a

Six carpenters entered the *Queen's Head* and ordered a 'quart of wine, and a pennyworth of bread, amounting to 8d and then they there did drink the said wine, and eat the bread, and upon request did refuse to pay for the same'. The question arose as to whether this refusal to pay rendered their original entry into the tavern tortious.

Held, it did not, as an omission cannot make a party a trespasser ab initio. (See also *Elias* v *Pasmore.*)

Slim v Daily Telegraph Ltd [1968] 1 All ER 497 (Court of Appeal)

The defendants published a letter from one of their readers which contained a statement which *might* have been capable of imputing dishonesty and insincerity to the plaintiffs. The defendants pleaded fair comment.

Held, allowing the defendants' appeal from a judgment awarding damages to the plaintiffs, the defence was entitled to succeed. If a person expresses an honest opinion about a matter of public interest, then, even though the words used might convey derogatory imputations, in the absence of malice no action for defamation will lie. 'The right to free speech is not to be whittled away by legal refinements, and newspapers should not be deterred from publishing letters for fear of libel actions. But the facts must be accurate, the opinion honestly held, and the comment fair ...' (per LORD DENNING MR). (See also *Lewis* v *Daily Telegraph Ltd* and *Telnikoff* v *Matusevitch*.)

Slipper v *British Broadcasting Corp* [1991] 1 All ER 165 (Court of Appeal)

The plaintiff detective chief superintendent alleged that, in a television film, the defendants had portrayed him as, inter alia, a ridiculous buffoon. The plaintiff brought one action for libel in respect of a press preview of the film and another in respect of its public broadcast. He contended that press reviews of the film, repeating the libel's defamatory sting, were relevant to the assessment of general damages in respect of the public broadcast.

Held, this claim would not be struck out. '... the questions raised on this appeal are, in my opinion: (i) did the reviews reproduce the sting of the libel? This is a question of fact for the jury. (ii) Did the defendants invite such reviews? The answer to this question depends on the facts concerning all the circumstances in which the preview was given to the press and, again, is a matter of fact for the jury. (iii) Did the defendants anticipate that such reviews would repeat the sting of the libel? It is at this point that the issue of natural and probable consequence or foreseeability arises. In my opinion this is a question of remoteness of damage and not liability and raises an issue of fact for the jury' (per STOCKER LJ). (See also *Weld-Blundell* v *Stephens*.)

Smith v *Baker (Charles) & Sons* [1891] AC 325 (House of Lords)

The plaintiff was employed by the defendants on the construction of a railway. He was engaged on drilling holes in rock and to his knowledge, while drilling was in progress, a crane on the top of the embankment was removing stones from the cutting. In spite of complaints by the workmen, without warning, the crane swung the stones over their heads. On one occasion some stones fell on the plaintiff and he claimed damages.

Held, he was entitled to succeed as the maxim volenti non fit injuria did not apply: the fact that he knew of the danger but nevertheless continued to do his work, notwithstanding the defendants' negligence, was not sufficient to defeat his claim as there was no evidence that he had voluntarily undertaken the risk of injury. (See also *Dann* v *Hamilton*.)

Smith v *Eric S Bush, Harris* v *Wyre Forest District Council* [1989] 2 All ER 514 (House of Lords)

In both cases the question arose whether a surveyor instructed by a mortgagee to value a house owed a duty of care to the prospective purchaser to carry out his valuation with reasonable skill and care and, if so, whether the surveyor's disclaimer of liability could be and had been effective.

Held, in the case of a typical house purchase, knowing that the purchaser would be relying on his valuation, the surveyor did owe the purchaser (but not subsequent purchasers) such a duty of care. In principle, a surveyor could exclude his liability by an express clause, but such a clause had to satisfy the requirement of reasonableness (see s2(2) of the Unfair Contract Terms Act 1977) and exclusion clauses in transactions of his kind failed that test. In both cases the purchasers recovered damages in negligence in respect of surveys carried out on the instructions of the mortgagee. 'It must, however, be remembered that this is a decision in respect of a dwelling house of modest value in which it is widely recognised by surveyors that purchasers are in fact relying on their care and skill. It will obviously be of general application in broadly similar circumstances. But I expressly reserve my position in respect of valuations of quite different types of property for mortgage purposes, such as industrial property, large blocks of flats or very expensive houses. In such cases it may well be that the general expectation of the behaviour of the purchaser is quite different ... and, in such circumstances with very much larger sums of money at stake, it may be reasonable for the surveyors valuing on behalf of those who are providing the finance either to exclude or limit their liability to the purchaser' (*per* LORD GRIFFITHS). (Approved: *Yianni v Edwin Evans & Sons.*)

Smith v Giddy [1904] 2 KB 448

Ash and elm trees growing on the defendant's land overhung that of the plaintiff and interfered with the growth of his fruit trees.

Held, apart from his right to cut back the defendant's trees, the plaintiff was entitled to maintain an action for damages for nuisance. (See also *Fay v Prentice*; but see *Mills v Brooker.*)

Smith v Leech Brain & Co Ltd [1961] 3 All ER 1159

In 1950 a galvaniser employed by the defendants was splashed by a piece of molten metal and he later contracted cancer from which he died. It was found that the defendants had been negligent and that the burn was the promoting agency, promoting cancer in tissues which already had a pre-malignant condition as a result of the plaintiff having worked at a gas works.

Held, the man's widow was entitled to damages under the Law Reform (Miscellaneous Provisions) Act 1934 and the Fatal Accidents Acts 1846 to 1908, as the type of injury which the man suffered was reasonably foreseeable, although the defendants could not have foreseen the ultimate consequences. 'The test is not whether these defendants could reasonably have foreseen that a burn would cause cancer and that [the man] would die. The question is whether these defendants could reasonably foresee the type of injury which he suffered, namely, the burn' (*per* LORD PARKER CJ). (But see *Doughty v Turner Manufacturing Co Ltd*; see also *Robinson v Post Office.*)

Smith v Littlewoods Organisation Ltd [1987] 1 All ER 710 (House of Lords)

The defendants bought a cinema intending to demolish it and build a supermarket. They took possession on 31 May; on 5 July a fire was started in the cinema deliberately by third parties, and it spread to and damaged the plaintiff's adjoining premises. The plaintiffs claimed damages for negligence.

Held, their claim would fail. While the defendants were under a general duty to exercise reasonable care to ensure that their premises were not a source of danger to neighbouring properties, the event which occurred had not, on the facts, been reasonably foreseeable. (See also *Lamb v London Borough of Camden*.)

Smith v London and South Western Railway Co (1870) LR 6 CP 14

The defendants' railway passed within 200 yards of the plaintiff's cottage. There was a grass strip and a hedge bordering the line and the plaintiff's cottage was separated from this hedge by a stubble-field and a road. During an exceptionally dry summer, the defendants trimmed the grass and the hedge but did not clear away the trimmings. About a fortnight later, shortly after two trains had passed, a fire broke out on the grass strip and, blown by a strong wind, the flames crossed the stubble-field and the road and destroyed the plaintiff's cottage.

Held, the defendants had been negligent and were liable for the injury which the plaintiff suffered as it was a natural consequence of the fire. It mattered not whether such a consequence could have been foreseen by a reasonable man. (See also *Polemis & Furness, Withy & Co Ltd, Re*; but see *Overseas Tankship (UK) Ltd v Morts Dock & Engineering Co Ltd*.)

Smith v Scott [1972] 3 All ER 645

The plaintiff householder sought an injunction against, inter alia, the Lewisham London Borough Council to restrain it from allowing its tenants in a neighbouring house to commit nuisance by damage to the plaintiff's property and by excessive noise. The council had placed the tenants in the neighbouring house while finding them permanent accommodation.

Held, (1) the council was not liable for nuisance since it had not expressly or impliedly authorised the nuisance. (2) The council was not liable under *Rylands v Fletcher* (qv) since a landlord cannot be regarded as the 'controller' of his tenants. (3) The council owed the plaintiff no duty of care in selecting its tenants since the law relating to the liability of owners of land cannot be reshaped by a reference to the duty principle. (See also *Baxter v Camden London Borough Council*; but see *Attorney-General v Corke*.)

Smith v Stages [1989] 1 All ER 833 (House of Lords)

A peripatetic lagger was working for his employers (the second defendants) at a power station in the Midlands. Urgent work was required at another power station in Wales: the lagger and another employee (the first defendant) were sent to carry it out and they were given eight hours' pay for travelling time in each direction, the mode of travel being left to their discretion. They travelled in the first defendant's car and, on the return journey, due to the first defendant's negligence, they crashed and the lagger sustained serious injuries.

Held, the second defendants were vicariously liable as the first defendant had been acting in the course of his employment. 'The paramount rule is that an employee travelling on the highway will be acting in the course of his employment if, and only if, he is at the material time going about his employer's business. One must not confuse the duty to turn up for one's work with the concept of already being "on duty" while travelling to it' (*per* LORD LOWRY). (Applied *Canadian Pacific Railway Co v Lockhart*.)

Smith Kline & French Laboratories Ltd v *Long* [1988] 3 All ER 887 (Court of Appeal)

The deceit of the defendant had the result of permanently depriving the plaintiffs of their goods.

Held, applying *Doyle v Olby (Ironmongers) Ltd* principles, by way of damages the plaintiffs were entitled to the market value of the goods, not the cost of replacing them.

Smith New Court Securities Ltd v *Scrimgeour Vickers (Asset Management) Ltd* [1996] 4 All ER 769 (House of Lords)

The plaintiffs' purchase of shares in Ferranti having been induced by the defendants' fraudulent misrepresentation and a previous unrelated fraud on Ferranti having been discovered after the shares had been purchased but before the plaintiffs sold them, the question arose as to how the plaintiffs' damages were to be assessed. The discovery of the unrelated fraud led to a dramatic fall in the value of Ferranti shares.

Held, the plaintiffs were entitled to the difference between the amount that they paid for the shares and the amount which they received on their sale. (Applied: *Doyle v Olby (Ironmongers) Ltd*.)

Smoker v *London Fire and Civil Defence Authority; Wood* v *British Coal Corp* [1991] 2 All ER 449 (House of Lords)

In both cases the question arose whether benefits payable under a contributory pension scheme were deductible from damages payable by the defendant employer to a plaintiff employee who had suffered loss of earnings as a result of an accident at work caused by the employer's negligence.

Held, they were not. '... the plaintiff has bought his pension, which is, in the words of Lord Reid [in *Parry v Cleaver*], "the fruit, through insurance, of all the money which was set aside in the past in respect of his past work." The fruit cannot be appropriated by the tortfeasor' (*per* LORD TEMPLEMAN).

Sochacki v *Sas* [1947] 1 All ER 344

Without any negligence on his part, a fire broke out in the plaintiff's room and spread to and destroyed the defendant's furniture in another room in the same house. The building was owned by the defendant and the plaintiff was a lodger. It seemed probable that the fire was caused by a spark from the fire which the plaintiff had left burning in the fireplace in his room. The defendant counterclaimed for damages.

Held, he was not entitled to succeed. The doctrine res ipsa loquitur was inapplicable, as was that of *Rylands* v *Fletcher* because, by having a fire in his grate, the plaintiff was using his room in an ordinary and natural way. (See also *Fish* v *Kapur*; but see *Crowhurst* v *Amersham Burial Board*.)

Sole v *W J Hallt Ltd* [1973] 1 All ER 1032

The plaintiff, a plasterer, orally contracted with the defendants to fix plasterboards to form ceilings in a house being built by the defendants on their own land. The plaintiff worked on an unguarded stair. While looking up at the ceiling, he stepped back and fell into the stair-well.

Held, the plaintiff could claim both in tort under s2(1) and in contract under s5(1) of the Occupiers' Liability Act 1957. The defendants were in breach of the common duty of care by not providing safety boards to cover the stair-well, since the plaintiff would have used them had they been provided. But the plaintiff was partly to blame for the accident. In contract his negligence in stepping back without looking broke the chain of causation. But in tort he was entitled to succeed as to two-thirds of his total damages.

Somasundaram v *M Julius Melchior & Co* [1989] 1 All ER 129 (Court of Appeal)

Originally intending to plead not guilty to a charge of unlawful and malicious wounding, the plaintiff changed his story and, in the light of counsel's advice, his plea. Following conviction in the Crown Court, he sued his solicitors for negligence alleging, inter alia, that they had overpersuaded him to change his story.

Held, his action had properly been struck out as no such action lies against a barrister or a solicitor in respect of the conduct of either civil or criminal proceedings if, as here, it involves an attack on the decision of a court of competent jurisdiction. (But see *Saif Ali* v *Sydney Mitchell & Co*.)

Sorrell v *Smith* [1925] AC 700 (House of Lords)

A trade union of retail newsagents wished to limit the number of retail newspaper shops in a certain area. This policy was enforced by inducing the members of the union to withdraw their custom from any wholesaler who supplied newspapers to a retailer who had opened a new shop within that particular area without first obtaining the union's consent. The appellant, who was a member of the union, obtained his supplies from Ritchie Brothers, but as they were also supplying newcomers who had opened shops without the union's permission, at the request of the union he transferred his custom to Watson & Sons. The respondents, who were the circulating managers of the principal London daily newspapers, threatened to withhold supplies to Watson & Sons unless the appellant returned his business to Ritchie Brothers. The appellant sought to restrain the respondents from interfering with his contractual relations with Watson & Sons.

Held, the action would fail as the respondents had not committed or threatened to commit any wrong. A combination of two or more persons for the purpose of injuring a man in his trade is unlawful and, if that man thereby suffers damage, is actionable. However, if the real purpose of the combination is not to injure another but to forward or defend the trade of those who enter into it, provided that purpose is not attained by illegal means, no wrong is committed and no action will lie, although damage to that other ensues. (See also *Rookes v Barnard*.)

South Australia Asset Management Corp v York Montague Ltd; United Bank of Kuwait plc v Prudential Property Services Ltd; Nykredit Mortgage Bank plc v Edward Erdman Group Ltd
[1996] 3 All ER 365 (House of Lords)

All three appeals raised a common question of principle: What is the extent of the liability of a valuer who has provided a lender with a negligent overvaluation of the property offered as security for a loan? The facts had two common features: first, if the lender had known the true value of the property, he would not have lent; second, a fall in the property market after the date of the valuation greatly increased the loss which the lender eventually suffered.

Held, the correct approach to the assessment of damages was to ascertain what element of the loss suffered as a result of the transaction going ahead was attributable to the inaccuracy of the information by comparing the valuation negligently provided and the correct property value at the time of the valuation, ie the figure which a reasonable valuer, using the information available at the relevant time, would have put forward as the amount which the property was most likely to fetch if sold on the open market. The valuer would not be liable for the amount of the lender's loss attributable to the fall in the property market. (Distinguished: *Banque Financière de la Cité SA v Westgate Insurance Co Ltd*; applied in *Nykredit Mortgage Bank plc v Edward Erdman Group Ltd (No 2)* and *Platform Home Loans Ltd v Oyston Shipways Ltd*.)

South Hetton Coal Co Ltd v North-Eastern News Association Ltd
[1894] 1 QB 133 (Court of Appeal)

The plaintiffs, a corporation, owned a number of cottages in connection with their collieries and it was found that the defendants had published a libel in their paper by suggesting that most of the plaintiffs' cottages were in a highly insanitary state and unfit for habitation.

Held, the plaintiffs were entitled to damages. (But see *Derbyshire County Council v Times Newspapers Ltd.*)

South Staffordshire Water Co v Sharman [1896] 2 QB 44

The plaintiffs employed the defendant to clean out a pool of water on their land. In the course of this work, the defendant found two gold rings in the mud at the bottom of the pool. The real owner of the rings could not be found.

Held, the defendant should pass the rings to the plaintiffs. (But see *Hannah v Peel.*)

Southwark London Borough Council v Williams [1971] 2 All ER 175 (Court of Appeal)

The defendants were homeless. They occupied empty houses owned by the plaintiff Council, which brought proceedings for possession.

Held, the defence of necessity is not available on the ground of homelessness. Even if the Council were in breach of their duty to provide temporary accommodation under s21(1) of the National Assistance Act 1948, this did not entitle the defendants to take the law into their own hands, the proper machinery under the statute being an approach to the Minister.

Spittle v Bunney [1988] 3 All ER 1031 (Court of Appeal)

As a result of the defendant's negligent driving, his van mounted the pavement, injured three-year-old Kate and killed her mother. The plaintiffs, the administrators of the mother's estate, brought proceedings under the Fatal Accidents Act 1976 and the judge awarded £47,500.

Held, when assessing damages for loss of a mother's services on the basis of hiring a nanny, a judge ought to take account of the fact that a child needed a nanny less as he got older and reduce the award accordingly. Here, adopting this approach, a jury would not have awarded more than £25,000 and the damages would therefore be reduced to that amount. (See also *Corbett v Barking Havering and Brentwood Health Authority.*)

Spring v Guardian Assurance plc [1994] 3 All ER 129 (House of Lords)

The plaintiff was dismissed by the defendants who gave such a bad reference to a prospective employer that it refused to have anything to do with him. In the plaintiff's action for damages the trial judge found, inter alia, that the defendants had been negligent in preparing the reference.

Held, the plaintiff's action would be successful as, inter alia, an employer who provided a reference in respect of an employee, whether past or present, to a prospective future employer ordinarily owed a duty of care to the employee in respect of the preparation of the reference and was liable in damages to the employee in respect of economic loss suffered by him by reason of the reference being prepared negligently. Although it did not add anything to the duty of care arising in negligence, such a duty could also be expressed as arising from an implied term of the contract of employment. 'I consider that in the instant case damage stemming from the defendants' careless mis-statement when giving a reference *was* foreseeable and that the proximity between the defendants and the plaintiff imposed a duty of care on the former for the protection of the latter.' (*per* LORD LOWRY). 'I wish ... to add that it does not necessarily follow that, because the employer owes ... a duty of care to his employee, he also owes a duty of care to the recipient of the reference' (*per* LORD GOFF OF CHIEVELEY). (Applied: *Hedley Byrne & Co Ltd v Heller and Partners Ltd.*)

Stafford v *Conti Commodity Services Ltd* [1981] 1 All ER 691

The plaintiff, an investor on the unpredictable London commodities futures market, gave the defendant brokers a substantial sum to invest. The defendants gave the plaintiff advice, but he often rejected it, usually making his own decisions. They carried out 46 transactions on the plaintiff's behalf, but only 10 of them made a profit. In an action for damages the plaintiff relied on the doctrine res ipsa loquitur – the losses showed that there had been a failure by the defendants to exercise due care and diligence.

Held, his action would be dismissed as an error of judgment in such circumstances would not necessarily amount to negligence and, in any case, as the plaintiff usually made his own decisions, it could not be said that his losses had been caused by any bad advice by the defendants. Losses in such an unpredictable market could not of themselves provide evidence of negligence on the part of a broker. (See also *Bolam v Friern Hospital Management Committee*; but see *Scott v London and St Katherine Docks Co.*)

Stanley v *Powell* [1891] 1 QB 86

The defendant was a member of a pheasant shooting party and the plaintiff was employed to carry cartridges and such game as was shot. Without any negligence on his part, one of the defendant's shots glanced off the bough of a tree and struck the plaintiff, who sought to recover damages in respect of the injury which he suffered as a result.

Held, the defendant was entitled to judgment as he had not been negligent and was not liable for trespass to the person as the wound was inflicted accidentally. (See also *National Coal Board v J E Evans & Co (Cardiff) Ltd.*)

Stanley v *Saddique* [1991] 1 All ER 529 (Court of Appeal)

In 1982 the plaintiff's mother left her husband and three young children and went to live with the plaintiff's father. In 1984, the year after the plaintiff's birth, the mother was killed in a motor accident for which the defendant admitted liability. Shortly afterwards the plaintiff's father met and married Tracey. The plaintiff claimed damages under the Fatal Accidents Act 1976 for loss of dependency on his mother and the judge found that Tracey provided 'excellent motherly services to the plaintiff ... of a higher quality than could foreseeably have been expected to have been provided by the plaintiff's mother ... [which] would have been of an indifferent quality and lacking in continuity.'

Held, in assessing damages, by virtue of s4 of the 1976 Act the court had to disregard the fact that the plaintiff was now living in a better home. However, in view of the mother's apparent unreliability, the multiplier/multiplicand approach to the calculation of damages was inappropriate. Instead, damages should be assessed on a jury award basis, making a proper discount for the lack of security and continuity in the provision of the mother's services. (See also *Watson v Willmott*; but see *Hayden v Hayden*.)

Stansbie v Troman [1948] 1 All ER 599 (Court of Appeal)

The plaintiff, a decorator, was doing some work under contract in the defendant's house. While the defendant and his wife were at work, the plaintiff, who was then alone in the house, left the front door unlocked for about two hours while he went to get some wallpaper. During this period a thief walked in and stole some jewellery. The plaintiff sued to recover his charges and the defendant counter-claimed for damages for negligence.

Held, the defendant was entitled to succeed as the entry of the thief was the direct consequence of the plaintiff's negligent act.

Stephens v Myers [1830] 4 C & P 349

In view of his conduct, it was resolved that the defendant, who was a member of a parish meeting, should be turned out. The defendant thereupon threatened to pull the chairman, the plaintiff, out of the chair and advanced with clenched fist with the apparent intention of carrying out his threat. He was stopped by a churchwarden who was sitting next but one to the plaintiff. The plaintiff claimed damages for assault.

Held, he was entitled to recover as the defendant was advancing with intent to strike him. (See also *R v St George*.)

Stern v Piper [1996] 3 All ER 385 (Court of Appeal)

The defendant's newspaper published an article containing quotations from an affirmation prepared in connection with a pending High Court action for debt against the plaintiff. In the plaintiff's action for libel, the defendant pleaded justification by reference exclusively to the statements in the affirmation and not the underlying facts.

Held, this plea of justification would be struck out: the statements were essentially hearsay and therefore within the repetition rule. (In *Shah v Standard Chartered Bank* [1998] 4 All ER 155 HIRST LJ said: 'I am satisfied that [the repetition rule] is a rule of law which governs not only meaning, but also the pleading and proof of a defence of justification. *Stern v Piper* is a very good illustration ... Moreover, I consider that the repetition rule reflects a fundamental canon of legal policy ... that words must be interpreted, and the imputations they contain justified, by reference to the underlying allegations of fact and not merely by reliance upon some second-hand report or assertion of them.')

Stovin v Wise (Norfolk County Council, third party)
[1996] 3 All ER 801 (House of Lords)

The plaintiff sustained serious injuries when his motor cycle collided with the defendant's car as it (the defendant's car) emerged from a side road. A bank of earth on British Rail land restricted the defendant's view to about 100 feet. The highway authority (the council) had offered to remove part of the bank at its own expense, but by the time of the accident (11 months after the offer had been made) British Rail had not responded and no action had been taken. In his action for damages the plaintiff alleged that the council had been in breach of its statutory duty to maintain the highway by virtue of s41 of the Highways Act 1980. This claim was rejected since the bank was not part of the highway. However, the trial judge and the Court of Appeal found that the council owed the plaintiff a duty of care at common law and that the council had been in breach of this duty. Had this decision been correct?

Held, it had not. 'I think that the minimum pre-conditions for basing a duty of care upon the existence of a statutory power, if it can be done at all, are, first, that it would in the circumstances have been irrational not to have exercised the power, so that there was in effect a public law duty to act, and secondly, that there are exceptional grounds for holding that the policy of the statute requires compensation to be paid to persons who suffer loss because the power was not exercised. ... Since the only basis for [a duty of care requiring the council to take steps to improve the junction] is the [council's] statutory powers ... to carry out works of improvement with the consent of British Rail, I will start by asking whether, in the light of what the council knew or ought to have known about the junction, it would have had a duty in public law to undertake the work. This requires that it would have been irrational not to exercise its discretion to do so. ... There was no suggestion [that the council's] was an unreasonable, let alone irrational, attitude to take. It seems to me, therefore, that the question of whether anything should be done about the junction was at all times firmly within the area of the council's discretion. As they were therefore not under a public law duty to do the work, the first condition for the imposition of a duty of care was not satisfied. But even if it were, I do not think that the second condition would be satisfied. Assuming that the [council] ought, as a matter of public law, to have done the work, I do not think that there are any grounds upon which it can be said that the public law duty should give rise to an obligation to compensate persons who have suffered loss because it was not performed. There is no question here of reliance on the council having improved the junction. Everyone could see that it was still the same. [The plaintiff] was not arbitrarily denied a benefit which was routinely provided to others. In respect of the junction, he was treated in exactly the same way as any other road user' (*per* LORD HOFFMANN). (See also *Capital and Counties plc v Hampshire County Council*.)

Stubbings v Webb [1993] 1 All ER 322 (House of Lords)

In August 1987, when over 30, the respondent issued a writ against her adoptive father and brother claiming damages for mental illness and psychological disturbance allegedly caused by the appellants' abuse of her between the ages of two and 14. It was not until September 1984 that she appreciated that her present problems might be linked with her experiences as a child. The appellants contended that her action (for trespass to the person) was statute-barred.

Held, this was the case. '[The phrase] "breach of duty" ... lying in juxtaposition with "negligence" and "nuisance" carries with it the implication of a breach of duty of care not to cause personal injury, rather than an obligation not to infringe any legal right of another person ... cases of deliberate assault ... are not actions for breach of duty within the meaning of s11(1) of the 1980 Act ... It thus follows that the respondent's causes of action against both appellants were subject to a six-year limitation period. This period was suspended during her infancy but commenced to run when she attained her majority: see s28 of the 1980 Act. This period expired many years before she issued her writ ... There are no provisions for extending this period and her actions are therefore statute-barred and cannot proceed' (*per* LORD GRIFFITHS). (See also *Letang v Cooper.*)

Sturge v Hackett [1962] 3 All ER 166 (Court of Appeal)

The defendant, a tenant of a flat in Henbury Manor, attached a paraffin rag to the end of a stick, lit it and, while standing on the roof of the porch, applied it to the bottom of a sparrows' nest in a part of the premises of which he was the occupier. The nest caught fire and a piece of straw from the nest was blown up into a crevice and the house was burnt down.

Held, the starting point of the relevant fire was the sparrows' nest (not the paraffin rag) and the fire which caused the damage was therefore started on, and escaped from, premises of which the defendant was occupier. The fire in the nest was started negligently and it followed that the defendant was liable as occupier for damage caused by its escape, quite apart from his liability as the actual person whose own negligent act started the fire. (See also *Musgrove v Pandelis.*)

Sturges v Bridgman (1879) 11 ChD 852 (Court of Appeal)

A confectioner and a physician occupied adjoining premises. In connection with his business for more than 20 years the confectioner used two large pestles and mortars and the noise and vibration had not seemed to the physician to be a nuisance until he built a consulting room at the end of his garden against the wall of the confectioner's kitchen in which the pestles and mortars were operated. The physician sought an injunction to restrain the use of the pestles and mortars in such a manner as to cause him annoyance.

Held, he would succeed. The confectioner could not plead that he was protected by prescription as until the consulting room was built there had been no actionable nuisance. (See also *Liverpool Corporation v H. Coghill & Son Ltd* and *Miller v Jackson.*)

Sun Life Assurance Co of Canada v W H Smith & Son Ltd (1933) 150 LT 211 (Court of Appeal)

The defendants, who were newsagents, displayed a poster which contained a libel of the plaintiffs. The poster had been supplied to the defendants by a third party and they did not know that its contents were defamatory.

Held, the plaintiffs were entitled to judgment. In such a case, the jury should be asked: (i) did the defendant know, or (ii) ought he to have known, ie if he carried on his business carefully, that the publication was one which was likely to contain a libel? (See also *Vizetelly v Mudie's Select Library Ltd.*)

Sutcliffe v *Pressdram Ltd* [1990] 1 All ER 269 (Court of Appeal)

The plaintiff wife of 'the Yorkshire Ripper' was awarded libel damages of £600,000 against the defendant publishers of *Private Eye*. The defendants appealed.

Held, the jury's award was so substantially in excess of any sum that could reasonably have been thought appropriate to compensate the plaintiff, even allowing for the fact that she was entitled to aggravated damages, that the award would be set aside and a new trial ordered on the issue of damages only. (See also *Rantzen* v *Mirror Group Newspapers (1986) Ltd*.)

Sutcliffe v *Thackrah* [1974] 1 All ER 859 (House of Lords)

The plaintiff appointed the defendants as the architects for the purposes of a building contract between the plaintiff as building owner and a firm of contractors. The defendants issued interim certificates in respect of work done by the contractors, and the plaintiff paid the contractors the sums so certified. The plaintiff, having discovered that the interim certificates covered much defective work, sued the defendants for negligence.

Held, on a question of law, that an architect appointed as such for the purposes of a standard RIBA building contract owes a duty of care to his client in respect of loss caused by his negligent over-certification in interim certificates for payment. While an action in negligence does not lie against an arbitrator for negligence in making his award, the defendants did not act as an arbitrator, for there was no reference of a dispute to them and no agreement to be bound by their decisions. 'Each case will depend upon its own facts and circumstances, and upon the particular provisions of the relevant contract' (per LORD MORRIS). Semble, an expert employed to make a valuation of property for the purposes of sale is not without more to be treated as an arbitrator. (See also *Arenson* v *Casson, Beckman Rutley & Co.*)

Sutherland Shire Council v *Heyman* (1985) 60 ALR 1 (High Court of Australia)

The plaintiffs claimed against the defendant authority the loss or damage represented by the inadequacy of the foundations of their house, ie the cost of remedying a structural defect which existed when they acquired it.

Held, declining to follow *Anns* v *Merton London Borough Council*, their claim could not succeed. In such circumstances a duty of care could only be based on the principle of reliance and there was nothing in the ordinary relationship of a local authority, as statutory supervisor of building operations, and the purchaser of a defective building, capable of giving rise to such a duty. 'It is preferable in my view, that the law should develop novel categories of negligence incrementally and by analogy with established categories, rather than by a massive extension of a prima facie duty of care restrained only by indefinable "considerations which ought to negative, or to reduce or limit the scope of the duty or the class of person to whom it is owed" ' (per BRENNAN J). (See also *Murphy* v *Brentwood District Council*.)

Swingcastle Ltd v Alastair Gibson [1991] 2 All ER 353 (House of Lords)

The respondents lent £10,000 on the basis of the appellant's negligent valuation of the borrowers' house at £18,000. The mortgage interest rate was 36.5% or, in default, 45.6%. The borrowers defaulted and the respondents sold the house for £12,000 leaving a shortfall, including default rate interest, of £7,136.41. The respondents sought to recover this sum from the appellant, contending that it was the loss caused by his negligence.

Held, the respondents were entitled to be placed in the same position as if the negligence had not occurred. If the appellant had not been negligent, the respondents would not have made the loan but would have employed their money elsewhere. The interest element of their damages would therefore be assessed at 12%. 'The fallacy of the [respondents'] case is that they have been trying to obtain from the [appellant] compensation for the borrowers' failure and not the proper damages for the [appellant's] negligence' (*per* LORD LOWRY). (See also *Perry* v *Sidney Phillips & Son.*)

Swordheath Properties Ltd v Tabet [1979] 1 All ER 241 (Court of Appeal)

A county court judge found that the plaintiffs were entitled to an order for possession of their residential property, but declined to award damages for trespass against the two defendants as they (the plaintiffs) had not adduced any evidence that they could or would have relet the premises if the defendants had not been in occupation.

Held, such evidence was not required and the plaintiffs were entitled by way of damages to the proper letting value of the property for the material period.

Taittinger v Allbev Ltd [1994] 4 All ER 75 (Court of Appeal)

In England, the defendants produced and marketed a non-alcoholic drink which they called 'Elderflower Champagne' and they sold it in bottles the size, colour and shape usually associated with champagne. The plaintiffs, French champagne producers, brought an action in passing off.

Held, they were entitled to an injunction, both at common law and under Community law. 'I do not think the defendants' product would reduce the ... plaintiffs' sales in any significant and direct way. But this is not ... the end of the matter. The ... plaintiffs' reputation and goodwill in the description "Champagne" derive not only from the quality of their wine and its glamorous associations, but also from the very singularity and exclusiveness of the description, the absence of qualifying epithets and imitative descriptions. Any product which is not Champagne but is allowed to describe itself as such must inevitably, in my view, erode the singularity and exclusiveness of the description "Champagne" and so cause the ... plaintiffs damage of an insidious but serious kind' (*per* SIR THOMAS BINGHAM MR). (Applied: *Erven Warnink BV* v *J Townend & Sons (Hull) Ltd.*)

Targett v Torfaen Borough Council [1992] 3 All ER 27 (Court of Appeal)

The plaintiff was tenant of a house designed and built by the defendants: access was by two flights of steps which had no handrail or immediate lighting. After dark, the plaintiff fell on the steps and injured his leg.

Held, the defendants were liable as they were in breach of their duty of care, even though the plaintiff had known of the dangerous defects. On the facts, it had not been unreasonable for the plaintiff to run the risk of injury by using the steps, but he could have taken greater care for his own safety and his damages would be reduced by 25% on account of his contributory negligence. (See also *Denny v Supplies & Transport Co Ltd*.)

Tarry v Ashton (1876) 1 QBD 314

The defendant was in occupation of a house from the front of which a heavy lamp projected over the pavement. As the lamp was becoming dangerous the defendant employed an independent contractor, one Chappell, an experienced gasfitter, to repair it. Nevertheless, as a result of Chappell's negligent work, the lamp fell down and injured the plaintiff.

Held, the plaintiff was entitled to damages as the defendant was in breach of his duty to make the lamp reasonably safe. (See also *Bower v Peate*; but see *Noble v Harrison* and *Mint v Good*.)

Taylor v Serious Fraud Office [1998] 4 All ER 801 (House of Lords)

Money involved in a fraud had passed through the plaintiffs' hands. When investigating the fraud, the defendants sought and obtained statements from the Isle of Man Attorney-General and the Law Society. The plaintiffs were not amongst those charged with conspiracy to defraud. However, in the course of those proceedings, honouring their obligation to disclose to the defence all unused material, the defendants sent the statements to the defence solicitors. The solicitors disclosed the statements to the plaintiffs and they sought damages for libel.

Held, their action could not succeed: the statements were protected by absolute immunity. 'In recent years the procedure has developed whereby very full disclosure is given to the defendant in a criminal case, so that he will become aware, and others may become aware, of what has been said by investigators and those who speak to them in the course of the investigation which preceded the prosecution. Therefore, just as the preliminary examination of a witness by a party's solicitor out of court is a step towards the administration of justice which requires to be protected, I consider that the investigation of a suspected crime is a step towards the administration of justice so that the protection of absolute privilege should be given to those who, in the course of their public duty in investigating a suspected crime, speak or write to persons who may be able to provide relevant information, and to such persons in respect of what they say or write to the investigators, and to the giving of information by investigators to their colleagues who are also concerned with the investigation' (*per* LORD HUTTON). (See also *Evans v London Hospital Medical College*.)

Telnikoff v Matusevitch [1991] 4 All ER 817 (House of Lords)

The plaintiff, a Russian emigré, wrote an article for the *Daily Telegraph* critical of the BBC's

Russian service. The defendant, also a Russian emigré, had a letter published in the same newspaper in which he indicated that the article was racialist and anti-semetic. The plaintiff sued for libel and the defendant pleaded fair comment on a matter of public interest. In reply, the plaintiff alleged that the defendant had been actuated by express malice.

Held, the question whether the letter constituted pure comment or contained defamatory statements of fact should have been left to the jury, without reference to the article. On the facts, there was no evidence of express malice and the plaintiff had failed to discharge the burden of proving that the defendant did not honestly hold the belief which he had expressed in his letter. (See also *Slim* v *Daily Telegraph Ltd*.)

Tetley v *Chitty* [1986] 1 All ER 663

Medway Borough Council granted planning permission for a go-cart track on its land and subsequently a seven-year lease of the land to a go-cart club. Go-cart noise could be heard in the plaintiffs' houses and they sought damages and an injunction against, inter alia, the council.

Held, their claims would be successful. The council were liable in nuisance and, in the circumstances, damages alone would have been a wholly insufficient remedy. (But see *Kennaway* v *Thompson*.)

Thake v *Maurice* [1986] 1 All ER 497 (Court of Appeal)

As a couple did not wish to have any more children, in 1975 the husband had a vasectomy: the defendant surgeon did not warn them of the small risk of the husband again becoming fertile. In 1978 the wife became pregnant and the couple claimed damages for, inter alia, negligence.

Held, their action would be successful as the failure of the defendant to give his usual warning was a breach of his duty of care to the couple. Even though the baby when born was healthy, the damages awarded included compensation for the discomfort and pain of a normal pregnancy and delivery. (But see *Gold* v *Haringey Health Authority*.)

Theaker v *Richardson* [1962] 1 All ER 299 (Court of Appeal)

The defendant wrote a letter which was highly defamatory of the plaintiff, enclosed and sealed it in a cheap manilla envelope addressed by typewriter to the plaintiff and put it through her letter box. Believing that the envelope contained an election address, the plaintiff's husband opened the envelope and read the letter. The defendant's allegations were without foundation and in an action for libel the jury found that the defendant anticipated that someone other than the plaintiff would open and read the letter and that it was a natural and probable consequence of the defendant's writing and delivery of the letter that the plaintiff's husband would open and read it. In view of these findings the trial judge properly directed that there had been publication of the libel and the jury assessed damages at £500.

Held, the jury were not perverse in their findings and there was therefore no reason why the verdict in favour of the plaintiff should be set aside. Although there was no evidence that the plaintiff's husband believed any of the highly scurrilous accusations made by the defendant and although the jury's award of £500 by way of damages was 'on the high side' (*per* PEARSON LJ), the assessment of damages was not wholly out of proportion to the gravity of the libel and the court would not interfere with it. (See also *Delacroix v Thevenot*; but see *Sutcliffe v Pressdram Ltd*.)

Thomas v Bradbury, Agnew & Co Ltd [1906] 2 KB 627 (Court of Appeal)

The plaintiff published a book entitled *Fifty Years of Fleet Street,* and *Punch,* which was owned by the defendants, published a very critical review of the work. The plaintiff sued for libel and the defence was fair comment.

Held, the plaintiff was entitled to judgment as there was evidence that the writer of the review was actuated by malice towards him. (But see *Lyon v Daily Telegraph Ltd*.)

Thomas v Brighton Health Authority See Wells v Wells

Thomas v Bunn [1991] 1 All ER 193 (House of Lords)

In an action for damages for personal injuries sustained by the respondent in a road traffic accident caused by the appellant's negligence, an interlocutory judgment was entered for damages to be assessed. Did interest on the judgment, pursuant to s17 of the Judgments Act 1838, run from the date of the interlocutory judgment or from the date on which damages were assessed and final judgment entered?

Held, in split trials such as this interest ran only from the date of final judgment.

Thomson (D C) & Co Ltd v Deakin [1952] 2 All ER 361 (Court of Appeal)

The plaintiffs, printers and publishers, required all their employees to undertake not to become members of a trade union and dismissed one who disregarded this undertaking. In view of this, a strike by the other members of this union employed by the plaintiffs was called and help was requested from other unions. The company which supplied the plaintiffs with paper noticed that their drivers were reluctant to deliver further supplies to the plaintiffs and maintained that they (the company) were prevented from continuing to perform their contract to do so 'by the action of trade unions'. They decided that in the prevailing situation they would not require their employees to handle paper for the plaintiffs, who thereupon sought an injunction to restrain the unions from causing or procuring this alleged breach of contract.

Held, they would fail as they had not succeeded in showing that the unions, with actual knowledge of the contract in question and with the intention of damaging the plaintiffs, had, by means of a wrongful act, persuaded or procured the employees of the company which supplied the plaintiffs with paper to make it impossible for that company to carry out its contractual obligations. (But see *GWK Ltd v Dunlop Rubber Co Ltd* and the Trade Union and Labour Relations Act 1974, ss13 and 29.)

Thorogood v *Van Den Berghs and Jurgens Ltd* [1951] 1 All ER 682 (Court of Appeal)

The plaintiff was employed by the defendants, who were margarine manufacturers, as an electrician. He injured his hand while repairing an electric fan and claimed damages for negligence.

Held, negligence having been established, the plaintiff was entitled to recover damages as his injury was the direct consequence of that negligence, foreseeability of the particular injury actually sustained being irrelevant. In the view of the court the decision in *Re Polemis & Furness, Withy & Co Ltd* had not been overruled. (See also *Pigney* v *Pointers Transport Services Ltd*; but see *Overseas Tankship (UK) Ltd* v *Morts Dock & Engineering Co Ltd.*)

Tolley v *J S Fry & Sons Ltd* [1931] AC 333 (House of Lords)

The plaintiff was a leading amateur golfer. Without his knowledge or consent the defendants issued an advertisement showing the plaintiff playing golf with a packet of their chocolate protruding from his pocket. By means of a limerick, a caddy was depicted as saying that the chocolate advertised was as excellent as the plaintiff's drive. The plaintiff brought an action for libel and alleged that the advertisement meant that the plaintiff had, for gain and reward, agreed to its publication, and thereby prostituted his reputation as an amateur golf player.

Held, the plaintiff would succeed as the advertisement was capable of bearing the meaning alleged in the innuendo. (See also *Astaire* v *Campling*.)

Topp v *London Country Bus (South West) Ltd* [1993] 3 All ER 448 (Court of Appeal)

The defendants' minibus had been stolen from outside a public house by an unknown person who had, while driving the minibus, shortly afterwards knocked down and killed the plaintiff's wife. The vehicle had been left unattended with the ignition key in the lock.

Held, the plaintiff's action in negligence had properly been dismissed. The parked minibus did not fall within a special category of risk as a source of danger on the highway as the acts of the wrongdoer were to be regarded as a novus actus interveniens which broke the chain of causation. Further, there was probably not sufficient proximity between the plaintiff's wife and the defendants such as to give rise to a duty of care. (See also *P Perl (Exporters) Ltd* v *Camden London Borough Council.*)

Trapp v *Mackie* [1979] 1 All ER 489 (House of Lords)

A headmaster of a school in Scotland having been dismissed, pursuant to the relevant Act of Parliament he petitioned the Secretary of State for Scotland to set up an inquiry into the reasons for his dismissal. The inquiry was ordered and held in public and the function of the commissioner (a Queen's Counsel) appointed was to report to the Minister. In the light of the commissioner's report the Minister upheld the dismissal and the former headmaster sued the chairman of the education authority, alleging that the evidence which he had given at the inquiry had been maliciously false.

Held, his action had properly been dismissed because absolute privilege attached to evidence given at the inquiry. 'To decide whether a tribunal acts in a manner similar to courts of justice and thus is of such a kind as will attract absolute, as distinct from qualified, privilege for witnesses when they give testimony before it, one must consider first, under what authority the tribunal acts, secondly, the nature of the question into which it is its duty to inquire, thirdly, the procedure adopted by it in carrying out the inquiry and, fourthly, the legal consequences of the conclusion reached by the tribunal as a result of the inquiry' (*per* LORD DIPLOCK). (See s14 of the Defamation Act 1996.)

Tremain v Pike [1969] 3 All ER 1303

The plaintiff contracted a very rare disease through contact with rats' urine while working on the defendant's farm. Rat infestation was such that a prudent farmer would have called in the rodent officer to protect the farm and its produce, but the farm workers were not in foreseeable danger.

Held, the employer was not in breach of his duty of care to the plaintiff. Even if he were in breach he would not be liable because the damage was too remote, the disease being different in kind from the ordinary risks of rat infestation, namely bites and food poisoning. (See also *Hughes v Lord Advocate*; compare *Robinson v Post Office*.)

Turner v Metro-Goldwyn-Mayer Pictures Ltd [1950] 1 All ER 449 (House of Lords)

The defendants wrote to the BBC and suggested that one of their film critics, the plaintiff, was 'out of touch with the tastes and entertainment requirements of the picture-going millions who are also radio listeners, and her criticisms are on the whole unnecessarily harmful to the film industry'. They requested the BBC to restrain the plaintiff from reviewing their films. The plaintiff brought an action for libel and admitted that the letter was written on an occasion of qualified privilege.

Held, her action would fail as the defendants' words were a genuine expression of opinion and not malicious. (See also *Kemsley v Foot*.)

Twine v Bean's Express Ltd (1946) 175 LT 131 (Court of Appeal)

An employee of the defendants, a van driver, had been forbidden to give lifts to unauthorised persons and a notice to this effect was displayed on the dashboard. The driver gave a lift to such a person and, due to his negligence, the passenger was killed. His widow sued the defendants.

Held, her action would not succeed as, at the time of the accident, the driver was not acting within the scope of his employment. (But see *Young v Edward Box & Co Ltd*.)

Union Transport Finance Ltd v British Car Auctions Ltd
[1978] 2 All ER 385 (Court of Appeal)

The plaintiffs bought an Audi car and let it on hire purchase to a man who called himself Harry Smith. In breach of the agreement, Smith instructed the defendants to sell the car and, without knowledge of the agreement, they did so. Both the car and Smith disappeared.

Held, the plaintiffs were entitled to damages for conversion. The agreement had been terminated and the plaintiffs had acquired the right to immediate possession of the vehicle as soon as Smith had instructed the defendants to sell it, in breach of the agreement. (See also *Willis (R H) & Son* v *British Car Auctions Ltd.*)

United Africa Co Ltd v Saka Owoade [1957] 3 All ER 216 (Privy Council)

The appellants were general merchants and the respondent a transport contractor. The appellants expressly committed some cigarettes and brandy to two of the respondent's servants for carriage up country, but the goods were never delivered and the respondent's servants were subsequently convicted of stealing them.

Held, the respondent was liable as the conversion of the appellants' goods took place in the course of the employment of the respondent's servants. (See also *Morris* v *C W Martin & Sons Ltd*; but see *General Engineering Services Ltd* v *Kingston and St Andrew Corp.*)

United Bank of Kuwait plc v Prudential Property Services Ltd See South Australia Asset Management Corp v York Montague Ltd

Uxbridge Permanent Benefit Building Society v Pickard
[1939] 2 All ER 344 (Court of Appeal)

A managing clerk employed by the appellant, a solicitor, fraudulently obtained an advance from the respondents, a building society, by using a forged deed.

Held, the appellant was liable for the damage suffered by the respondents as throughout the transaction the clerk had acted within his ostensible authority. (See also *Pettersson* v *Royal Oak Hotel Ltd.*)

Van Oppen v Clerk to the Bedford Charity Trustees
[1989] 3 All ER 389 (Court of Appeal)

The plaintiff pupil was seriously injured playing rugby at his (the defendants') school. He alleged, inter alia, that the defendants had been negligent in failing to insure him against accidental injury or to advise his father to effect such cover.

Held, this was not the case. The proximity between a school and a pupil did not give rise to a general duty on the school to have regard to the pupil's economic welfare and it would not be just or reasonable to impose such a duty. (See also *Reid* v *Rush & Tompkins Group plc.*)

Vaughan v Menlove (1837) 3 Bing NC 468

The defendant had been warned that a hayrick on his land was liable to catch fire, but he decided to take the risk. The rick did catch fire and the fire spread to and destroyed some cottages nearby owned by the plaintiff.

Held, the plaintiff was entitled to damages as the defendant, who had been negligent, was liable for this consequence of his neglect.

Videan v British Transport Commission [1963] 2 All ER 860
(Court of Appeal)

The two-year-old son of a stationmaster strayed on to the railway line near a barrow crossing and his father leaped from the platform in the path of the defendants' trolley to save him. The stationmaster was killed and the boy badly injured and it was found that the trolley driver was guilty of negligence in the driving of the trolley. The boy sought damages in respect of his injuries and the stationmaster's widow claimed damages under the Fatal Accidents Acts 1846 to 1959, and the Law Reform (Miscellaneous Provisions) Act 1934.

Held, the boy's claim should fail as he was a trespasser on the railway line and the trolley driver owed him no duty of care as his presence there was not reasonably foreseeable. However, the widow was entitled to succeed as the stationmaster (an employee of the defendants) was not a trespasser on the line, his presence there was within the sphere of contemplation and the trolley driver owed him a duty of care. 'It is not necessary that the particular accident which happened should have been foreseeable. It is enough that it was foreseeable that some situation requiring the stationmaster to go on the line might arise' (*per* PEARSON LJ). (See also *Horsley v MacLaren* and *Revill v Newbery*.)

Vizetelley v Mudie's Select Library Ltd [1900] 2 QB 170
(Court of Appeal)

The proprietors of a circulating library, the defendants, lent and sold copies of a book which, unknown to them, contained a libel on the plaintiff. The publishers of the book had previously advertised in the recognised trade papers asking that all copies should be returned to them in order that one page should be cancelled and replaced, but this advertisement had been overlooked by the defendants.

Held, the plaintiff's action for libel would succeed. (See also *Sun Life Assurance Co of Canada v W H Smith Son Ltd.*)

Wadey v Surrey County Council [1999] 2 All ER 334 (Court of Appeal)

The plaintiff firefighter sustained injuries in the course of his employment with the defendants. The county court judge deducted social security benefits received by the plaintiff before calculating interest on special damages. Had he been right to do this?

Held, he had not. 'To my mind, the scheme of the Social Security (Recovery of Benefits) Act 1997 is clear and straightforward and leads to only one conclusion: not only should benefits be disregarded from the assessment of damages, but also from the assessment of interest. ... I have come to this conclusion primarily because of the absence of a provision on interest similar to s103 [of the Social Security Administration Act 1992] in the new Act, coupled with the enactment of s17 [of the 1997 Act] with its unambiguous direction as to the treatment of benefits in relation to damages. The 1997 Act was not meant as a piecemeal amendment to the existing law, but was redrafted in its entirety, fitting with Parliament's intention of setting up a new scheme. The omission of a provision such as s103 cannot, therefore, have been unintentional' (*per* OTTON LJ).

Wagon Mound, The See *Overseas Tankship (UK) Ltd v Morts Docks & Engineering Co Ltd, The Wagon Mound (No 1)*

Walker v Geo H Medlicott & Son [1999] 1 All ER 685 (Court of Appeal)

The defendant solicitors drew up the testatrix's will. The plaintiff, the testatrix's nephew, alleged that the defendants had been negligent in preparing the will: they had not carried out her instructions, to his cost. The trial judge dismissed the claim: the plaintiff appealed.

Held, the appeal would be dismissed. 'The facts of the present case ... differ from those of *Ross v Caunters*, *White v Jones* and *Carr-Glynn v Frearsons*. The alleged negligence (if any) of the defendants consists not of failure to see that a will is properly attested, or of the failure to draw it up at all, or of the failure to advise the testator to take some action to ensure that the relevant asset will fall into his estate, but of the failure to draft the will in accordance with the testatrix's instructions. ... A claim against solicitors brought by a disappointed beneficiary who claims that the will was negligently drafted could be said to give rise to questions of principle that did not arise in *Ross v Caunters*, *White v Jones* or *Carr-Glynn v Frearsons*. In none of those cases would the disappointed beneficiary have had any remedy at all if he had none in negligence. On the other hand, in circumstances such as those of the present case, the claim in negligence is by no means the disappointed beneficiary's only remedy, because of the existence of the remedy of rectification – a remedy not available or considered in any of the three earlier cases. ... The issue in relation to liability is whether or not [the plaintiff] has proved by convincing evidence on the balance of probabilities that the testatrix instructed [the defendants] to include in her will a gift of the house to [him] and [they] failed to carry out those instructions in circumstances which constituted negligence. The judge found that this has not been proved and I see no sufficient grounds upon which this court would be entitled to reach a different finding. ... There is ... a further or alternative ground on which I reach the same conclusion. ... if [the plaintiff's] case as presented at the trial was well founded, he would have had a valid claim for rectification of the will under s20(1) of the [Administration of Justice Act 1982]. ... since [the plaintiff] has failed to mitigate his damages (if any) by first issuing proceedings for rectification of the will, he should on this ground, if no other, recover nothing in this action' (*per* SIR CHRISTOPHER SLADE). (Distinguished in *Horsfall v Haywards*.)

Walker (John) & Sons Ltd v Henry Ost & Co Ltd [1970] 2 All ER 106

The first defendants registered trade marks in respect of Scotch Whisky. Under an agreement they shipped bottles, labels and whisky to the second defendants, a company in Ecuador. The second defendants mixed this whisky with local cane spirit and, with the aid of the labels, sold it in Ecuador as Scotch Whisky, to the knowledge of the first defendants. The plaintiffs, blenders and bottlers of Scotch Whisky who exported to Ecuador, sought injunctions to restrain the passing off of the mixture as Scotch Whisky.

Held, 'Scotch Whisky' is a trade description. To maintain an action for passing off the plaintiffs need not have an exclusive right to a trade description. The first defendants had committed a tort in England by selling the labels in England knowing they would be used to practise a deception abroad. Both defendants had committed a tort by the passing off in Ecuador, because the wrong was actionable in England. (See also *Bollinger (J) v Costa Brava Wine Co Ltd.*)

Walkley v Precision Forgings Ltd See Shapland v Palmer

Wallace v Newton [1982] 2 All ER 106

The plaintiff groom was employed by the defendant to look after several horses one of which, *Lord Justice*, was known to have a nervous and unpredictable temperament. One day, as the plaintiff was loading *Lord Justice* onto a trailer, the animal became violent and uncontrollable and crushed her arm against a breast bar.

Held, the plaintiff was entitled to damages for breach of duty under s2(2) of the Animals Act 1971 as she had proved that, to the defendant's knowledge, *Lord Justice* had characteristics of a kind not normally found in horses.

Walsh v Holst & Co Ltd [1958] 3 All ER 33 (Court of Appeal)

Some contractors employed by the occupiers of a building in Blackburn were carrying out a conversion when a brick, which came from the building, fell on and injured the plaintiff who was walking along the pavement on the other side of the street. The contractors had taken precautions to prevent bricks falling into the highway and it was inexplicable how one came to do so.

Held, the maxim res ipsa loquitur applied, but as the occupiers and the contractors had satisfied the court that they had not been negligent, the plaintiff's action for damages should not succeed. (See also *Byrne v Boadle.*)

Wandsworth District Board of Works v United Telephone Co Ltd (1884) 13 QBD 904 (Court of Appeal)

A telephone company erected telephone wires at chimney level over streets owned by the board of works.

Held, the board of works were not entitled to an injunction to restrain this activity on the grounds of trespass. (But see *Clifton v Viscount Bury.*)

Waple v *Surrey County Council* [1998] 1 All ER 624 (Court of Appeal)

The plaintiff and her husband were the adoptive parents of a boy and, problems having arisen between the boy and his adopters, the defendant council placed the boy with foster parents. The husband having declined to supply the council with details of his means, the council served on him a contribution notice requiring him to contribute to the boy's maintenance. In response to inquiries made by the adoptive parents' solicitor as to the decision to remove the boy from them, the council's solicitor wrote a letter which allegedly defamed the plaintiff. In proceedings for defamation the judge decided that the letter had been written on an occasion of absolute privilege. The plaintiff appealed against this decision.

Held, the appeal would be allowed since the letter did not have an immediate link with possible proceedings. Indeed, it did not follow from the mere service of a contribution notice that proceedings would ever be commenced.

Ward v *T E Hopkins & Son Ltd* [1959] 3 All ER 225 (Court of Appeal)

The defendant company was engaged to clean out a well and they used a petrol driven pump for this purpose. The working of the pump created a dangerous concentration of carbon monoxide and the engine stopped. Two of the defendants' servants went down the well, but they were overcome by fumes. A doctor was called to the well and he went down with a rope round his waist to see if he could rescue the men but he, too, was overcome by fumes and all three lost their lives. The widow of one of the men and the executors of the doctor brought actions for damages for negligence.

Held, the defendants were liable in respect of the death of their former employee as they had not discharged their legal duty to take reasonable care not to expose him to unnecessary risk. They were also liable for negligently causing the death of the doctor, who had not acted recklessly or negligently, because it was a natural and proper consequence of the defendants' negligence towards the two men that someone would attempt to rescue them, and they should have foreseen that consequence, and neither the principle novus actus interveniens nor volenti non fit injuria afforded them any defence. (See also *Videan* v *British Transport Commission.*)

Warren v *Henlys Ltd* [1948] 2 All ER 935

A pump attendant, one Beaumont, mistakenly thought that a customer, the plaintiff, was driving away from the defendants' garage without paying for some petrol. Beaumont used violent language to the plaintiff who, in view of this, threatened to report him to the defendants. Beaumont then 'gave him one on the chin to get on with' and the plaintiff brought an action for damages.

Held, the defendants were not liable as Beaumont's assault, an act of personal vengeance, was not within the course of his employment. (See also *Keppel Bus Co Ltd* v *Ahmad.*)

Watson v *Willmott* [1991] 1 All ER 473

The plaintiff's mother was killed in a car accident with the defendant's car when he (the plaintiff) was two and, as a result, his father suffered depressive illness and four months later committed suicide. The plaintiff went to live with his aunt and uncle and they adopted him when he was nearly five. In actions by the plaintiff and his father's estate under the Fatal Accidents Act 1976, the plaintiff included a claim for loss of dependency on both parents and the question arose as to the effect of the adoption.

Held, no loss of dependency on the natural mother could be claimed from the date of the adoption and the loss of dependency on his natural father was to be calculated by subtracting the acquired dependency on his uncle from the loss of dependency on his father. (See also *Stanley* v *Saddique*.)

Watt v *Hertfordshire County Council* [1954] 2 All ER 368 (Court of Appeal)

In an emergency the officer in charge of the defendants' fire station at Watford ordered a heavy lifting jack to be loaded on to a lorry, the only vehicle available which was capable of carrying it, although it was not specially equipped to do so. There was only one vehicle properly fitted to carry the jack and that was properly engaged on other work. Because it was insufficiently secured, on the way to the accident the jack moved and injured one of the firemen and he claimed damages for negligence. There was evidence that calls for the use of the jack were extremely rare.

Held, the fireman's action would fail as the risk taken was one which, in an emergency, might normally be encountered in the fire service and was not unduly great in relation to the end which it was hoped to achieve, ie the rescue of a woman trapped under a heavy vehicle. (But see *Smith* v *Baker (Charles) & Sons*.)

Watt v *Longsdon* [1930] 1 KB 130 (Court of Appeal)

The foreign manager of a company wrote to a director, the defendant, and said that the managing director, the plaintiff, was 'a blackguard, a thief, a liar … who lived and lives exclusively to satisfy his own passions and lust'. The defendant showed this letter to the plaintiff's wife and to the chairman of the board of directors. The allegations contained in the letter were unfounded, but the defendant believed them to be true. The plaintiff sued for libel.

Held, he was entitled to damages as the publication of the letter to his wife was not upon a privileged occasion as the defendant did not have a sufficient interest or duty, legal, moral or social, to make the communication. Publication to the chairman of the board of directors was privileged. (See also *Wenman* v *Ash*; but see *Osborn* v *Boulter (Thomas) and Son*.)

Weld-Blundell v *Stephens* [1920] AC 956 (House of Lords)

The appellant employed the respondent, a chartered accountant, to investigate the affairs of a company in which he had invested a considerable amount of money. In a letter to the respondent the appellant made severe reflections upon the conduct of the manager and two other gentlemen who had taken part in the conduct of the company's business. The respondent's partner negligently dropped this letter in the manager's office and the two other gentlemen brought successful actions for libel against the appellant in respect of the statements which it contained. The appellant then sued the respondent alleging that the actions for libel had been brought in consequence of the negligence of the respondent and his partner.

Held, the appellant's liability for damages in libel did not result from the respondent's breach of duty and he was therefore liable for nominal damages only. (See also *Clark* v *Chambers* and *Slipper* v *British Broadcasting Corp*.)

Weldon v Home Office See Hague v Deputy Governor of Parkhurst Prison

Weller & Co v Foot and Mouth Disease Research Institute
[1965] 3 All ER 560

In consequence, it was assumed, of the escape of a virus imported by the defendants and used by them for experimental work on foot and mouth disease in premises owned and occupied by them, cattle in the vicinity of the premises became infected with the disease. Because of the disease an order was made under statutory powers closing cattle markets in the district and as a result the plaintiff auctioneers were temporarily unable to carry on their business at those markets and suffered loss. The court was required to assume that the loss to the plaintiffs was foreseeable and that there was neglect on the part of the defendants which caused the escape of the virus.

Held, the defendants were not liable in negligence as the plaintiffs were not the owners of the cattle and the defendants did not owe them (as opposed to owners of cattle in the neighbourhood) a duty to take care to avoid the escape of the virus which arose from the foreseeable fact that the virus might affect cattle in the vicinity. Further, the plaintiffs could not recover damages under the rule in *Rylands* v *Fletcher* because they had no interest in the cattle endangered by the escape of the virus and the loss suffered by the plaintiffs was not a sufficiently proximate and direct consequence of such escape. 'The decision in *Hedley Byrne & Co Ltd* v *Heller & Partners Ltd* does not depart in any way from the fundamental that there can be no claim for negligence in the absence of a duty of care owed to the plaintiff. It recognises that a duty of care may arise in the giving of advice even though no contract or fiduciary relationship exists between the giver of the advice and the person who may act on it, and having recognised the existence of the duty it goes on to recognise that indirect or economic loss will suffice to support the plaintiff's claim. What the case does not decide is that an ability to foresee indirect or economic loss to another as a result of one's conduct automatically imposes a duty to take care to avoid that loss' (*per* WIDGERY J). (See also *SCM (UK) Ltd* v *W J Whittall & Son Ltd*.)

Wells v Wells; Thomas v Brighton Health Authority; Page v Sheerness Steel Co plc [1998] 3 All ER 481 (House of Lords)

These appeals in actions for personal injuries raised the same question, ie what is the correct method of calculating lump sum damages for the loss of future earnings and the cost of future care? Negligence was admitted in all three cases.

Held, 'Under our present system of law the compensation to which each plaintiff is entitled must, unless the parties agree otherwise, be paid in a lump sum and there is no power for the courts to award periodical payments. Therefore each plaintiff must receive a lump sum to provide compensation for the annual cost of lifetime nursing case and for the loss of future earning capacity. ... The multiplier which the courts apply to the annual cost of nursing care and the annual loss of earning capacity to produce a lump sum of compensation is determined by reference to the respective periods in the future for which the cost will be incurred and the loss will be sustained, but discounted to allow for the immediate receipt of the lump sum rather than the receipt of periodical payments over a number of years. The discount is assessed by reference to the assumed rate of return on the lump sum when invested, so that the higher the rate of interest assumed the smaller the multiplier. Two principal questions have been debated in this appeal. One question is whether allowance should be made for future inflation to take account of the fact that in future years the cost of nursing care will rise and that the earnings of the plaintiff would have increased. The other question relates to the rate of interest which the courts should assume the capital sum awarded will earn in order to arrive at the multiplier. ... [with] the introduction of [index-linked government securities (ILGS)] providing an income which is protected against inflation it is now appropriate to make allowance for the risk of future inflation by fixing the multiplier by reference to the rate of return on ILGS. ... Accordingly I have reached the conclusion that under the present principles which govern the assessment of compensation and having regard to the availability of ILGS, the plaintiffs are entitled to compensation assessed by taking a discount rate based on the return on ILGS. The return on ILGS fluctuates but the schedules of the month end returns during the past three years show a net average return of about 3 per cent. Therefore I consider that this rate should be adopted as the rate to arrive at the multiplier in the present cases ... the rate of 3 per cent taken by this House in the present appeals should be applied in other cases notwithstanding fluctuations in the return on ILGS until the Lord Chancellor prescribes a different rate pursuant to his power under s1 of the Damages Act 1996 or unless there is a very considerable change in economic circumstances' (*per* LORD HUTTON).

Welsh v Chief Constable of the Merseyside Police [1993] 1 All ER 692

The plaintiff alleged that the Crown Prosecution Service (CPS) had negligently failed to inform a magistrates' court, from which he had been bailed on charges of theft, that those offences had subsequently been taken into consideration at the Crown Court and that, as a result of that failure, he had been arrested and detained and thereby suffered loss, damage and distress. The registrar struck out the plaintiff's claim on the ground that the CPS did not owe the plaintiff any duty of care.

Held, the claim would be reinstated as immunity did not extend to the CPS's general administrative responsibilities. 'By every one of the agreed tokens by which to test the existence of a duty, a duty is found to exist' (*per* TUDOR EVANS J). (Applied: *Saif Ali v Sydney Mitchell & Co* and *Kirkham v Chief Constable of the Greater Manchester Police.*)

Welton v North Cornwall District Council See Harris v Evans

Wenman v Ash (1853) 13 CB 836

The defendant wrote to Sabrina Wenman, the plaintiff's wife, and the letter contained statements which were defamatory of her husband.

Held, the libel had been published to the plaintiff's wife and her husband was entitled to damages. (See also *Watt v Longsdon.*)

Wentworth v Wiltshire County Council [1993] 2 WLR 175 (Court of Appeal)

The plaintiff's dairy farm was served by a road used by the Milk Marketing Board's tankers. The road having become dangerous to traffic because of its disrepair, the Board refused to use it and to collect the plaintiff's milk. As a result, the plaintiff gave up his dairy herd and suffered financial loss. Resorting to procedures under the Highways Act 1959, the plaintiff established that the defendant highway authority had been under a duty to repair the road. In the present action, he sued the defendants, maintaining that s1(1) of the Highways (Miscellaneous Provisions) Act 1961 had removed highway authorities' exemption from liability for non-repair and therefore that the defendants were liable for breach of statutory duty.

Held, the plaintiff's action would fail and his only remedy was in accordance with the 1959 Act's procedures. 'The sole question is whether the respondent can claim for economic loss which admittedly flowed from the breach ... the matter is in the end one of statutory construction and in my judgment the intention of Parliament, to be gathered from the wording of the two Acts and the pre-existing state of the law, is clear. It is (1) to replace the remedy for non-repair by way of indictment by the new remedy under s59 [of the 1959 Act] and (2) to replace the previous exemption from civil liability for damage resulting from non-repair by an action for damage to the person or property of a road user from the dangerous condition of a highway, subject only to the statutory defence' (*per* PARKER LJ). (See also *Atkinson v Newcastle and Gateshead Waterworks Co.*)

West (H) & Son Ltd v Shephard [1963] 2 All ER 625 (House of Lords)

The appellants were liable in respect of serious injuries suffered by the respondent, a woman of 41 years of age and the mother of three children. As a result of her injuries the respondent was permanently bedridden and unable to speak, although she could show some sign of recognising her relatives, and her expectation of life had been reduced to seven years from the date of the accident. She was awarded by the trial judge, inter alia, £17,500 by way of general damages and the appeal was against this assessment.

Held, the award should stand. While it might seem high, everything that life held for the respondent had been taken away from her and the award was neither unreasonable nor so excessive as to justify an appellate court's interference. 'If damages are assessed on a correct basis, there should not then be paring down of the award because of some thought that a particular plaintiff will not be able to use the money' (*per* LORD MORRIS).

Westripp v Baldock [1938] 2 All ER 779; affd [1939] 1 All ER 279 (Court of Appeal)

On his own land, the defendant, a jobbing builder, placed ladders, planks and building materials against the plaintiff's wall.

Held, the plaintiff could bring a successful action in trespass. (See also *Gregory v Piper* and *League Against Cruel Sports Ltd v Scott.*)

Whatman v Pearson (1868) LR 3 CP 422

The defendant was constructing a sewer. He allowed his employees one hour for dinner, but stipulated that they should not, during this period, go home or leave their horses and carts. An employee went home to dinner and in his absence his horse ran away and damaged the plaintiff's railings.

Held, the defendant was liable as the employee had acted within the scope of his employment. (But see *Storey v Ashton.*)

Wheat v E Lacon & Co Ltd [1966] 1 All ER 582 (House of Lords)

The Golfers' Arms was owned by the defendants and a Mr Richardson, the licensee of the inn, was employed by them and under the terms of a written agreement occupied the whole of the premises. Mr Richardson and his wife lived on the first floor and with the defendants' unwritten consent Mrs Richardson carried on a boarding house business in that part of the premises. Mr Wheat engaged two rooms for himself, his wife and family, and because there was no bulb in the light on the staircase leading from the first floor to the ground floor and the handrail stopped three steps from the bottom, he fell and was killed. His widow, the plaintiff, sought to recover damages under the Fatal Accidents Acts 1846 to 1959, on the basis that the defendants were in 'occupation or control' of the staircase and that her husband was their 'visitor' within s1(2) of the Occupiers' Liability Act 1957. It was found that the defendants had a right of entry to view the state of repair of the whole of the premises but that they did not in fact exercise any control over the way in which Mr Richardson used the first floor flat.

Held, the defendants were not liable as, on the facts, they were not in actual or immediate control of the staircase and although Mr Wheat was the defendants' 'visitor' they were not, on the facts, in breach of the common duty of care under ss1(2) and s2(1), (2) of the Act of 1957. (See also *Fisher v CHT Ltd* and *Harris v Birkenhead Corporation.*)

Wheeler v Copas [1981] 3 All ER 405

The defendant farmer wished to build a house on his land and he negotiated a labour-only contract whereby the plaintiff and his partner would lay bricks and erect and dismantle scaffolding, the defendant providing the building materials and any necessary equipment. When erecting the scaffolding, the partners were offered two of the defendant's farm ladders. The defendant did not ask them whether the ladders were adequate for the purpose, nor was he told that they were unsuitable. The partners chose one of the ladders; it gave way and the plaintiff fell off and suffered injuries. The ladder was too flimsy for building work and this was the cause of the accident.

Held, although s1(3)(a) of the Occupiers' Liability Act 1957 could apply to a ladder, once the defendant had handed the ladder over to the partners it could not be said that he was still the occupier of the ladder for the purposes of that Act. However, the defendant was obliged to take reasonable care to see that the ladder was fit and safe for the purpose for which it was to be used. He had failed in this duty and he was therefore liable to the plaintiff in negligence, but as the plaintiff, an experienced builder, had accepted use of the ladder in spite of its apparent inadequacy, he had been contributorily negligent and the damages awarded were reduced by 50 per cent.

White v Chief Constable of the South Yorkshire Police
[1999] 1 All ER 1 (House of Lords)

The plaintiff police officers were on duty at the ground at the time of the Hillsborough Stadium disaster (see *Alcock* v *Chief Constable of the South Yorkshire Police*). They became much involved in helping the injured and dealing with the dead. As a result, they suffered post-traumatic stress disorder and, as employees and rescuers, they sought damages for negligence.

Held, their claims could not succeed on either ground. '*The employment argument* ... The argument was that the present case can be decided on conventional employer's liability principles. And counsel relies on the undoubted duty of an employer to protect employees from harm through work. ... When analysed this argument breaks down. It is a non sequitur to say that because an employer is under a duty to an employee not to cause him physical injury, the employer should as a necessary consequence of that duty (of which there is no breach) be under a duty not to cause the employee psychiatric injury ... The rules to be applied when an employee brings an action against his employer for harm suffered at his workplace are the rules of tort. One is therefore thrown back to the ordinary rules of the law of tort which contain restrictions on the recovery of compensation for psychiatric harm. [His Lordship had already observed that *Alcock,* the leading case, had established that a person who suffers reasonably foreseeable psychiatric illness as a result of another person's death or injury cannot recover damages unless he can satisfy three requirements, viz: (i) that he had a close tie of love and affection with the person killed, injured or imperilled; (ii) that he was close to the incident in time and space; (iii) that he directly perceived the incident rather than, for example, hearing about it from a third person. His Lordship also said that *Page* v *Smith* was plainly intended, in the context of pure psychiatric harm, to narrow the range of potential secondary victims.] *The rescue argument* … The law has long recognised the moral imperative of encouraging citizens to rescue persons in peril. Those who altruistically expose themselves to danger in an emergency to save others are favoured by the law. The specific difficulty counsel [for the plaintiffs] faces is that it is common ground that none of the … police officers were at any time exposed to personal danger and none thought they were so exposed. On the judge's findings [in *Chadwick v British Transport Commission*] the rescuer had passed the threshold of being in personal danger … in order to contain the concept of rescuer in reasonable bounds for the purposes of the recovery of compensation for pure psychiatric harm the plaintiff must at least satisfy the threshold requirement that he objectively exposed himself to danger or reasonably believed that he was doing so. … For my part the limitation of actual or apprehended dangers is what proximity in this special situation means. In my judgment it would be an unwarranted extension of the law to uphold the claims of the police officers' (*per* LORD STEYN). (See also *Hunter v British Coal Corp.*)

White v Jones [1995] 1 All ER 691 (House of Lords)

The defendant solicitors negligently took two months to respond to the testator's instructions to prepare him a new will. Three days before the defendants responded, the testator died. The plaintiffs would have benefited under the new will: they sought damages against the defendants.

Held, their action would be successful. 'In my opinion … your Lordships' House should in cases such as these extend to the intended beneficiary a remedy under the *Hedley Byrne & Co Ltd v Heller & Partners Ltd* principle by holding that the assumption of responsibility by the solicitor towards his client should be held in law to extend to the intended beneficiary who (as the solicitor can reasonably foresee) may, as a result of the solicitor's negligence, be deprived of his intended legacy in circumstances in which neither the testator nor his estate will have a remedy against the solicitor. Such liability will not of course arise in cases in which the defect in the will comes to light before the death of the testator, and the testator either leaves the will as it is or otherwise continues to exclude the previously intended beneficiary from the relevant benefit. I only wish to add that, with the benefit of experience during the 15 years in which *Ross v Caunters* has been regularly applied, we can say with some confidence that a direct remedy by the intended beneficiary against the solicitor appears to create no problems in practice' (*per* LORD GOFF OF CHIEVELEY). (See also *Carr-Glynn v Frearsons.*)

White v London Transport Executive [1982] 1 All ER 411

A motor mechanic was killed at work due to his employers' admitted negligence. He was 25 years of age and unmarried and he lived with his mother and stepfather. The question arose as to the correct measure of damages recoverable by his estate under s1(1) of the Law Reform (Miscellaneous Provisions) Act 1934, for loss of earnings in 'the lost years'.

Held, the loss to be measured was the loss to the deceased (as opposed to his estate) arising out of the loss of future earnings. It was not limited to what he would have been likely to save and no deduction should be made on account of money he would have spent on his dependant mother. The loss, therefore, was to be measured by the difference between his estimated net earnings and the estimated cost of his maintenance and providing for himself a reasonably satisfying and enjoyable life: the notional surplus had to be large enough to cover a substantial part of the cost of maintaining a family. It was agreed that the multiplier was 15 years' purchase and, in this case, the award was one-third of his net earnings for the first five years and one-quarter for the remaining 10. (See also *Rose v Ford* and s1 of the Administration of Justice Act 1982.)

White Hudson & Co Ltd v Asian Organisation Ltd [1965] 1 All ER 1040 (Privy Council)

Since 1953 the appellants had sold cough sweets in Singapore. Each sweet was wrapped in red cellophane bearing the word 'Hacks' and the respondents began importing similar sweets wrapped in red paper bearing the word 'Pecto'. The trial judge found that the vast majority of non-English speaking customers were unable to read and asked simply for 'red paper cough sweets' (by which they meant the appellants' goods) and, therefore, as far as these customers were concerned, the 'get-up' was all-important, while the name was insignificant. Although no actual deception was proved, the trial judge also found that the get-up of 'Pecto' sweets was such as to be calculated to deceive.

Held, on the evidence, the trial judge's findings were fully justified and the appellants were entitled to an injunction to restrain passing off by the respondents. (See also *Erven Warnink BV v J Townend & Sons (Hull) Ltd*.)

Whitehouse v Jordan [1981] 1 All ER 267 (House of Lords)

A senior hospital registrar took charge of the delivery of a baby, guided by notes made by the consultant professor in charge of the hospital's maternity unit. He embarked on a trial of forceps delivery, pulling on the baby six times, but after some 25 minutes he abandoned this procedure and delivered the baby successfully by Caesarian section. Soon after delivery the baby was found to have suffered severe brain damage and it was alleged that the registrar had pulled too long and too hard with the forceps on the baby's head and therefore that he had been negligent. The trial judge found that the registrar had been guilty of negligence, but the Court of Appeal reversed this decision on the ground, inter alia, that his finding was based on an unjustified interpretation of the evidence.

Held, the trial judge's conclusion had been open to reassessment by the appellate court and it had been entitled to find that the evidence did not justify the inference that the registrar had negligently pulled too hard and too long with the forceps. 'Merely to describe something as an error of judgment tells us nothing about whether it is negligent or not. The true position is that an error of judgment may, or may not, be negligent; it depends on the nature of the error. If it is one that would not have been made by a reasonably competent professional man professing to have the standard and type of skill that the defendant held himself out as having, and acting with ordinary care, then it is negligent. If, on the other hand, it is an error that a man with ordinary care might have made, then it is not negligence' (*per* LORD FRASER OF TULLYBELTON). (See also *Stafford v Conti Commodity Services Ltd* and *Maynard v West Midlands Regional Health Authority*.)

Wieland v Cyril Lord Carpets Ltd [1969] 3 All ER 1006

The plaintiff suffered an injury caused by the defendants' admitted negligence, and as a result the plaintiff was obliged to wear a collar, which restricted the movement of her head and prevented the proper use of her bifocal glasses. She fell while descending some stairs.

Held, the injury sustained in the first accident was the cause of the second accident, and was not too remote in that it was foreseeable that one injury might affect a person's ability to cope with the vicissitudes of life and thereby be a cause of another injury. (But see *McKew v Holland and Hannen and Cubitts (Scotland) Ltd*.)

Wilkinson v Downton [1897] 2 QB 57

By way of a practical joke, the defendant falsely told the plaintiff that her husband had met with a serious accident. As a result, she experienced a violent nervous shock and weeks of suffering and incapacity.

Held, she was entitled to damages as the defendant had wilfully done an act which was calculated to do and did in fact cause harm to her. (See also *Janvier v Sweeney*.)

Wilks v Cheltenham Homeguard Motor Cycle and Light Car Club [1971] 2 All ER 369 (Court of Appeal)

The plaintiffs were spectators at a motor-cycle scramble organised by a club. During one race a rider left the course for no explicable reason, and went into the spectators' enclosure, injuring the plaintiffs. An action for negligence was brought against the club and the rider. The judge exempted the club but found the rider liable.

Held, the rider was not liable because there was no evidence of negligence. 'In a race the rider is, I think, liable if his conduct is such as to evince a reckless disregard of the spectators' safety: in other words, if his conduct is foolhardy' (*per* LORD DENNING MR). (See *Wooldridge v Sumner*.)

Williams v Curzon Syndicate Ltd (1919) 35 TLR 475 (Court of Appeal)

The defendants, proprietors of a residential club, employed one Lister, an old and dangerous criminal, as a night porter. Lister stole the plaintiff's jewellery from a safe in the club manager's office and the plaintiff alleged that the defendants were guilty of negligence in employing such a man without taking proper care to ascertain his record.

Held, the defendants were liable to make good her loss as they had not used due care in engaging Lister. (See also *Uxbridge Permanent Benefit Building Society v Pickard*.)

Williams v *Natural Life Health Foods Ltd* [1998] 2 All ER 577 (House of Lords)

Mr Mistlin, the second defendant, formed the defendant company, of which he was managing director and the principal shareholder, in order to franchise the concept of retail health food shops. The plaintiffs entered into a franchise agreement, but their business failed. They were awarded damages for negligent advice. The defendant company having been dissolved, the question was whether Mr Mistlin was personally liable.

Held, this was not the case: Mr Mistlin had not assumed personal responsibility for the advice given to the plaintiffs and the plaintiffs had not relied on such an assumption of responsibility. (Applied: *Henderson* v *Merrett Syndicates Ltd.*)

Willson v *Ministry of Defence* [1991] 1 All ER 638

The plaintiff sustained injury at work and, in an action against his former employers, he applied for an award of provisional damages under s32A of the Supreme Court Act 1981 in the light of medical evidence that there would be degeneration of the ankle joint and the possibility of arthritis.

Held, his application would be unsuccessful and damages would be awarded on a lump sum basis. In s32A of the 1981 Act 'chance' had to be a possibility that was measurable rather than fanciful (the possibility of arthritis satisfied this test) and 'serious deterioration' denoted a clear and severable risk, rather than continuing or ordinary deterioration, and the arthritis possibility did not come within this category.

Wilsher v *Essex Area Health Authority* [1988] 1 All ER 871 (House of Lords)

When the infant plaintiff was born prematurely he was suffering from various illnesses. In the defendants' baby unit he was given excess oxygen and it was later discovered that he had an incurable condition of the retina. This condition could have been caused by excess oxygen; it also occurred in premature babies suffering from the plaintiff's illnesses. At the trial of the plaintiff's action for negligence the medical evidence was inconclusive as to the cause of the plaintiff's condition.

Held, there should be a new trial as (contrary to the view of the courts below) the plaintiff had not discharged the burden of proving the causitive link between the defendants' negligence and his injury. (See also *Pickford* v *Imperial Chemical Industries plc*; but see *Bonnington Castings Ltd* v *Wardlaw*.)

Wilson v *Pringle* [1986] 2 All ER 440 (Court of Appeal)

Arising out of an incident in the school corridor, the plaintiff schoolboy sued the defendant schoolboy for trespass to the person. The defendant admitted horseplay but not a hostile act.

Held, the plaintiff was not entitled to summary judgment. 'In our view, the authorities lead one to the conclusion that in a battery there must be an intentional touching or contact in one form or another of the plaintiff by the defendant. That touching must be proved to be a hostile touching. That still leaves unanswered the question, when is a touching to be called hostile? Hostility cannot be equated with ill-will or malevolence. It cannot be governed by the obvious intention shown in acts like punching, stabbing or shooting. It cannot be solely governed by an expressed intention, although that may be strong evidence. But the element of hostility, in the sense in which it is now to be considered, must be a question of fact for the tribunal of fact. It may be imported from the circumstances' (*per* CROOM-JOHNSON LJ). (See also *Letang v Cooper*.)

Wilsons & Clyde Coal Co Ltd v *English* [1937] 3 All ER 628 (House of Lords)

A miner brought an action for damages for personal injuries against his employers and the question arose as to whether they were liable in respect of these injuries as they had delegated to a competent servant the duty of taking due care in the provision of a reasonably safe system of working in the mine.

Held, the miner was entitled to succeed as the employers could not avoid by delegation their duty to provide a competent staff of men, adequate material and a proper system of working and effective supervision. (See also *Kubach v Hollands* and *McDermid v Nash Dredging and Reclamation Co Ltd*.)

Winkfield, The [1902] P 42 (Court of Appeal)

As a result of a collision at sea which occurred in fog off Table Bay certain letters and parcels in transit by post were lost. The Postmaster-General sought damages from the owners of the ship which had negligently caused the accident.

Held, the Postmaster General would succeed although he was not liable to the senders of the mail in respect of its loss. However, he was bound to pay them that which he received above his own interest. (Applied in *O'Sullivan v Williams*.)

Wood v *British Coal Corp* See *Smoker* v *London Fire and Civil Defence Authority*

Woods v *Martins Bank Ltd* [1958] 3 All ER 166

Acting on the advice of the manager of a branch of the defendant bank, the plaintiff invested the sum of £14,800 in a certain company. This advice was given honestly, but there was no reasonable ground for advising the plaintiff in his own interest to make this investment and the whole sum so invested was lost.

Held, the defendant bank and the manager were liable for the loss occasioned by the advice as it was within the scope of their business to advise on financial matters and they owed a duty to the plaintiff to advise him with reasonable care and skill. (But see *Hedley Byrne & Co Ltd v Heller & Partners Ltd*.)

Wooldridge v Sumner [1962] 2 All ER 978 (Court of Appeal)

During a horse show at the White City Stadium the plaintiff, a professional photographer, was knocked down and severely injured by a horse owned by the defendant which ran out of the competition arena. The plaintiff sought damages on the ground of negligence and it was found that the accident occurred because the rider of the horse, a competitor of great experience and skill, attempted to take a corner 'too fast'.

Held, his action should fail as, on the facts, the rider was guilty of an error of judgment as opposed to negligence. (But see *Cleghorn v Oldham*; see also *Wilks v Cheltenham Homeguard Motor Cycle Club.*)

Woollerton and Wilson Ltd v Richard Costain Ltd [1970] 1 All ER 483

The plaintiffs sought an injunction to restrain trespass by the defendant building contractors of the air space above the plaintiffs' premises. The jib of the defendants' crane overhung the plaintiffs' premises 50 ft above roof level. The defendants admitted the trespass and offered the plaintiffs compensation.

Held, the plaintiffs were entitled to an injunction although they had suffered no damage, but its operation was suspended until a date by when the trespass would in any event have ceased. The judge took into account the offer of compensation and the fact that the air space had only assumed any value by reason of the defendants' needs. (But see *Bernstein (Lord) v Skyviews and General Ltd.*)

Wright v Cheshire County Council [1952] 2 All ER 789 (Court of Appeal)

A group of boy pupils in the defendants' school was engaged in vaulting the 'buck'. The boys had been taught that the last over was to wait to assist the next vaulter if the need arose, but because a boy failed to do this the next boy, the plaintiff, fell and sustained injuries. At the time of the accident the instructor was supervising other activities a little distance away, but evidence showed that it was the generally approved practice to leave boys to vault by themselves.

Held, for this reason, the defendants had not been negligent and the plaintiff's action for damages would fail. (But see *Cavanagh v Ulster Weaving Co Ltd.*)

Wright v Lodge [1993] 4 All ER 299 (Court of Appeal)

A Mini driven by the respondent, Miss Shepherd, broke down on an unlit dual carriageway at night when visibility was very poor owing to fog. The car came to a stop in the nearside lane of the carriageway and, while the respondent was attempting to start it, a Scania articulated container lorry driven by the appellant, Mr Lodge, crashed into the back of it, causing a passenger in the rear seat of the Mini to be seriously injured. The lorry then veered out of control across the central reservation and came to rest on its side in the opposite westbound carriageway where it was struck by three cars and a lorry. The driver of one of the cars was killed and another driver was injured. At the time of the collision the appellant's lorry was travelling at 60 mph. The injured driver and the personal representatives of the dead driver sued the appellant and the respondent while the injured passenger in the respondent's car sued the appellant who joined the respondent as a third party. The appellant admitted liability but claimed contribution from the respondent. The trial judge found that the appellant was driving recklessly and ordered that the respondent should contribute 10 per cent in respect of the claim by her passenger but dismissed the contribution claims relating to the injured and dead drivers. The appellant appealed contending that the judge should have ordered a 10 per cent contribution in respect of those claims.

Held, the appeal would be dismissed as, on the facts, although the respondent had been negligent in not removing her car from the carriageway onto the verge, the sole cause of the lorry ending up on the westbound carriageway and the drivers' consequent death and injuries was the appellant's reckless driving, which was the only relevant legal cause of that event. (But see *Rouse* v *Squires*.)

Wringe v *Cohen* [1939] 4 All ER 241 (Court of Appeal)

A wall to the defendant's house collapsed and damaged the plaintiff's shop. The house was let to a weekly tenant, but the defendant was liable to keep the premises in repair. He did not know that the wall, by reason of which the property had become a nuisance, was in a dangerous condition.

Held, the defendant was liable whether or not he knew, or ought to have known, of the danger. However, neither the defendant nor his tenant would have been liable if the injury had been attributed to the act of a trespasser or the secret and unobservable process of nature but this would not apply if he had knowledge or means of knowledge and he allowed the danger to continue. (See also *Mint* v *Good*.)

X and Others (Minors) v *Bedfordshire County Council* See *Barrett* v *Enfield London Borough Council*

Yianni v *Edwin Evans & Sons* [1981] 3 All ER 592

The plaintiffs decided to buy a house, provided they could obtain a building society loan. They applied for a loan and paid the society's survey fee. The society instructed the defendant valuers and surveyors to inspect the house and value it, naming the plaintiffs as prospective purchasers and stating the purchase price and the loan required. After carrying out their inspection, the defendants reported to the society that the house was an adequate security for the loan. After accepting the report, the society told the plaintiffs that it was willing to make the loan; it also advised them to instruct an independent surveyor if they required a report for their own information and protection. The plaintiffs did not take this step, but accepted the society's loan offer and completed the purchase. Later in the same year they discovered that the foundations of the house were cracked and that the necessary work would cost £18,000: they sued the defendants for damages for negligence.

Held, their action would succeed as the defendants owed the plaintiffs a duty of care, the relationship between them being sufficiently proximate to establish that it was within the defendants' reasonable contemplation that carelessness on their part might be likely to cause the plaintiffs damage, and the defendants had been in breach of that duty. As it had been reasonable for the plaintiffs to rely on the defendants' valuation, they had not been guilty of contributory negligence in not having an independent survey. (See also *Ministry of Housing and Local Government* v *Sharp* and *Smith* v *Eric S Bush*.)

Young v *Edward Box & Co Ltd* [1951] I TLR 789 (Court of Appeal)

The defendants' foreman gave his consent to the giving of a lift to the plaintiff in one of the defendants' lorries. The lorry driver negligently caused injury to the plaintiff.

Held, the defendants were liable as the granting of permission for the ride was within the foreman's ostensible authority. (But see *Conway* v *George Wimpey & Co Ltd*.)

Youssoupoff v *Metro-Goldwyn-Mayer Pictures Ltd* (1934) 50 TLR 581 (Court of Appeal)

A Russian princess alleged that a film made by the defendants suggested that she had been raped or seduced by a monk called Rasputin. She claimed damages for libel.

Held, she would succeed as to say that a woman had been ravished was defamatory of her as it tended to cause her to be shunned and avoided although it involved no moral turpitude on her part. (But see *Sim* v *Stretch*.)

Yuen Kun-yeu v *Attorney-General of Hong Kong* [1987] 2 All ER 705 (Privy Council)

The appellants, four Hong Kong residents, made substantial deposits with a registered deposit-taking company there: the company went into liquidation and they lost their money. By statute, the Hong Kong Commissioner of Deposit-taking Companies had regulatory functions and he could grant, refuse or revoke registrations. The appellants maintained that the company had been run fraudulently and that the commissioner had been negligent in the discharge of his functions.

Held, the appellants' action would fail as there was no special relationship between the commissioner and the company or between the commissioner and the depositors capable of giving rise to a duty of care owed by the commissioner to the depositors. (Applied in *Davis* v *Radcliffe*.)

Statutes

Fires Prevention (Metropolis) Act 1774
(14 Geo 3 c 78)

86 No action to lie against a person where the fire accidentally begins

And no action, suit or process whatever shall be had, maintained or prosecuted against any person in whose house, chamber, stable, barn or other building, or on whose estate any fire shall accidentally begin, nor shall any recompense be made by such person for any damage suffered thereby, any law, usage or custom to the contrary notwithstanding provided that no contract or agreement made between landlord and tenant shall be hereby defeated or made void.

Libel Act 1792
(32 Geo 3 c 60)

Whereas doubts have arisen whether on the trial of an indictment or information for the making or publishing any libel, where an issue or issues are joined between the King and the defendant or defendants, on the plea of not guilty pleaded, it be competent to the jury impanelled to try the same to give their verdict upon the whole matter in issue:

1 On the trial of an indictment for a libel the jury may give a general verdict upon the whole matter put in issue

On every such trial the jury sworn to try the issue may give a general verdict of guilty or not guilty upon the whole matter out in issue upon such indictment or information, and shall not be required or directed by the court or judge before whom such indictment or information shall be tried to find the defendant or defendants guilty merely on the proof of the publication by such defendant or defendants of the paper charged to be a libel, and of the sense ascribed to the same in such indictment or information.

2 The court shall give their opinion and directions

Provided always, that on every such trial the court or judge before whom such indictment or information shall be tried shall, according to their or his discretion, give their or his opinion and directions to the jury on the matter in issue between the King and the defendant or defendants, in like manner as in other criminal cases.

Statute of Frauds Amendment Act 1828
(9 Geo 4 c 14)

6 Action not maintainable on representations of character, etc, unless they be in writing signed by the party chargeable

No action shall be brought whereby to charge any person upon or by reason of any representation or assurance made or given concerning or relating to the character, conduct, credit, ability, trade, or dealings of any other person, to the intent or purpose that such other person may obtain credit, money, or goods upon, unless such representation or assurance be made in writing, signed by the party to be charged therewith.

Judgments Act 1838
(1 & 2 Vict c 110)

17 Judgment debts to carry interest

(1) Every judgment debt shall carry interest at the rate of 8 per cent per annum from the time of entering up the judgment until the same shall be satisfied, and such interest may be levied under a writ of execution on such judgment.

(2) Rules of court may provide for the court to disallow all or part of any interest otherwise payable under subsection (1).

[As amended by the Statute Law Revision (No 2) Act 1888; Civil Procedure Acts Repeal Act 1879, s2, Schedule, Pt I; Judgment Debts (Rate of Interest) Order 1993; Civil Procedure (Modifiction of Enactments) Order 1998, art 3.]

Parliamentary Papers Act 1840
(3 & 4 Vict c 9)

1 Proceedings, criminal or civil, against persons for publication of papers printed by order of Parliament, to be stayed upon delivery of a certificate and affidavit to the effect that such publication is by order of either House of Parliament

It shall and may be lawful for any person or persons who now is or are, or hereafter shall be, a defendant or defendants in any civil or criminal proceeding commenced or prosecuted in any manner soever, for or on account or in respect of the publication of any such report, paper, votes, or proceedings by such person or persons, or by his, her, or their servant or servants, by or under the authority of either House of Parliament, to bring before the court in which such proceeding shall have been or shall be so commenced or prosecuted, or before any judge of the same (if one of the superior courts at Westminster), first giving twenty-four hours' notice of his intention so to do to the prosecutor or plaintiff in such proceeding, a certificate under the hand of the lord high chancellor of Great Britain, or the lord keeper of the great seal, or of the speaker of the House of Lords, for the time being, or of the clerk of the Parliaments, or of the speaker of the House of Commons, or of the clerk of the same house, stating that the report, paper, votes, or proceedings, as the case may be, in respect whereof such civil or criminal proceeding shall have been commended or prosecuted, was published by such person or persons, or by his, her, or their servant or servants, by order or under the authority of the House of Lords or of the House of Commons, as the case may be, together with an affidavit verifying such certificate, and such court or judge shall thereupon immediately stay such civil or criminal proceeding; and the same, and every writ or process issued therein, shall be deemed and taken to be finally put an end to, determined, and superseded by virtue of this Act.

2 Proceedings to be stayed when commenced in respect of a copy of an authenticated report, etc

In case of any civil or criminal proceeding hereafter to be commenced or prosecuted for or on account or in respect of the publication of any copy of such report, paper, votes, or proceedings, it shall be lawful for the defendant or defendants at any stage of the proceedings to lay before the court or judge such report, paper, votes, or proceedings, and such copy, with an affidavit verifying such report, paper, votes or proceedings, and the correctness of such copy, and the court or judge shall immediately stay such civil or criminal proceeding; and the same, and every writ or process issued therein, shall be and shall be deemed and taken to be finally put an end to, determined and superseded by virtue of this Act.

3 In proceedings for printing any extract or abstract of a paper, it may be shewn that such extract was bona fide made

It shall be lawful in any civil or criminal proceeding to be commenced or prosecuted for printing any extract from or abstract of such report, paper, votes, or proceedings, to give in evidence such report, paper, votes or proceedings, and to show that such extract or abstract was published bona fide and without malice; and if such shall be the opinion of the jury, a verdict of not guilty shall be entered for the defendant or defendants.

4 Act not to affect the privileges of Parliament

Provided always that nothing herein contained shall be deemed or taken, or held or construed, directly or indirectly, by implication or otherwise, to affect the privileges of Parliament in any manner whatsoever.

[As amended by the Statute Law Revision (No 2) Act 1888; Statute Law Revision (No 2) Act 1890; Statute Law Revision Act 1958.]

Libel Act 1843
(6 & 7 Vict c 96)

1 Offer of an apology admissible in evidence in mitigation of damages in action for defamation

In any action for defamation it shall be lawful for the defendant (after notice in writing of his intention so to do, duly given to the plaintiff at the time of filing or delivering the plea in such action,) to give evidence, in mitigation of damages, that he made or offered an apology to the plaintiff for such defamation before the commencement of the action, or as soon afterwards as he had an opportunity of doing so, in case the action shall have been commenced before there was an opportunity of making or offering such apology.

2 In an action against a newspaper for libel, the defendant may plead that it was inserted without malice and without negligence, and that he has published or offered to publish an apology

In an action for libel contained in any public newspaper or other periodical publication it shall be competent to the defendant to plead that such libel was inserted in such newspaper or other periodical publication without actual malice, and without gross negligence, and that before the commencement of the action, or at the earliest opportunity afterwards, he inserted in such newspaper or other periodical publication a full apology for the said libel, or, if the newspaper or periodical publication in which the said libel appeared should be ordinarily published at intervals exceeding one week, had offered to publish the said apology in any newspaper or periodical publication to be selected by the plaintiff in such action; and to such plea to such action it shall be competent to the plaintiff to reply generally, denying the whole of such plea.

[As amended by the Statute Law Revision Acts 1891 and 1892.]

Libel Act 1845
(8 & 9 Vict c 75)

2 Defendant not to plead matters allowed by the Libel Act 1843 without payment into court

It shall not be competent to any defendant in such action, whether in England or Ireland, to file any such plea, without at the same time making a payment of money into court by way of amends, but every such plea so filed without payment of money into court shall be deemed a nullity, and may be treated as such by the plaintiff in the action.

[As amended by the Statute Law Revision Act 1891.]

Newspaper Libel and Registration Act 1881
(44 & 45 Vict c 60)

1 Interpretation ...

The word 'newspaper' shall mean any paper containing public news, intelligence, or occurrences, or any remarks or observations therein printed for sale, and published in England or Ireland periodically, or in parts or numbers at intervals not exceeding twenty-six days between the publication of any two such papers, parts, or numbers. ...

Law of Libel Amendment Act 1888
(51 & 52 Vict c 64)

1 Interpretation

In the construction of this Act the word 'newspaper' shall have the same meaning as in the Newspaper Libel and Registration Act 1881.

5 Consolidation of actions

It shall be competent for a judge or the court, upon an application by or on behalf of two or more defendants in actions in respect to the same, or substantially the same, libel brought by one and the same person, to make an order for the consolidation of such actions, so that they shall be tried together; and after such order has been made, and before the trial of the said actions, the defendants in any new actions instituted in respect to the same, or substantially the same, libel shall also be entitled to be joined in a common action upon a joint application being made by such new defendants and the defendants in the actions already consolidated. In a consolidated action under this section the jury shall assess the whole amount of the damages (if any) in one sum, but a separate verdict shall be taken for or against each defendant in the same way as if the actions consolidated had been tried separately; and if the jury shall have found a verdict against the defendant or defendants in more than one of the actions so consolidated, they shall proceed to apportion the amount of damages which they shall have so found between and against the said last-mentioned defendants; and the judge at the trial, if he awards to the plaintiff the costs of the action, shall thereupon make such order as he shall deem just for the apportionment of such costs between and against such defendants.

Partnership Act 1890
(53 & 54 Vict c 39)

10 Liability of the firm for wrongs

Where, by any wrongful act or omission of any partner acting in the ordinary course of the business of the firm, or with the authority of his co-partners, loss or injury is caused to any person not being a partner in the firm, or any penalty is incurred, the firm is liable therefore to the same extent as the partner so acting or omitting to act.

11 Misapplication of money or property received for or in custody of the firm

In the following cases; namely –

(a) Where one partner acting within the scope of his apparent authority receives the money or property of a third person and misapplies it; and

(b) Where a firm in the course of its business receives money or property of a third person, and the money or property so received is misapplied by one or more of the partners while it is in the custody of the firm;

the firm is liable to make good the loss.

12 Liability for wrongs joint and several

Every partner is liable jointly with his co-partners and also severally for everything for which the firm while he is a partner therein becomes liable under either of the two last preceding sections.

Slander of Women Act 1891
(54 & 55 Vict c 51)

1 Amendment of law

Words spoken and published which impute unchastity or adultery to any woman or girl shall not require special damage to render them actionable. Provided always, that in any action for words spoken and made actionable by this Act, a plaintiff shall not recover more costs than damages, unless the judge shall certify that there was reasonable ground for bringing the action.

[As amended by the Statute Law Revision Act 1908.]

Railway Fires Act 1905
(5 Edw 7 c 11)

1 Liability of railway companies to make good damage to crops by their engines

(1) When, after this Act comes into operation, damage is caused to agricultural land or to agricultural crops, as in this Act defined, by fire arising from sparks or cinders emitted from any locomotive engine used on a railway, the fact that the engine was used under statutory powers shall not affect liability in an action for such damage.

(2) Where any such damage has been caused through the use of an engine by one company

on a railway worked by another company, either company shall be liable in such an action; but, if the action is brought against the company working the railway, that company shall be entitled to be indemnified in respect of their liability by the company by whom the engine was used.

(3) This section shall not apply in the case of any action for damage unless the claim for damage in the action does not exceed £3,000 or such greater sum as may for the time being be prescribed by order made by the Secretary of State.

(3A) An order under subsection (3) above shall be made by statutory instrument which shall be subject to annulment in pursuance of a resolution of either House of Parliament. ...

4 Definitions and application

In this Act –

The expression 'agricultural land' includes arable and meadow land and ground used for pastoral purposes or for market or nursery gardens, and plantations and woods and orchards, and also includes any fences on such land, but does not include any moorland or buildings; The expression 'agricultural crops' includes any crops on agricultural land, whether growing or severed, which are not led or stacked; The expression 'railway' includes any light railway and any tramway worked by steam power. ... This Act shall apply to agricultural land under the management of the Commissioners of Woods, and to agricultural crops thereon.

[As amended by s38(1) of the Transport Act 1981.]

Law Reform (Miscellaneous Provisions) Act 1934
(24 & 25 Geo 5 c 41)

1 Effect of death on certain causes of action

(1) Subject to the provisions of this section, on the death of any person after the commencement of this Act all causes of action subsisting against or vested in him shall survive against, or, as the case may be, for the benefit of, his estate. Provided that this subsection shall not apply to causes of action for defamation.

(1A) The right of a person to claim under section 1A of the Fatal Accidents Act 1976 (bereavement) shall not survive for the benefit of his estate on his death.

(2) Where a cause of action survives as aforesaid for the benefit of the estate of a deceased person, the damages recoverable for the benefit of the estate of that person –

(a) shall not include –

(i) any exemplary damages;
(ii) any damages for loss of income in respect of any period after that person's death;

(c) where the death of that person has been caused by the act or omission which gives rise to the cause of action, shall be calculated without reference to any loss or gain to his estate consequent on his death, except that a sum in respect of funeral expenses may be included.

(4) Where damage has been suffered by reason of any act or omission in respect of which a cause of action would have subsisted against any person if that person had not died before or at the same time as the damage was suffered, there shall be deemed, for the purposes of this Act, to have been subsisting against him before his death such cause of action in respect of that act or omission as would have subsisted if he had died after the damage was suffered.

(5) The rights conferred by this Act for the benefit of the estates of deceased persons shall be in addition to and not in derogation of any rights conferred on the dependants of deceased persons by the Fatal Accidents Act 1976, and so much of this Act as relates to causes of action against the estates of deceased persons shall apply in relation to causes of action under the said Acts as it applies in relation to other causes of action not expressly excepted from the operation of subsection (1) of this section.

(6) In the event of the insolvency of an estate against which proceedings are maintainable by virtue of this section, any liability in respect of the cause of action in respect of which the proceedings are maintainable shall be deemed to be a debt provable in the administration of the estate, notwithstanding that it is a demand in the nature of unliquidated damages arising otherwise than by a contract, promise or breach of trust.

[As amended by the Statute Law Revision Act 1950; Carriage by Air Act 1961, s14(3), Schedule 2; Law Reform (Miscellaneous Provisions) Act 1970, s7, Schedule; Proceedings Against Estates Act 1970, s1; Administration of Justice Act 1982, ss4(1), (2), 75(1), Schedule 9.]

Law Reform (Married Women and Tortfeasors) Act 1935
(25 & 26 Geo 5 c 30)

Part I

Capacity, Property, and Liabilities of Married Women, and Liabilities of Husbands

1 Capacity of married women

Subject to the provisions of this Part of this Act, a married woman shall –

(a) be capable of acquiring, holding, and disposing of, any property; and
(b) be capable of rendering herself, and being rendered, liable in respect of any tort, contract, debt, or obligation; and
(c) be capable of suing and being sued, either in tort or in contract or otherwise; and
(d) be subject to the law relating to bankruptcy and to the enforcement of judgments and orders.

in all respects as if she were a feme sole.

2 *Property of married women*

(1) Subject to the provisions of this Part of this Act all property which –

(a) immediately before the passing of this Act was the separate property of a married woman or held for her separate use in equity; or

(b) belongs at the time of her marriage to a woman married after the passing of this Act; or

(c) after the passing of this Act is acquired by or devolves upon a married woman,

shall belong to her in all respects as if she were a feme sole and may be disposed of accordingly.

3 *Abolition of husband's liability for wife's torts and ante-nuptial contracts, debts and obligations*

Subject to the provisions of this Part of this Act, the husband of a married woman shall not, by reason only of his being her husband, be liable –

(a) in respect of any tort committed by her whether before or after the marriage, or in respect of any contract entered into, or debt or obligation incurred, by her before the marriage; or

(b) to be sued, or made a party to any legal proceeding brought, in respect of any such tort, contract, debt, or obligation.

4 *Savings*

(1) Nothing in this Part of this Act shall –

(a) during converture which began before the first day of January eighteen hundred and eighty-three, affect any property to which the title (whether vested or contingent, and whether in possession, reversion, or remainder) of a married woman accrued before that date, except property held for her separate use in equity;

(b) affect any legal proceeding in respect of any tort if proceedings had been instituted in respect thereof before the passing of this Act;

(c) enable any judgment or order against a married woman in respect of a contract entered into, or debt or obligation incurred, before the passing of this Act, to be enforced in bankruptcy or to be enforced otherwise than against her property.

(2) For the avoidance of doubt it is hereby declared that nothing in this Part of this Act –

(a) renders the husband of a married woman liable in respect of any contract entered into, or debt or obligation incurred, by her after the marriage in respect of which he would not have been liable if this Act had not been passed;

(b) exempts the husband of a married woman from liability in respect of any contract entered into, or debt or obligation (not being a debt or obligation arising out of the commission of a tort) incurred by her after the marriage in respect of which he would have been liable if this Act had not been passed;

(c) prevents a husband and wife from acquiring, holding, and disposing of, any property jointly or as tenants in common, or from rendering themselves, or being rendered, jointly liable in respect of any tort, contract, debt or obligation, and of suing and being sued either in tort or in contract or otherwise, in like manner as if they were not married;

(d) prevents the exercise of any joint power given to a husband and wife.

[As amended by the Married Women (Restraint upon Anticipation) Act 1949, s1(2), (4), Schedule 2; Law Reform (Husband and Wife) Act 1962, s3(2), Schedule.]

Law Reform (Contributory Negligence) Act 1945
(8 & 9 Geo 6 c 28)

1 Apportionment of liability in case of contributory negligence

(1) Where any person suffers damage as the result partly of his own fault and partly of the fault of any other person or persons, a claim in respect of that damage shall not be defeated by reason of the fault of the person suffering the damage, but the damages recoverable in respect thereof shall be reduced to such extent as the court thinks just and equitable having regard to the claimant's share in the responsibility for the damage:

Provided that –

(a) this subsection shall not operate to defeat any defence arising under a contract;

(b) where any contract or enactment providing for the limitation of liability is applicable to the claim, the amount of damages recoverable by the claimant by virtue of this subsection shall not exceed the maximum limit so applicable.

(2) Where damages are recoverable by any person by virtue of the foregoing subsection subject to such reduction as is therein mentioned, the court shall find and record the total damages which would have been recoverable if the claimant had not been at fault.

(5) Where, in any case to which subsection (1) of this section applies, one of the persons at fault avoids liability to any other such person or his personal representative by pleading the Limitation Act 1939, or any other enactment limiting the time within which proceedings may be taken, he shall not be entitled to recover any damages from that other person or representative by virtue of the said subsection.

(6) Where any case to which subsection (1) of this section applies is tried with a jury, the jury shall determine the total damages which would have been recoverable if the claimant had not been at fault and the extent to which those damages are to be reduced.

3 Saving for Maritime Conventions Act 1911 and past cases

(1) This Act shall not apply to any claim to which section one of the Maritime Conventions Act 1911 applies and that Act shall have effect as if this Act had not passed.

(2) This Act shall not apply to any case where the acts or omissions giving rise to the claim occurred before the passing of this Act.

4 *Interpretation*

The following expressions have the meanings hereby respectively assigned to them, that is to say –

'court' means, in relation to any claim, the court or arbitrator by or before whom the claim falls to be determined;

'damage' includes loss of life and personal injury;

'fault' means negligence, breach of statutory duty or other act or omission which gives rise to a liability in tort or would, apart from this Act, give rise to the defence of contributory negligence.

[As amended by the National Insurance (Industrial Injuries) Act 1946, s89(1), Schedule 9; Carriage by Air Act 1961, s14(3), Schedule 2; Fatal Accidents Act 1976, s6(2), Schedul;e 2; Civil Liability (Contribution) Act 1978, s9(2), Schedule 2.]

Fire Services Act 1947
(10 & 11 Geo 6 c 41)

30 *Powers of firemen and police in extinguishing fires*

(1) Any member of a fire brigade maintained in pursuance of this Act who is on duty, any member of any other fire brigade who is acting in pursuance of any arrangements made under this Act, or any constable, may enter and if necessary break into any premises or place in which a fire has or is reasonably believed to have broken out, or any premises or place which it is necessary to enter for the purposes of extinguishing a fire or of protecting the premises or place from acts done for fire-fighting purposes, without the consent of the owner or occupier thereof, and may do all such things as he may deem necessary for extinguishing the fire or for protecting from fire, or from acts done as aforesaid, any such premises or place or for rescuing any person or property therein.

(2) Any person who wilfully obstructs or interferes with any member of a fire brigade maintained in pursuance of this Act who is engaged in operations for fire-fighting purposes shall be liable on summary conviction to a fine not exceeding level 3 on the standard scale.

(3) At any fire the senior fire brigade officer present shall have the sole charge and control of all operations for the extinction of the fire, including the fixing of the positions of fire engines and apparatus, the attaching of hose to any water pipes or the use of any water supply, and the selection of the parts of the premises, object or place where the fire is, or of adjoining premises, objects or places, against which the water is to be directed. ...

[As amended by the Criminal Justice Act 1982, ss38, 46.]

Crown Proceedings Act 1947
(10 & 11 Geo 6 c 44)

Part I
Substantive Law

1 Right to sue the Crown

Where any person has a claim against the Crown after the commencement of this Act, and, if this Act had not been passed, the claim might have been enforced, subject to the grant of His Majesty's fiat, by petition of right, or might have been enforced by a proceeding provided by any statutory provision repealed by this Act, then, subject to the provisions of this Act, the claim may be enforced as of right, and without the fiat of His Majesty, by proceedings taken against the Crown for that purpose in accordance with the provisions of this Act.

2 Liability of the Crown in tort

(1) Subject to the provisions of this Act, the Crown shall be subject to all those liabilities in tort to which, if it were a private person of full age and capacity, it would be subject –

(a) in respect of torts committed by its servants or agents;
(b) in respect of any breach of those duties which a person owes to his servants or agents at common law by reason of being their employer; and
(c) in respect of any breach of the duties attaching at common law to the ownership, occupation, possession or control of property:

Provided that no proceedings shall lie against the Crown by virtue of paragraph (a) of this subsection in respect of any act or omission of a servant or agent of the Crown unless the act or omission would apart from the provisions of this Act have given rise to a cause of action in tort against that servant or agent or his estate.

(2) Where the Crown is bound by a statutory duty which is binding also upon persons other than the Crown and its officers, then, subject to the provisions of this Act, the Crown shall, in respect of a failure to comply with that duty, be subject to all those liabilities in tort (if any) to which it would be so subject if it were a private person of full age and capacity.

(3) Where any functions are conferred or imposed upon an officer of the Crown as such either by any rule of the common law or by statute, and that officer commits a tort while performing or purporting to perform those functions, the liabilities of the Crown in respect of the tort shall be such as they would have been if those functions had been conferred or imposed solely by virtue of instructions lawfully given by the Crown.

(4) Any enactment which negatives or limits the amount of the liability of any Government department or officer of the Crown in respect of any tort committed by that department or officer shall, in the case of proceedings against the Crown under this section in respect of a tort committed by that department or officer, apply in relation to the Crown as it would

have applied in relation to that department or officer if the proceedings against the Crown had been proceedings against that department or officer.

(5) No proceedings shall lie against the Crown by virtue of this section in respect of anything done or omitted to be done by any person while discharging or purporting to discharge any responsibilities of a judicial nature vested in him, or any responsibilities which he has in connection with the execution of judicial process.

(6) No proceedings shall lie against the Crown by virtue of this section in respect of any act, neglect or default of any officer of the Crown, unless that officer has been directly or indirectly appointed by the Crown and was at the material time paid in respect of his duties as an officer of the Crown wholly out of the Consolidated Fund of the United Kingdom, moneys provided by Parliament, or any other Fund certified by the Treasury for the purposes of this subsection or was at the material time holding an office in respect of which the Treasury certify that the holder thereof would normally be so paid.

4 Application of law as to indemnity, contribution, joint and several tortfeasors, and contributory negligence

(1) Where the Crown is subject to any liability by virtue of this Part of this Act, the law relating to indemnity and contribution shall be enforceable by or against the Crown in respect of the liability to which it is so subject as if the Crown were a private person of full age and capacity.

(3) Without prejudice to the general effect of section one of this Act, the Law Reform (Contributory Negligence) Act 1945 (which amends the law relating to contributory negligence) shall bind the Crown.

11 Saving in respect of acts done under prerogative and statutory power

(1) Nothing in Part I of this Act shall extinguish or abridge any powers or authorities which, if this Act had not been passed, would have been exercisable by virtue of the prerogative of the Crown, or any powers or authorities conferred on the Crown by any statute, and, in particular, nothing in the said Part I shall extinguish or abridge any powers or authorities exercisable by the Crown, whether in time of peace or of war, for the purpose of the defence of the realm or of training, or maintaining the efficiency of, any of the armed forces of the Crown.

(2) Where in any proceedings under this Act it is material to determine whether anything was properly done or omitted to be done in the exercise of the prerogative of the Crown, a Secretary of State may, if satisfied that the act or omission was necessary for any such purpose as is mentioned in the last preceding subsection, issue a certificate to the effect that the act or omission was necessary for that purpose; and the certificate shall, in those proceedings, be conclusive as to the matter so certified.

Part II
Jurisdiction and Procedure

21 Nature of relief

(1) In any civil proceedings by or against the Crown the court shall, subject to the provisions of this Act, have power to make all such orders as it has power to make in proceedings between subjects, and otherwise to give such appropriate relief as the case may require:

Provided that –

(a) where in any proceedings against the Crown any such relief is sought as might in proceedings between subjects be granted by way of injunction or specific performance, the court shall not grant an injunction or make an order for specific performance, but may in lieu thereof make an order declaratory of the rights of the parties; and

(b) in any proceedings against the Crown for the recovery of land or other property the court shall not make an order for the recovery of the land or the delivery of the property, but may in lieu thereof make an order declaring that the plaintiff is entitled as against the Crown to the land or property or to the possession thereof.

(2) The court shall not in any civil proceedings grant any injunction or make any order against an officer of the Crown if the effect of granting the injunction or making the order would be to give any relief against the Crown which could not have been obtained in proceedings against the Crown.

Part IV
Miscellaneous and Supplemental

38 Interpretation

(1) Any reference in this Act to the provisions of this Act shall, unless the context otherwise requires, include a reference to rules of court or county court rules made for the purposes of this Act.

(2) In this Act, except in so far as the context otherwise requires or it is otherwise expressly provided, the following expressions have the meanings hereby respectively assigned to them, that is to say –

'Agent', when used in relation to the Crown, includes an independent contractor employed by the Crown;

'Civil proceedings' includes proceedings in the High Court or the county court for the recovery of fines or penalties, but does not include proceedings on the Crown side of the King's Bench Division; ...

'Officer', in relation to the Crown, includes any servant of His Majesty, and accordingly (but without prejudice to the generality of the foregoing provision) includes a Minister of the Crown and a member of the Scottish Executive;

'Order' includes a judgment, decree, rule, award or declaration;

'Prescribed' means prescribed by rules of court or county court rules, as the case may be;

'Proceedings against the Crown' includes a claim by way of set-off or counter-claim raised in proceedings by the Crown;

'Ship' has the same meaning as in the Merchant Shipping Act 1995;

'Statutory duty' means any duty imposed by or under any Act of Parliament.

(3) Any reference in this Act to His Majesty in His private capacity shall be construed as including a reference to His Majesty in right of His Duchy of Lancaster and to the Duke of Cornwall.

(4) Any reference in Parts III or IV of this Act to civil proceedings by or against the Crown, or to civil proceedings to which the Crown is a party, shall be construed as including a reference to civil proceedings to which the Attorney-General, or any Governmental department, or any officer of the Crown as such is a party:

Provided that the Crown shall not for the purposes of Parts III and IV of this Act be deemed to be a party to any proceedings by reason only that they are brought by the Attorney-General upon the relation of some other person. …

40 Savings

(1) Nothing in this Act shall apply to proceedings by or against, or authorise proceedings in tort to be brought against, His Majesty in His private capacity.

[As amended by the Defence (Transfer of Functions) (No 1) Order 1964; Civil Liability (Contribution) Act 1978, s9(2), Schedule 2; Statute Law (Repeals) Act 1981; Armed Forces Act 1981, s28(2), Schedule 5, Pt I; Merchant Shipping Act 1995, s314(2), Schedule 13, para 21; Scotland Act 1998, s125(1), Schedule 8, para 7(1), (2).]

Law Reform (Personal Injuries) Act 1948
(11 & 12 Geo 6 c 41)

1 Common employment

(1) It shall not be a defence to an employer who is sued in respect of personal injuries caused by the negligence of a person employed by him, that that person was at the time the injuries were caused in common employment with the person injured …

(3) Any provision contained in a contract of service or apprenticeship, or in an agreement collateral thereto (including a contract or agreement entered into before the commencement of this Act) shall be void in so far as it would have the effect of excluding or limiting any liability of the employer in respect of personal injuries caused to the person employed or apprenticed by the negligence of persons in common employment with him.

2 *Measure of damages*

(4) In an action for damages for personal injuries (including any such action arising out of a contract), there shall be disregarded, in determining the reasonableness of any expenses, the possibility of avoiding these expenses or part of them by taking advantage of facilities available under the National Health Service Act 1977 ...

3 *Definition of 'personal injury'*

In this Act the expression 'personal injury' includes any disease and any impairment of a person's physical or mental condition, and the expression 'injured' shall be construed accordingly.

4 *Application to Crown*

This Act shall bind the Crown.

[As amended by the Fatal Accidents Act 1959, s3(3), Schedule; National Health Service Act 1977, s129, Schedule 15, para 8; Social Security (Recovery of Benefits) Act 1997, s33(1), (2), Schedule 3, para 1, Schedule 4.]

Defamation Act 1952
(15 & 16 Geo & Eliz 2 c 66)

2 *Slander affecting official, professional or business reputation*

In an action for slander in respect of words calculated to disparage the plaintiff in any office, profession, calling, trade or business held or carried on by him at the time of the publication, it shall not be necessary to allege or prove special damage, whether or not the words are spoken of the plaintiff in the way of his office, profession, calling, trade or business.

3 *Slander of title, etc*

(1) In an action for slander of title, slander of goods or other malicious falsehood, it shall not be necessary to allege or prove special damage –

(a) if the words upon which the action is founded are calculated to cause pecuniary damage to the plaintiff and are published in writing or other permanent form; or
(b) if the said words are calculated to cause pecuniary damage to the plaintiff in respect of any office, profession, calling, trade or business held or carried on by him at the time of the publication.

4 *Unintentional defamation*

(1) A person who has published words alleged to be defamatory of another person may, if he claims that the words were published by him innocently in relation to that other person, make an offer of amends under this section; and in any such case –

(a) if the offer is accepted by the party aggrieved and is duly performed, no proceedings for libel or slander shall be taken or continued by that party against the person making the offer in respect of the publication in question (but without prejudice to any cause of action against any other person jointly responsible for that publication);

(b) if the offer is not accepted by the party aggrieved, then, except as otherwise provided by this section, it shall be a defence, in any proceedings by him for libel or slander against the person making the offer in respect of the publication in question, to prove that the words complained of were published by the defendant innocently in relation to the plaintiff and that the offer was made as soon as practicable after the defendant received notice that they were or might be defamatory of the plaintiff, and has not been withdrawn.

(2) An offer of amends under this section must be expressed to be made for the purposes of this section, and must be accompanied by an affidavit specifying the facts relied upon by the person making it to show that the words in question were published by him innocently in relation to the party aggrieved; and for the purposes of a defence under paragraph (b) of subsection (1) of this section no evidence, other than evidence of facts specified in the affidavit, shall be admissible on behalf of that person to prove that the words were so published.

(3) An offer of amends under this section shall be understood to mean an offer –

(a) in any case, to publish or join in the publication of a suitable correction of the words complained of, and a sufficient apology to the party aggrieved in respect of those words;

(b) where copies of a document or record containing the said words have been distributed by or with the knowledge of the person making the offer, to take such steps as are reasonably practicable on his part for notifying persons to whom copies have been so distributed that the words are alleged to be defamatory of the party aggrieved.

(4) Where an offer of amends under this section is accepted by the party aggrieved –

(a) any question as to the steps to be taken in fulfilment of the offer as so accepted shall in default of agreement between the parties be referred to and determined by the High Court, whose decision thereon shall be final;

(b) the power of the court to make orders as to costs in proceedings by the party aggrieved against the person making the offer in respect of the publication in question, or in proceedings in respect of the offer under paragraph (a) of this subsection, shall include power to order the payment by the person making the offer to the party aggrieved of costs on an indemnity basis and any expenses reasonably incurred or to be incurred by that party in consequence of the publication in question;

and if no such proceedings as aforesaid are taken, the High Court may, upon application made by the party aggrieved, make any such order for the payment of such costs and expenses as aforesaid as could be made in such proceedings

(5) For the purposes of this section words shall be treated as published by one person (in this subsection referred to as the publisher) innocently in relation to another person if and only if the following conditions are satisfied, that is to say –

(a) that the publisher did not intend to publish them of and concerning that other person, and did not know of circumstances by virtue of which they might be understood to refer to him; or

(b) that the words were not defamatory on the face of them, and the publisher did not know of circumstances by virtue of which they might be understood to be defamatory of that other person,

and in either case that the publisher exercised all reasonable care in relation to the publication; and any reference in this subsection to the publisher shall be construed as including a reference to any servant or agent of his who was concerned with the contents of the publication.

(6) Paragraph (b) of subsection (1) of this section shall not apply in relation to the publication by any person of words of which he is not the author unless he proves that the words were written by the author without malice.

5 Justification

In an action for libel or slander in respect of words containing two or more distinct charges against the plaintiff, a defence of justification shall not fail by reason only that the truth of every charge is not proved if the words not proved to be true do not materially injure the plaintiff's reputation having regard to the truth of the remaining charges.

6 Fair comment

In an action for libel or slander in respect of words consisting partly of allegations of fact and partly of expression of opinion, a defence of fair comment shall not fail by reason only that the truth of every allegation of fact is not proved if the expression of opinion is fair comment having regard to such of the facts alleged or referred to in the words complained of as are proved.

9 Extension of certain defences to broadcasting

(1) Section three of the Parliamentary Papers Act 1840 (which confers protection in respect of proceedings for printing extracts from or abstracts of parliamentary papers) shall have effect as if the reference to printing included a reference to broadcasting by means of wireless telegraphy.

10 Limitation on privilege at elections

A defamatory statement published by or on behalf of a candidate in any election to a local government authority, to the Scottish Parliament or to Parliament shall not be deemed to be published on a privileged occasion on the ground that it is material to a question in issue in the election, whether or not the person by whom it is published is qualified to vote at the election.

11 Agreements for indemnity

An agreement for indemnifying any person against civil liability for libel in respect of the publication of any matter shall not be lawful unless at the time of the publication that person knows that the matter is defamatory, and does not reasonably believe there is a good defence to any action brought upon it.

12 Evidence of other damages recovered by plaintiff

In any action for libel or slander the defendant may give evidence in mitigation of damages that the plaintiff has recovered damages, or has brought actions for damages, for libel or slander in respect of the publication of words to the same effect as the words on which the action is founded, or has received or agreed to receive compensation in respect of any such publication.

13 Consolidation of actions for slander, etc

Section five of the Law of Libel Amendment Act 1888 (which provides for the consolidation, on the application of the defendants, of two or more actions for libel by the same plaintiff) shall apply to actions for slander and to actions for slander of title, slander of goods or other malicious falsehood as it applies to actions for libel; and references in that section to the same, or substantially the same, libel shall be construed accordingly.

16 Interpretation

(1) Any reference in this Act to words shall be construed as including a reference to pictures, visual images, gestures and other methods of signifying meaning.

(3) In this Act 'broadcasting by means of wireless telegraphy' means publication for general reception by means of wireless telegraphy within the meaning of the Wireless Telegraphy Act 1949, and 'broadcast by means of wireless telegraphy' shall be construed accordingly.

17 Proceedings affected and saving

(1) This Act applies for the purposes of any proceedings begun after the commencement of this Act, whenever the cause of action arose, but does not affect any proceedings begun before the commencement of this Act.

(2) Nothing in this Act affects the law relating to criminal libel.

[As amended by the Revision of the Army and Air Force Acts (Transitional Provisions) Act 1955, s3, Schedule 2, para 16; British Nationality Act 1981, s52(6), Schedule 7; Cable and Broadcasting Act 1984, s57(2), Schedule 6; Local Government (Access to Information) Act 1985, s3(1), Schedule 2, para 2; Defamation Act 1996, s16, Schedule 2; Scotland Act 1998, Schedule 8, para 10.]

Occupiers' Liability Act 1957
(5 & 6 Eliz 2 c 31)

1 Preliminary

(1) The rules enacted by the two next following sections shall have effect, in place of the rules of the common law, to regulate the duty which an occupier of premises owes to his visitors in respect of dangers due to the state of the premises or to things done or omitted to be done on them.

(2) The rules so enacted shall regulate the nature of the duty imposed by law in consequence of a person's occupation or control of premises and of any invitation or permission he gives (or is to be treated as giving) to another to enter or use the premises, but they shall not alter the rules of the common law as to the persons on whom a duty is so imposed or to whom it is owed; and accordingly for the purpose of the rules so enacted the persons who are to be treated as an occupier and as his visitors are the same (subject to subsection (4) of this section) as the persons who would at common law be treated as an occupier and as his invitees or licensees.

(3) The rules so enacted in relation to an occupier of premises and his visitors shall also apply, in like manner and to the like extent as the principles applicable at common law to an occupier of premises and his invitees or licensees would apply, to regulate –

(a) the obligations of a person occupying or having control over any fixed or movable structure, including any vessel, vehicle or aircraft; and

(b) the obligations of a person occupying or having control over any premises or structure in respect of damage to property, including the property of persons who are not themselves his visitors.

(4) A person entering any premises in exercise of rights conferred by virtue of an access agreement or order under the National Parks and Access to the Countryside Act 1949 is not, for the purposes of this Act, a visitor of the occupier of those premises.

2 Extent of occupier's ordinary duty

(1) An occupier of premises owes the same duty, the 'common duty of care', to all his visitors, except in so far as he is free and does extend, restrict, modify or exclude his duty to any visitor or visitors by agreement or otherwise.

(2) The common duty of care is a duty to take such care as in all the circumstances of the case is reasonable to see that the visitor will be reasonably safe in using the premises for the purposes for which he is invited or permitted by the occupier to be there.

(3) The circumstances relevant for the present purpose include the degree of care and want of care, which would ordinarily be looked for in such a visitor, so that (for example) in proper cases –

(a) an occupier must be prepared for children to be less careful than adults; and

(b) an occupier may expect that a person, in the exercise of his calling, will appreciate and guard against any special risks ordinarily incident to it, so far as the occupier leaves him free to do so.

(4) In determining whether the occupier of premises has discharged the common duty of care to a visitor, regard is to be had to all the circumstances so that (for example) –

(a) where damage is caused to a visitor by a danger of which he had been warned by the occupier, the warning is not to be treated without more as absolving the occupier from liability, unless in all the circumstances it was enough to enable the visitor to be reasonably safe; and

(b) where damage is caused to a visitor by a danger due to the faulty execution of any work of construction, maintenance or repair by an independent contractor employed by the occupier, the occupier is not to be treated without more as answerable for the danger if in all the circumstances he had acted reasonably in entrusting the work to an independent contractor and had taken such steps (if any) as he reasonably ought in order to satisfy himself that the contractor was competent and that the work had been properly done.

(5) The common duty of care does not impose on an occupier any obligation to a visitor in respect of risks willingly accepted as his by the visitor (the question whether a risk was so accepted to be decided on the same principles as in other cases in which one person owes a duty of care to another).

(6) For the purposes of this section, persons who enter premises for any purpose in the exercise of a right conferred by law are to be treated as permitted by the occupier to be there for that purpose, whether they in fact have his permission or not.

3 Effect of contract on occupier's liability to third party

(1) Where an occupier of premises is bound by contract to permit persons who are strangers to the contract to enter or use the premises, the duty of care which he owes to them as his visitors cannot be restricted or excluded by that contract, but (subject to any provision of the contract to the contrary) shall include the duty to perform his obligations under the contract, whether undertaken for their protection or not, in so far as those obligations go beyond the obligations otherwise involved in that duty.

(2) A contract shall not by virtue of this section have the effect, unless it expressly so provides, of making an occupier who has taken all reasonable care answerable to strangers to the contract for dangers due to the faulty execution of any work of construction, maintenance or repair or other like operation by persons other than himself, his servants and persons acting under his direction and control.

(3) In this section 'stranger to the contract' means a person not for the time being entitled to the benefit of the contract as a party to it or as the successor by assignment or otherwise of a party to it, and accordingly includes a party to the contract who has ceased to be so entitled.

(4) Where by the terms or conditions governing any tenancy (including a statutory tenancy which does not in law amount to a tenancy) either the landlord or the tenant is bound,

though not by contract, to permit persons to enter or use premises of which he is the occupier, this section shall apply as if the tenancy were a contract between the landlord and the tenant.

(5) This section, in so far as it prevents the common duty of care from being restricted or excluded, applies to contracts entered into and tenancies created before the commencement of this Act, as well as to those entered into or created after its commencement; but, in so far as it enlarges the duty owed by an occupier beyond the common duty of care, it shall have effect only in relation to obligations which are undertaken after that commencement or which are renewed by agreement (whether express or implied) after that commencement.

5 Implied term in contracts

(1) Where persons enter or use, or bring or send goods to, any premises in exercise of a right conferred by contract with a person occupying or having control of the premises, the duty he owes them in respect of dangers due to the state of the premises or to things done or omitted to be done on them, in so far as the duty depends on a term to be implied in the contract by reason of its conferring that right, shall be the common duty of care.

(2) The foregoing subsection shall apply to fixed and movable structures as it applies to premises.

(3) This section does not affect the obligations imposed on a person by or by virtue of any contract for the hire of, or for the carriage for reward of persons or goods in, any vehicle, vessel, aircraft or other means of transport, or by or by virtue of any contract of bailment.

6 Application to Crown

This Act shall bind the Crown, but as regards the Crown's liability in tort shall not bind the Crown further than the Crown is made liable in tort by the Crown Proceedings Act 1947, and that Act and in particular section two of it shall apply in relation to duties under sections two to four of this Act as statutory duties.

Law Reform (Husband and Wife) Act 1962
(10 & 11 Eliz 2 c 48)

1 Actions in tort between husband and wife

(1) Subject to the provisions of this section, each of the parties to a marriage shall have the like right of action in tort against the other as if they were not married.

(2) Where an action in tort is brought by one of the parties to a marriage against the other during the subsistence of the marriage, the court may stay the action if it appears – (a) that no substantial benefit would accrue to either party from the continuation of the proceedings; or (b) that the question or questions in issue could more conveniently be disposed of on an application made under section seventeen of the Married Women's Property Act 1882 (determination of questions between husband and wife as to the title to or

possession of property); and without prejudice to paragraph (b) of this subsection the court may, in such an action, either exercise any power which could be exercised on an application under the said section seventeen, or give such directions as it thinks fit for the disposal under that section of any question arising in the proceedings. ...

3 Short title, repeal, interpretation, saving and extent ...

(3) The references in subsection (1) of section one of this Act to the parties to a marriage include references to the persons who were parties to a marriage which has been dissolved. ...

[As amended by the Civil Procedure (Modification of Enactments) Order 1998, art 4.]

Misrepresentation Act 1967
(1967 c 7)

2 Damages for misrepresentation

(1) Where a person has entered into a contract after a mis-representation has been made to him by another party thereto and as a result thereof he has suffered loss, then, if the person making the misrepresentation would be liable to damages in respect thereof had the misrepresentation been made fraudulently, that person shall be so liable notwithstanding that the misrepresentation was not made fraudulently, unless he proves that he had reasonable ground to believe and did believe up to the time the contract was made that the facts represented were true.

(2) Where a person has entered into a contract after a mis-representation has been made to him otherwise than fraudulently, and he would be entitled, by reason of the misrepresentation, to rescind the contract, then, if it is claimed, in any proceedings arising out of the contract, that the contract ought to be or has been rescinded the court or arbitrator may declare the contract subsisting and award damages in lieu of rescission, if of opinion that it would be equitable to do so, having regard to the nature of the misrepresentation and the loss that would be caused by it if the contract were upheld, as well as to the loss that rescission would cause to the other party.

(3) Damages may be awarded against a person under subsection (2) of this section whether or not he is liable to damages under subsection (1) thereof, but where he is so liable any award under the said subsection (2) shall be taken into account in assessing his liability under the said subsection (1).

3 Avoidance of certain provisions excluding liability for misrepresentation

If a contract contains a term which would exclude or restrict –

(a) any liability to which a party to a contract may be subject by reason of any misrepresentation made by him before the contract was made; or

(b) any remedy available to another party to the contract by reason of such a misrepresentation;

that term shall be of no effect in so far as it satisfies the requirement of reasonableness as stated in section 11(1) of the Unfair Contract Terms Act 1977; and it is for those claiming that the term satisfies that requirement to show that it does.

[As substituted by the Unfair Contract Terms Act 1977, s8(1).]

Criminal Law Act 1967
(1967 c 58)

3 *Use of force in making arrest, etc*

(1) A person may use such force as is reasonable in the circumstances in the prevention of crime, or in effecting or assisting in the lawful arrest of offenders or suspected offenders or of persons unlawfully at large.

(2) Subsection (1) above shall replace the rules of the common law on the question when force used for a purpose mentioned in the subsection is justified by that purpose.

Theatres Act 1968
(1967 c 58)

4 *Amendment of the law of defamation*

(1) For the purposes of the law of libel and slander (including the law of criminal libel so far as it relates to the publication of defamatory matter) the publication of words in the course of a performance of a play shall, subject to section 7 of this Act, be treated as publication in permanent form.

(2) The foregoing subsection shall apply for the purposes of section 3 (slander of title, etc) of the Defamation Act 1952, as it applies for the purposes of the law of libel and slander.

(3) In this section 'words' includes pictures, visual images, gestures and other methods of signifying meaning.

7 *Exceptions for performances given in certain circumstances*

(1) Nothing in sections 2 to 4 of this Act shall apply in relation to a performance of a play given on a domestic occasion in a private dwelling.

(2) Nothing in sections 2 to 6 of this Act shall apply in relation to a performance of a play given solely or primarily for one or more of the following purposes, that is to say –

    (a) rehearsal; or
    (b) to enable –

        (i) a record or cinematograph film to be made from or by means of the performance; or

(ii) the performance to be broadcast; or

(iii) the performance to be included in a programme service (within the meaning of the Broadcasting Act 1990) other than a sound or television broadcasting service;

but in any proceedings for an offence under section 2 or 6 of this Act alleged to have been committed in respect of a performance of a play or an offence at common law alleged to have been committed in England and Wales by the publication of defamatory matter in the course of a performance of a play, if it is proved that the performance was attended by persons other than persons directly connected with the giving of the performance or the doing in relation thereto of any of the things mentioned in paragraph (b) above, the performance shall be taken to not have been given solely or primarily for one or more of the said purposes unless the contrary is shown.

(3) In this section –

'broadcast' means broadcast by wireless telegraphy (within the meaning of the Wireless Telegraphy Act 1949), whether by way of sound broadcasting or television;

'cinematograph film' means any print, negative, tape or other article on which a performance of a play or any part of such a performance is recorded for the purposes of visual reproduction;

'record' means any record or similar contrivance for reproducing sound, including the sound-track of a cinematograph film.

[As amended by the Cable and Broadcasting Act 1984, s57, Schedule 5, para 21, Schedule 6; Public Order Act 1986, s40(3), Schedule 3; Broadcasting Act 1990, s203(1), Schedule 20, para 13.]

Civil Evidence Act 1968
(1968 c 64)

13 Conclusiveness of convictions for purposes of defamation actions

(1) In an action for libel or slander in which the question whether the plaintiff did or did not commit a criminal offence is relevant to an issue arising in the action, proof that, at the date when that issue falls to be determined, he stands convicted of that offence shall be conclusive evidence that he committed that offence; and his conviction thereof shall be admissible in evidence accordingly.

(2) In any such action as aforesaid in which by virtue of this section the plaintiff is proved to have been convicted of an offence, the contents of any document which is admissible as evidence of the conviction, and the contents of the information, complaint, indictment or charge-sheet on which he was convicted, shall, without prejudice to the reception of any other admissible evidence for the purpose of identifying the facts on which the conviction was based, be admissible in evidence for the purpose of identifying those facts.

(2A) In the case of an action for libel or slander in which there is more than one plaintiff –

(a) the references in subsections (1) and (2) above to the plaintiff shall be construed as references to any of the plaintiffs, and

(b) proof that any of the plaintiffs stands convicted of an offence shall be conslusive evidence that he committed that offence so far as that fact is relevant to any issue arising in relation to his cause of action or that of any other plaintiff.

(3) For the purposes of this section a person shall be taken to stand convicted of an offence if but only if there subsists against him a conviction of that offence by or before a court in the United Kingdom or by a court-martial there or elsewhere. ...

[As amended by the Defamation Act 1996, s12(1).]

Employers' Liability (Defective Equipment) Act 1969
(1969 c 37)

1 Extension of employer's liability for defective equipment

(1) Where after the commencement of this Act –

(a) an employee suffers personal injury in the course of his employment in consequence of a defect in equipment provided by his employer for the purposes of the employer's business; and

(b) the defect is attributable wholly or partly to the fault of a third party (whether identified or not),

the injury shall be deemed to be also attributable to negligence on the part of the employer (whether or not he is liable in respect of the injury apart from this subsection), but without prejudice to the law relating to contributory negligence and to any remedy by way of contribution or in contract or otherwise which is available to the employer in respect of the injury.

(2) In so far as any agreement purports to exclude or limit any liability of an employer arising under subsection (1) of this section, the agreement shall be void.

(3) In this section –

'business' includes the activities carried on by any public body;

'employee' means a person who is employed by another person under a contract of service or apprenticeship and is so employed for the purposes of a business carried on by that other person, and 'employer' shall be construed accordingly; 'equipment' includes any plant and machinery, vehicle, aircraft and clothing;

'fault' means negligence, breach of statutory duty or other act or omission which gives rise to liability in tort in England and Wales or which is wrongful and gives rise to liability in damages in Scotland; and

'personal injury' includes loss of life, any impairment of a person's physical or mental condition and any disease.

(4) This section binds the Crown, and persons in the service of the Crown shall accordingly

be treated for the purposes of this section as employees of the Crown if they would not be so treated apart from this subsection.

Animals Act 1971
(1971 c 22)

1 New provisions as to strict liability for damage done by animals

(1) The provisions of sections 2 to 5 of this Act replace –

(a) the rules of the common law imposing a strict liability in tort for damage done by an animal on the ground that the animal is regarded as ferae naturae or that its vicious or mischievous propensities are known or presumed to be known;

(b) subsections (1) and (2) of section I of the Dogs Act 1906 as amended by the Dogs (Amendment) Act 1928 (injury to cattle or poultry); and

(c) the rules of the common law imposing a liability for cattle trespass.

(2) Expressions used in those sections shall be interpreted in accordance with the provisions of section 6 (as well as those of section 11) of this Act.

2 Liability for damage done by dangerous animals

(1) Where any damage is caused by an animal which belongs to a dangerous species, any person who is a keeper of the animal is liable for the damage, except as otherwise provided by this Act.

(2) Where damage is caused by an animal which does not belong to a dangerous species, a keeper of the animal is liable for the damage, except as otherwise provided by this Act, if –

(a) the damage is of a kind which the animal, unless restrained, was likely to cause or which, if caused by the animal, was likely to be severe; and

(b) the likelihood of the damage or of its being severe was due to characteristics of the animal which are not normally found in animals of the same species or are not normally so found except at particular times or in particular circumstances; and

(c) those characteristics were known to that keeper or were at any time known to a person who at that time had charge of the animal as that keeper's servant or, where that keeper is the head of a household, were known to another keeper of the animal who is a member of that household and under the age of sixteen.

3 Liability for injury done by dogs to livestock

Where a dog causes damage by killing or injuring livestock, any person who is a keeper of the dog is liable for the damage, except as otherwise provided by this Act.

4 Liability for damage and expenses due to trespassing livestock

(1) Where livestock belonging to any person strays on to land in the ownership or occupation of another and –

(a) damage is done by the livestock to the land or to any property on it which is in the ownership or possession of the other person; or

(b) any expenses are reasonably incurred by that other person in keeping the livestock while it cannot be restored to the person to whom it belongs or while it is detained in pursuance of section 7 of this Act, or in ascertaining to whom it belongs;

the person to whom the livestock belongs is liable for the damage or expenses, except as otherwise provided by this Act.

(2) For the purposes of this section any livestock belongs to the person in whose possession it is.

5 Exceptions from liability under sections 2 to 4

(1) A person is not liable under sections 2 to 4 of this Act for any damage which is due wholly to the fault of the person suffering it.

(2) A person is not liable under section 2 of this Act for any damage suffered by a person who has voluntarily accepted the risk thereof.

(3) A person is not liable under section 2 of this Act for any damage caused by an animal kept on any premises or structure to a person trespassing there, if it is proved either –

(a) that the animal was not kept there for the protection of persons or property; or

(b) (if the animal was kept there for the protection of persons or property) that keeping it there for that purpose was not unreasonable.

(4) A person is not liable under section 3 of this Act if the livestock was killed or injured on land on to which it had strayed and either the dog belonged to the occupier or its presence on the land was authorised by the occupier.

(5) A person is not liable under section 4 of this Act where the livestock strayed from a highway and its presence there was a lawful use of the highway.

(6) In determining whether any liability for damage under section 4 of this Act is excluded by subsection (1) of this section the damage shall not be treated as due to the fault of the person suffering it by reason only that he could have prevented it by fencing; but a person is not liable under that section where it is proved that the straying of the livestock on to the land would not have occurred but for a breach by any other person, being a person having an interest in the land, of a duty to fence.

6 Interpretation of certain expressions used in sections 2 to 5

(1) The following provisions apply to the interpretation of sections 2 to 5 of this Act.

(2) A dangerous species is a species –

(a) which is not commonly domesticated in the British Islands; and

(b) whose fully grown animals normally have such characteristics that they are likely, unless restrained, to cause severe damage or that any damage they may cause is likely to be severe.

(3) Subject to subsection (4) of this section, a person is a keeper of an animal if –

(a) he owns the animal or has it in his possession; or

(b) he is the head of a household of which a member under the age of sixteen owns the animal or has it in his possession;

and if at any time an animal ceased to be owned by or to be in the possession of a person, any person who immediately before that time was a keeper thereof by virtue of the preceding provisions of this subsection continues to be a keeper of the animal until another person becomes a keeper thereof by virtue of those provisions.

(4) Where an animal is taken into and kept in possession for the purpose of preventing it from causing damage or of restoring it to its owner, a person is not a keeper of it by virtue only of that possession.

(5) Where a person employed as a servant by a keeper of an animal incurs a risk incidental to his employment he shall not be treated as accepting it voluntarily.

7 Detention and sale of trespassing livestock

(1) The right to seize and detain any animal by way of distress damage feasant is hereby abolished.

(2) Where any livestock strays on to any land and is not then under the control of any person the occupier of the land may detain it, subject to subsection (3) of this section, unless ordered to return it by a court.

(3) Where any livestock is detained in pursuance of this section the right to detain it ceases –

(a) at the end of a period of forty-eight hours, unless within that period notice of the detention has been given to the officer in charge of a police station and also, if the person detaining the livestock knows to whom it belongs, to that person; or

(b) when such amount is tendered to the person detaining the livestock as is sufficient to satisfy any claim he may have under section 4 of this Act in respect of the livestock; or

(c) if he has no such claim, when the livestock is claimed by a person entitled to its possession.

(4) Where livestock has been detained in pursuance of this section for a period of not less than fourteen days the person detaining it may sell it at a market or by public auction, unless proceedings are then pending for the return of the livestock or for any claim under section 4 of this Act in respect of it.

(5) Where any livestock is sold in the exercise of the right conferred by this section and the proceeds of the sale, less the costs thereof and any costs incurred in connection with it, exceed the amount of any claim under section 4 of this Act which the vendor had in respect of the livestock, the excess shall be recoverable from him by the person who would be entitled to the possession of the livestock but for the sale.

(6) A person detaining any livestock in pursuance of this section is liable for any damage caused to it by a failure to treat it with reasonable care and supply it with adequate food and water while it is so detained.

(7) References in this section to a claim under section 4 of this Act in respect of any livestock do not include any claim under that section for damage done by or expenses incurred in respect of the livestock before the straying in connection with which it is detained under this section.

8 Duty to take care to prevent damage from animals straying on to the highway

(1) So much of the rules of the common law relating to liability for negligence as excludes or restricts the duty which a person might owe to others to take such care as is reasonable to see that damage is not caused by animals straying on to a highway is hereby abolished.

(2) Where damage is caused by animals straying from unfenced land to a highway a person who placed them on the land shall not be regarded as having committed a breach of the duty to take care by reason only of placing them there if –

(a) the land is common land, or is land situated in an area where fencing is not customary, or is a town or village green; and
(b) he had a right to place the animals on that land.

9 Killing of or injury to dogs worrying livestock

(1) In any civil proceedings against a person (in this section referred to as the defendant) for killing or causing injury to a dog it shall be a defence to prove –

(a) that the defendant acted for the protection of any livestock and was a person entitled to act for the protection of that livestock; and
(b) that within forty-eight hours of the killing or injury notice thereof was given by the defendant to the officer in charge of a police station.

(2) For the purposes of this section a person is entitled to act for the protection of any livestock if, and only if –

(a) the livestock or the land on which it is belongs to him or to any person under whose express or implied authority he is acting; and
(b) the circumstances are not such that liability for killing or causing injury to the livestock would be excluded by section 5(4) of this Act.

(3) Subject to subsection (4) of this section, a person killing or causing injury to a dog shall be deemed for the purposes of this section to act for the protection of any livestock if, and only if; either –

(a) the dog is worrying or is about to worry the livestock and there are no other reasonable means of ending or preventing the worrying; or
(b) the dog has been worrying livestock, has not left the vicinity and is not under the control of any person and there are no practicable means of ascertaining to whom it belongs.

(4) For the purposes of this section the condition stated in either of the paragraphs of the preceding subsection shall be deemed to have been satisfied if the defendant believed that it was satisfied and had reasonable ground for that belief.

(5) For the purposes of this section –

(a) an animal belongs to any person if he owns it or has it in his possession; and

(b) land belongs to any person if he is the occupier thereof.

10 Application of certain enactments to liability under sections 2 to 4

For the purposes of the Fatal Accidents Act 1976, the Law Reform (Contributory Negligence) Act 1945 and the Limitation Act 1980 any damage for which a person is liable under sections 2 to 4 of this Act shall be treated as due to his fault.

11 General interpretation

In this Act –

'common land', and 'town or village green' have the same meanings as in the Commons Registration Act 1965;

'damage' includes the death of, or injury to, any person (including any disease and any impairment of physical or mental condition);

'fault' has the same meaning as in the Law Reform (Contributory Negligence) Act 1945;

'fencing' includes the construction of any obstacle designed to prevent animals from straying;

'livestock' means cattle, horses, asses, mules, hinnies, sheep, pigs, goats and poultry, and also deer not in the wild state and, in sections 3 and 9, also, while in captivity, pheasants, partridges and grouse; 'poultry' means the domestic varieties of the following, that is to say, fowls, turkeys, geese, ducks, guineafowls, pigeons, peacocks and quails; and

'species' includes sub-species and variety.

12 Application to Crown

(1) This Act binds the Crown, but nothing in this section shall authorise proceedings to be brought against Her Majesty in her private capacity.

(2) Section 38 (3) of the Crown Proceedings Act 1947 (interpretation of references to Her Majesty in her private capacity) shall apply as if this section were contained in that Act.

[As amended by the Limitation Act 1980, s40(2), Schedule 3, para 10.]

Defective Premises Act 1972
(1972 c 35)

1 Duty to build dwellings properly

(1) A person taking on work for or in connection with the provision of a dwelling (whether the dwelling is provided by the erection or by the conversion or enlargement of a building) owes a duty –

(a) if the dwelling is provided to the order of any person, to that person; and
(b) without prejudice to paragraph (a) above, to every person who acquires an interest (whether legal or equitable) in the dwelling;

to see that the work which he takes on is done in a workmanlike or, as the case may be, professional manner, with proper materials and so that as regards that work the dwelling will be fit for habitation when completed.

(2) A person who takes on any such work for another on terms that he is to do it in accordance with instructions given by or on behalf of that other shall, to the extent to which he does it properly in accordance with those instructions, be treated for the purposes of this section as discharging the duty imposed on him by subsection (1) above except where he owes a duty to that other to warn him of any defects in the instructions and fails to discharge that duty.

(3) A person shall not be treated for the purposes of subsection (2) above as having given instructions for the doing of work merely because he has agreed to the work being done in a specified manner, with specified materials or to a specified design.

(4) A person who –

(a) in the course of a business which consists of or includes providing or arranging for the provision of dwellings or installations in dwellings; or
(b) in the exercise of a power of making such provision or arrangements conferred by or by virtue of any enactment;

arranges for another to take on work for or in connection with the provision of a dwelling shall be treated for the purposes of this section as included among the persons who have taken on the work.

(5) Any cause of action in respect of a breach of the duty imposed by this section shall be deemed, for the purposes of the Limitation Act 1980, to have accrued at the time when the dwelling was completed, but if after that time a person who has done work for or in connection with the provision of the dwelling does further work to rectify the work he has already done, any such cause of action in respect of that further work shall be deemed for those purposes to have accrued at the time when the further work was finished.

2 Cases excluded from the remedy under section 1

(1) Where –

(a) in connection with the provision of a dwelling or its first sale or letting for habitation any rights in respect of defects in the state of the dwelling are conferred by an approved scheme to which this section applies on a person having or acquiring an interest in the dwelling; and

(b) it is stated in a document of a type approved for the purposes of this section that the requirements as to design or construction imposed by or under the scheme have, or appear to have, been substantially complied with in relation to the dwelling;

no action shall be brought by any person having or acquiring an interest in the dwelling for breach of the duty imposed by section 1 above in relation to the dwelling.

(2) A scheme to which this section applies –

(a) may consist of any number of documents and any number of agreements or other transactions between any number of persons; but

(b) must confer, by virtue of agreements entered into with persons having or acquiring an interest in the dwellings to which the scheme applies, rights on such persons in respect of defects in the state of the dwellings.

(3) In this section 'approved' means approved by the Secretary of State, and the power of the Secretary of State to approve a scheme or document for the purposes of this section shall be exercisable by order, except that any requirements as to construction or design imposed under a scheme to which this section applies may be approved by him without making any order or, if he thinks fit, by order.

(4) The Secretary of State –

(a) may approve a scheme or document for the purposes of this section with or without limiting the duration of his approval; and

(b) may by order revoke or vary a previous order under this section or, without such an order, revoke or vary a previous approval under this section given otherwise than by order.

(5) The production of a document purporting to be a copy of an approval given by the Secretary of State otherwise than by order and certified by an officer of the Secretary of State to be a true copy of the approval shall be conclusive evidence of the approval, and without proof of the handwriting or official position of the person purporting to sign the certificate.

(6) The power to make an order under this section shall be exercisable by statutory instrument which shall be subject to annulment in pursuance of a resolution by either House of Parliament.

(7) Where an interest in a dwelling is compulsorily acquired –

(a) no action shall be brought by the acquiring authority for breach of the duty imposed by section 1 above in respect of the dwelling; and

(b) if any work for or in connection with the provision of the dwelling was done otherwise than in the course of a business by the person in occupation of the dwelling at the time of the compulsory acquisition, the acquiring authority and not that person shall be treated as the person who took on the work and accordingly as owing that duty.

3 Duty of care with respect to work done on premises not abated by disposal of premises

(1) Where work of construction, repair, maintenance or demolition or any other work is done on or in relation to premises, any duty of care owed, because of the doing of the work, to persons who might reasonably be expected to be affected by defects in the state of the premises created by the doing of the work shall not be abated by the subsequent disposal of the premises by the person who owed the duty.

(2) This section does not apply –

(a) in the case of premises which are let, where the relevant tenancy of the premises commenced, or the relevant tenancy agreement of the premises was entered into, before the commencement of this Act;

(b) in the case of premises disposed of in any other way, when the disposal of the premises was completed, or a contract for their disposal was entered into, before the commencement of this Act; or

(c) in either case, where the relevant transaction disposing of the premises is entered into in pursuance of an enforceable option by which the consideration for the disposal was fixed before the commencement of this Act.

4 Landlord's duty of care in virtue of obligation or right to repair premises demised

(1) Where premises are let under a tenancy which puts on the landlord an obligation to the tenant for the maintenance or repair of the premises, the landlord owes to all persons who might reasonably be expected to be affected by defects in the state of the premises a duty to take such care as is reasonable in all the circumstances to see that they are reasonably safe from personal injury or from damage to their property caused by a relevant defect.

(2) The said duty is owed if the landlord knows (whether as the result of being notified by the tenant or otherwise) or if he ought in all the circumstances to have known of the relevant defect.

(3) In this section 'relevant defect' means a defect in the state of the premises existing at or after the material time and arising from, or continuing because of, an act or omission by the landlord which constitutes or would if he had had notice of the defect have constituted a failure by him to carry out his obligation to the tenant for the maintenance or repair of the premises; and for the purposes of the foregoing provision 'the material time' means –

(a) where the tenancy commenced before this Act, the commencement of this Act; and

(b) in all other cases, the earliest of the following times, that is to say –

(i) the time when the tenancy commences;

(ii) the time when the tenancy agreement is entered into;

(iii) the time when possession is taken of the premises in contemplation of the letting.

(4) Where premises are let under a tenancy which expressly or impliedly gives the landlord the right to enter the premises to carry out any description of maintenance or repair of the premises, then, as from the time when he first is, or by notice or otherwise can put himself,

in a position to exercise the right and so long as he is or can put himself in that position, he shall be treated for the purposes of subsections (1) to (3) above (but for no other purpose) as if he were under an obligation to the tenant for that description of maintenance or repair of the premises; but the landlord shall not owe the tenant any duty by virtue of this subsection in respect of any defect in the state of the premises arising from, or continuing because of, a failure to carry out an obligation expressly imposed on the tenant by the tenancy.

(5) For the purposes of this section obligations imposed or rights given by any enactment in virtue of a tenancy shall be treated as imposed or given by the tenancy.

(6) This section applies to a right of occupation given by contract or any enactment and not amounting to a tenancy as if the right were a tenancy, and 'tenancy' and cognate expressions shall be construed accordingly.

5 Application to Crown

This Act shall bind the Crown, but as regards the Crown's liability in tort shall not bind the Crown further than the Crown is made liable in tort by the Crown Proceedings Act 1947.

6 Supplemental

(1) In this Act –

'disposal', in relation to premises, includes a letting, and an assignment or surrender of a tenancy, of the premises and the creation by contract of any other right to occupy the premises and 'dispose' shall be construed accordingly;

'personal injury' includes any disease and any impairment of a person's physical or mental condition;

'tenancy' means –

> (a) a tenancy created either immediately or derivatively out of the freehold, whether by a lease or underlease, by an agreement for a lease or underlease or by a tenancy agreement, but not including a mortgage term or any interest arising in favour of a mortgagor by his attorning tenant to his mortgagee; or
> (b) a tenancy at will or a tenancy on sufferance; or
> (c) a tenancy, whether or not constituting a tenancy at common law, created by or in pursuance of any enactment; and cognate expressions shall be construed accordingly.

(2) Any duty imposed by or enforceable by virtue of any provision of this Act is in addition to any duty a person may owe apart from that provision.

(3) Any term of an agreement which purports to exclude or restrict, or has the effect of excluding or restricting, the operation of any of the provisions of this Act, or any liability arising by virtue of any such provision, shall be void.

Guard Dogs Act 1975
(1975 c 50)

1 Control of guard dogs

(1) A person shall not use or permit the use of a guard dog at any premises unless a person ('the handler') who is capable of controlling the dog is present on the premises and the dog is under the control of the handler at all times while it is being so used except while it is secured so that it is not at liberty to go freely about the premises.

(2) The handler of a guard dog shall keep the dog under his control at all times while it is being used as a guard dog at any premises except –

(a) while another handler has control over the dog; or
(b) while the dog is secured so that it is not at liberty to go freely about the premises.

(3) A person shall not use or permit the use of a guard dog at any premises unless a notice containing a warning that a guard dog is present is clearly exhibited at each entrance to the premises.

5 Offences, penalties and civil liability

(1) A person who contravenes section 1 or 2 of this Act shall be guilty of an offence and liable on summary conviction to a fine not exceeding level 5 on the standard scale.

(2) The provisions of this Act shall not be construed as –

(a) conferring a right of action in any civil proceedings (other than proceedings for the recovery of a fine or any prescribed fee) in respect of any contravention of this Act or of any regulations made under this Act or of any of the terms or conditions of a licence granted under section 3 of this Act; or
(b) derogating from any right of action or other remedy (whether civil or criminal) in proceedings instituted otherwise than by virtue of this Act.

7 Interpretation

In this Act unless the context otherwise requires – ...

'guard dog' means a dog which is being used to protect –

(a) premises; or
(b) property kept on the premises; or
(c) a person guarding the premises of such property; ...

'premises' means land other than agricultural land and land within the curtilage of a dwelling-house, and buildings, including parts of buildings, other than dwellinghouses. ...

Congenital Disabilities (Civil Liability) Act 1976
(1976 c 28)

1 Civil liability to child born disabled

(1) If a child is born disabled as the result of such an occurrence before its birth as is mentioned in subsection (2) below, and a person (other than the child's own mother) is under this section answerable to the child in respect of the occurrence, the child's disabilities are to be regarded as damage resulting from the wrongful act of that person and actionable accordingly at the suit of the child.

(2) An occurrence to which this section applies is one which –

(a) affected either parent of the child in his or her ability to have a normal, healthy child; or

(b) affected the mother during her pregnancy, or affected her or the child in the course of its birth, so that the child is born with disabilities which would not otherwise have been present.

(3) Subject to the following subsections, a person (here referred to as 'the defendant') is answerable to the child if he was liable in tort to the parent or would, if sued in due time, have been so; and it is no answer that there could not have been such liability because the parent suffered no actionable injury, if there was a breach of legal duty which, accompanied by injury, would have given rise to the liability.

(4) In the case of an occurrence preceding the time of conception, the defendant is not answerable to the child if at that time either or both of the parents knew the risk of their child being born disabled (that is to say, the particular risk created by the occurrence); but should it be the child's father who is the defendant, this subsection does not apply if he knew of the risk and the mother did not.

(5) The defendant is not answerable to the child, for anything he did or omitted to do when responsible in a professional capacity for treating or advising the parent, if he took reasonable care having due regard to then received professional opinion applicable to the particular class of case; but this does not mean that he is answerable only because he departed from received opinion.

(6) Liability to the child under this section may be treated as having been excluded or limited by contract made with the parent affected, to the same extent and subject to the same restrictions as liability in the parent's own case; and a contract term which could have been set up by the defendant in an action by the parent, so as to exclude or limit his liability to him or her, operates in the defendant's favour to the same, but no greater, extent in an action under this section by the child.

(7) If in the child's action under this section it is shown that the parent affected shared the responsibility for the child being born disabled, the damages are to be reduced to such extent as the court thinks just and equitable having regard to the extent of the parent's responsibility.

1A Extension of section 1 to cover infertility treatments

(1) In any case where –

(a) a child carried by a woman as the result of the placing in her of an embryo or of sperm and eggs or her artificial insemination is born disabled,

(b) the disability results from an act or omission in the course of the selection, or the keeping or use outside the body, of the embryo carried by her or of the gametes used to bring about the creation of the embryo, and

(c) a person is under this section answerable to the child in respect of the act or omission,

the child's disabilities are to be regarded as damage resulting from the wrongful act of that person and actionable accordingly at the suit of the child.

(2) Subject to subsection (3) below and the applied provisions of section 1 of this Act, a person (here referred to as 'the defendant') is answerable to the child if he was liable in tort to one or both of the parents (here referred to as 'the parent or parents concerned') or would, if sued in due time, have been so; and it is no answer that there could not have been such liability because the parent or parents concerned suffered no actionable injury, if there was a breach of legal duty which, accompanied by injury, would have given rise to the liability.

(3) The defendant is not under this section answerable to the child if at the time the embryo, or the sperm and eggs, are placed in the woman or the time of her insemination (as the case may be) either or both of the parents knew the risk of their child being born disabled (that is to say, the particular risk created by the act or omission).

(4) Subsections (5) to (7) of section 1 of this Act apply for the purposes of this section as they apply for the purposes of that but as if references to the parent or the parent affected were references to the parent or parents concerned.

2 Liability of women driving when pregnant

A woman driving a motor vehicle when she knows (or ought reasonably to know) herself to be pregnant is to be regarded as being under the same duty to take care for the safety of her unborn child as the law imposes on her with respect to the safety of other people; and if in consequence of her breach of that duty her child is born with disabilities which would not otherwise have been present, those disabilities are to be regarded as damage resulting from her wrongful act and actionable accordingly at the suit of the child.

3 Disabled birth due to radiation

(1) Section 1 of this Act does not affect the operation of the Nuclear Installations Act 1965 as to liability for, and compensation in respect of, injury or damage caused by occurrences involving nuclear matter or the emission of ionising radiations.

(2) For the avoidance of doubt anything which –

(a) affects a man in his ability to have a normal, healthy child; or

(b) affects a woman in that ability, or so affects her when she is pregnant that her child is born with disabilities which would not otherwise have been present, is an injury for the purposes of that Act.

(3) If a child is born disabled as the result of an injury to either of its parents caused in breach of a duty imposed by any of sections 7 to 11 of that Act (nuclear site licensees and others to secure that nuclear incidents do not cause injury to persons, etc), the child's disabilities are to be regarded under the subsequent provisions of that Act (compensation and other matters) as injuries caused on the same occasion, and by the same breach of duty, as was the injury to the parent.

(4) As respects compensation to the child, section 13(6) of that Act (contributory fault of person injured by radiation) is to be applied as if the reference there to fault were to the fault of the parent.

(5) Compensation is not payable in the child's case if the injury to the parent preceded the time of the child's conception and at that time either or both of the parents knew the risk of their child being born disabled (that is to say, the particular risk created by the injury).

4 Interpretation and other supplementary provisions

(1) References in this Act to a child being born disabled or with disabilities are to its being born with any deformity, disease or abnormality, including predisposition (whether or not susceptible of immediate prognosis) to physical or mental defect in the future.

(2) In this Act –

(a) 'born' means born alive (the moment of a child's birth being when it first has a life separate from its mother), and 'birth' has a corresponding meaning; and
(b) 'motor vehicle' means a mechanically propelled vehicle intended or adapted for use on roads

and references to embryos shall be construed in accordance with section 1 of the Human Fertilisation and Embryology Act 1990.

(3) Liability to a child under section 1, 1A or 2 of this Act is to be regarded –

(a) as respects all its incidents and any matters arising or to arise out of it; and
(b) subject to any contrary context or intention, for the purpose of construing references in enactments and documents to personal or bodily injuries and cognate matters,

as liability for personal injuries sustained by the child immediately after its birth.

(4) No damages shall be recoverable under any of those sections in respect of any loss of expectation of life, nor shall any such loss be taken into account in the compensation payable in respect of a child under the Nuclear Installations Act 1965 as extended by section 3, unless (in either case) the child lives for at least 48 hours.

(4A) In any case where a child carried by a woman as the result of the placing in her of an embryo or of sperm and eggs or her artificial insemination is born disabled, any reference in section 1 of this Act to a parent includes a reference to a person who would be a parent but for sections 27 to 29 of the Human Fertilisation and Embryology Act 1990.

(5) This Act applies in respect of births after (but not before) its passing, and in respect of any such birth it replaces any law in force before its passing, whereby a person could be liable to a child in respect of disabilities with which it might be born; but in section 1(3) of this Act the expression 'liable in tort' does not include any reference to liability by virtue of this Act, or to liability by virtue of any such law.

(6) References to the Nuclear Installations Act 1965 are to that Act as amended; and for the purposes of section 28 of that Act (power by Order in Council to extend the Act to territories outside the United Kingdom) section 3 of this Act is to be treated as if it were a provision of that Act.

5 Crown application

This Act binds the Crown.

[As amended by the Human Fertilisation and Embryology Act 1990, ss35(4), 44(1), (2).]

Fatal Accidents Act 1976
(1976 c 30)

1 Right of action for wrongful act causing death

(1) If death is caused by any wrongful act, neglect or default which is such as would (if death had not ensued) have entitled the person injured to maintain an action and recover damages in respect thereof, the person who would have been liable if death had not ensued shall be liable to an action for damages, notwithstanding the death of the person injured.

(2) Subject to section 1A(2) below, every such action shall be for the benefit of the dependants of the person ('the deceased') whose death has been so caused.

(3) In this Act 'dependant' means –

  (a) the wife or husband or former wife or husband of the deceased;
  (b) any person who –

    (i) was living with the deceased in the same household immediately before the date of the death; and
    (ii) had been living with the deceased in the same household for at least two years before that date; and
    (iii) was living during the whole of that period as the husband or wife of the deceased;

  (c) any parent or other ascendant of the deceased;
  (d) any person who was treated by the deceased as his parent;
  (e) any child or other descendant of the deceased;
  (f) any person (not being a child of the deceased) who, in the case of any marriage to which the deceased was at any time a party was treated by the deceased as a child of the family in relation to that marriage;
  (g) any person who is, or is the issue of, a brother, sister, uncle or aunt of the deceased.

(4) The reference to the former wife or husband of the deceased in subsection (3) (a) above

includes a reference to a person whose marriage to the deceased has been annulled or declared void as well as a person whose marriage to the deceased has been dissolved.

(5) In deducing any relationship for the purposes of subsection (3) above –

(a) any relationship by affinity shall be treated as a relationship by consanguinity, any relationship of the half blood as a relationship of the whole blood, and the stepchild of any person as his child, and

(b) an illegitimate person shall be treated as the legitimate child of his mother and reputed father.

(6) Any reference in this Act to injury includes any disease and any impairment of a person's physical or mental condition.

IA Bereavement

(1) An action under this Act may consist of or include a claim for damages for bereavement.

(2) A claim for damages for bereavement shall only be for the benefit –

(a) of the wife or husband of the deceased; and

(b) where the deceased was a minor who was never married –

(i) of his parents, if he was legitimate; and

(ii) of his mother, if he was illegitimate.

(3) Subject to subsection (5) below, the sum to be awarded as damages under this section shall be £7,500.

(4) Where there is a claim for damages under this section for the benefit of both the parents of the deceased, the sum awarded shall be divided equally between them (subject to any deduction falling to be made in respect of costs not recovered from the defendant).

(5) The Lord Chancellor may by order made by statutory instrument, subject to annulment in pursuance of a resolution of either House of Parliament, amend this section by varying the sum for the time being specified in subsection (3) above.

2 Persons entitled to bring the action

(1) The action shall be brought by and in the name of the executor or administrator of the deceased.

(2) If –

(a) there is no executor or administrator of the deceased, or

(b) no action is brought within six months after the death by and in the name of an executor or administrator of the deceased,

the action may be brought by and in the name of all or any of the persons for whose benefit an executor or administrator could have brought it.

(3) Not more than one action shall lie for and in respect of the same subject matter of complaint.

(4) The plaintiff in the action shall be required to deliver to the defendant or his solicitor full

particulars of the persons for whom and on whose behalf the action is brought and of the nature of the claim in respect of which damages are sought to be recovered.

3 Assessment of damages

(1) In the action such damages, other than damages for bereavement, may be awarded as are proportioned to the injury resulting from the death to the dependants respectively.

(2) After deducting the costs not recovered from the defendant any amount recovered otherwise than as damages for bereavement shall be divided among the dependants in such shares as may be directed.

(3) In an action under this Act where there fall to be assessed damages payable to a widow in respect of the death of her husband there shall not be taken into account the re-marriage of the widow or her prospects of re-marriage.

(4) In an action under this Act where there fall to be assessed damages payable to a person who is a dependant by virtue of section 1(3)(b) above in respect of the death of the person with whom the dependant was living as husband or wife there shall be taken into account (together with any other matter that appears to the court to be relevant to the action) the fact that the dependant had no enforceable right to financial support by the deceased as a result of their living together.

(5) If the dependants have incurred funeral expenses in respect of the deceased, damages may be awarded in respect of those expenses.

(6) Money paid into court in satisfaction of a cause of action under this Act may be in one sum without specifying any person's share.

4 Assessment of damages: disregard of benefits

In assessing damages in respect of a person's death in an action under this Act, benefits which have accrued or will or may accrue to any person from his estate or otherwise as a result of his death shall be disregarded.

5 Contributory negligence

Where any person dies as the result partly of his own fault and partly of the fault of any other person or persons, and accordingly if an action were brought for the benefit of the estate under the Law Reform (Miscellaneous Provisions) Act 1934 the damages recoverable would be reduced under section 1(1) of the Law Reform (Contributory Negligence) Act 1945, any damages recoverable in an action under this Act shall be reduced to a proportionate extent.

[As amended by the Administration of Justice Act 1982, ss3(1), (2), 75, Schedule 9, Pt I; Damages for Bereavement (Variation of Sum) (England and Wales) Order 1990.]

Torts (Interference with Goods) Act 1977
(1977 c 32)

1 Definition of 'wrongful interference with goods'

In this Act 'wrongful interference', or 'wrongful interference with goods', means –

(a) conversion of goods (also called trover),
(b) trespass to goods,
(c) negligence so far as it results in damage to goods or to an interest in goods,
(d) subject to section 2, any other tort so far as it results in damage to goods or to an interest in goods

and reference in this Act (however worded) to proceedings for wrongful interference or to a claim or right to claim for wrongful interference shall include references to proceedings by virtue of Part I of the Consumer Protection Act 1987 ... (product liability) in respect of any damage to goods or to an interest in goods or, as the case may be, to a claim or right to claim by virtue of that Part in respect of any such damage.

2 Abolition of detinue

(1) Detinue is abolished.

(2) An action lies in conversion for loss or destruction of goods which a bailee has allowed to happen in breach of his duty to his bailor (that is to say it lies in a case which is not otherwise conversion, but would have been detinue before detinue was abolished).

3 Form of judgment where goods are detained

(1) In proceedings for wrongful interference against a person who is in possession or in control of the goods relief may be given in accordance with this section, so far as appropriate.

(2) The relief is –

(a) an order for delivery of the goods, and for payment of any consequential damages, or
(b) an order for delivery of the goods, but giving the defendant the alternative of paying damages by reference to the value of the goods, together in either alternative with payment of any consequential damages, or
(c) damages.

(3) Subject to rules of court –

(a) relief shall be given under only one of paragraphs (a), (b) and (c) of subsection (2),
(b) relief under paragraph (a) of subsection (2) is at the discretion of the court, and the claimant may choose between the others.

(4) If it is shown to the satisfaction of the court that an order under subsection (2)(a) has not been complied with, the court may –

(a) revoke the order, or the relevant part of it, and

(b) make an order for payment of damages by reference to the value of the goods.

(5) Where an order is made under subsection (2)(b) the defendant may satisfy the order by returning the goods at any time before execution of judgment, but without prejudice to liability to pay any consequential damages.

(6) An order for delivery of the goods under subsection (2)(a) or (b) may impose such conditions as may be determined by the court, or pursuant to rules of court, and in particular, where damages by reference to the value of the goods would not be the whole of the value of the goods, may require an allowance to be made by the claimant to reflect the difference.

For example, a bailor's action against the bailee may be one in which the measure of damages is not the full value of the goods, and then the court may order delivery of the goods, but require the bailor to pay the bailee a sum reflecting the difference.

(7) Where under subsection (1) or subsection (2) of section 6 an allowance is to be made in respect of an improvement of the goods, and an order is made under subsection (2)(a) or (b), the court may assess the allowance to be made in respect of the improvement, and by the order require, as a condition for delivery of the goods, that allowance to be made by the claimant.

(8) This section is without prejudice –

(a) to the remedies afforded by section 133 of the Consumer Credit Act 1974, or
(b) to the remedies afforded by section 35, 42 and 44 of the Hire-Purchase Act 1965, ... (so long as those sections respectively remain in force), or
(c) to any jurisdiction to afford ancillary or incidental relief.

4 Interlocutory relief where goods are detained

(1) In this section 'proceedings' means proceedings for wrong interference.

(2) On the application of any person in accordance with rules of court, the High Court shall, in such circumstances as may be specified in the rules, have power to make an order providing for the delivery up of any goods which are or may become the subject matter of subsequent proceedings in the court, or as to which any question may arise in proceedings.

(3) Delivery shall be, as the order may provide, to the claimant or to a person appointed by the court for the purpose, and shall be on such terms and conditions as may be specified in the order. ...

5 Extinction of title on satisfaction of claim for damages

(1) Where damages for wrongful interference are, or would fall to be, assessed on the footing that the claimant is being compensated –

(a) for the whole of his interest in the goods, or
(b) for the whole of his interest in the goods subject to a reduction for contributory negligence,

payment of the assessed damages (under all heads), or as the case may be settlement of a claim for damages for the wrong (under all heads), extinguishes the claimant's title to that interest.

(2) In subsection (1) the reference to the settlement of the claim includes –

(a) where the claim is made in court proceedings, and the defendant has paid a sum into court to meet the whole claim, the taking of that sum by the claimant, and

(b) where the claim is made in court proceedings, and the proceedings are settled or compromised, the payment of what is due in accordance with the settlement or complomlse, and

(c) where the claim is made out of court and is settled or compromised, the payment of what is due in accordance with the settlement or compromise.

(3) It is hereby declared that subsection (1) does not apply where damages are assessed on the footing that the claimant is being compensated for the whole of his interest in the goods, but the damages paid are limited to some lesser amount by virtue of any enactment or rule of law.

(4) Where under section 7(3) the claimant accounts over to another person (the 'third party') so as to compensate (under all heads) the third party for the whole of his interest in the goods, the third party's title to that interest is extinguished.

(5) This section has effect subject to any agreement varying the respective rights of the parties to the agreement, and where the claim is made in court proceedings has effect subject to any order of the court.

6 *Allowances for improvement of the goods*

(1) If in proceedings for wrongful interference against a person (the 'improver') who has improved the goods, it is shown that the improver acted in the mistaken but honest belief that he had a good title to them, an allowance shall be made for the extent to which, at the time as at which the goods fall to be valued in assessing damages, the value of the goods is attributable to the improvement.

(2) If, in proceedings for wrongful interference against a person ('the purchaser') who has purported to purchase the goods –

(a) from the improver, or

(b) where after such a purported sale the goods passed by a further purported sale on one or more occasions, on any such occasion,

it is shown that the purchaser acted in good faith, an allowance shall be made on the principle set out in subsection (1).

For example, where a person in good faith buys a stolen car from the improver and is sued in conversion by the true owner the damages may be reduced to reflect the improvement, but if the person who bought the stolen car from the improver sues the improver for failure of consideration, and the improver acted in good faith, subsection (3) below will ordinarily make a comparable reduction in the damages he recovers from the improver.

(3) If in a case within subsection (2) the person purporting to sell the goods acted in good faith, then in proceedings by the purchaser for recovery of the purchase price because of

failure of consideration, or in any other proceedings founded on that failure of consideration, an allowance shall, where appropriate, be made on the principle set out in subsection (1).

(4) This section applies, with the necessary modifications, to a purported bailment or other disposition of goods as it applies to a purported sale of goods.

7 Double liability

(1) In this section 'double liability' means the double liability of the wrongdoer which can arise–

(a) where one of two or more rights of action for wrongful interference is founded on a possessory title, or

(b) where the measure of damages in an action for wrongful interference founded on a proprietary title is or includes the entire value of the goods, although the interest is one of two or more interests in the goods.

(2) In proceedings to which any two or more claimants are parties, the relief shall be such as to avoid double liability of the wrongdoer as between those claimants.

(3) On satisfaction, in whole or in part, of any claim for an amount exceeding that recoverable if subsection (2) applied, the claimant is liable to account over to the other person having a right to claim to such extent as will avoid double liability.

(4) Where, as the result of enforcement of a double liability, any claimant is unjustly enriched to any extent, he shall be liable to reimburse the wrongdoer to that extent.

For example, if a converter of goods pays damages first to a finder of the goods, and then to the true owner, the finder is unjustly enriched unless he accounts over to the true owner under subsection (3); and then the true owner is unjustly enriched and becomes liable to reimburse the converter of the goods.

8 Competing rights to the goods

(1) The defendant in an action for wrongful interference shall be entitled to show, in accordance with rules of court, that a third party has a better right than the plaintiff as respects all or any part of the interest claimed by the plaintiff, or in right of which he sues, and any rule of law (sometimes called jus tertii) to the contrary is abolished.

(2) Rules of court relating to proceedings for wrongful interference may –

(a) require the plaintiff to give particulars of his title,

(b) require the plaintiff to identify any person who, to his knowledge, has or claims any interest in the goods,

(c) authorise the defendant to apply for directions as to whether any person should be joined with a view to establishing whether he has a better right than the plaintiff, or has a claim as a result of which the defendant might be doubly liable,

(d) where a party fails to appear on an application within paragraph (c), or to comply with any direction given by the court on such an application, authorise the court to deprive him of any right of action against the defendant for the wrong either unconditionally, or subject to such terms or conditions as may be specified.

(3) Subsection (2) is without prejudice to any other power of making rules of court.

9 Concurrent actions

(1) This section applies where goods are the subject of two or more claims for wrongful interference (whether or not the claims are founded on the same wrongful act, and whether or not any of the claims relates also to other goods).

(2) Where goods are the subject of two or more claims under section 6 this section shall apply as if any claim under section 6(3) were a claim for wrongful interference.

(3) If proceedings have been brought in a county court on one of those claims, county court rules may waive, or allow a court to waive, any limit (financial or territorial) on the jurisdiction of county courts in the County Courts Act 1984 so as to allow another of those claims to be brought in the same county court.

(4) If proceedings are brought on one of the claims in the High Court and proceedings on any other are brought in a county court, whether prior to the High Court proceedings or not, the High Court may, on the application of the defendant, after notice has been given to the claimant in the county court proceedings –

(a) order that the county court proceedings be transferred to the High Court, and
(b) order security for costs or impose such other terms as the court thinks fit.

10 Co-owners

(1) Co-ownership is no defence to an action founded on conversion or trespass to goods where the defendant without the authority of the other co-owner –

(a) destroys the goods, or disposes of the goods in a way giving a good title to the entire property in the goods, or otherwise does anything equivalent to the destruction of the other's interest in the goods, or
(b) purports to dispose of the goods in a way which would give a good title to the entire property in the goods if he was acting with the authority of all co-owners of the goods.

(2) Subsection (1) shall not effect the law concerning execution or enforcement of judgments, or concerning any form of distress.

(3) Subsection (1)(a) is by way of restatement of existing law so far as it relates to conversion.

11 Minor amendments

(1) Contributory negligence is no defence in proceedings founded on conversion, or on intentional trespass to goods.

(2) Receipt of goods by way of pledge is conversion if the delivery of the goods is conversion.

(3) Denial of title is not of itself conversion.

12 Bailee's power of sale

(1) This section applies to goods in the possession or under the control of a bailee where –

(a) the bailor is in breach of an obligation to take delivery of the goods or, if the terms of the bailment so provide, to give directions as to their delivery, or

(b) the bailee could impose such an obligation by giving notice to the bailor, but is unable to trace or communicate with the bailor, or

(c) the bailee can reasonably expect to be relieved of any duty to safeguard the goods on giving notice to the bailor, but is unable to trace or communicate with the bailor.

(2) In the cases in Part I of Schedule 1 to this Act a bailee may, for the purposes of subsection (1), impose an obligation on the bailor to take delivery of the goods, or as the case may be to give directions as to their delivery, and in those cases the said Part I sets out the methods of notification.

(3) If the bailee –

(a) has in accordance with Part II of Schedule 1 to this Act given notice to the bailor of his intention to sell the goods under this subsection, or

(b) has failed to trace or communicate with the bailor with a view to giving him such a notice, after having taken reasonable steps for the purpose,

and is reasonably satisfied that the bailor owns the goods, he shall be entitled, as against the bailor, to sell the goods.

(4) Where subsection (3) applies but the bailor did not in fact own the goods, a sale under this section, or under section 13, shall not give a good title as against the owner, or as against a person claiming under the owner.

(5) A bailee exercising his powers under subsection (3) shall be liable to account to the bailor for the proceeds of sale, less any costs of sale, and –

(a) the account shall be taken on the footing that the bailee should have adopted the best method of sale reasonably available in the circumstances, and

(b) where subsection (3)(a) applies, any sum payable in respect of the goods by the bailor to the bailee which accrued due before the bailee gave notice of intention to sell the goods shall be deductible from the proceeds of sale.

(6) A sale duly made under this section gives a good title to the purchaser as against the bailor.

(7) In this section, section 13, and Schedule 1 to this Act,

(a) 'bailor' and 'bailee' include their respective successors in title, and

(b) references to what is payable, paid or due to the bailee in respect of the goods include references to what would be payable by the bailor to the bailee as a condition of delivery of the goods at the relevant time.

(8) This section, and Schedule 1 to this Act, have effect subject to the terms of the bailment.

(9) This section shall not apply where the goods were bailed before the commencement of this Act.

13 Sale authorised by the court

(1) If a bailee of the goods to which section 12 applies satisfies the court that he is entitled to sell the goods under section 12, or that he would be so entitled if he had given any notice required in accordance with Schedule 1 to this Act, the court –

(a) may authorise the sale of the goods subject to such terms and conditions, if any, as may be specified in the order, and
(b) may authorise the bailee to deduct from the proceeds of sale any costs of sale and any amount due from the bailor to the bailee in respect of the goods, and
(c) may direct the payment into court of the net proceeds of sale, less any amount deducted under paragraph (b), to be held to the credit of the bailor.

(2) A decision of the court authorising a sale under this section shall, subject to any right of appeal, be conclusive, as against the bailor, of the bailee's entitlement to sell the goods, and gives a good title to the purchaser as against the bailor.

(3) In this section 'the court' means the High Court or a county court …

14 Interpretation

(1) In this Act, unless the context otherwise requires – …

'goods' includes all chattels personal other than things in action and money, …

16 Extent and application to the Crown …

(3) This Act shall bind the Crown, but as regards the Crown's liability in tort shall not bind the Crown further than the Crown is made liable in tort by the Crown Proceedings Act 1947.

Schedule 1

Uncollected Goods

Part I

Power to Impose Obligations to Collect Goods

1. – (1) For the purposes of section 12(1) a bailee may, in the circumstances specified in this Part of this Schedule, by notice given to the bailor impose on him an obligation to take delivery of the goods.

(2) The notice shall be in writing, and may be given either –

(a) by delivering it to the bailor, or
(b) by leaving it at his proper address, or
(c) by post.

(3) The notice shall –

(a) specify the name and address of the bailee, and give suffficient particulars of the goods and the address or place where they are held, and

(b) state that the goods are ready for delivery to the bailor, or where combined with a notice terminating the contract of bailment, will be ready for delivery when the contract is terminated, and

(c) specify the amount, if any, which is payable by the bailor to the bailee in respect of the goods and which became due before the giving of the notice.

(4) Where the notice is sent by post it may be combined with a notice under Part II of this Schedule if the notice is sent by post in a way complying with paragraph 6(4).

(5) References in this Part of this Schedule to taking delivery of the goods include, where the terms of the bailment admit, references to giving directions as to their delivery.

(6) This Part of this Schedule is without prejudice to the provisions of any contract requiring the bailor to take delivery of the goods.

2. If a bailee has accepted goods for repair or other treatment on the terms (expressed or implied) that they will be re-delivered to the bailor when the repair or other treatment has been carried out, the notice may be given at any time after the repair or other treatment has been carried out.

3. If a bailee has accepted goods in order to value or appraise them, the notice may be given at any time after the bailee has carried out the valuation or appraisal.

4. – (1) If a bailee is in possession of goods which he has held as custodian, and his obligation as custodian has come to an end, the notice may be given at any time after the ending of the obligation, or may be combined with any notice terminating his obligation as custodian.

(2) This paragraph shall not apply to goods held by a person as mercantile agent, that is to say by a person having in the customary course of his business as a mercantile agent authority either to sell goods or to consign goods for the purpose of sale, or to buy goods, or to raise money on the security of goods.

5. Paragraphs 2, 3 and 4 apply whether or not the bailor has paid any amount due to the bailee in respect of the goods, and whether or not the bailment is for reward, or in the course of business, or gratuitous.

Part II

Notice of Intention to Sell Goods

6. – (1) A notice under section 12(3) shall –

(a) specify the name and address of the bailee, and give sufficient particulars of the goods and the address or place where they are held, and

(b) specify the date on or after which the bailee proposes to sell the goods, and

(c) specify the amount, if any, which is payable by the bailor to the bailee in respect of the goods, and which became due before the giving of the notice.

(2) The period between giving of the notice and the date specified in the notice as that on or after which the bailee proposes to exercise the power of sale shall be such as will afford the bailor a reasonable opportunity of taking delivery of the goods.

(3) If any amount is payable in respect of the goods by the bailor to the bailee, and became due before giving of the notice, the said period shall be not less than three months.

(4) This notice shall be in writing and shall be sent by post in a registered letter, or by the recorded delivery service.

7. – (1) The bailee shall not give a notice under section 12(3), or exercise his right to sell the goods pursuant to such a notice, at a time when he has notice that, because of a dispute concerning the goods, the bailor is questioning or refusing to pay all or any part of what the bailee claims to be due to him in respect of the goods.

(2) This paragraph shall be left out of account in determining under section 13(1) whether a bailee of goods is entitled to sell the goods under section 12, or would be so entitled if he had given any notice required in accordance with this Schedule.

8. For the purposes of this Schedule, and of section 26 of the Interpretation Act 1889 in its application to this Schedule, the proper address of the person to whom a notice is to be given shall be –

(a) in the case of a body corporate, a registered or principal office of the body corporate, and

(b) in any other case, the last known address of the person.

[As amended by the Consumer Protection Act 1987, s48(1), Schedule 4, para 5; High Court and County Courts Jurisdiction Order 1991, art 2(8), Schedule.]

Unfair Contract Terms Act 1977
(1977 c 50)

1 Scope of Part I

(1) For the purposes of this Part of this Act, 'negligence' means the breach –

(a) of any obligation, arising from the express or implied terms of a contract, to take reasonable care or exercise reasonable skill in the performance of the contract;

(b) of any common law duty to take reasonable care or exercise reasonable skill (but not stricter duty);

(c) of the common duty of care imposed by the Occupiers' Liability Act 1957 or the Occupiers' Liability Act (Northern Ireland) 1957.

(2) This part of this Act is subject to Part III; and in relation to contracts, the operation of sections 2 to 4 and 7 is subject to the exceptions made by Schedule 1.

(3) In the case of both contract and tort, sections 2 to 7 apply (except where the contrary is stated in section 6(4)) only to business liability, that is liability for breach of obligations or duties arising –

(a) from things done or to be done by a person in the course of a business (whether his own business or another's); or

(b) from the occupation of premises used for business purposes of the occupier;

and references to liability are to be read accordingly but liability of an occupier of premises for breach of an obligation or duty towards a person obtaining access to the premises for recreational or educational purposes, being liability for loss or damage suffered by reason of the dangerous state of the premises, is not a business liability of the occupier unless granting that person such access for the purposes concerned falls within the business purposes of the occupier.

(4) In relation to any breach of duty or obligation, it is immaterial for any purpose of this Part of this Act whether the breach was inadvertent or intentional, or whether liability for it arises directly or vicariously.

2 *Negligence liability*

(1) A person cannot by reference to any contract term or to a notice given to persons generally or to particular persons exclude or restrict his liability for death or personal injury resulting from negligence.

(2) In the case of other loss or damage, a person cannot so exclude or restrict his liability for negligence except in so far as the term or notice satisfies the requirement of reasonableness.

(3) Where a contract term or notice purports to exclude or restrict liability for negligence a person's agreement to or awareness of it is not of itself to be taken as indicating his voluntary acceptance of any risk.

4 *Unreasonable indemnity clauses*

(1) A person dealing as consumer cannot by reference to any contract term be made to indemnify another person (whether a party to the contract or not) in respect of liability that may be incurred by the other for negligence or breach of contract, except in so far as the contract term satisfies the requirement of reasonableness.

(2) This section applies whether the liability in question –

    (a) is directly that of the person to be indemnified or is incurred by him vicariously;

    (b) is to the person dealing as consumer or to someone else.

5 *'Guarantee' of consumer goods*

(1) In the case of goods of a type ordinarily supplied for private use or consumption, where loss or damage –

    (a) arises from the goods proving defective while in consumer use; and

    (b) results from the negligence of a person concerned in the manufacture or distribution of the goods,

liability for the loss or damage cannot be excluded or restricted by reference to any contract term or notice contained in or operating by reference to a guarantee of the goods.

(2) For these purposes –

    (a) goods are to be regarded as 'in consumer use' when a person is using them, or has them in his possession for use, otherwise than exclusively for the purposes of a business; and

    (b) anything in writing is a guarantee if it contains or purports to contain some promise or assurance (however worded or presented) that defects will be made good by complete or partial replacement, or by repair, monetary compensation or otherwise.

(3) This section does not apply as between the parties to a contract under or in pursuance of which possession or ownership of the goods passed.

11 The 'reasonableness' test

(1) In relation to a contract term, the requirement of reasonableness for the purposes of this Part of this Act, section 3 of the Misrepresentation Act 1967 and section 3 of the Misrepresentation Act (Northern Ireland) 1967 is that the term shall have been a fair and reasonable one to be included having regard to the circumstances which were, or ought reasonably to have been, known to or in the contemplation of the parties when the contract was made …

(3) In relation to a notice (not being a notice having contractual effect), the requirement of reasonableness under this Act is that it should be fair and reasonable to allow reliance on it, having regard to all the circumstances obtaining when the liability arose or (but for the notice) would have arisen.

(4) Where by reference to a contract term or notice a person seeks to restrict liability to a specified sum of money, and the question arises (under this or any other Act) whether the term or notice satisfies the requirement of reasonableness, regard shall be had in particular (but without prejudice to subsection (2) above in the case of contract terms) to –

    (a) the resources which he could expect to be available to him for the purpose of meeting the liability should it arise; and
    (b) how far it was open to him to cover himself by insurance.

(5) It is for those claiming that a contract term or notice satisfies the requirements of reasonableness to show that it does.

13 Varieties of exemption clause

(1) To the extent that this Part of this Act prevents the exclusion or restriction of any liability it also prevents –

    (a) making the liability or its enforcement subject to restrictive or onerous conditions;
    (b) excluding or restricting any right or remedy in respect of the liability, or subjecting a person to any prejudice in consequence of his pursuing any such right or remedy;
    (c) excluding or restricting rules of evidence or procedure;

and (to that extent) sections 2 and 5 to 7 also prevent excluding or restricting liability by reference to terms and notices which exclude or restrict the relevant obligation or duty.

(2) But an agreement in writing to submit present or future differences to arbitration is not to be treated under this Part of this Act as excluding or restricting any liability.

14 Interpretation of Part I

In this Part of this Act –

'business' includes a profession and the activities of any government department or local or public authority; ...

'negligence' has the meaning given by section 1(1);

'notice' includes an announcement, whether or not in writing, and any other communication or pretended communication; and

'personal injury' includes any disease and any impairment of physical or mental condition.

[As amended by the Occupiers' Liability Act 1984, s2.]

Civil Liability (Contribution) Act 1978
(1978 c 47)

1 Entitlement to contribution

(1) Subject to the following provisions of this section, any person liable in respect of any damage suffered by another person may recover contribution from any other person liable in respect of the same damage (whether jointly with him or otherwise).

(2) A person shall be entitled to recover contribution by virtue of subsection (1) above notwithstanding that he has ceased to be liable in respect of the damage in question since the time when the damage occurred, provided that he was so liable immediately before he made or was ordered or agreed to make the payment in respect of which the contribution is sought.

(3) A person shall be liable to make contribution by virtue of subsection (1) above notwithstanding that he has ceased to be liable in respect of the damage in question since the time when the damage occurred, unless he ceased to be liable by virtue of the expiry of a period of limitation or prescription which extinguished the right on which the claim against him in respect of the damage was based.

(4) A person who has made or agreed to make any payment in bona fide settlement or compromise of any claim made against him in respect of any damage (including a payment into court which has been accepted) shall be entitled to recover contribution in accordance with this section without regard to whether or not he himself is or ever was liable in respect of the damage provided, however, that he would have been liable assuming that the factual basis of the claim against him could be established.

(5) A judgment given in any action brought in any part of the United Kingdom by or on behalf of the person who suffered the damage in question against any person from whom contribution is sought under this section shall be conclusive in the proceedings for contribution as to any issue determined by that judgment in favour of the person from whom the contribution is sought.

(6) References in this section to a person's liability in respect of any damage are references to any such liability which has been or could be established in an action brought against him in England and Wales by or on behalf of the person who suffered the damage; but it is immaterial whether any issue arising in any such action was or would be determined (in

accordance with the rules of private international law) by reference to the law of a country outside England and Wales.

2 Assessment of contribution

(1) Subject to subsection (3) below, in any proceedings for contribution under section 1 above the amount of the contribution recoverable from any person shall be such as may be found by the court to be just and equitable having regard to the extent of that person's responsibility for the damage in question.

(2) Subject to subsection (3) below, the court shall have power in any such proceedings to exempt any person from liability to make contribution, or to direct that the contribution to be recovered from any person shall amount to a complete indemnity.

(3) Where the amount of the damages which have or might have been awarded in respect of the damage in question in any action brought in England and Wales by or on behalf of the person who suffered it against the person from whom the contribution is sought was or would have been subject to –

  (a) any limit imposed by or under any enactment or by any agreement made before the damage occurred;
  (b) any reduction by virtue of section 1 of the Law Reform (Contributory Negligence) Act 1945 or section 5 of the Fatal Accidents Act 1976; or
  (c) any corresponding limit or reduction under the law of a country outside England and Wales; the person from whom the contribution is sought shall not by virtue of any contribution awarded under section 1 above be required to pay in respect of the damage a greater amount than the amount to those damages as so limited or reduced.

3 Proceedings against persons jointly liable for the same debt or damage

Judgment recovered against any person liable in respect of any debt or damage shall not be a bar to an action, or to the continuance of an action, against any other person who is (apart from any such bar) jointly liable with him in respect of the same debt or damage.

4 Successive actions against persons liable (jointly or otherwise) for the same damage

If more than one action is brought in respect of any damage by or on behalf of the person by whom it was suffered against persons liable in respect of the damage (whether jointly or otherwise) the plaintiff shall not be entitled to costs in any of those actions, other than that in which judgment is first given, unless the court is of the opinion that there was reasonable ground for bringing the action.

5 Application to Crown

Without prejudice to section 4(1) of the Crown Proceedings Act 1947 (indemnity and contribution), this Act shall bind the Crown, but nothing in this Act shall be construed as in any way affecting Her Majesty in Her private capacity (including in right of Her Duchy of Lancaster) or the Duchy of Cornwall.

6 *Interpretation*

(1) A person is liable in respect of any damage for the purposes of this Act if the person who suffered it (or anyone representing his estate or dependants) is entitled to recover compensation from him in respect of that damage (whatever the legal basis of his liability, whether tort, breach of contract, breach of trust or otherwise).

(2) References in this Act to an action brought by or on behalf of the person who suffered any damage include references to an action brought for the benefit of his estate or dependants.

(3) In this Act 'dependants' has the same meaning as in the Fatal Accidents Act 1976.

(4) In this Act, except in section 1(5) above, 'action' means an action brought in England and Wales.

7 *Savings*

(1) Nothing in this Act shall affect any case where the debt in question became due or (as the case may be) the damage in question occurred before the date on which it comes into force.

(2) A person shall not be entitled to recover contribution or liable to make contribution in accordance with section 1 above by reference to any liability based on breach of any obligation assumed by him before the date on which this Act comes into force.

(3) The right to recover contribution in accordance with section 1 above supersedes any right, other than an express contractual right, to recover contribution (as distinct from indemnity) otherwise than under this Act in corresponding circumstances; but nothing in this Act shall affect –

    (a) any express or implied contractual or other right to indemnity; or
    (b) any express contractual provision regulating or excluding contribution;

which would be enforceable apart from this Act (or render enforceable any agreement for indemnity or contribution which would not be enforceable apart from this Act).

Limitation Act 1980
(1980 c 58)
Part I
Ordinary TIme Limits for Different Classes of Action

1 Time limits under Part I subject to extension or exclusion under Part II

(1) This Part of this Act gives the ordinary time limits for bringing actions of the various classes mentioned in the following provisions of this Part.

(2) The ordinary time limits given in this Part of this Act are subject to extension or exclusion in accordance with the provisions of Part II of this Act.

2 Time limit for actions founded on tort

An action founded on tort shall not be brought after the expiration of six years from the date on which the cause of action accrued.

3 Time limit in case of successive conversions and extinction of title of owner of converted goods

(1) Where any cause of action in respect of the conversion of a chattel has accrued to any person and, before he recovers possession of the chattel, a further conversion takes place, no action shall be brought in respect of the further conversion after the expiration of six years from the accrual of the cause of action in respect of the original conversion.

(2) Where any such cause of action has accrued to any person and the period prescribed for bringing that action has expired and he has not during that period recovered possession of the chattel, the title of that person to the chattel shall be extinguished.

4 Special time limit in case of theft

(1) The right of any person from whom a chattel is stolen to bring an action in respect of the theft shall not be subject to the time limits under sections 2 and 3(1) of this Act, but if his title to the chattel is extinguished under section 3(2) of this Act he may not bring an action in respect of a theft preceding the loss of his title, unless the theft in question preceded the conversion from which time began to run for the purposes of section 3(2).

(2) Subsection (1) above shall apply to any conversion related to the theft of a chattel as it applies to the theft of a chattel; and, except as provided below, every conversion following the theft of a chattel before the person from whom it is stolen recovers possession of it shall be regarded for the purposes of this section as related to the theft. If anyone purchases the stolen chattel in good faith neither the purchase nor any conversion following it shall be regarded as related to the theft.

(3) Any cause of action accruing in respect of the theft or any conversion related to the theft

of a chattel to any person from whom the chattel is stolen shall be disregarded for the purpose of applying section 3(1) or (2) of this Act to his case.

(4) Where in any action brought in respect of the conversion of a chattel it is proved that the chattel was stolen from the plaintiff or anyone through whom he claims it shall be presumed that any conversion following the theft is related to the theft unless the contrary is shown.

(5) In this section 'theft' includes –

(a) any conduct outside England and Wales which would be theft if committed in England and Wales; and

(b) obtaining any chattel (in England and Wales or elsewhere) in the circumstances described in section 15(1) of the Theft Act 1968 (obtaining by deception) or by blackmail within the meaning of section 21 of that Act;

and references in this section to a chattel being 'stolen' shall be construed accordingly.

4A Time limit for actions for defamation or malicious falsehood

The time limit under section 2 of this Act shall not apply to an action for –

(a) libel or slander, or

(b) slander of title, slander of goods or other malicious falsehood,

but no such action shall be brought after the expiration of one year from the date on which the cause of action accrued.

10 Special time limit for claiming contribution

(1) Where under section 1 of the Civil Liability (Contribution) Act 1978 any person becomes entitled to a right to recover contribution in respect of any damage from any other person, no action to recover contribution by virtue of that right shall be brought after the expiration of two years from the date on which that right accrued.

(2) For the purposes of this section the date on which a right to recover contribution in respect of any damage accrues to any person (referred to below in this section as 'the relevant date') shall be ascertained as provided in subsections (3) and (4) below.

(3) If the person in question is held liable in respect of that damage –

(a) by a judgment given in any civil proceedings; or

(b) by an award made on any arbitration;

the relevant date shall be the date on which the judgment is given, or the date of the award (as the case may be).

For the purposes of this subsection no account shall be taken of any judgment or award given or made on appeal in so far as it varies the amount of damages awarded against the person in question.

(4) If, in any case not within subsection (3) above, the person in question makes or agrees to make any payment to one or more persons in compensation for that damage (whether he

admits any liability in respect of the damage or not), the relevant date shall be the earliest date on which the amount to be paid by him is agreed between him (or his representative) and the person (or each of the persons, as the case may be) to whom the payment is to be made.

(5) An action to recover contribution shall be one to which sections 28, 32 and 35 of this Act apply, but otherwise Parts II and III of this Act (except sections 34, 37 and 38) shall not apply for the purposes of this section.

11 Special time limit for actions in respect of personal injuries

(1) This section applies to any action for damages for negligence, nuisance or breach of duty (whether the duty exists by virtue of a contract or of provision made by or under a statute or independently of any contract or any such provision) where the damages claimed by the plaintiff for the negligence, nuisance or breach of duty consist of or include damages in respect of personal injuries to the plaintiff or any other person.

(1A) This section does not apply to any action brought for damages under section 3 of the Protection from Harassment Act 1997.

(2) None of the time limits given in the preceding provisions of this Act shall apply to an action to which this section applies.

(3) An action to which this section applies shall not be brought after the expiration of the period applicable in accordance with subsection (4) or (5) below.

(4) Except where subsection (5) below applies, the period applicable is three years from –

   (a) the date on which the cause of action accrued; or
   (b) the date of knowledge (if later) of the person injured.

(5) If the person injured dies before the expiration of the period mentioned in subsection (4) above, the period applicable as respects the cause of action surviving for the benefit of his estate by virtue of section 1 of the Law Reform (Miscellaneous Provisions) Act 1934 shall be three years from –

   (a) the date of death; or
   (b) the date of the personal representative's knowledge;

whichever is the later.

(6) For the purposes of this section 'personal representative' includes any person who is or has been a personal representative of the deceased, including an executor who has not proved the will (whether or not he has renounced probate) but not anyone appointed only as a special personal representative in relation to settled land; and regard shall be had to any knowledge acquired by any such person while a personal representative or previously.

(7) If there is more than one personal representative, and their dates of knowledge are different, subsection (5)(b) above shall be read as referring to the earliest of those dates.

11A *Actions in respect of defective products*

(1) This section shall apply to an action for damages by virtue of any provision of Part I of the Consumer Protection Act 1987.

(2) None of the time limits given in the preceeding provisions of this Act shall apply to an action to which this section applies.

(3) An action to which this section applies shall not be brought after the expiration of the period of ten years from the relevant time, within the meaning of section 4 of the said Act of 1987; and this subsection shall operate to extinguish a right of action and shall do so whether or not that right of action had accrued, or time under the following provisions of this Act had begun to run, at the end of the said period of ten years.

(4) Subject to subsection (5) below, an action to which this section applies in which the damages claimed by the plaintiff consist of or include damages in respect of personal injuries to the plaintiff or any other person or loss of or damage to any property, shall not be brought after the expiration of the period of three years from whichever is the later of –

    (a) the date on which the cause of action accrued; and

    (b) the date of knowledge of the injured person or, in the case of loss of or damage to property, the date of knowledge of the plaintiff or (if earlier) of any person in whom his cause of action was previously vested.

(5) If in a case where the damages claimed by the plaintiff consist of or include damages in respect of personal injuries to the plaintiff or any other person the injured person died before the expiration of the period mentioned in subsection (4) above, that subsection shall have effect as respects the cause of action surviving for the benefit of his estate by virtue of section 1 of the Law Reform (Miscellaneous Provisions) Act 1934 as if for the reference to that period there were substituted a reference to the period of three years from whichever is the later of –

    (a) the date of death; and

    (b) the date of the personal representative's knowledge.

(6) For the purposes of this section 'personal representative' includes any person who is or has been a personal representative of the deceased, including an executor who has not proved the will (whether or not he had renounced probate) but not anyone appointed only as a special personal representative in relation to settled land; and regard shall be had to any knowledge acquired by any such person while a personal representative or previously.

(7) If there is more than one personal representative and their dates of knowledge are different, subsection (5)(b) above shall be read as referring to the earliest of those dates.

(8) Expressions used in this section or section 14 of this Act and in Part I of the Consumer Protection Act 1987 have the same meanings in this section or that section as in that Part; and section 1(1) of that Act (Part I to be construed as enacted for the purpose of complying with the product liability Directive) shall apply for the purpose of construing this section and the following provisions of this Act so far as they relate to an action by virtue of any provision of that Part as it applies for the purpose of construing that Part.

12 Special time limit for actions under Fatal Accidents legislation

(1) An action under the Fatal Accidents Act 1976 shall not be brought if the death occurred when the person injured could no longer maintain an action and recover damages in respect of the injury (whether because of a time limit in this Act or in any other Act, or for any other reason).

Where any such action by the injured person would have been barred by the time limit in section 11 or 11A of this Act, no account shall be taken of the possibility of that time limit being overridden under section 33 of this Act.

(2) None of the time limits given in the preceding provisions of this Act shall apply to an action under the Fatal Accidents Act 1976, but no such action shall be brought after the expiration of three years from –

(a) the date of death; or
(b) the date of knowledge of the person for whose benefit the action is brought; whichever is the later.

(3) An action under the Fatal Accidents Act 1976 shall be one to which sections 28, 33 and 35 of this Act apply, and the application to any such action of the time limit under subsection (2) above shall be subject to section 39; but otherwise Parts II and III of this Act shall not apply to any such action.

13 Operation of time limit under section 12 in relation to different dependants

(1) Where there is more than one person for whose benefit an action under the Fatal Accidents Act 1976 is brought, section 12(2)(b) of this Act shall be applied separately to each of them.

(2) Subject to subsection (3) below, if by virtue of subsection (1) above the action would be outside the time limit given by section 12(2) as regards one or more, but not all, of the persons for whose benefit it is brought, the court shall direct that any person as regards whom the action would be outside that limit shall be excluded from those for whom the action is brought.

(3) The court shall not give such a direction if it is shown that if the action were brought exclusively for the benefit of the person in question it would not be defeated by a defence of limitation (whether in consequence of section 28 of this Act or an agreement between the two parties not to raise the defence, or otherwise).

14 Definition of date of knowledge for purposes of sections 11 and 12

(1) Subject to subsection (1A) below, in sections 11 and 12 of this Act references to a person's date of knowledge are references to the date on which he first had knowledge of the following facts –

(a) that the injury in question was significant; and

(b) that the injury was attributable in whole or in part to the act or omission which is alleged to constitute negligence, nuisance or breach of duty; and

(c) the identity of the defendant; and

(d) if it is alleged that the act or omission was that of a person other than the defendant, the identity of that person and the additional facts supporting the bringing of an action against the defendant;

and knowledge that any acts or omissions did or did not, as a matter of law, involve negligence, nuisance or breach of duty is irrelevant.

(1A) In section 11A of this Act and in section 12 of this Act so far as that section applies to an action by virtue of section 6(1)(a) of the Consumer Protection Act 1987 (death caused by defective product) references to a person's date of knowledge are references to the date on which he first had knowledge of the following facts –

(a) such facts about the damage caused by the defect as would lead a reasonable person who had suffered such damage to consider it sufficiently serious to justify his instituting proceedings for damages against a defendant who did not dispute liability and was able to satisfy a judgment; and

(b) that the damage was wholly or partly attributable to the facts and circumstances alleged to constitute the defect; and

(c) the identity of the defendant;

but, in determining the date on which a person first had such knowledge there shall be disregarded both the extent (if any) of that person's knowledge on any date of whether particular facts or circumstances would or would not, as a matter of law, constitute a defect and, in a case relating to loss of or damage to property, any knowledge which that person had on a date on which he had no right of action by virtue of Part I of that Act in respect of the loss or damage.

(2) For the purposes of this section an injury is significant if the person whose date of knowledge is in question would reasonably have considered it sufficiently serious to justify his instituting proceedings for damages against a defendant who did not dispute liability and was able to satisfy a judgment.

(3) For the purposes of this section a person's knowledge includes knowledge which he might reasonably have been expected to acquire –

(a) from facts observable or ascertainable by him; or

(b) from facts ascertainable by him with the help of medical or other appropriate expert advice which it is reasonable for him to seek;

but a person shall not be fixed under this subsection with knowledge of a fact ascertainable only with the help of expert advice so long as he has taken all reasonable steps to obtain (and, where appropriate, to act on) that advice.

14A Special time limit for negligence actions where facts relevant to cause of action are not known at date of accrual

(1) This section applies to any action for damages for negligence, other than one to which

section 11 of this Act applies, where the starting date for reckoning the period of limitation under subsection (4)(b) below falls after the date on which the cause of action accrued.

(2) Section 2 of this Act shall not apply to an action to which this section applies.

(3) An action to which this section applies shall not be brought after the expiration of the period applicable in accordance with subsection (4) below.

(4) That period is either –

(a) six years from the date on which the cause of action accrued; or

(b) three years from the starting date as defined by subsection (5) below, if that period expires later than the period mentioned in paragraph (a) above.

(5) For the purposes of this section, the starting date for reckoning the period of limitation under subsection (4)(b) above is the earliest date on which the plaintiff or any person in whom the cause of action was vested before him first had both the knowledge required for bringing an action for damages in respect of the relevant damage and a right to bring such an action.

(6) In subsection (5) above 'the knowledge required for bringing an action for damages in respect of the relevant damage' means knowledge both –

(a) of the material facts about the damage in respect of which damages are claimed; and

(b) of the other facts relevant to the current action mentioned in subsection (8) below.

(7) For the purposes of subsection (6)(a) above, the material facts about the damage are such facts about the damage as would lead a reasonable person who had suffered such damage to consider it sufficiently serious to justify his instituting proceedings for damages against the defendant who did not dispute liability and was able to satisfy a judgment.

(8) The other facts referred to in subsection (6)(b) above are –

(a) that the damage was attributable in whole or in part to the act or omission which is alleged to constitute negligence; and

(b) the identity of the defendant; and

(c) if it is alleged that the act or omission was that of a person other than the defendant, the identity of that person and the additional facts supporting the bringing of an action against the defendant.

(9) Knowledge that any acts or omissions did or did not, as a matter of law, involve negligence is irrelevant for the purposes of subsection (5) above.

(10) For the purposes of this section a person's knowledge includes knowledge which he might reasonably have been expected to acquire –

(a) from facts observable or ascertainable by him; or

(b) from facts ascertainable by him with the help of appropriate expert advice which it is reasonable for him to seek;

but a person shall not be taken by virtue of this subsection to have knowledge of a fact ascertainable only with the help of expert advice so long as he has taken all reasonable steps to obtain (and, where appropriate, to act on) that advice.

14B Overriding time limit for negligence actions not involving personal injuries

(1) An action for damages for negligence, other than one to which section 11 of this Act applies, shall not be brought after the expiration of fifteen years from the date (or, if more than one, from the last of the dates) on which there occurred any act or omission –

(a) which is alleged to constitute negligence; and

(b) to which the damage in respect of which damages are claimed is alleged to be attributable (in whole or in part).

(2) This section bars the right of action in a case to which subsection (1) above applies notwithstanding that –

(a) the cause of action has not yet accrued; or

(b) where section 14A of this Act applies to the action, the date which is for the purposes of that section the starting date for reckoning the period mentioned in subsection (4)(b) of that section has not yet occurred;

before the end of the period of limitation prescribed by this section.

24 Time limit for actions to enforce judgments

(1) An action shall not be brought upon any judgment after the expiration of six years from the date on which the judgment became enforceable.

(2) No arrears of interest in respect of any judgment debt shall be recovered after the expiration of six years from the date on which the interest became due.

Part II

Extension or Exclusion of Ordinary Time Limits

28 Extension of limitation period in case of disability

(1) Subject to the following provisions of this section, if on the date when any right of action accrued for which a period of limitation is prescribed by this Act, the person to whom it accrued was under a disability, the action may be brought at any time before the expiration of six years from the date when he ceased to be under a disability or died (whichever first occurred) notwithstanding that the period of limitation has expired.

(2) This section shall not affect any case where the right of action first accrued to some person (not under a disability) through whom the person under a disability claims.

(3) When a right of action which has accrued to a person under a disability accrues, on the death of that person while still under a disability, to another person under a disability, no further extension of time shall be allowed by reason of the disability of the second person.

(4) No action to recover land or money charged on land shall be brought by virtue of this section by any person after the expiration of thirty years from the date on which the right of action accrued to that person or some person through whom he claims.

(4A) If the action is one to which section 4A of this Act applies, subsection (1) above shall have direct effect –

(a) in the case of an action for libel or slander, as if for the words from 'at any time' to 'occurred' there were substituted the words 'by him at any time before the expiration of one year from the date on which he ceased to be under a disability', and

(b) in the case of an action for slander of title, slander of goods or other malicious falsehood, as if for the words 'six years' there were substituted the words 'one year'.

(5) If the action is one to which section 10 of this Act applies, subsection (1) above shall have effect as if for the words 'six years' there were substituted the words 'two years'.

(6) If the action is one to which section 11 or 12(2) of this Act applies, subsection (1) above shall have effect as if for the words 'six years' there were substituted the words 'three years'.

(7) If the action is one to which section 11A of this Act applies or one by virtue of section 6(1)(a) of the Consumer Protection Act 1987 (death caused by defective product), subsection (1) above –

(a) shall not apply to the time limit prescribed by subsection (3) of the said section 11A or to that time limit as applied by virtue of section 12(1) of this Act; and

(b) in relation to any other time limit prescribed by this Act shall have effect as if for the words 'six years' there were substituted the words 'three years'.

28A Extension for cases where the limitation period is the period under section 14A(4)(b)

(1) Subject to subsection (2) below, if in the case of any action for which a period of limitation is prescribed by section 14A of this Act –

(a) the period applicable in accordance with subsection (4) of that section is the period mentioned in paragraph (b) of that subsection;

(b) on the date which is for the purposes of that section the starting date for reckoning that period the person by reference to whose knowledge that date fell to be determined under subsection (5) of that section was under a disability; and

(c) section 28 of this Act does not apply to the action;

the action may be brought at any time before the expiration of three years from the date when he ceased to be under a disability or died (whichever first occurred) notwithstanding that the period mentioned above has expired.

(2) An action may not be brought by virtue of subsection (1) above after the end of the period of limitation prescribed by section 14B of this Act.

32 Postponement of limitation period in case of fraud, concealment or mistake

(1) Subject to subsections (3) and (4A) below, where in the case of any action for which a period of limitation is prescribed by this Act, either –

(a) the action is based upon the fraud of the defendant; or

(b) any fact relevant to the plaintiff's right of action has been deliberately concealed from him by the defendant; or

(c) the action is for relief from the consequences of a mistake;

the period of limitation shall not begin to run until the plaintiff has discovered the fraud, concealment or mistake (as the case may be) or could with reasonable diligence have discovered it.

References in this subsection to the defendant include references to the defendant's agent and to any person through whom the defendant claims and his agent.

(2) For the purposes of subsection (1) above, deliberate commission of a breach of duty in circumstances in which it is unlikely to be discovered for some time amounts to deliberate concealment of the facts involved in that breach of duty.

(3) Nothing in this section shall enable any action –

(a) to recover, or recover the value of, any property; or

(b) to enforce any charge against, or set aside any transaction affecting, any property; to be brought against the purchaser of the property or any person claiming through him in any case where the property has been purchased for valuable consideration by an innocent third party since the fraud or concealment or (as the case may be) the transaction in which the mistake was made took place.

(4) A purchaser is an innocent third party for the purposes of this section –

(a) in the case of fraud or concealment of any fact relevant to the plaintiff's right of action, if he was not a party to the fraud or (as the case may be) to the concealment of that fact and did not at the time of the purchase know or have reason to believe that the fraud or concealment had taken place; and

(b) in the case of mistake, if he did not at the time of the purchase know or have reason to believe that the mistake had been made.

(4A) Subsection (1) above shall not apply in relation to the time limit prescribed by section 11A(3) of this Act or in relation to that time limit as applied by virtue of section 12(1) of this Act.

(5) Sections 14A and 14B of this Act shall not apply to any action to which subsection (1)(b) above applies (and accordingly the period of limitation referred to in that subsection, in any case to which either of those sections would otherwise apply, is the period applicable under section 2 of this Act).

32A Discretionary exclusion of time limit for actions for defamation or malicious falsehood

(1) If it appears to the court that it would be equitable to allow an action to proceed having regard to the degree to which –

(a) the operation of section 4A of this Act prejudices the plaintiff or any person whom he represents, and

(b) any decision of the court under this subsection would prejudice the defendant or any person whom he represents, the court may direct that that section shall not apply to the action or shall not apply to any specified cause of action to which the action relates.

(2) In acting under this section the court shall have regard to all the circumstances of the case and in particular to –

(a) the length of, and the reasons for, the delay on the part of the plaintiff;

(b) where the reason or one of the reasons for the delay was that all or any of the facts relevant to the cause of action did not become known to the plaintiff until after the end of the period mentioned in section 4A –

(i) the date on which any such facts did become known to him, and

(ii) the extent to which he acted promptly and reasonably once he knew whether or not the facts in question might be capable of giving rise to an action; and

(c) the extent to which, having regard to the delay, relevant evidence is likely –

(i) to be unavailable, or

(ii) to be less cogent than if the action had been brought within the period mentioned in section 4A.

(3) In the case of an action for slander of title, slander of goods or other malicious falsehood brought by a personal representative –

(a) the references in subsection (2) above to the plaintiff shall be construed as including the deceased person to whom the cause of action accrued and any previous personal representative of that person; and

(b) nothing in section 28(3) of this Act shall be construed as affecting the court's discretion under this section.

(4) In this section 'the court' means the court in which the action has been brought.

33 Discretionary exclusion of time limit for actions in respect of personal injuries or death

(1) If it appears to the court that it would be equitable to allow an action to proceed having regard to the degree to which –

(a) the provisions of section 11 or 11A or 12 of this Act prejudice the plaintiff or any person whom he represents; and

(b) any decision of the court under this subsection would prejudice the defendant or any person whom he represents;

the court may direct that those provisions shall not apply to the action, or shall not apply to any specified cause of action to which the action relates.

(1A) The court shall not under this section disapply –

(a) subsection (3) of section 11A; or

(b) where the damages claimed by the plaintiff are confined to damages for loss of or damage to any property, any other provision in its application to an action by virtue of Part I of the Consumer Protection Act 1987.

(2) The court shall not under this section disapply section 12(1) except where the reason

why the person injured could no longer maintain an action was because of the time limit in section 11 or subsection (4) of section 11A.

If, for example, the person injured could at his death no longer maintain an action under the Fatal Accidents Act 1976 because of the time limit in Article 29 in Schedule I to the Carriage by Air Act 1961, the court has no power to direct that section 12(1) shall not apply.

(3) In acting under this section the court shall have regard to all the circumstances of the case and in particular to –

(a) the length of, and the reasons for, the delay on the part of the plaintiff;

(b) the extent to which, having regard to the delay, the evidence adduced or likely to be adduced by the plaintiff or the defendant is or is likely to be less cogent than if the action had been brought within the time allowed by section 11, by section 11A or (as the case may be) by section 12;

(c) the conduct of the defendant after the cause of action arose, including the extent (if any) to which he responded to requests reasonably made by the plaintiff for information or inspection for the purpose of ascertaining facts which were or might be relevant to the plaintiff's cause of action against the defendant;

(d) the duration of any disability of the plaintiff arising after the date of the accrual of the cause of action;

(e) the extent to which the plaintiff acted promptly and reasonably once he knew whether or not the act or omission of the defendant, to which the injury was attributable, might be capable at that time of giving rise to an action for damages;

(f) the steps, if any, taken by the plaintiff to obtain medical, legal or other expert advice and the nature of any such advice he may have received.

(4) In a case where the person injured died when, because of section 11 or subsection (4) of section 11A, he could no longer maintain an action and recover damages in respect of the injury, the court shall have regard in particular to the length of, and the reasons for, the delay on the part of the deceased.

(5) In a case under subsection (4) above, or any other case where the time limit, or one of the time limits, depends on the date of knowledge of a person other than the plaintiff, subsection (3) above shall have effect with appropriate modifications, and shall have effect in particular as if references to the plaintiff included references to any person whose date of knowledge is or was relevant in determining a time limit.

(6) A direction by the court disapplying the provisions of section 12(1) shall operate to disapply the provisions to the same effect in section 1(1) of the Fatal Accidents Act 1976.

(7) In this section 'the court' means the court in which the action has been brought.

(8) References in this section to section 11 or 11A include references to that section as extended by any of the preceding provisions of this Part of this Act or by any provision of Part III of this Act.

Part III

Miscellaneous and General

36 *Equitable jurisdiction and remedies*

(1) The following time limits under this Act, that is to say –

(a) the time limit under section 2 for actions founded on tort;

(aa) the time limit under section 4A for actions for libel or slander, or for slander of title, slander of goods or other malicious falsehood;

(b) the time limit under section 5 for actions founded on simple contract

(c) the time limit under section 7 for actions to enforce awards where the submission is not by an instrument under seal;

(d) the time limit under section 8 for actions on a specialty;

(e) the time limit under section 9 for actions to recover a sum recoverable by virtue of any enactment; and

(f) the time limit under section 24 for actions to enforce a judgment;

shall not apply to any claim for specific performance of a contract or for an injunction or for other equitable relief, except in so far as any such time limit may be applied by the court by analogy in like manner as the corresponding time limit under any enactment repealed by the Limitation Act 1939 was applied before 1 July 1940.

(2) Nothing in this Act shall affect any equitable jurisdiction to refuse relief on the ground of acquiescence or otherwise.

37 *Application to the Crown and the Duke of Cornwall*

(1) Except as otherwise expressly provided in this Act, and without prejudic to section 39 [saving for other limitation enactments], this Act shall apply to proceedings by or against the Crown in like manner as it applies to proceedings between subjects. ...

(3) For the purposes of this section, proceedings by or against the Crown include –

(a) proceedings by or against Her Majesty in right of the Duchy of Lancaster;

(b) proceedings by or against any Government department or any officer of the Crown as such or any person acting on behalf of the Crown; and

(c) proceedings by or against the Duke of Cornwall. ...

38 *Interpretation*

(1) In this Act, unless the context otherwise requires –

'action' includes any proceeding in a court of law, including an ecclesiastical court; ...

'personal injuries' includes any disease and any impairment of a person's physical or mental condition, and 'injury' and cognate expressions shall be construed accordingly; ...

(2) For the purposes of this Act a person shall be treated as under a disability while he is an infant, or of unsound mind.

(3) For the purposes of subsection (2) above a person is of unsound mind if he is a person who, by reason of mental disorder within the meaning of the Mental Health Act 1983, is incapable of managing and administering his property and affairs.

(4) Without prejudice to the generality of subsection (3) above, a person shall be conclusively presumed for the purposes of subsection (2) above to be of unsound mind –

(a) while he is liable to be detained or subject to guardianship under the Mental Health Act 1983 (otherwise than by virtue of section 35 or 89); and
(b) while he is receiving treatment as an in-patient in any hospital within the meaning of the Mental Health Act 1983 or mental nursing home within the meaning of the Nursing Homes Act 1975 without being liable to be determined under the said Act of 1983 (otherwise than by virtue of section 35 or 89), being treatment which follows without any interval a period during which he was liable to be detained or subject to guardianship under the Mental Health Act 1959, or the said Act of 1983 (otherwise than by virtue of section 35 or 80) or by virtue of any enactment repealed or excluded by the Mental Health Act 1959.

(5) Subject to subsection (6) below, a person shall be treated as claiming through another person if he became entitled by, through, under, or by the act of that other person to the right claimed, and any person whose estate or interest might have been barred by a person entitled to an entailed interest in possession shall be treated as claiming through the person so entitled.

(9) References in Part II of this Act to a right of action shall include references to –

(a) a cause of action; …

(10) References in Part II to the date of the accrual of a right of action shall be construed –

(a) in the case of an action upon a judgment, as references to the date on which the judgment became enforceable; and
(b) in the case of an action to recover arrears of rent or interest, or damages in respect of arrears of rent or interest, as references to the date on which the rent or interest became due.

[As amended by the Mental Health Act 1983, s148, Schedule 4, para 55; Latent Damage Act 1986, ss1, 2(1), (2); Consumer Protection Act 1987, s6(6), Schedule 1, paras 1, 2, 5, 6; Defamation Act 1996, s5; Protection from Harassment Act 1997, s6.]

Highways Act 1980
(1980 c 66)

41 Duty to maintain highways maintainable at public expense

(1) The authority who are for the time being the highway authority for a highway maintainable at the public expense are under a duty … to maintain the highway. …

58 Special defence in action against a highway authority for damages for non-repair of highway

(1) In an action against a highway authority in respect of damage resulting from their failure to maintain a highway maintainable at the public expense it is a defence (without prejudice to any other defence or the application of the law relating to contributory negligence) to prove that the authority had taken such care as in all the circumstances was reasonably required to secure that the part of the highway to which the action relates was not dangerous for traffic.

(2) For the purposes of a defence under subsection (1) above, the court shall in particular have regard to the following matters –

(a) the character of the highway, and the traffic which was reasonably to be expected to use it;

(b) the standard of maintenance appropriate for a highway of that character and used by such traffic;

(c) the state of repair in which a reasonable person would have expected to find the highway;

(d) whether the highway authority knew, or could reasonably have been expected to know, that the condition of the part of the highway to which the action relates was likely to cause danger to users of the highway;

(e) where the highway authority could not reasonably have been expected to repair that part of the highway before the cause of action arose, what warning notices of its condition had been displayed;

but for the purposes of such a defence it is not relevant to prove that the highway authority had arranged for a competent person to carry out or supervise the maintenance of the part of the highway to which the action relates unless it is also proved that the authority had given him proper instructions with regard to the maintenance of the highway and that he had carried out the instructions.

(3) This sections binds the Crown.

328 Meaning of 'highway'

(1) In this Act, except where the context otherwise requires, 'highway' means the whole or a part of a highway other than a ferry or waterway.

(2) Where a highway passes over a bridge or through a tunnel, that bridge or tunnel is to be taken for the purposes of this Act to be a part of the highway.

(3) In this Act, 'highway maintainable at the public expense' and any other expression defined by references to a highway is to be construed in accordance with the foregoing provisions of this section.

329 Further provision as to interpretation

(1) In this Act, except where the context otherwise requires – ...

'maintenance' includes repair, and 'maintain' and 'maintainable' are to be construed accordingly; ...

'traffic' includes pedestrians and animals; ...

[As amended by the New Roads and Street Works Act 1991, s168(2), Schedule 9.]

Supreme Court Act 1981
(1981 c 54)

32 Orders for interim payment

(1) As regards proceedings pending in the High Court, provision may be made by rules of court for enabling the court, in such circumstances as may be prescribed, to make an order requiring a party to the proceedings to make an interim payment of such amount as may be specified in the order, with provision for the payment to be made to such other party to the proceedings as may be so specified or, if the order so provides, by paying it into court.

(2) Any rules of court which make provision in accordance with subsection (1) may include provision for enabling a party to any proceedings who, in pursuance of such an order, has made an interim payment to recover the whole or part of the amount of the payment in such circumstances, and from such other party to the proceedings, as may be determined in accordance with the rules.

(3) Any rules made by virtue of this section may include such incidental, supplementary and consequential provisions as the rule-making authority may consider necessary or expedient.

(4) Nothing in this section shall be construed as affecting the exercise of any power relating to costs, including any power to make rules of court relating to costs.

(5) In this section 'interim payment', in relation to a party to any proceedings, means a payment on account of any damages, debt or other sum (excluding any costs) which that party may be held liable to pay to or for the benefit of another party to the proceedings if a final judgment or order of the court in the proceedings is given or made in favour of that other party.

32A Orders for provisional damages for personal injuries

(1) This section applies to an action for damages for personal injuries in which there is proved or admitted to be a chance that at some definite or indefinite time in the future the injured person will, as a result of the act or omission which gave rise to the cause of action, develop some serious disease or suffer some serious deterioration in his physical or mental condition.

(2) Subject to subsection (4) below, as regards any action for damages to which this section applies in which a judgment is given in the High Court, provision may be made by rules of court for enabling the court, in such circumstances as may be prescribed, to award the injured person –

(a) damages assessed on the assumption that the injured person will not develop the disease or suffer the deterioration in his condition; and

(b) further damages at a future date if he develops the disease or suffers the deterioration.

(3) Any rules made by virtue of this section may include such incidental, supplementary and consequential provisions as the rule-making authority may consider necessary or expedient.

(4) Nothing in this section shall be construed –

(a) as affecting the exercise of any power relating to costs, including any power to make rules of court relating to costs; or

(b) as prejudicing any duty of the court under any enactment or rule of law to reduce or limit the total damages which would have been recoverable apart from any such duty.

35A Power of High Court to award interest on debts and damages

(1) Subject to rules of court, in proceedings (whenever instituted) before the High Court for the recovery of a debt or damages there may be included in any sum for which judgment is given simple interest, at such rate as the court thinks fit or as rules of court may provide, on all or any part of the debt or damages in respect of which judgment is given, or payment is made before judgment, for all or any part of the period between the date when the cause of action arose and –

(a) in the case of any sum paid before judgment, the date of the payment; and

(b) in the case of the sum for which judgment is given, the date of the judgment.

(2) In relation to a judgment given for damages for personal injuries or death which exceed £200 subsection (1) shall have effect –

(a) with the substitution of 'shall be included' for 'may be included'; and

(b) with the addition of 'unless the court is satisfied that there are special reasons to the contrary' after 'given', where first occurring.

(3) Subject to rules of court, where –

(a) there are proceedings (whenever instituted) before the High Court for the recovery of a debt; and

(b) the defendant pays the whole debt to the plaintiff (otherwise than in pursuance of a judgment in the proceedings),

the defendant shall be liable to pay the plaintiff simple interest at such rate as the court thinks fit or as rules of court may provide on all or any part of the debt for all or any part of the period between the date when the cause of action arose and the date of the payment.

(4) Interest in respect of a debt shall not be awarded under this section for a period during which, for whatever reason, interest on the debt already runs.

(5) Without prejudice to the generality of section 84, rules of court may provide for a rate of interest by reference to the rate specified in section 17 of the Judgments Act 1838 as that section has effect from time to time or by reference to a rate for which any other enactment provides.

(6) Interest under this section may be calculated at different rates in respect of different periods.

(7) In this section 'plaintiff' means the person seeking the debt or damages and 'defendant' means the person from whom the plaintiff seeks the debt or damages and 'personal injuries' includes any disease and any impairment of a person's physical or mental condition.

(8) Nothing in this section affects the damages recoverable for the dishonour of a bill of exchange.

37 Powers of High Court with respect to injunctions and receivers

(1) The High Court may by order (whether interlocutory or final) grant an injunction or appoint a receiver in all cases in which it appears to the court to be just and convenient to do so.

(2) Any such order may be made either unconditionally or on such terms and conditions as the court thinks just.

(3) The power of the High Court under subsection (1) to grant an interlocutory injunction restraining a party to any proceedings from removing from the jurisdiction of the High Court, or otherwise dealing with, assets located within that jurisdiction shall be exercisable in cases where that party is, as well as in cases where he is not, domiciled resident or present within that jurisdiction.

(4) The power of the High Court to appoint a receiver by way of equitable execution shall operate in relation to all legal estates and interests in land; and that power –

(a) may be exercised in relation to an estate or interest in land whether or not a charge has been imposed on that land under section 1 of the Charging Orders Act 1979 for the purpose of enforcing the judgment, order or award in question; and
(b) shall be in addition to, and not in derogation of, any power of any court to appoint a receiver in proceedings for enforcing such a charge.

(5) Where an order under the said section 1 imposing a charge for the purpose of enforcing a judgment, order or award has been, or has effect as if, registered under section 6 of the Land Charges Act 1972, subsection (4) of the said section 6 (effect of non-registration of writs and orders registrable under that section) shall not apply to an order appointing a receiver made either –

(a) in proceedings for enforcing the charge; or
(b) by way of equitable execution of the judgment, order or award or, as the case may be, of so much of it as requires payment of moneys secured by the charge.

[Sections 32A and 35A were inserted by the Administration of Justice Act 1982, ss6(1) and 15(1) respectively.]

Administration of Justice Act 1982
(1982 c 53)

1 Abolition of right of damages for loss of expectation of life

(1) In an action under the law of England and Wales or the law of Northern Ireland for damages for personal injuries –

(a) no damages shall be recoverable in respect of any loss of expectation of life caused to the injured person by the injuries; but

(b) if the injured person's expectation of life has been reduced by the injuries, the court, in assessing damages in respect of pain and suffering caused by the injuries, shall take account of any suffering caused or likely to be caused to him by awareness that his expectation of life has been so reduced.

(2) The reference in subsection (1)(a) above to damages in respect of loss of expectation of life does not include damages in respect of loss of income.

2 Abolition of actions for loss of services, etc

No person shall be liable in tort under the law of England and Wales or the law of Northern Ireland –

(a) to a husband on the ground only of his having deprived him of the services or society of his wife;

(b) to a parent (or person standing in the place of a parent) on the ground only of his having deprived him of the services of a child; or

(c) on the ground only –

(i) of having deprived another of the services of his menial servant;

(ii) of having deprived another of the services of his female servant by raping or seducing her; or

(iii) of enticement of a servant or harbouring a servant.

5 Maintenance at public expense to be taken into account in assessment of damages

In an action under the law of England and Wales or the law of Northern Ireland for damages for personal injuries (including any such action arising out of a contract) any saving to the injured person which is attributable to his maintenance wholly or partly at public expense in a hospital, nursing home or other institution shall be set off against any income lost by him as a result of his injuries.

Occupiers' Liability Act 1984
(1984 c 3)

1 Duty of occupier to persons other than his visitors

(1) The rules enacted by this section shall have effect, in place of the rules of the common law, to determine –

(a) whether any duty is owed by a person as occupier of premises to persons other than his visitors in respect of any risk of their suffering injury on the premises by reason of any danger due to the state of the premises or to things done or omitted to be done on them; and
(b) if so, what that duty is.

(2) For the purposes of this section, the persons who are to be treated respectively as an occupier of any premises (which, for those purposes, include any fixed or movable structure) and as his visitors are –

(a) any person who owes in relation to the premises the duty referred to in section 2 of the Occupiers' Liability Act 1957 (the common duty of care), and
(b) those who are his visitors for the purposes of that duty.

(3) An occupier of premises owes a duty to another (not being his visitor) in respect of any such risk as is referred to in subsection (1) above if –

(a) he is aware of the danger or has reasonable grounds to believe that it exists;
(b) he knows or has reasonable grounds to believe that the other is in the vicinity of the danger concerned or that he may come into the vicinity of the danger (in either case, whether the other has lawful authority for being in that vicinity or not); and
(c) the risk is one against which, in all the circumstances of the case, he may reasonably be expected to offer the other some protection.

(4) Where, by virtue of this section, an occupier of premises owes a duty to another in respect of such a risk, the duty is to take such care as is reasonable in all the circumstances of the case to see that he does not suffer injury on the premises by reason of the danger concerned.

(5) Any duty owed by virtue of this section in respect of a risk may, in an appropriate case, be discharged by taking such steps as are reasonable in all the circumstances of the case to give warning of the danger concerned or to discourage persons from incurring the risk.

(6) No duty is owed by virtue of this section to any person in respect of risks willingly accepted as his by that person (the question whether a risk was so accepted to be decided on the same principles as in other cases in which one person owes a duty of care to another).

(7) No duty is owed by virtue of this section to persons using the highway, and this section does not affect any duty owed to such persons.

(8) Where a person owes a duty by virtue of this section, he does not, by reason of any breach of the duty, incur any liability in respect of any loss of or damage to property.

(9) In this section –

'highway' means any part of a highway other than a ferry or waterway;

'injury' means anything resulting in death or personal injury, including any disease and any impairment of physical or mental condition; and

'movable structure' includes any vessel, vehicle or aircraft.

3 Application to Crown

Section 1 of this Act shall bind the Crown, but as regards the Crown's liability in tort shall not bind the Crown further than the Crown is made liable in tort by the Crown Proceedings Act 1947.

Police and Criminal Evidence Act 1984
(1984 c 60)

117 Power of constable to use reasonable force

Where any provision of this Act –

(a) confers a power on a constable; and

(b) does not provide that the power may only be exercised with the consent of some person, other than a police officer,

the officer may use reasonable force, if necessary, in the exercise of the power.

Latent Damage Act 1986
(1986 c 37)

3 Accrual of cause of action to successive owners in respect of latent damage to property

(1) Subject to the following provisions of this section, where –

(a) a cause of action ('the original cause of action') has accrued to any person in respect of any negligence to which damage to any property in which he has an interest is attributable (in whole or in part); and

(b) another person acquires an interest in that property after the date on which the original cause of action occurred but before the material facts about the damage have become known to any person who, at the time when he first has knowledge of those facts, has any interest in the property;

a fresh cause of action in respect of that negligence shall accrue to that other person on the date on which he acquires his interest in the property.

(2) A cause of action accruing to any person by virtue of subsection (1) above –

(a) shall be treated as if based on breach of a duty of care at common law owed to the person to whom it accrues; and

(b) shall be treated for the purposes of section 14A of the 1980 Act (special time limit for negligence actions where facts relevant to cause of action are not known at date of accrual) as having accrued on the date on which the original cause of action accrued.

(3) Section 28 of the 1980 Act (extension of limitation period in case of disability) shall not apply in relation to any such cause of action.

(4) Subsection (1) above shall not apply in any case where the person acquiring an interest in the damaged property is either –

(a) a person in whom the original cause of action vests by operation of law; or
(b) a person in whom the interest in that property vests by virtue of any order made by a court under section 538 of the Companies Act 1985 (vesting of company property in liquidator).

(5) For the purposes of subsection (1)(b) above, the material facts about the damage are such facts about the damage as would lead a reasonable person who has an interest in the damaged property at the time when those facts became known to him to consider it sufficiently serious to justify his instituting proceedings for damages against a defendant who did not dispute liability and was able to satisfy a judgment.

(6) For the purposes of this section a person's knowledge includes knowledge which he might reasonably have been expected to acquire –

(a) from facts observable or ascertainable by him; or
(b) from facts ascertainable by him with the help of appropriate expert advice which it is reasonable for him to seek;

but a person shall not be taken by virtue of this subsection to have knowledge of a fact ascertainable by him only with the help of expert advice so long as he has taken all reasonable steps to obtain (and, where appropriate, to act on) that advice.

(7) This section shall bind the Crown, but as regards the Crown's liability in tort shall not bind the Crown further than the Crown is made liable in tort by the Crown Proceedings Act 1947.

4 Transitional provisions

(1) Nothing in section 1 or 2 of this Act [these sections inserted ss14A, 14B and 28A, 32(5) of the Limitation Act 1980 respectively] shall –

(a) enable any action to be brought which was barred by the 1980 Act or (as the case may be) by the Limitation Act 1939 before this Act comes into force; or
(b) affect any action commenced before this Act comes into force.

(2) Subject to subsection (1) above, sections 1 and 2 of this Act shall have effect in relation to causes of action accruing before, as well as in relation to causes of action accruing after, this Act comes into force.

(3) Section 3 of this Act shall only apply in cases where an interest in damaged property is acquired after this Act comes into force but shall so apply, subject to subsection (4) below, irrespective of whether the original cause of action accrued before or after this Act comes into force.

(4) Where –

(a) a person acquires an interest in damaged property in circumstances to which section 3 would apart from this subsection apply; but

(b) the original cause of action accrued more than six years before this Act comes into force;

a cause of action shall not accrue to that person by virtue of subsection (1) of that section unless section 32(1)(b) of the 1980 Act (postponement of limitation period in case of deliberate concealment of relevant facts) would apply to any action founded on the original cause of action.

5 Citation, interpretation, commencement and extent ...

(3) This act shall come into force at the end of the period of two months beginning with the date on which it is passed. ...

Consumer Protection Act 1987
(1987 c 43)
Part I
Product Liability

1 Purpose and construction of Part I

(1) This part shall have effect for the purpose of making such provision as is necessary in order to comply with the product liability Directive and shall be construed accordingly.

(2) In this Part, except in so far as the context otherwise requires –

'agricultural produce' means any produce of the soil, of stockfarming or of fisheries;

'dependant' and 'relative' have the same meaning as they have in, respectively, the Fatal Accidents Act 1976 and the Damages (Scotland) Act 1976;

'producer', in relation to a product, means –

(a) the person who manufactured it;

(b) in the case of a substance which has not been manufactured but has been won or abstracted, the person who won or abstracted it;

(c) in the case of a product, which has not been manufactured, won or abstracted but essential characteristics of which are attributable to an industrial or other process having been carried out (for example, in relation to agricultural produce), the person who carried out that process;

'product' means any goods or electricity and (subject to subsection (3) below) includes a product which is comprised in another product, whether by virtue of being a component part or raw material or otherwise; and

'the product liability Directive' means the Directive of the Council of the European Communities, dated 25 July 1985, (No 85/374/EEC) on the approximation of the laws, regulations and administrative provisions of the member States concerning liability for defective products.

(3) For the purposes of this Part a person who supplies any product in which products are comprised, whether by virtue of being component parts or raw materials or otherwise, shall not be treated by reason only of his supply of that product as supplying any of the products so comprised.

2 Liability for defective products

(1) Subject to the following provisions of this Part, where any damage is caused wholly or partly by a defect in a product, every person to whom subsection (2) below applies shall be liable for the damage.

(2) This subsection applies to –

(a) the producer of the product;
(b) any person who, by putting his name on the product or using a trade mark or other distinguishing mark in relation to the product, has held himself out to be the producer of the product;
(c) any person who has imported the product into a member State from a place outside the member States in order, in the course of any business of his, to supply it to another.

(3) Subject as aforesaid, where any damage is caused wholly or partly by a defect in a product, any person who supplied the product (whether to the person who suffered the damage, to the producer of any product in which the product in question is comprised or to any other person) shall be liable for the damage if –

(a) the person who suffered the damage requests the supplier to identify one or more of the persons (whether still in existence or not) to whom subsection (2) above applies in relation to the product;
(b) that request is made within a reasonable period after the damage occurs and at a time when it is not reasonably practicable for the person making the request to identify all those persons; and
(c) the supplier fails, within a reasonable period after receiving the request, either to comply with the request or to identify the person who supplied the product to him.

(4) Neither subsection (2) nor subsection (3) above shall apply to a person in respect of any defect in any game or agricultural produce if the only supply of the game or produce by that person to another was at a time when it had not undergone an industrial process.

(5) Where two or more persons are liable by virtue of this Part for the same damage, their liability shall be joint and several.

(6) This section shall be without prejudice to any liability arising otherwise than by virtue of this Part.

3 Meaning of 'defect'

(1) Subject to the following provisions of this section, there is a defect in a product for the

purposes of this Part if the safety of the product is not such as persons generally are entitled to expect; and for those purposes 'safety', in relation to a product, shall include safety with respect to products comprised in that product and safety in the context of risks of damage to property, as well as in the context of risks of death or personal injury.

(2) In determining for the purposes of subsection (1) above what persons generally are entitled to expect in relation to a product all the circumstances shall be taken into account, including –

(a) the manner in which, and purposes for which, the product has been marketed, its get-up, the use of any mark in relation to the product and any instructions for, or warnings with respect to, doing or refraining from doing anything with or in relation to the product;
(b) what might reasonably be expected to be done with or in relation to the product; and
(c) the time when the product was supplied by its producer to another;

and nothing in this section shall require a defect to be inferred from the fact alone that the safety of a product which is supplied after that time is greater than the safety of the product in question.

4 Defences

(1) In any civil proceedings by virtue of this Part against any person ('the person proceeded against') in respect of a defect in a product it shall be a defence for him to show –

(a) that the defect is attributable to compliance with any requirement imposed by or under any enactment or with any Community obligation; or
(b) that the person proceeded against did not at any time supply the products to another; or
(c) that the following conditions are satisfied, that is to say –

(i) that the only supply of the product to another by the person proceeded against was otherwise than in the course of a business of that person's;
(ii) that section 2(2) above does not apply to that person or applies to him by virtue only of things done otherwise than with a view to profit; or

(d) that the defect did not exist in the product at the relevant time; or
(e) that the state of scientific and technical knowledge at the relevant time was not such that a producer of products of the same description as the product in question might be expected to have discovered the defect if it had existed in his products while they were under his control; or
(f) that the defect –

(i) constituted a defect in a product ('the subsequent product') in which the product in question had been comprised; and
(ii) was wholly attributable to the design of the subsequent product or to compliance by the producer of the product in question with instructions given by the producer of the subsequent product.

(2) In this section 'the relevant time', in relation to electricity, means the time at which it

was generated, being a time before it was transmitted or distributed, and in relation to any other product, means –

(a) if the person proceeded against is a person to whom subsection (2) of section 2 above applies in relation to the product, the time when he supplied the product to another;
(b) if that subsection does not apply to that person in relation to the product, the time when the product was last supplied by a person to whom that subsection does apply in relation to the product.

5 Damage giving rise to liability

(1) Subject to the following provisions of this section, in this Part 'damage' means death or personal injury or any loss of or damage to any property (including land).

(2) A person shall not be liable under section 2 above in respect of any defect in a product for the loss of or any damage to the product itself or for the loss of or any damage to the whole or any part of any product which has been supplied with the product in question comprised in it.

(3) A person shall not be liable under section 2 above for any loss of or damage to any property which, at the time it is lost or damaged, is not –

(a) of a description of property ordinarily intended for private use, occupation or consumption; and
(b) intended by the person suffering the loss or damage mainly for his own private use, occupation or consumption.

(4) No damages shall be awarded to any person by virtue of this Part in respect of any loss of or damage to any property if the amount which would fall to be so awarded to that person, apart from this subsection and any liability for interest, does not exceed £275.

(5) In determining for the purposes of this Part who has suffered any loss of or damage to property and when any such loss or damage occurred, the loss or damage shall be regarded as having occurred at the earliest time at which a person with an interest in the property had knowledge of the material facts about the loss or damage.

(6) For the purposes of subsection (5) above the material facts about any loss of or damage to any property are such facts about the loss or damage as would lead a reasonable person with an interest in the property to consider the loss or damage sufficiently serious to justify his instituting proceedings for damages against a defendant who did not dispute liability and was able to satisfy a judgment.

(7) For the purposes of subsection (5) above a person's knowledge includes knowledge which he might reasonably have been expected to acquire –

(a) from facts observable or ascertainable by him; or
(b) from facts ascertainable by him with the help of appropriate expert advice which it is reasonable for him to seek;

but a person shall not be taken by virtue of this subsection to have knowledge of a fact ascertainable by him only with the help of expert advice unless he has failed to take all reasonable steps to obtain (and, where appropriate, to act on) that advice.

6 *Application of certain enactments*

(1) Any damage for which a person is liable under section 2 above shall be deemed to have been caused –

(a) for the purposes of the Fatal Accidents Act 1976, by that person's wrongful act, neglect or default; ...

(2) Where –

(a) a person's death is caused wholly or partly by a defect in a product, or a person dies after suffering damage which has been so caused;

(b) a request such as mentioned in paragraph (a) of subsection (3) of section 2 above is made to a supplier of the product by that person's personal representatives or, in the case of a person whose death is caused wholly or partly by the defect, by any dependant or relative of that person; and

(c) the conditions specified in paragraphs (b) and (c) of that subsection are satisfied in relation to that request;

this Part shall have effect for the purposes of the Law Reform (Miscellaneous Provisions) Act 1934, the Fatal Accidents Act 1976 and the Damages (Scotland) Act 1976 as if liability of the supplier to that person under that subsection did not depend on that person having requested the supplier to identify certain persons or on the said conditions having been satisfied in relation to a request made by that person.

(3) Section 1 of the Congenital Disabilities (Civil Liability) Act 1976 shall have effect for the purposes of this Part as if –

(a) a person were answerable to a child in respect of an occurrence caused wholly or partly by a defect in a product if he is or has been liable under section 2 above in respect of any effect of the occurrence on a parent of the child, or would be so liable if the occurrence caused a parent of the child to suffer damage;

(b) the provisions of this Part relating to liability under section 2 above applied in relation to liability by virtue of paragraph (a) above under the said section 1; and

(c) subsection (6) of the said section 1 (exclusion of liability) were omitted.

(4) Where any damage is caused partly by a defect in a product and partly by the fault of the person suffering the damage, the Law Reform (Contributory Negligence) Act 1945 and section 5 of the Fatal Accidents Act 1976 (contributory negligence) shall have effect as if the defect were the fault of every person liable by virtue of this Part for the damage caused by the defect.

(5) In subsection (4) above 'fault' has the same meaning as in the said Act of 1945.

(6) Schedule 1 to this Act shall have effect for the purpose of amending the Limitation Act 1980 and the Prescription and Limitation (Scotland) Act 1973 in their application in relation to the bringing of actions by virtue of this Part.

(7) It is hereby declared that liability by virtue of this Part is to be treated as liability in tort for the purposes of any enactment conferring jurisdiction on any court with respect to any matter.

(8) Nothing in this Part shall prejudice the operation of section 12 of the Nuclear

Installations Act 1965 (rights to compensation for certain breaches of duties confined to rights under that Act).

7 Prohibition on exclusions from liability

The liability of a person by virtue of this Part to a person who has suffered damage caused wholly or partly by a defect in a product, or to a dependant or relative of such a person, shall not be limited or excluded by any contract term, by any notice or by any other provision.

8 Power to modify Part I

(1) Her Majesty may by Order in Council make such modifications of this Part and of another enactment (including an enactment contained in the following Parts of this Act, or in an Act passed after this Act) as appear to Her Majesty in Council to be necessary or expedient in consequence of any modification of the product liability Directive which is made at any time after the passing of this Act.

(2) An Order in Council under subsection (1) above shall not be submitted to Her Majesty in Council unless a draft of the Order has been laid before, and approved by a resolution of, each House of Parliament.

9 Application of Part I to Crown

(1) Subject to subsection (2) below, this Part shall bind the Crown.

(2) The Crown shall not, as regards the Crown's liability by virtue of this Part, be bound by this Part further than the Crown is made liable in tort or in reparation under the Crown Proceedings Act 1947, as that Act has effect from time to time.

Part V

Miscellaneous and Supplemental

45 Interpretation

(1) In this Act, except in so far as the context otherwise requires –

'aircraft' includes gliders, balloons and hovercraft;

'business' includes a trade or profession and the activities of a professional or trade association or of a local authority or other public authority;

'conditional sale agreement', 'credit-sale agreement' and 'hire-purchase agreement' have the same meanings as in the Consumer Credit Act 1974 but as if in the definitions of that Act 'goods' had the same meaning as in this Act; ...

'gas' has the same meaning as in Part I of the Gas Act 1986;

'goods' includes substances, growing crops and things comprised in land by virtue of being attached to it and any ship, aircraft or vehicle;

'information' includes accounts, estimates and returns; ...

'modifications' includes additions, alterations and omissions, and cognate expressions shall be construed accordingly;

'motor vehicle' has the same meaning as in the Road Traffic Act 1988;

'notice' means a notice in writing; ...

'personal injury' includes any disease and any other impairment of a person's physical or mental condition;

'premises' includes any place and any ship, aircraft or vehicle; ...

'records' includes any books or documents and any records in non-documentary form; ...

'ship' includes any boat and any other description of vessel used in navigation;

'substance' means any natural or artificial substance, whether in solid, liquid or gaseous form or in the form of a vapour, and includes substances that are comprised in or mixed with other goods;

'supply' and cognate expressions shall be construed in accordance with section 46 below; ...

(2) Except in so far as the context otherwise requires, reference in this Act to a contravention of a safety provision shall, in relation to any goods, include references to anything which would constitute such a contravention if the goods were supplied to any person.

(3) Reference in this Act to any goods in relation to which any safety provision has been or may have been contravened shall include references to any goods which it is not reasonably practicable to separate from any such goods.

46 Meaning of 'supply'

(1) Subject to the following provisions of this section, references in this Act to supplying goods shall be construed as references to doing any of the following, whether as principal or agent, that is to say –

(a) selling, hiring out or lending the goods;
(b) entering into a hire-purchase agreement to furnish the goods;
(c) the performance of any contract for work and materials to furnish the goods;
(d) providing the goods in exchange for any consideration (including trading stamps) other than money;
(e) providing the goods in or in connection with the performance of any statutory function; or
(f) giving the goods as a prize or otherwise making a gift of the goods;

and, in relation to gas or water, those references shall be construed as including references to providing the service by which the gas or water is made available for use.

(2) For the purposes of any reference in this Act to supplying goods, where a person ('the ostensible supplier') supplies goods to another person ('the customer') under a hire-purchase agreement, conditional sale agreement or credit-sale agreement or under an

agreement for the hiring of goods (other than a hire-purchase agreement) and the ostensible supplier –

(a) carries on the business of financing the provision of goods for others by means of such agreements; and

(b) in the course of that business acquired his interest in the goods supplied to the customer as a means of financing the provision of them for the customer by a further person ('the effective supplier'), the effective supplier and not the ostensible supplier shall be treated as supplying the goods to the customer.

(3) Subject to subsection (4) below, the performance of any contract by the erection of any building or structure on any land or by the carrying out of any other building works shall be treated for the purposes of this Act as a supply of goods in so far as, but only in so far as, it involves the provision of any goods to any person by means of their incorporation into the building, structure or works.

(4) Except for the purposes of, and in relation to, notices to warn or any provision made by or under Part III of this Act, references in this Act to supplying goods shall not include references to supplying goods comprised in land where the supply is effected by the creation or disposal of an interest in the land.

(5) Except in Part I of this Act references in this Act to a person's supplying goods shall be confined to references to that person's supplying goods in the course of a business of his, but for the purposes of this subsection it shall be immaterial whether the business is a business of dealing in the goods.

(6) For the purposes of subsection (5) above goods shall not be treated as supplied in the course of a business if they are supplied, in pursuance of an obligation arising under or in connection with the insurance of the goods, to the person with whom they were insured.

(7) Except for the purposes of, and in relation to, prohibition notices or suspension notices, references in Parts II to IV of this Act to supplying goods shall not include –

(a) references to supplying goods where the person supplied carries on a business of buying goods of the same description as those goods and repairing or reconditioning them';

(b) references to supplying goods by a sale of articles as scrap (that is to say, for the value of materials included in the articles rather than for the value of the articles themselves).

(8) Where any goods have at any time been supplied by being hired out or lent to any person, neither a continuation or renewal of the hire or loan (whether on the same or different terms) nor any transaction for the transfer after that time of any interest in the goods to the person to whom they were hired or lent shall be treated for the purposes of this Act as a further supply of the goods to that person.

(9) A ship, aircraft or motor vehicle shall not be treated for the purposes of this Act as supplied to any person by reason only that services consisting in the carriage of goods or passengers in that ship, aircraft or vehicle, or in its use for any other purpose, are provided to that person in pursuance of an agreement relating to the use of the ship, aircraft or vehicle for a particular period or for particular voyages, flights or journeys.

[As amended by the Road Traffic (Consequential Provisions) Act 1988, s4, Schedule 3, para 35; Trade Marks Act 1994, s106(2), Schedule 5.]

Road Traffic Act 1988
(1988 c 52)

149 *Avoidance of certain agreements as to liability towards passengers*

(1) This section applies where a person uses a motor vehicle in circumstances such that under section 143 of this Act there is required to be in force in relation to his use of it such a policy of insurance or such a security in respect of third-party risks as complies with the requirements of this Part of this Act.

(2) If any other person is carried in or upon the vehicle while the user is so using it, any antecedent agreement or understanding between them (whether intended to be legally binding or not) shall be of no effect so far as it purports or might be held –

(a) to negative or restrict any such liability of the user in respect of persons carried in or upon the vehicle as is required by section 145 of this Act to be covered by a policy of insurance, or
(b) to impose any conditions with respect to the enforcement of any such liability of the user.

(3) The fact that a person so carried has willingly accepted as his the risk of negligence on the part of the user shall not be treated as negativing any such liability of the user.

(4) For the purposes of this section –

(a) references to a person being carried in or upon a vehicle include references to a person entering or getting on to, or alighting from, the vehicle, and
(b) the reference to an antecedent agreement is to one made at any time before the liability arose.

Human Fertilisation and Embryology Act 1990
(1990 c 37)

35 *Disclosure in interests of justice: congenital disabilities, etc*

(1) Where for the purpose of instituting proceedings under section 1 of the Congenital Disabilities (Civil Liability) Act 1976 (civil liability to child born disabled) it is necessary to identify a person who would or might be the parent of a child but for sections 27 to 29 of this Act, the court may, on the application of the child, make an order requiring the [Human Fertilisation and Embryology] Authority to disclose any information contained in the register kept in pursuance of section 31 of this Act identifying that person.

Courts and Legal Services Act 1990
(1990 c 41)

8 Powers of Court of Appeal to award damages

(1) In this section 'case' means any case where the Court of Appeal has power to order a new trial on the ground that damages awarded by a jury are excessive or inadequate.

(2) Rules of court may provide for the Court of Appeal, in such classes of case as may be specified in the rules, to have power, in place of ordering a new trial, to substitute for the sum awarded by the jury such sum as appears to the court to be proper.

(3) This section is not to be read as prejudicing in any way any other power to make rules of court.

62 Immunity of advocates from actions in negligence and for breach of contract

(1) A person –

    (a) who is not a barrister; but
    (b) who lawfully provides any legal services in relation to any proceedings,

shall have the same immunity from liability for negligence in respect of his acts or omissions as he would have if he were a barrister lawfully providing those services.

(2) No act or omission on the part of any barrister or other person which is accorded immunity from liability for negligence shall give rise to an action for breach of any contract relating to the provision by him of the legal services in question.

69 Exemption from liability for damages, etc

(1) Neither the Lord Chancellor nor any of the designated judges shall be liable in damages for anything done or omitted in the discharge or purported discharge of any of their functions under this Part [legal services].

(2) For the purposes of the law of defamation, the publication by the Lord Chancellor, a designated judge or the Director of any advice or reasons given by or to him in the exercise of functions under this Part shall be absolutely privileged.

119 Interpretation

(1) In this Act – ...

'designated judge' means the Lord Chief Justice, the Master of the Rolls, the President of the Family Division or the Vice-Chancellor;

'the Director' means the Director General of Fair Trading; ...

Broadcasting Act 1990
(1990 c 42)

166 Defamatory material

(1) For the purposes of the law of libel and slander (including the law of criminal libel so far as it relates to the publication of defamatory matter) the publication of works in the course of any programme included in a programme service shall be treated as publication in permanent form.

(2) Subsection (1) above shall apply for the purposes of section 3 of each of the Defamation Acts (slander of title, etc) as it applies for the purposes of the law of libel and slander.

(4) In this section 'the Defamation Acts' means the Defamation Act 1952 and the Defamation Act (Northern Ireland) 1955.

203 Consequential and transitional provisions ...

(2) Unless the context otherwise requires, in any enactment amended by this Act –

'programme', in relation to a programme service, includes any items included in that service; and

'television programme' includes a teletext transmission. ...

Schedule 20
Minor and Consequential Amendments
Parliamentary Papers Act 1840 (c 9)

1. Section 3 (protection in respect of proceedings for printing extracts from or abstracts of parliamentary papers) shall have effect as if the reference to printing included a reference to including in a programme service.

[As amended by the Defamation Act 1996, s16, Schedule 2.]

Environmental Protection Act 1990
(1990 c 43)

33 Prohibition on unauthorised or harmful deposit, treatment or disposal, etc, of waste ...

(7) It shall be a defence for a person charged with an offence under this section to prove –

(a) that he took all reasonable precautions and exercised all due diligence to avoid the commission of the offence; or

(b) that he acted under instructions from his employer and neither knew nor had reason to suppose that the acts done by him constituted a contravention of subsection (1) above; or

(c) that the acts alleged to constitute the contravention were done in an emergency in order to avoid danger to human health in a case where –

(i) he took all such steps as were reasonably practicable in the circumstances for minimising pollution of the environment and harm to human health; and
(ii) particulars of the acts were furnished to the waste regulation authority as soon as reasonably practicable after they were done.

73 Appeals and other provisions relating to legal proceedings and civil liability ...

(6) Where any damage is caused by waste which has been deposited in or on land, any person who deposited it, or knowingly caused or knowingly permitted it to be deposited, in either case so as to commit an offence under section 33(1) or 63(2) above, is liable for the damage except where the damage –

(a) was due wholly to the fault of the person who suffered it; or
(b) was suffered by a person who voluntarily accepted the risk of the damage being caused;

but without prejudice to any liability arising otherwise than under this subsection.

(7) The matters which may be proved by way of defence under section 33(7) above may be proved also by way of defence to an action brought under subsection (6) above.

(8) In subsection (6) above –

'damage' includes the death of, or injury to, any person (including any disease and any impairment of physical or mental condition); and

'fault' has the same meaning as in the Law Reform (Contributory Negligence) Act 1945.

(9) For the purposes of the following enactments –

(a) the Fatal Accidents Act 1976;
(b) the Law Reform (Contributory Negligence) Act 1945; and
(c) the Limitation Act 1980; ...

any damage for which a person is liable under subsection (6) above shall be treated as due to his fault.

75 Meaning of 'waste' and household, commercial and industrial waste and special waste ...

(2) 'Waste' includes –

(a) any substance which constitutes a scrap material or any effluent or other unwanted surplus substance arising from the application of any process; and
(b) any substance or article which requires to be disposed of as being broken, worn out, contaminated or otherwise spoiled;

but does not include a substance which is an explosive within the meaning of the Explosives Act 1875.

(3) Any thing which is discarded or otherwise dealt with as if it were waste shall be presumed to be waste unless the contrary is proved.

[As amended by the Environment Act 1995, s120(1), Schedule 22, para 64.]

Water Resources Act 1991
(1991 c 57)

208 Civil liability of the Agency for escapes of water, etc

(1) Where an escape of water, however caused, from a pipe vested in the Agency causes loss or damage, the Agency shall be liable, except as otherwise provided in this section, for the loss or damage.

(2) The Agency shall not incur any liability under subsection (1) above if the escape was due wholly to the fault of the person who sustained the loss or damage or of any servant, agent or contractor of his.

(3) The Agency shall not incur any liability under subsection (1) above in respect of any loss or damage for which the Agency would not be liable apart from that subsection and which is sustained –

(a) by any water undertaker or sewerage undertaker or by any statutory undertakers, within the meaning of section 336(1) of the Town and Country Planning Act 1990;
(b) by any public gas supplier within the meaning of Part I of the Gas Act 1986 or the holder of a licence under section 6(1) of the Electricity Act 1989;
(c) by any highway authority; or
(d) by any person on whom a right to compensation is conferred by section 82 of the New Roads and Street Works Act 1991.

(4) The Law Reform (Contributory Negligence) Act 1945, the Fatal Accidents Act 1976 and the Limitation Act 1980 shall apply in relation to any loss or damage for which the Agency is liable under this section, but which is not due to the Agency's fault, as if it were due to its fault.

(5) Nothing in subsection (1) above affects any entitlement which the Agency may have to recover contribution under the Civil Liability (Contribution) Act 1978; and for the purposes of that Act, any loss for which the Agency is liable under that subsection shall be treated as if it were damage.

(6) Where the Agency is liable under any enactment or agreement passed or made before 1 April 1982 to make any payment in respect of any loss or damage the Agency shall not incur liability under subsection (1) above in respect of the same loss or damage.

(7) In this section 'fault' has the same meaning as in the Law Reform (Contributory Negligence) Act 1945. ...

221 *General interpretation*

(1) In this Act, except in so far as the context otherwise requires – ...

'the Agency' means the Environment Agency;

'damage', in relation to individuals, includes death and any personal injury (including any disease or impairment of physical or mental condition).

[As amended by the Environment Act 1995, s120(1), (3), Schedule 22, paras 130, 177(1), (3), Schedule 24.]

[NB The civil liability of water undertakers for escapes of water, etc, is in similar terms: see s209 of the Water Industry Act 1991, as amended.]

Trade Union and Labour Relations (Consolidation) Act 1992
(1992 c 52)

1 *Meaning of 'trade union'*

In this Act a 'trade union' means an organisation (whether temporary or permanent) –

(a) which consists wholly or mainly or workers of one or more descriptions and whose principal purposes include the regulation of relations between workers of that description or those descriptions and employers or employers' associations; or
(b) which consists wholly or mainly of –

(i) constituent or affiliated organisations which fulfil the conditions in paragraph (a) (or themselves consist wholly or mainly of constituent or affiliated organisations which fulfil those conditions), or
(ii) representatives of such constituent or affiliated organisations,

and whose principal purposes include the regulation of relations between workers and employers or between workers and employers' associations, or the regulation of relations between its constituent or affiliated organisations.

10 *Quasi-corporate status of trade unions*

(1) A trade union is not a body corporate but –

(a) it is capable of making contracts;
(b) it is capable of suing and being sued in its own name, whether in proceedings relating to property or founded on contract or tort or any other cause of action; and
(c) proceedings for an offence alleged to have been committed by it or on its behalf may be brought against it in its own name.

(2) A trade union shall not be treated as if it were a body corporate except to the extent authorised by the provisions of this Part. ...

12 *Property to be vested in trustees*

(1) All property belonging to a trade union shall be vested in trustees in trust for it.

(2) A judgment, order or award made in proceedings of any description brought against a trade union is enforceable, by way of execution, diligence, punishment for contempt or otherwise, against any property held in trust for it to the same extent and in the same manner as if it were a body corporate.

(3) Subsection (2) has effect subject to section 23 (restriction on enforcement of awards against certain property.)

20 *Liability of trade union in certain proceedings in tort*

(1) Where proceedings in tort are brought against a trade union –

(a) on the ground that an act –

(i) induces another person to break a contract or interferes or induces another person to interfere with its performance, or

(ii) consists in threatening that a contract (whether one to which the union is a party or not) will be broken or its performance interfered with, or that the union will induce another person to break a contract or interfere with its performance, or

(b) in respect of an agreement or combination by two or more persons to do or to procure the doing of an act which, if it were done without any such agreement or combination, would be actionable in tort on such a ground,

then, for the purpose of determining in those proceedings whether the union is liable in respect of the act in question, that act shall be taken to have been done by the union if, but only if, it is to be taken to have been authorised or endorsed by the trade union in accordance with the following provisions.

(2) An act shall be taken to have been authorised or endorsed by a trade union if it was done, or was authorised or endorsed –

(a) by any person empowered by the rules to do, authorise or endorse acts of the kind in question, or

(b) by the principal executive committee or the president or general secretary, or

(c) by any other committee of the union or any other official of the union (whether employed by it or not).

(3) For the purposes of paragraph (c) of subsection (2) –

(a) any group of persons constituted in accordance with the rules of the union is a committee of the union; and

(b) an act shall be taken to have been done, authorised or endorsed by an official if it was done, authorised or endorsed by, or by any member of, any group of persons of which he was at the material time a member, the purposes of which included organising or co-ordinating industrial action.

(4) The provisions of paragraphs (b) and (c) of subsection (2) apply notwithstanding

anything in the rules of the union, or in any contract or rule of law, but subject to the provisions of section 21 (repudiation by union of certain acts).

(5) Where for the purposes of any proceedings an act is by virtue of this section taken to have been done by a trade union, nothing in this section shall affect the liability of any other person, in those or any other proceedings, in respect of that act.

(6) In proceedings arising out of an act which is by virtue of this section taken to have been done by a trade union, the power of the court to grant an injunction or interdict includes power to require the union to take such steps as the court considers appropriate for ensuring –

(a) that there is no, or no further, inducement of persons to take part or to continue to take part in industrial action, and
(b) that no person engages in any conduct after the granting of the injunction or interdict by virtue of having been induced before it was granted to take part or to continue to take part in industrial action.

The provisions of subsection (2) to (4) above apply in relation to proceedings for failure to comply with any such injunction or interdict as they apply in relation to the original proceedings.

(7) In this section 'rules', in relation to a trade union, means the written rules of the union and any other written provision forming part of the contract between a member and the other members.

21 Repudiation by union of certain acts

(1) An act shall not be taken to have been authorised or endorsed by a trade union by virtue only of paragraph (c) of section 20(2) if it was repudiated by the executive, president or general secretary as soon as reasonably practicable after coming to the knowledge of any of them.

(2) Where an act is repudiated –

(a) written notice of the repudiation must be given to the committee or official in question, without delay, and
(b) the union must do its best to give individual written notice of the fact and date of repudiation, without delay –

(i) to every member of the union who the union has reason to believe is taking part, or might otherwise take part, in industrial action as a result of the act, and
(ii) to the employer of every such member.

(3) The notice given to members in accordance with paragraph (b)(i) of subsection (2) must contain the following statement –

'Your union has repudiated the call (or calls) for industrial action to which this notice relates and will give no support to unofficial industrial action taken in response to it (or them). If you are dismissed while taking unofficial industrial action, you will have no right to complain of unfair dismissal.'

(4) If subsection (2) or (3) is not complied with, the repudiation shall be treated as ineffective.

(5) An act shall not be treated as repudiated if at any time after the union concerned purported to repudiate it the executive, president or general secretary has behaved in a manner which is inconsistent with the purported repudiation.

(6) The executive, president or general secretary shall be treated as so behaving if, on a request made to any of them within three months of the purported repudiation by a person who –

(a) is a party to a commercial contract whose performance has been or may be interfered with as a result of the act in question, and
(b) has not been given written notice by the union of the repudiation,

it is not forthwith confirmed in writing that the act has been repudiated.

(7) In this section 'commercial contract' means any contract other than –

(a) a contract of employment, or
(b) any other contract under which a person agrees personally to do work or perform services for another.

22 Limit on damages awarded against trade unions in actions in tort

(1) This section applies to any proceedings in tort brought against a trade union, except –

(a) proceedings for personal injury as a result of negligence, nuisance or breach of duty;
(b) proceedings for breach of duty in connection with the ownership, occupation, possession, control or use of property;
(c) proceedings brought by virtue of Part I of the Consumer Protection Act 1987 (product liability).

(2) In any proceedings in tort to which this section applies the amount which may be awarded against the union by way of damages shall not exceed the following limit –

Number of members of union	*Maximum award of damages*
Less than 5,000	£10,000
5,000 or more but less than 25,000	£50,000
25,000 or more but less than 100,000	£125,000
100,000 or more	£250,000

(3) The Secretary of State may by order amend subsection (2) so as to vary any of the sums specified; and the order may make such transitional provision as the Secretary of State considers appropriate.

(4) Any such order shall be made by statutory instrument which shall be subject to annulment in pursuance of a resolution of either House of Parliament.

(5) In this section –

'breach of duty' means breach of a duty imposed by any rule of law or by or under any enactment;

'personal injury' includes any disease and any impairment of a person's physical or mental condition; and

'property' means any property, whether real or personal (or in Scotland, heritable or moveable).

23 *Restriction on enforcement of awards against certain property*

(1) Where in any proceedings an amount is awarded by way of damages, costs or expenses –

(a) against a trade union,
(b) against trustees in whom property is vested in trust for a trade union, in their capacity as such (and otherwise than in respect of a breach of trust on their part), or
(c) against members or officials of a trade union on behalf of themselves and all of the members of the union,

no part of that amount is recoverable by enforcement against any protected property.

(2) The following is protected property –

(a) property belonging to the trustees otherwise than in their capacity as such;
(b) property belonging to any member of the union otherwise than jointly or in common with the other members;
(c) property belonging to an official of the union who is neither a member nor a trustee;
(d) property comprised in the union's political fund where that fund –

(i) is subject to rules of the union which prevent property which is or has been comprised in the fund from being used for financing strikes or other industrial action, and
(ii) was so subject at the time when the act in respect of which the proceedings are brought was done;

(e) property comprised in a separate fund maintained in accordance with the rules of the union for the purpose only of providing provident benefits.

(3) For this purpose 'provident benefits' includes –

(a) any payment expressly authorised by the rules of the union which is made –

(i) to a member during sickness or incapacity from personal injury or while out of work, or
(ii) to an aged member by way of superannuation, or
(iii) to a member who has met with an accident or has lost his tools by fire or theft;

(b) a payment in discharge or aid of funeral expenses on the death of a member or the wife of a member or as provision for the children of a deceased member.

119 Expressions relating to trade unions

In this Act, in relation to a trade union – …

'branch or section', except where the context otherwise requires, includes a branch or section which is itself a trade union;

'executive' means the principal committee of the union exercising executive functions, by whatever name it is called; …

'general secretary' means the official of the union who holds the office of general secretary or, where there is no such office, holds an office which is equivalent, or (except in section 14(4)) the nearest equivalent, to that of general secretary;

'officer' includes –

(a) any member of the governing body of the union, and
(b) any trustee of any fund applicable for the purposes of the union;

'official' means –

(a) an officer of the union or of a branch or section of the union, or
(b) a person elected or appointed in accordance with the rules of the union to be a representative of its members or of some of them,

and includes a person so elected or appointed who is an employee of the same employer as the members or one or more of the members whom he is to represent;

'president' means the official of the union who holds the office of president or, where there is no such office, who holds an office which is equivalent, or (except in section 14(4) or Chapter IV) the nearest equivalent, to that of president; and

'rules', except where the context otherwise requires, includes the rules of any branch or section of the union.

121 Meaning of 'the court'

In this Part 'the court' (except where the reference is expressed to be to the county court or sheriff court) means the High Court or the Court of Session.

122 Meaning of 'employers' association'

(1) In this Act an 'employers' association' means an organisation (whether temporary or permanent) –

(a) which consists wholly or mainly of employers or individual owners of undertakings of one or more descriptions and whose principal purposes include the regulation of relations between employers of that description or those descriptions and workers or trade unions; or
(b) which consists wholly or mainly of –

(i) constituent or affiliated organisations which fulfil the conditions in paragraph (a) (or themselves consist wholly or mainly of constituent or affiliated organisations which fulfil those conditions), or

(ii) representatives of such constituent or affiliated organisations,

and whose principal purposes include the regulation of relations between employers and workers or between employers and trade unions, or the regulation of relations between its constituent or affiliated organisations.

(2) References in this Act to employers' associations include combinations of employers and employers' associations.

127 Corporate or quasi-corporate status of employers' associations

(1) An employers' association may be either a body corporate or an unincorporated association.

(2) Where an employers' association is unincorporated –

(a) it is capable of making contracts;
(b) it is capable of suing and being sued in its own name, whether in proceedings relating to property or founded on contract or tort or any other cause of action; and
(c) proceedings for an offence alleged to have been committed by it or on its behalf may be brought against it in its own name.

(3) Nothing in section 716 of the Companies Act 1985 (associations of over 20 members to be incorporated or otherwise formed in special ways) shall be taken to prevent the formation of an employers' association which is neither registered as a company under that Act nor otherwise incorporated.

130 Restriction on enforcement of awards against certain property

(1) Where in any proceedings an amount is awarded by way of damages, costs or expenses –

(a) against an employers' association,
(b) against trustees in whom property is vested in trust for an employers' association, in their capacity as such (and otherwise than in respect of a breach of trust on their part), or
(c) against members or officials of an employers' association on behalf of themselves and all of the members of the association,

no part of that amount is recoverable by enforcement against any protected property.

(2) The following is protected property –

(a) property belonging to the trustees otherwise than in their capacity as such;
(b) property belonging to any member of the association otherwise than jointly or in common with the other members;
(c) property belonging to an official of the association who is neither a member nor a trustee.

219 Protection from certain tort liabilities

(1) An act done by a person in contemplation or furtherance of a trade dispute is not actionable in tort on the ground only –

(a) that it induces another person to break a contract or interferes or induces another person to interfere with its performance, or

(b) that it consists in his threatening that a contract (whether one to which he is a party or not) will be broken or its performance interfered with, or that he will induce another person to break a contract or interfere with its performance.

(2) An agreement or combination by two or more persons to do or procure the doing of an act in contemplation or furtherance of a trade dispute is not actionable in tort if the act is one which if done without any such agreement or combination would not be actionable in tort.

(3) Nothing in subsection (1) and (2) prevents an act done in the course of picketing from being actionable in tort unless it is done in the course of attendance declared lawful by section 220 (peaceful picketing).

(4) Subsections (1) and (2) have effect subject to sections 222 to 225 (action excluded from protection) and to sections 226 (requirement of ballot before action by trade union) and 234A (requirement of notice to employer of industrial action); and in those sections 'not protected' means excluded from the protection afforded by this section or, where the expression is used with reference to a particular person, excluded from that protection as respects that person.

220 Peaceful picketing

(1) It is lawful for a person in contemplation or furtherance of a trade dispute to attend –

(a) at or near his own place of work, or

(b) if he is an official of a trade union, at or near the place of work of a member of the union whom he is accompanying and whom he represents,

for the purpose only of peacefully obtaining or communicating information, or peacefully persuading any person to work or abstain from working.

(2) If a person works or normally works –

(a) otherwise than at any one place, or

(b) at a place the location of which is such that attendance there for a purpose mentioned in subsection (1) is impracticable,

his place of work for the purposes of that subsection shall be any premises of his employer from which he works or from which his work is administered.

(3) In the case of a worker not in employment where –

(a) his last employment was terminated in connection with a trade dispute, or

(b) the termination of his employment was one of the circumstances giving rise to a trade dispute, in relation to that dispute his former place of work shall be treated for the purposes of subsection (1) as being his place of work.

(4) A person who is an official of a trade union by virtue only of having been elected or appointed to be a representative of some of the members of the union shall be regarded for the purposes of subsection (1) as representing only those members; but otherwise an official of a union shall be regarded for those purposes as representing all its members.

221 Restrictions on grant of injunctions ...

(1) Where –

(a) an application for an injunction ... is made to a court in the absence of the party against whom it is sought or any representative of his, and

(b) he claims, or in the opinion of the court would be likely to claim, that he acted in contemplation or furtherance of a trade dispute,

the court shall not grant the injunction ... unless satisfied that all steps which in the circumstances were reasonable have been taken with a view to securing that notice of the application and an opportunity of being heard with respect to the application have been given to him.

(2) Where –

(a) an application for an interlocutory injunction is made to a court pending the trial of an action, and

(b) the party against whom it is sought claims that he acted in contemplation or furtherance of a trade dispute,

the court shall, in exercising its discretion whether or not to grant the injunction, have regard to the likelihood of that party's succeeding at the trial of the action in establishing any matter which would afford a defence to the action under section 219 (protection from certain tort liabilities) or section 220 (peaceful picketing) ...

222 Action to enforce trade union membership

(1) An act is not protected if the reason, or one of the reasons, for which it is done is the fact or belief that a particular employer –

(a) is employing, has employed or might employ a person who is not a member of a trade union, or

(b) is failing, has failed or might fail to discriminate against such a person.

(2) For the purposes of subsection (1)(b) an employer discriminates against a person if, but only if, he ensures that his conduct in relation to –

(a) persons, or persons of any description, employed by him, or who apply to be, or are, considered by him for employment, or

(b) the provision of employment for such persons,

is different, in some or all cases, according to whether or not they are members of a trade union, and is more favourable to those who are.

(3) An act is not protected if it constitutes, or is one of a number of acts which together constitute, an inducement or attempted inducement of a person –

(a) to incorporate in a contract to which that person is a party, or a proposed contract to which he intends to be a party, a term or condition which is or would be void by virtue of section 144 (union membership requirement in contract for goods or services), or

(b) to contravene section 145 (refusal to deal with person on grounds relating to union membership).

(4) References in this section to an employer employing a person are to a person acting in the capacity of the person for whom a worker works or normally works.

(5) References in this section to not being a member of a trade union are to not being a member of any trade union, of a particular trade union or of one of a number of particular trade unions. Any such reference includes a reference to not being a member of a particular branch or section of a trade union or of one of a number of particular branches or sections of a trade union.

223 Action taken because of dismissal for taking unofficial action

An act is not protected if the reason, or one of the reasons, for doing it is the fact or belief that an employer has dismissed one or more employees in circumstances such that by virtue of section 237 (dismissal in connection with unofficial action) they have no right to complain of unfair dismissal.

224 Secondary action

(1) An act is not protected if one of the facts relied on for the purpose of establishing liability is that there has been secondary action which is not lawful picketing.

(2) There is secondary action in relation to a trade dispute when, and only when, a person –

(a) induces another to break a contract of employment or interferes or induces another to interfere with its performance, or

(b) threatens that a contract of employment under which he or another is employed will be broken or its performance interfered with, or that he will induce another to break a contract of employment or to interfere with its performance,

and the employer under the contract of employment is not the employer party to the dispute.

(3) Lawful picketing means acts done in the course of such attendance as is declared lawful by section 220 (peaceful picketing) –

(a) by a worker employed (or, in the case of a worker not in employment, last employed) by the employer party to the dispute, or

(b) by a trade union official whose attendance is lawful by virtue of subsection (1)(b) of that section.

(4) For the purposes of this section an employer shall not be treated as party to a dispute between another employer and workers of that employer; and where more than one

employer is in dispute with his workers, the dispute between each employer and his workers shall be treated as a separate dispute. In this subsection 'worker' has the same meaning as in section 244 (meaning of 'trade dispute').

(5) An act in contemplation or furtherance of a trade dispute which is primary action in relation to that dispute may not be relied on as secondary action in relation to another trade dispute.

Primary action means such action as is mentioned in paragraph (a) or (b) of subsection (2) where the employer under the contract of employment is the employer party to the dispute.

(6) In this section 'contract of employment' includes any contract under which one person personally does work or performs services for another, and related expressions shall be construed accordingly.

225 Pressure to impose union recognition requirement

(1) An act is not protected if it constitutes, or is one of a number of acts which together constitute, an inducement or attempted inducement of a person –

(a) to incorporate in a contract to which that person is a party, or a proposed contract to which he intends to be a party, a term or condition which is or would be void by virtue of section 186 (recognition requirement in contract for goods or services), or
(b) to contravene section 187 (refusal to deal with person on grounds of union exclusion).

(2) An act is not protected if –

(a) it interferes with the supply (whether or not under a contract) of goods or services, or can reasonably be expected to have that effect, and
(b) one of the facts relied upon for the purpose of establishing liability is that a person has –

(i) induced another to break a contract of employment or interfered or induced another to interfere with its performance, or
(ii) threatened that a contract of employment under which he or another is employed will be broken or its performance interfered with, or that he will induce another to break a contract of employment or to interfere with its performance, and

(c) the reason, or one of the reasons, for doing the act is the fact or belief that the supplier (not being the employer under the contract of employment mentioned in paragraph (b)) does not, or might not –

(i) recognise one or more trade unions for the purpose of negotiating on behalf of workers, or any class of worker, employed by him, or
(ii) negotiate or consult with, or with an official of, one or more trade unions.

226 Requirement of ballot before action by trade union

(1) An act done by a trade union to induce a person to take part, or continue to take part, in industrial action –

(a) is not protected unless the industrial action has the support of a ballot, and

(b) where section 226A falls to be complied with in relation to the person's employer, is not protected as respects the employer unless the trade union has complied with section 226A in relation to him.

In this section 'the relevant time', in relation to an act by a trade union to induce a person to take part, or continue to take part, in industrial action, means the time at which proceedings are commenced in respect of the act.

(2) Industrial action shall be regarded as having the support of a ballot only if –

(a) the union has held a ballot in respect of the action –

(i) in relation to which the requirements of section 226B [appointment of scrutineer] so far as applicable before and during the holding of the ballot were satisfied,

(ii) in relation to which the requirements of sections 227 to 231A were satisfied, and

(iii) in which the majority voting in the ballot answered 'Yes' to the question applicable in accordance with section 229(2) to industrial action of the kind to which the act of inducement relates;

(b) such of the requirements of the following sections as have fallen to be satisfied at the relevant time have been satisfied, namely –

(i) section 226B so far as applicable after the holding of the ballot, and

(ii) section 231B; and

(c) the requirements of section 233 (calling of industrial action with support of ballot) are satisfied.

Any reference in this subsection to a requirement of a provision which is disapplied or modified by section 232 has effect subject to that section.

(3) Where separate workplace ballots are held by virtue of section 228(1) –

(a) industrial action shall be regarded as having the support of a ballot if the conditions specified in subsection (2) are satisfied, and

(b) the trade union shall be taken to have complied with the requirements relating to a ballot imposed by section 226A [notice of ballot and sample voting paper for employers] if those requirements are complied with,

in relation to the ballot for the place of work of the person induced to take part, or continue to take part, in the industrial action.

(4) For the purposes of this section an inducement, in relation to a person, includes an inducement which is or would be ineffective, whether because of his unwillingness to be influenced by it or for any other reason.

244 Meaning of 'trade dispute' in Part V

(1) In this Part [ss219-246] a 'trade dispute' means a dispute between workers and their employer which relates wholly or mainly to one or more of the following –

(a) terms and conditions of employment, or the physical conditions in which any workers are required to work;

(b) engagement or non-engagement, or termination or suspension of employment or the duties of employment, of one or more workers;

(c) allocation of work or the duties of employment between workers or groups of workers;

(d) matters of discipline;

(e) a worker's membership or non-membership of a trade union;

(f) facilities for officials of trade unions; and

(g) machinery for negotiation or consultation, and other procedures, relating to any of the above matters, including the recognition by employers or employers' associations of the right of a trade union to represent workers in such negotiation or consultation or in the carrying out of such procedures.

(2) A dispute between a Minister of the Crown and any workers shall, notwithstanding that he is not the employer of those workers, be treated as a dispute between those workers and their employer if the dispute relates to matters which –

(a) have been referred for consideration by a joint body on which, by virtue of provision made by or under any enactment, he is represented, or

(b) cannot be settled without him exercising a power conferred on him by or under an enactment.

(3) There is a trade dispute even though it relates to matters occurring outside the United Kingdom, so long as the person or persons whose actions in the United Kingdom are said to be in contemplation or furtherance of a trade dispute relating to matters occurring outside the United Kingdom are likely to be affected in respect of one or more of the matters specified in subsection (1) by the outcome of the dispute.

(4) An act, threat or demand done or made by one person or organisation against another which, if resisted, would have led to a trade dispute with that other, shall be treated as being done or made in contemplation of a trade dispute with that other, notwithstanding that because that other submits to the act or threat or accedes to the demand no dispute arises.

(5) In this section –

'employment' includes any relationship whereby one person personally does work or performs services for another; and

'worker', in relation to a dispute with an employer, means –

(a) a worker employed by that employer; or

(b) a person who has ceased to be so employed if his employment was terminated in connection with the dispute or if the termination of his employment was one of the circumstances giving rise to the dispute.

298 Minor definitions: general

In this Act, unless the context otherwise requires –

'act' and 'action' each includes omission, and references to doing an act or taking action shall be construed accordingly;

'contravention' includes a failure to comply, and cognate expressions shall be construed accordingly; ...

[As amended by the Trade Union Reform and Employment Rights Act 1993, ss18(1), 49(1), (2), Schedules 7, para 17, 8, paras 72, 73.]

Police Act 1996
(1996 c 16)

88 Liability for wrongful acts of constables

(1) The chief officer of police for a police area shall be liable in respect of torts committed by constables under his direction and control in the performance or purported performance of their functions in like manner as a master is liable in respect of torts committed by his servants in the course of their employment, and accordingly shall in respect of any such tort be treated for all purposes as a joint tortfeasor.

(2) There shall be paid out of the police fund –

(a) any damages or costs awarded against the chief officer of police in any proceedings brought against him by virtue of this section and any costs incurred by him in any such proceedings so far as not recovered by him in the proceedings; and

(b) any sum required in connection with the settlement of any claim made against the chief officer of police by virtue of this section, if the settlement is approved by the police authority.

(3) Any proceedings in respect of a claim made by virtue of this section shall be brought against the chief officer of police for the time being or, in the case of a vacancy in that office, against the person for the time being performing the functions of the chief officer of police and references in subsections (1) and (2) to the chief officer of police shall be construed accordingly.

(4) A police authority may, in such cases and to such extent as appear to it to be appropriate, pay out of the police fund –

(a) any damages or costs awarded against a person to whom this subsection applies in proceedings for a tort committed by that person,

(b) any costs incurred and not recovered by such a person in such proceedings, and

(c) any sum required in connection with the settlement of a claim that has or might have given rise to such proceedings.

(5) Subsection (4) applies to a person who is –

(a) a member of the police force maintained by the police authority,

(b) a constable for the time being required to serve with that force by virtue of section 24 [provision of special services] or 98 [cross-border aid of one police force by another] of this Act or section 23 of the Police Act 1997 [aid by and for NCIS], or

(c) a special constable appointed for the authority's police area.

[As amended by the Police Act 1997, s134(1), Schedule 9, para 85.]

Defamation Act 1996
(1996 c 31)

1 Responsibility for publication

(1) In defamation proceedings a person has a defence if he shows that –

(a) he was not the author, editor or publisher of the statement complained of,

(b) he took reasonable care in relation to its publication, and

(c) he did not know, and had no reason to believe, that what he did caused or contributed to the publication of a defamatory statement.

(2) For this purpose 'author', 'editor' and 'publisher' have the following meanings, which are further explained in subsection (3) –

'author' means the originator of the statement, but does not include a person who did not intend that his statement be published at all;

'editor' means a person having editorial or equivalent responsibility for the content of the statement or the decision to publish it; and

'publisher' means a commercial publisher, that is, a person whose business is issuing material to the public, or a section of the public, who issues material containing the statement in the course of that business.

(3) A person shall not be considered the author, editor or publisher of a statement if he is only involved –

(a) in printing, producing, distributing or selling printed material containing the statement;

(b) in processing, making copies of, distributing, exhibiting or selling a film or sound recording (as defined in Part I of the Copyright, Designs and Patents Act 1988) containing the statement;

(c) in processing, making copies of, distributing or selling any electronic medium in or on which the statement is recorded, or in operating or providing any equipment, system or service by means of which the statement is retrieved, copied, distributed or made available in electronic form;

(d) as the broadcaster of a live programme containing the statement in circumstances in which he has no effective control over the maker of the statement;

(e) as the operator of or provider of access to a communications system by means of which the statement is transmitted, or made available, by a person over whom he has no effective control.

In a case not within paragraphs (a) to (e) the court may have regard to those provisions by way of analogy in deciding whether a person is to be considered the author, editor or publisher of a statement.

(4) Employees or agents of an author, editor or publisher are in the same position as their employer or principal to the extent that they are responsible for the content of the statement or the decision to publish it.

(5) In determining for the purposes of this section whether a person took reasonable care, or

had reason to believe that what he did caused or contributed to the publication of a defamatory statement, regard shall be had to –

(a) the extent of his responsibility for the content of the statement or the decision to publish it,

(b) the nature or circumstances of the publication, and

(c) the previous conduct or character of the author, editor or publisher.

(6) This section does not apply to any cause of action which arose before the section came into force.

13 *Evidence concerning proceedings in Parliament*

(1) Where the conduct of a person in or in relation to proceedings in Parliament is in issue in defamation proceedings, he may waive for the purposes of those proceedings, so far as concerns him, the protection of any enactment or rule of law which prevents proceedings in Parliament being impeached or questioned in any court or place out of Parliament.

(2) Where a person waives that protection –

(a) any such enactment or rule of law shall not apply to prevent evidence being given, questions being asked or statements, submissions, comments or findings being made about his conduct, and

(b) none of those things shall be regarded as infringing the privilege of either House of Parliament.

(3) The waiver by one person of that protection does not affect its operation in relation to another person who has not waived it.

(4) Nothing in this section affects any enactment or rule of law so far as it protects a person (including a person who has waived the protection referred to above) from legal liability for words spoken or things done in the course of, or for the purposes of or incidental to, any proceedings in Parliament.

(5) Without prejudice to the generality of subsection (4), that subsection applies to –

(a) the giving of evidence before either House or a committee;

(b) the presentation or submission of a document to either House or a committee;

(c) the preparation of a document for the purposes of or incidental to the transacting of any such business;

(d) the formulation, making or publication of a document, including a report, by or pursuant to an order of either House or a committee; and

(e) any communication with the Parliamentary Commissioner for Standards or any person having functions in connection with the registration of members' interests.

In this subsection 'a committee' means a committee of either House or a joint committee of both Houses of Parliament.

14 *Reports of court proceedings absolutely privileged*

(1) A fair and accurate report of proceedings in public before a court to which this section applies, if published contemporaneously with proceedings, is absolutely privileged.

(2) A report of proceedings which by an order of the court, or as a consequence of any statutory provision, is required to be postponed shall be treated as published contemporaneously if it is published as soon as practicable after publication is permitted.

(3) This section applies to –

(a) any court in the United Kingdom,
(b) the European Court of Justice or any court attached to that court,
(c) the European Court of Human Rights, and
(d) any international criminal tribunal established by the Security Council of the United Nations or by an international agreement to which the United Kingdom is a party.

In paragraph (a) 'court' includes any tribunal or body exercising the judicial power of the State. ...

15 *Reports, etc protected by qualified privilege*

(1) The publication of any report or other statement mentioned in Schedule 1 to this Act is privileged unless the publication is shown to be made with malice, subject as follows.

(2) In defamation proceedings in respect of the publication of a report or other statement mentioned in Part II of that Schedule, there is no defence under this section if the plaintiff shows that the defendant –

(a) was requested by him to publish in a suitable manner a reasonable letter or statement by way of explanation or contradiction, and
(b) refused or neglected to do so.

For this purpose 'in a suitable manner' means in the same manner as the publication complained of or in a manner that is adequate and reasonable in the circumstances.

(3) This section does not apply to the publication to the public, or a section of the public, of matter which is not of public concern and the publication of which is not for the public benefit.

(4) Nothing in this section shall be construed –

(a) as protecting the publication of matter the publication of which is prohibited by law, or
(b) as limiting or abridging any privilege subsisting apart from this section.

17 *Interpretation*

(1) In this Act –

'publication' and 'publish', in relation to a statement, have the meaning they have for the purposes of the law of defamation generally, but 'publisher' is specially defined for the purposes of section 1;

'statement' means words, pictures, visual images, gestures or any other method of signifying meaning; and

'statutory provision' means –

(a) a provision contained in an Act or in subordinate legislation within the meaning of the Interpretation Act 1978, ...

19 Commencement

(1) Sections 18 to 20 (extent, commencement and other general provisions) come into force on Royal Assent.

(2) The following provisions of this Act come into force at the end of the period of two months beginning with the day on which this Act is passed –

section 1 (responsibility for publication),
sections 5 and 6 (time limit for actions for defamation or malicious falsehood),
section 12 (evidence of convictions),
section 13 (evidence concerning proceedings in Parliament),
section 16 and the repeals in Schedule 2, so far as consequential on the above provisions, and
section 17 (interpretation), so far as relating to the above provisions.

(3) The provisions of this Act otherwise come into force on such day as may be appointed –

(a) for England and Wales ... by order of the Lord Chancellor ...

and different days may be appointed for different purposes. ...

20 Short title and saving ...

(2) Nothing in this Act affects the law relating to criminal libel.

Schedule 1

Qualified Privilege

Part I

Statements Having Qualified Privilege without Explanation or Contradiction

1. A fair and accurate report of proceedings in public of a legislature anywhere in the world.

2. A fair and accurate report of proceedings in public before a court anywhere in the world.

3. A fair and accurate report of proceedings in public of a person appointed to hold a public inquiry by a government or legislature anywhere in the world.

4. A fair and accurate report of proceedings in public anywhere in the world of an international organisation or an international conference.

5. A fair and accurate copy of or extract from any register or other document required by law to be open to public inspection.

6. A notice or advertisement published by or on the authority of a court, or of a judge or officer of a court, anywhere in the world.

7. A fair and accurate copy of or extract from matter published by or on the authority of a government or legislature anywhere in the world.

8. A fair and accurate copy of or extract from matter published anywhere in the world by an international organisation or an international conference.

Part II

Statements Privileged Subject to Explanation or Contradiction

9. (1) A fair and accurate copy of or extract from a notice or other matter issued for the information of the public by or on behalf of –

(a) a legislature in any member State or the European Parliament;
(b) the government of any member State, or any authority performing governmental functions in any member State or part of a member State, or the European Commission;
(c) an international organisation or international conference.

(2) In this paragraph 'governmental functions' includes police functions.

10. A fair and accurate copy of or extract from a document made available by a court in any member State or the European Court of Justice (or any court attached to that court), or by a judge or officer of any such court.

11. (1) A fair and accurate report of proceedings at any public meeting or sitting in the United Kingdom of –

(a) a local authority or local authority committee;
(b) a justice or justices of the peace acting otherwise than as a court exercising judicial authority;
(c) a commission, tribunal, committee or person appointed for the purposes of any inquiry by any statutory provision, by Her Majesty or by a Minister of the Crown, a member of the Scottish Executive or a Northern Ireland Department;
(d) a person appointed by a local authority to hold a local inquiry in pursuance of any statutory provision;
(e) any other tribunal, board, committee or body constituted by or under, and exercising functions under, any statutory provision.

(2) In sub-paragraph (1)(a) –

'local authority' means –

(a) in relation to England and Wales, a principal council within the meaning of the Local Government Act 1972, any body falling within any paragraph of section 100J(1) of that Act or an authority or body to which the Public Bodies (Admission to Meetings) Act 1960 applies, … and

'local authority committee' means any committee of a local authority or of local authorities, and includes –

(a) any committee or sub-committee in relation to which sections 100A to 100D of the Local Government Act 1972 apply by virtue of section 100E of that Act (whether or not also by virtue of section 100J of that Act), ...

(3) A fair and accurate report of any corresponding proceedings in any of the Channel Islands or the Isle of Man or in another member State.

12. (1) A fair and accurate report of proceedings at any public meeting held in a member State.

(2) In this paragraph a 'public meeting' means a meeting bona fide and lawfully held for a lawful purpose and for the furtherance or discussion of a matter of public concern, whether admission to the meeting is general or restricted.

13. (1) A fair and accurate report of proceedings at a general meeting of a UK public company.

(2) A fair and accurate copy of or extract from any document circulated to members of a UK public company –

(a) by or with the authority of the board of directors of the company,
(b) by the auditors of the company, or
(c) by any member of the company in pursuance of a right conferred by any statutory provision.

(3) A fair and accurate copy of or extract from any document circulated to members of a UK public company which relates to the appointment, resignation, retirement or dismissal of directors of the company.

(4) In this paragraph 'UK public company' means –

(a) a public company within the meaning of section 1(3) of the Companies Act 1985 or Article 12(3) of the Companies (Northern Ireland) Order 1986, or
(b) a body corporate incorporated by or registered under any other statutory provision, or by Royal Charter, or formed in pursuance of letters patent.

(5) A fair and accurate report of proceedings at any corresponding meeting of, or copy of or extract from any corresponding document circulated to members of, a public company formed under the law of any of the Channel Islands or the Isle of Man or of another member State.

14. A fair and accurate report of any finding or decision of any of the following descriptions of association, formed in the United Kingdom or another member State, or of any committee or governing body of such an association –

(a) an association formed for the purpose of promoting or encouraging the exercise of or interest in any art, science, religion or learning, and empowered by its constitution to exercise control over or adjudicate on matters of interest or concern to the association, or the actions or conduct of any person subject to such control or adjudication;
(b) an association formed for the purpose of promoting or safeguarding the interests of any trade, business, industry or profession, or of the persons carrying on or engaged in any trade, business, industry or profession, and empowered by its constitution to exercise

control over or adjudicate upon matters connected with that trade, business, industry or profession, or the actions or conduct of those persons;

(c) an association formed for the purpose of promoting or safeguarding the interests of a game, sport or pastime to the playing or exercise of which members of the public are invited or admitted, and empowered by its constitution to exercise control over or adjudicate upon persons connected with or taking part in the game, sport or pastime;

(d) an association formed for the purpose of promoting charitable objects or other objects beneficial to the community and empowered by its constitution to exercise control over or to adjudicate on matters of interest or concern to the association, or the actions or conduct of any person subject to such control or adjudication.

15. (1) A fair and accurate report of, or copy of or extract from, any adjudication, report, statement or notice issued by a body, officer or other person designated for the purposes of this paragraph –

(a) for England and Wales or Northern Ireland, by order of the Lord Chancellor, …

(2) An order under this paragraph shall be made by statutory instrument which shall be subject to annulment in pursuance of a resolution of either House of Parliament.

Part III

Supplementary Provisions

16. (1) In this Schedule –

'court' includes any tribunal or body exercising the judicial power of the State;
'international conference' means a conference attended by representatives of two or more governments;
'international organisation' means an organisation of which two or more governments are members, and includes any committee or other subordinate body of such an organisation; and
'legislature' includes a local legislature.

(2) References in this Schedule to a member State include any European dependent territory of a member State.

(3) In paragraphs 2 and 6 'court' includes –

(a) the European Court of Justice (or any court attached to that court) and the Court of Auditors of the European Communities,
(b) the European Court of Human Rights,
(c) any international criminal tribunal established by the Security Council of the United Nations or by an international agreement to which the United Kingdom is a party, and
(d) the International Court of Justice and any other judicial or arbitral tribunal deciding matters in dispute between States.

(4) In paragraphs 1, 3 and 7 'legislature' includes the European Parliament.

17. (1) Provision may be made by order identifying –

(a) for the purposes of paragraph 11, the corresponding proceedings referred to in sub-paragraph (3);

(b) for the purposes of paragraph 13, the corresponding meetings and documents referred to in sub-paragraph (5).

(2) An order under this paragraph may be made –

(a) for England and Wales or Northern Ireland, by the Lord Chancellor, …

(3) An order under this paragraph shall be made by statutory instrument which shall be subject to annulment in pursuance of a resolution of either House of Parliament.

[As amended by the Scotland Act 1998, s125(1), Schedule 8, para 33(1), (3).]

Damages Act 1996
(1996 c 48)

1 Assumed rate of return on investment of damages

(1) In determining the return to be expected from the investment of a sum awarded as damages for future pecuniary loss in an action for personal injury the court shall, subject to and in accordance with rules of court made for the purposes of this section, take into account such rate of return (if any) as may from time to time be prescribed by an order made by the Lord Chancellor.

(2) Subsection (1) above shall not however prevent the court taking a different rate of return into account if any party to the proceedings shows that it is more appropriate in the case in question.

(3) An order under subsection (1) above may prescribe different rates of return for different classes of case.

(4) Before making an order under subsection (1) above the Lord Chancellor shall consult the Government Actuary and the Treasury; and any order under that subsection shall be made by statutory instrument subject to annulment in pursuance of a resolution of either House of Parliament. …

2 Consent orders for periodical payments

(1) A court awarding damages in an action for personal injury may, with the consent of the parties, make an order under which the damages are wholly or partly to take the form of periodical payments.

(2) In this section 'damages' includes an interim payment which the court, by virtue of rules of court in that behalf, orders the defendant to make to the plaintiff …

(3) This section is without prejudice to any powers exercisable apart from this section.

3 *Provisional damages and fatal accident claims*

(1) This section applies where a person –

(a) is awarded provisional damages; and

(b) subsequently dies as a result of the act or omission which gave rise to the cause of action for which the damages were awarded.

(2) The award of the provisional damages shall not operate as a bar to an action in respect of that person's death under the Fatal Accidents Act 1976.

(3) Such part (if any) of –

(a) the provisional damages; and

(b) any further damages awarded to the person in question before his death,

as was intended to compensate him for pecuniary loss in a period which in the event falls after his death shall be taken into account in assessing the amount of any loss of support suffered by the person or persons for whose benefit the action under the Fatal Accidents Act 1976 is brought.

(4) No award of further damages made in respect of that person after his death shall include any amount for loss of income in respect of any period after his death.

(5) In this section 'provisional damages' means damages awarded by virtue of subsection (2)(a) of section 32A of the Supreme Court Act 1981 or section 51 of the County Courts Act 1984 and 'further damages' means damages awarded by virtue of subsection (2)(b) of either of those sections.

(6) Subsection (2) above applies whether the award of provisional damages was before or after the coming into force of that subsection; and subsections (3) and (4) apply to any award of damages under the 1976 Act or, as the case may be, further damages after the coming into force of those subsections. ...

4 *Enhanced protection for structured settlement annuitants*

(1) In relation to an annuity purchased for a person pursuant to a structured settlement from an authorised insurance company within the meaning of the Policyholders Protection Act 1975 (and in respect of which that person as annuitant is accordingly the policyholder for the purposes of that Act) sections 10 and 11 of that Act (protection in the event of liquidation of the insurer) shall have effect as if any reference to ninety per cent of the amount of the liability, of any future benefit or of the value attributed to the policy were a reference to the full amount of the liability, benefit or value.

(2) Those sections shall also have effect as mentioned in subsection (1) above in relation to an annuity purchased from an authorised insurance company within the meaning of the 1975 Act pursuant to any order incorporating terms corresponding to those of a structured settlement which a court makes when awarding damages for personal injury.

(3) Those sections shall also have effect as mentioned in subsection (1) above in relation to an annuity purchased from or otherwise provided by an authorised insurance company within the meaning of the 1975 Act pursuant to terms corresponding to those of a structured settlement contained in an agreement made by –

(a) the Motor Insurers' Bureau; or

(b) a Domestic Regulations Insurer,

in respect of damages for personal injury which the Bureau or Insurer undertakes to pay in satisfaction of a claim or action against an uninsured driver.

(4) In subsection (3) above 'the Motor Insurers' Bureau' means the company of that name incorporated on 14th June 1946 under the Companies Act 1929 and 'a Domestic Regulations Insurer' has the meaning given in the Bureau's Domestic Regulations.

(5) This section applies if the liquidation of the authorised insurance company begins (within the meaning of the 1975 Act) after the coming into force of this section irrespective of when the annuity was purchased or provided.

5 *Meaning of structured settlement*

(1) In section 4 above a 'structured settlement' means an agreement settling a claim or action for damages for personal injury on terms whereby –

(a) the damages are to consist wholly or partly of periodical payments; and

(b) the person to whom the payments are to be made is to receive them as the annuitant under one or more annuities purchased for him by the person against whom the claim or action is brought or, if he is insured against the claim, by his insurer.

(2) The periodical payments may be for the life of the claimant, for a specified period or of a specified number or minimum number or include payments of more than one of those descriptions.

(3) The amounts of the periodical payments (which need not be at a uniform rate or payable at uniform intervals) may be –

(a) specified in the agreement, with or without provision for increases of specified amounts or percentages; or

(b) subject to adjustment in a specified manner so as to preserve their real value; or

(c) partly specified as mentioned in paragraph (a) above and partly subject to adjustment as mentioned in paragraph (b) above.

(4) The annuity or annuities must be such as to provide the annuitant with sums which as to amount and time of payment correspond to the periodical payments described in the agreement.

(5) Payments in respect of the annuity or annuities may be received on behalf of the annuitant by another person or received and held on trust for his benefit under a trust of which he is, during his lifetime, the sole beneficiary.

(6) The Lord Chancellor may by an order made by statutory instrument provide that there shall for the purposes of this section be treated as an insurer any body specified in the order, being a body which, though not an insurer, appears to him to fulfil corresponding functions in relation to damages for personal injury claimed or awarded against persons of any class or description, and the reference in subsection (1)(b) above to a person being insured against the claim and his insurer shall be construed accordingly. ...

(8) Where –

(a) an agreement is made settling a claim or action for damages for personal injury on terms whereby the damages are to consist wholly or partly of periodical payments;
(b) the person against whom the claim or action is brought (or, if he is insured against the claim, his insurer) purchases one or more annuities; and
(c) a subsequent agreement is made under which the annuity is, or the annuities are, assigned in favour of the person entitled to the payments (so as to secure that from a future date he receives the payments as the annuitant under the annuity or annuities),

then, for the purposes of section 4 above, the agreement settling the claim or action shall be treated as a structured settlement and any such annuity assigned in favour of that person shall be treated as an annuity purchased for him pursuant to the settlement.

(9) Subsections (2) to (7) [Scotland] above shall apply to an agreement to which subsection (8) above applies as they apply to a structured settlement as defined in subsection (1) above (the reference in subsection (6) to subsection (1)(b) being read as a reference to subsection (8)(b)).

6 Guarantees for public sector settlements

(1) This section applies where –

(a) a claim or action for damages for personal injury is settled on terms corresponding to those of a structured settlement as defined in section 5 above except that the person to whom the payments are to be made is not to receive them as mentioned in subsection (1)(b) of that section; or
(b) a court awarding damages for personal injury makes an order incorporating such terms.

(2) If it appears to a Minister of the Crown that the payments are to be made by a body in relation to which he has, by virtue of this section, power to do so, he may guarantee the payments to be made under the agreement or order.

(3) The bodies in relation to which a Minister may give such a guarantee shall, subject to subsection (4) below, be such bodies as are designated in relation to the relevant government department by guidelines agreed upon between that department and the Treasury.

(4) A guarantee purporting to be given by a Minister under this section shall not be invalidated by any failure on his part to act in accordance with such guidelines as are mentioned in subsection (3) above.

(5) A guarantee under this section shall be given on such terms as the Minister concerned may determine but those terms shall in every case require the body in question to reimburse the Minister, with interest, for any sums paid by him in fulfilment of the guarantee.

(6) Any sums required by a Minister for fulfilling a guarantee under this section shall be defrayed out of money provided by Parliament and any sums received by him by way of reimbursement or interest shall be paid into the Consolidated Fund.

(7) A Minister who has given one or more guarantees under this section shall, as soon as possible after the end of each financial year, lay before each House of Parliament a statement showing what liabilities are outstanding in respect of the guarantees in that year, what sums have been paid in that year in fulfilment of the guarantees and what sums (including interest) have been recovered in that year in respect of the guarantees or are still owing.

(8) In this section 'government department' means any department of Her Majesty's government in the United Kingdom and for the purposes of this section a government department is a relevant department in relation to a Minister if he has responsibilities in respect of that department. ...

7 Interpretation

(1) Subject to subsection (2) below, in this Act 'personal injury' includes any disease and any impairment of a person's physical or mental condition and references to a claim or action for personal injury include references to such a claim or action brought by virtue of the Law Reform (Miscellaneous Provisions) Act 1934 and to a claim or action brought by virtue of the Fatal Accidents Act 1976. ...

Social Security (Recovery of Benefits) Act 1997
(1997 c 27)

1 Cases in which this Act applies

(1) This Act applies in cases where –

(a) a person makes a payment (whether on his own behalf or not) to or in respect of any other person in consequence of any accident, injury or disease suffered by the other, and
(b) any listed benefits have been, or are likely to be, paid to or for the other during the relevant period in respect of the accident, injury or disease.

(2) The reference above to a payment in consequence of any accident, injury or disease is to a payment made –

(a) by or on behalf of a person who is, or is alleged to be, liable to any extent in respect of the accident, injury or disease, or
(b) in pursuance of a compensation scheme for motor accidents;

but does not include a payment mentioned in Part I of Schedule 1.

(3) Subsection (1)(a) applies to a payment made –

(a) voluntarily, or in pursuance of a court order or an agreement, or otherwise, and
(b) in the United Kingdom or elsewhere.

(4) In a case where this Act applies –

(a) the 'injured person' is the person who suffered the accident, injury or disease,
(b) the 'compensation payment' is the payment within subsection (1)(a), and
(c) 'recoverable benefit' is any listed benefit which has been or is likely to be paid as mentioned in subsection (1)(b).

2 Compensation payments to which this Act applies

This Act applies in relation to compensation payments made on or after the day on which this section comes into force, unless they are made in pursuance of a court order or agreement made before that day.

3 'The relevant period'

(1) In relation to a person ('the claimant') who has suffered any accident, injury or disease, 'the relevant period' has the meaning given by the following subsections.

(2) Subject to subsection (4), if it is a case of accident or injury, the relevant period is the period of five years immediately following the day on which the accident or injury in question occurred.

(3) Subject to subsection (4), if it is a case of disease, the relevant period is the period of five years beginning with the date on which the claimant first claims a listed benefit in consequence of the disease.

(4) If at any time before the end of the period referred to in subsection (2) or (3) –

(a) a person makes a compensation payment in final discharge of any claim made by or in respect of the claimant and arising out of the accident, injury or disease, or
(b) an agreement is made under which an earlier compensation payment is treated as having been made in final discharge of any such claim,

the relevant period ends at that time.

4 Applications for certificates of recoverable benefits

(1) Before a person ('the compensator') makes a compensation payment he must apply to the Secretary of State for a certificate of recoverable benefits.

(2) Where the compensator applies for a certificate of recoverable benefits, the Secretary of State must –

(a) send to him a written acknowledgement of receipt of his application, and
(b) subject to subsection (7), issue the certificate before the end of the following period.

(3) The period is –

(a) the prescribed period, or
(b) if there is no prescribed period, the period of four weeks,

which begins with the day following the day on which the application is received.

(4) The certificate is to remain in force until the date specified in it for that purpose.

(5) The compensator may apply for fresh certificates from time to time.

(6) Where a certificate of recoverable benefits ceases to be in force, the Secretary of State may issue a fresh certificate without an application for one being made.

(7) Where the compensator applies for a fresh certificate while a certificate ('the existing certificate') remains in force, the Secretary of State must issue the fresh certificate before the end of the following period.

(8) The period is –

(a) the prescribed period, or
(b) if there is no prescribed period, the period of four weeks,

which begins with the day following the day on which the existing certificate ceases to be in force.

(9) For the purposes of this Act, regulations may provide for the day on which an application for a certificate of recoverable benefits is to be treated as received.

5 *Information contained in certificates*

(1) A certificate of recoverable benefits must specify, for each recoverable benefit –

(a) the amount which has been or is likely to have been paid on or before a specified date, and
(b) if the benefit is paid or likely to be paid after the specified date, the rate and period for which, and the intervals at which, it is or is likely to be so paid.

(2) In a case where the relevant period has ended before the day on which the Secretary of State receives the application for the certificate, the date specified in the certificate for the purposes of subsection (1) must be the day on which the relevant period ended.

(3) In any other case, the date specified for those purposes must not be earlier than the day on which the Secretary of State received the application.

(4) The Secretary of State may estimate, in such manner as he thinks fit, any of the amounts, rates or periods specified in the certificate.

(5) Where the Secretary of State issues a certificate of recoverable benefits, he must provide the information contained in the certificate to –

(a) the person who appears to him to be the injured person, or
(b) any person who he thinks will receive a compensation payment in respect of the injured person.

(6) A person to whom a certificate of recoverable benefits is issued or who is provided with information under subsection (5) is entitled to particulars of the manner in which any amount, rate or period specified in the certificate has been determined, if he applies to the Secretary of State for those particulars.

6 *Liability to pay Secretary of State amount of benefits*

(1) A person who makes a compensation payment in any case is liable to pay to the Secretary of State an amount equal to the total amount of the recoverable benefits.

(2) The liability referred to in subsection (1) arises immediately before the compensation payment or, if there is more than one, the first of them is made.

(3) No amount becomes payable under this section before the end of the period of 14 days following the day on which the liability arises.

(4) Subject to subsection (3), an amount becomes payable under this section at the end of

the period of 14 days beginning with the day on which a certificate of recoverable benefits is first issued showing that the amount of recoverable benefit to which it relates has been or is likely to have been paid before a specified date.

7 Recovery of payments due under section 6

(1) This section applies where a person has made a compensation payment but –

(a) has not applied for a certificate of recoverable benefits, or

(b) has not made a payment to the Secretary of State under section 6 before the end of the period allowed under that section.

(2) The Secretary of State may –

(a) issue the person who made the compensation payment with a certificate of recoverable benefits, if none has been issued, or

(b) issue him with a copy of the certificate of recoverable benefits or (if more than one has been issued) the most recent one,

and (in either case) issue him with a demand that payment of any amount due under section 6 be made immediately.

(3) The Secretary of State may, in accordance with subsections (4) and (5), recover the amount for which a demand for payment is made under subsection (2) from the person who made the compensation payment.

(4) If the person who made the compensation payment resides or carries on business in England and Wales and a county court so orders, any amount recoverable under subsection (3) is recoverable by execution issued from the county court or otherwise as if it were payable under an order of that court.

(5) If the person who made the payment resides or carries on business in Scotland, any amount recoverable under subsection (3) may be enforced in like manner as an extract registered decree arbitral bearing a warrant for execution issued by the sheriff court of any sheriffdom in Scotland.

(6) A document bearing a certificate which –

(a) is signed by a person authorised to do so by the Secretary of State, and

(b) states that the document, apart from the certificate, is a record of the amount recoverable under subsection (3),

is conclusive evidence that that amount is so recoverable.

(7) A certificate under subsection (6) purporting to be signed by a person authorised to do so by the Secretary of State is to be treated as so signed unless the contrary is proved.

8 Reduction of compensation payment

(1) This section applies in a case where, in relation to any head of compensation listed in column 1 of Schedule 2 –

(a) any of the compensation payment is attributable to that head, and

(b) any recoverable benefit is shown against that head in column 2 of the Schedule.

(2) In such a case, any claim of a person to receive the compensation payment is to be treated for all purposes as discharged if –

(a) he is paid the amount (if any) of the compensation payment calculated in accordance with this section, and

(b) if the amount of the compensation payment so calculated is nil, he is given a statement saying so by the person who (apart from this section) would have paid the gross amount of the compensation payment.

(3) For each head of compensation listed in column 1 of the Schedule for which paragraphs (a) and (b) of subsection (1) are met, so much of the gross amount of the compensation payment as is attributable to that head is to be reduced (to nil, if necessary) by deducting the amount of the recoverable benefit or, as the case may be, the aggregate amount of the recoverable benefits shown against it.

(4) Subsection (3) is to have effect as if a requirement to reduce a payment by deducting an amount which exceeds that payment were a requirement to reduce that payment to nil.

(5) The amount of the compensation payment calculated in accordance with this section is –

(a) the gross amount of the compensation payment, less

(b) the sum of the reductions made under subsection (3),

(and, accordingly, the amount may be nil).

9 Section 8: supplementary

(1) A person who makes a compensation payment calculated in accordance with section 8 must inform the person to whom the payment is made –

(a) that the payment has been so calculated, and

(b) of the date for payment by reference to which the calculation has been made.

(2) If the amount of a compensation payment calculated in accordance with section 8 is nil, a person giving a statement saying so is to be treated for the purposes of this Act as making a payment within section 1(1)(a) on the day on which he gives the statement.

(3) Where a person –

(a) makes a compensation payment calculated in accordance with section 8, and

(b) if the amount of the compensation payment so calculated is nil, gives a statement saying so,

he is to be treated, for the purpose of determining any rights and liabilities in respect of contribution or indemnity, as having paid the gross amount of the compensation payment.

(4) For the purposes of this Act –

(a) the gross amount of the compensation payment is the amount of the compensation payment apart from section 8, and

(b) the amount of any recoverable benefit is the amount determined in accordance with the certificate of recoverable benefits.

10 Review of certificates of recoverable benefits

(1) The Secretary of State may review any certificate of recoverable benefits if he is satisfied –

(a) that it was issued in ignorance of, or was based on a mistake as to, a material fact, or
(b) that a mistake (whether in computation or otherwise) has occurred in its preparation.

(2) On a review under this section the Secretary of State may either –

(a) confirm the certificate, or
(b) (subject to subsection (3)) issue a fresh certificate containing such variations as he considers appropriate.

(3) The Secretary of State may not vary the certificate so as to increase the total amount of the recoverable benefits unless it appears to him that the variation is required as a result of the person who applied for the certificate supplying him with incorrect or insufficient information.

11 Appeals against certificates of recoverable benefits

(1) An appeal against a certificate of recoverable benefits may be made on the ground –

(a) that any amount, rate or period specified in the certificate is incorrect, or
(b) that listed benefits which have been, or are likely to be, paid otherwise than in respect of the accident, injury or disease in question have been brought into account.

(2) An appeal under this section may be made by –

(a) the person who applied for the certificate of recoverable benefits, or
(b) (in a case where the amount of the compensation payment has been calculated under section 8) the injured person or other person to whom the payment is made.

(3) No appeal may be made under this section until –

(a) the claim giving rise to the compensation payment has been finally disposed of, and
(b) the liability under section 6 has been discharged.

(4) For the purposes of subsection (3)(a), if an award of damages in respect of a claim has been made under or by virtue of –

(a) section 32A(2)(a) of the Supreme Court Act 1981,
(b) section 12(2)(a) of the Administration of Justice Act 1982, or
(c) section 51(2)(a) of the County Courts Act 1984,

(orders for provisional damages in personal injury cases), the claim is to be treated as having been finally disposed of. ...

12 Reference of questions to medical appeal tribunal

(1) The Secretary of State must refer to a medical appeal tribunal any question mentioned in subsection (2) arising for determination on an appeal under section 11.

(2) The questions are any concerning –

(a) any amount, rate or period specified in the certificate of recoverable benefits, or

(b) whether listed benefits which have been, or are likely to be, paid otherwise than in respect of the accident, injury or disease in question have been brought into account.

(3) In determining any question referred to it under subsection (1), the tribunal must take into account any decision of a court relating to the same, or any similar, issue arising in connection with the accident, injury or disease in question. ...

13 Appeal to Social Security Commissioner

(1) An appeal may be made to a Commissioner against any decision of a medical appeal tribunal under section 12 on the ground that the decision was erroneous in point of law.

(2) An appeal under this section may be made by –

(a) the Secretary of State,
(b) the person who applied for the certificate of recoverable benefits, or
(c) (in a case where the amount of the compensation payment has been calculated in accordance with section 8) the injured person or other person to whom the payment is made. ...

15 Court orders

(1) This section applies where a court makes an order for a compensation payment to be made in any case, unless the order is made with the consent of the injured person and the person by whom the payment is to be made.

(2) The court must, in the case of each head of compensation listed in column 1 of Schedule 2 to which any of the compensation payment is attributable, specify in the order the amount of the compensation payment which is attributable to that head.

17 Benefits irrelevant to assessment of damages

In assessing damages in respect of any accident, injury or disease, the amount of any listed benefits paid or likely to be paid is to be disregarded.

21 Compensation payments to be disregarded

(1) If, when a compensation payment is made, the first and second conditions are met, the payment is to be disregarded for the purposes of sections 6 and 8.

(2) The first condition is that the person making the payment –

(a) has made an application for a certificate of recoverable benefits which complies with subsection (3), and
(b) has in his possession a written acknowledgment of the receipt of his application.

(3) An application complies with this subsection if it –

(a) accurately states the prescribed particulars relating to the injured person and the accident, injury or disease in question, and
(b) specifies the name and address of the person to whom the certificate is to be sent.

(4) The second condition is that the Secretary of State has not sent the certificate to the person, at the address, specified in the application, before the end of the period allowed under section 4.

(5) In any case where –

(a) by virtue of subsection (1), a compensation payment is disregarded for the purposes of sections 6 and 8, but
(b) the person who made the compensation payment nevertheless makes a payment to the Secretary of State for which (but for subsection (1)) he would be liable under section 6,

subsection (1) is to cease to apply in relation to the compensation payment.

(6) If, in the opinion of the Secretary of State, circumstances have arisen which adversely affect normal methods of communication –

(a) he may by order provide that subsection (1) is not to apply during a specified period not exceeding three months, and
(b) he may continue any such order in force for further periods not exceeding three months at a time.

22 Liability of insurers

(1) If a compensation payment is made in a case where –

(a) a person is liable to any extent in respect of the accident, injury or disease, and
(b) the liability is covered to any extent by a policy of insurance,

the policy is also to be treated as covering any liability of that person under section 6.

(2) Liability imposed on the insurer by subsection (1) cannot be excluded or restricted.

(3) For that purpose excluding or restricting liability includes –

(a) making the liability or its enforcement subject to restrictive or onerous conditions,
(b) excluding or restricting any right or remedy in respect of the liability, or subjecting a person to any prejudice in consequence of his pursuing any such right or remedy, or
(c) excluding or restricting rules of evidence or procedure. ...

28 The Crown

This Act applies to the Crown.

29 General interpretation

In this Act –

'benefit' means any benefit under the Social Security Contributions and Benefits Act 1992, a jobseeker's allowance or mobility allowance,

'compensation scheme for motor accidents' means any scheme or arrangement under which funds are available for the payment of compensation in respect of motor accidents caused, or alleged to have been caused, by uninsured or unidentified persons,

'listed benefit' means a benefit listed in column 2 of Schedule 2,

'payment' means payment in money or money's worth, and related expressions are to be interpreted accordingly,

'prescribed' means prescribed by regulations, and 'regulations' means regulations made by the Secretary of State.

Schedule 1

Compensation Payments

Part I

Exempted Payments

1. Any small payment (defined in Part II of this Schedule).

2. Any payment made to or for the injured person under section 35 of the Powers of Criminal Courts Act 1973 ... (compensation orders against convicted persons). ...

5. Any payment made to the injured person by an insurance company within the meaning of the Insurance Companies Act 1982 under the terms of any contract of insurance entered into between the injured person and the company before –

(a) the date on which the injured person first claims a listed benefit in consequence of the disease in question, or
(b) the occurrence of the accident or injury in question.

6. Any redundancy payment falling to be taken into account in the assessment of damages in respect of an accident, injury or disease.

7. So much of any payment as is referable to costs.

8. Any prescribed payment.

Part II

Power to Disregard Small Payments

9. – (1) Regulations may make provision for compensation payments to be disregarded for the purposes of sections 6 and 8 in prescribed cases where the amount of the compensation payment, or the aggregate amount of two or more connected compensation payments, does not exceed the prescribed sum.

(2) A compensation payment disregarded by virtue of this paragraph is referred to in paragraph 1 as a 'small payment'.

(3) For the purposes of this paragraph –

(a) two or more compensation payments are 'connected' if each is made to or in respect of the same injured person and in respect of the same accident, injury or disease, and
(b) any reference to a compensation payment is a reference to a payment which would be such a payment apart from paragraph 1.

Schedule 2
Calculation of Compensation Payment

(1) *Head of compensation*	(2) *Benefit*
1. Compensation for earnings lost during the relevant period	Disability working allowance Disablement pension payable under section 103 of the 1992 Act Incapacity benefit Income support Invalidity pension and allowance Jobseeker's allowance Reduced earnings allowance Severe disablement allowance Sickness benefit Statutory sick pay Unemployability supplement Unemployment benefit
2. Compensation for cost of care incurred during the relevant period	Attendance allowance Care component of disability living allowance Disablement pension increase payable under section 104 or 105 of the 1992 Act
3. Compensation for loss of mobility during the relevant period	Mobility allowance Mobility component of disability living allowance

NOTES

1. – (1) References to incapacity benefit, invalidity pension and allowance, severe disablement allowance, sickness benefit and unemployment benefit also include any income support paid with each of those benefits on the same instrument of payment or paid concurrently with each of those benefits by means of an instrument for benefit payment.

(2) For the purpose of this Note, income support includes personal expenses addition, special transitional additions and transitional addition as defined in the Income Support (Transitional) Regulations 1987.

2. Any reference to statutory sick pay –

(a) includes only 80 per cent. of payments made between 6th April 1991 and 5th April 1994, and

(b) does not include payments made on or after 6th April 1994.

3. In this Schedule 'the 1992 Act' means the Social Security Contributions and Benefits Act 1992.

Protection from Harassment Act 1997
(1997 c 40)

1 Prohibition of harassment

(1) A person must not pursue a course of conduct –

(a) which amounts to harassment of another, and

(b) which he knows or ought to know amounts to harassment of the other.

(2) For the purposes of this section, the person whose course of conduct is in question ought to know that it amounts to harassment of another if a reasonable person in possession of the same information would think the course of conduct amounted to harassment of the other.

(3) Subsection (1) does not apply to a course of conduct if the person who pursued it shows –

(a) that it was pursued for the purpose of preventing or detecting crime,

(b) that it was pursued under any enactment or rule of law or to comply with any condition or requirement imposed by any person under any enactment, or

(c) that in the particular circumstances the pursuit of the course of conduct was reasonable.

3 Civil remedy

(1) An actual or apprehended breach of section 1 may be the subject of a claim in civil proceedings by the person who is or may be the victim of the course of conduct in question.

(2) On such a claim, damages may be awarded for (among other things) any anxiety caused by the harassment and any financial loss resulting from the harassment.

(3) Where –

(a) in such proceedings the High Court or a county court grants an injunction for the purpose of restraining the defendant from pursuing any conduct which amounts to harassment, and

(b) the plaintiff considers that the defendant has done anything which he is prohibited from doing by the injunction,

the plaintiff may apply for the issue of a warrant for the arrest of the defendant. ...

7 Interpretation of this group of sections

(1) This section applies for the interpretation of sections 1 to 5.

(2) References to harassing a person include alarming the person or causing the person distress.

(3) A 'course of conduct' must involve conduct on at least two occasions.

(4) 'Conduct' includes speech.

Government of Wales Act 1998
(1998 c 38)

77 Defamation

(1) For the purposes of the law of defamation –

(a) any statement made in, for the purposes of or for purposes incidental to proceedings of the Assembly (including proceedings of a committee of the Assembly or of a sub-committee of such a committee), and

(b) the publication by or under the authority of the Assembly of a report of such proceedings,

is absolutely privileged.

(2) Subsection (1)(a) applies, in particular, to any statement made in –

(a) evidence given before the Assembly, a committee of the Assembly or a sub-committee of such a committee,

(b) a document laid before the Assembly or such a committee or sub-committee,

(c) a document prepared for the purposes of, or for the purposes incidental to, the transaction of business by the Assembly or such a committee or sub-committee,

(d) a document (other than a report to which subsection (1)(b) applies) formulated, made or published by or under the authority of the Assembly or such a committee or sub-committee,

(e) any communication –

(i) between any person and a person having functions in connection with the registration of interests of Assembly members, or

(ii) between any person and an Assembly member,

in connection with such registration, or

(f) any communication –

(i) between any person and a person having functions in connection with the investigation of complaints about actions or failures on the part of the Assembly, or

(ii) between any person and an Assembly member,

in connection with any such complaint.

(3) In subsections (1) and (2) 'statement' has the same meaning as in the Defamation Act 1996.

(4) The Assembly –

(a) is a legislature for the purposes of Schedule 1 to that Act (qualified privilege for fair and accurate report of public proceedings of legislatures etc), and

(b) shall be treated as if it were a Minister of the Crown for the purposes of paragraph 11(1)(c) of that Schedule (report of proceedings of person appointed by a Minister etc for the purposes of an inquiry).

(5) Section 10 of the Defamation Act 1952 ... (limitation on privilege at elections) [has] effect in relation to elections of Assembly members as to elections to Parliament.

Glossary
of Latin and other words and phrases

Ab extra. From outside.

Ab inconvenienti. *See* ARGUMENTUM

Ab initio. From the beginning.

Accessio. Addition; appendage. The combination of two chattels belonging to different persons into a single article.

Acta exteriora indicant interiora secreta. A man's outward actions are evidence of his innermost thoughts and intentions.

Actio personalis moritur cum persona. A personal right of action dies on the death of the person by or against whom it could be enforced.

Actus non facit reum, nisi mens sit rea. The act itself does not make a man guilty, unless he does it with a guilty intention.

Ad colligenda bona. To collect the goods.

Ad hoc. Arranged for this purpose; special.

Ad idem. *See* CONSENSUS.

Ad infinitum. To infinity; without limit; for ever.

Ad litem. For the purpose of the law suit.

Ad opus. For the benefit of: on behalf of.

Ad valorem. Calculated in proportion to the value or price of the property.

Adversus extraneos vitiosa possessio prodesse solet. Possession, though supported only by a defective title, will prevail over the claims of strangers other than the true owner.

A fortiori (ratione). For a stronger reason; by even more convincing reasoning.

Aliter. Otherwise; the result would be different, if …; (also, used of a judge who thinks differently from his fellow judges).

Aliud est celare; aliud est tacere; neque enim id est celare quicquid reticeas. Mere silence is one thing but active concealment is quite another thing; for it is not disguising something when you say nothing about it.

Aliunde. From elsewhere; from other sources.

A mensa et thoro. A separation from the 'table and bed' of one's spouse.

Amicus curiae. A friend of the court.

Animo contrahendi. With the intention of contracting.

Animo revocandi. With the intention of revoking.

Animus deserendi. The intention of deserting.

Animus donandi. The intention of giving.

Animus possidendi. The intention of possessing.

Animus revertendi. The intention of returning.

Animus testandi. The intention of making a will.

Ante. Before; (also used of a case referred to earlier on a page or in a book).

A posteriori. From effect to cause; inductively; from subsequent conclusions.

A priori. From cause to effect; deductively; from previous assumptions or reasoning.

Argumentum ab inconvenienti. An argument devised because of the existence of an awkward problem so as to provide an explanation for it.

Asportatio. The act of carrying away.

Assensus. *See* CONSENSUS.

Assensus ad idem. Agreement as to the same terms.

Assumpsit (super se). He undertook.

Ats. (ad sectam). At the suit of. (The opposite of VERSUS.)

Autrefois acquit. Formerly acquitted.

Autrefois convict. Formerly convicted.

Bis dat qui cito dat. He gives doubly who gives swiftly; a quick gift is worth two slow ones.

Bona fide. In good faith; sincere.

Bona vacantia. Goods without an owner.

Brutum fulmen. A silent thunderbolt; an empty threat.

Cadit quaestio. The matter admits of no further argument.

Caeterorum. Of the things which are left.

Capias ad satisfaciendum. A writ commanding the sheriff to take the body of the defendant in order that he may make satisfaction for the plaintiff's claim.

Causa causans. The immediate cause of something; the last link in the chain of causation.

Causa proxima non remota spectatur. Regard is paid to the immediate, not to the remote cause.

Causa sine qua non. A preceding link in the chain of causation without which the causa causans could not be operative.

Caveat emptor. The buyer must look out for himself.

Cessante ratione legis, cessat lex ipsa. When the reason for its existence ceases, the law itself ceases to exist.

Cestui(s) que trust. A person (or persons) for whose benefit property is held on trust; a beneficiary (beneficiaries).

Cestui que vie. Person for the duration of whose life an estate is granted to another person.

Chose in action. Intangible personal property or rights, which can be enjoyed or enforced only by legal action, and not by taking physical possession (eg debts).

Chose jugée. Thing it is idle to discuss.

Coitus interruptus. Interrupted sexual intercourse, ie withdrawal before emission.

Colore officii. Under the pretext of a person's official position.

Commorientes. Persons who die at the same time.

Confusio. A mixture; union. The mixture of things of the same nature, but belonging to different persons so that identification of the original things becomes impossible.

Consensu. By general consent; unanimously.

Consensus ad idem. Agreement as to the same thing.

Consortium. Conjugal relations with and companionship of a spouse.

Contra. To the contrary. (Used of a case in which the decision was contrary to the doctrine or cases previously cited; also of a judge who delivers a dissenting judgment.)

Contra bonos mores. Contrary to good morals.

Contra mundum. Against the world.

Contra proferentem. Against the party who puts forward a clause in a document.

Cor. (coram). In the presence of; before (a judge).

Coram non judice. Before one who is not a judge. Corpus. Body; capital.

Corpus. Body; capital.

Coverture. Marriage.

Cri de coeur. Heartfelt cry.

Cujus est solum, ejus est usque ad coelum et ad inferos. Whosoever owns the soil also owns everything above it as far as the heavens and everything below it as far as the lower regions of the earth.

Culpa. Wrongful default.

Cum onere. Together with the burden.

Cum testamento annexo. With the will annexed.

Cur. adv. vult. (curia advisari vult). The court wishes time to consider the matter.

Cy-pres. For a purpose resembling as nearly as possible the purpose originally proposed.

Damage feasant. *See* DISTRESS.

Damnosa hereditas. An insolvent inheritance.

Damnum. Loss; damage.

Damnum absque injuria. *See* DAMNUM SINE INJURIA.

Damnum emergens. A loss which arises.

Damnum fatale. Damage resulting from the workings of fate for which human negligence is not to blame.

Damnum sine (or absque) injuria. Damage which is not the result of a legally remediable wrong.

De bene esse. Evidence or action which a court allows to be given or done provisionally, subject to further consideration at a later stage.

Debitor non praesumitur donare. A debtor is presumed to give a legacy to a creditor to discharge his debt and not as a gift.

Debitum in praesenti. A debt which is due at the present time.

Debitum in futuro solvendum. A debt which will be due to be paid at a future time.

De bonis asportatis. Of goods carried away.

De bonis non administratis. Of the assets which have not been administered .

De die in diem. From day to day.

De facto. In fact.

De futuro. Regarding the future; in the future; about something which will exist in the future.

Dehors. Outside (the document or matter in question); irrelevant.

De integro. As regards the whole; entirely.

De jure. By right; rightful.

Del credere agent. An agent who for an extra commission guarantees the due performance of contracts by persons whom he introduces to his principal.

Delegatus non potest delegare. A person who is entrusted with a duty has no right to appoint another person to perform it in his place.

De minimis non curat lex. The law does not concern itself with trifles.

De novo. Anew; starting afresh.

Deodand. A chattel which caused the death of a human being and was forfeited to the Crown.

De praerogativa regis. Concerning the royal prerogative.

De son tort. Of his wrong.

Deus est procurator fatuorum. God is the protector of the simpleminded.

Devastavit. Where an executor 'has squandered' the estate.

Dictum. Saying. *See* OBITER DICTUM.

Dies non (jurisdicus). Day on which no legal business can be transacted.

Dissentiente. Delivering a dissenting judgment.

Distress damage feasant. The detention by a landowner of an animal or chattel while it is doing damage on his land.

Distringas. That you may distrain.

Doli incapax. Incapable of crime.

Dolus qui dat locum contractui. A deception which clears the way for the other party to enter into a contract.

Dominium. Ownership.

Dominus litis. The principal in a suit.

Dominus pro tempore. The master for the time being.

Donatio mortis causa. A gift made in contemplation of death and conditional thereon.

Dubitante. Doubting the correctness of the decision.

Durante absentia. During an executor's absence abroad.

Durante minore aetate. While an executor remains an infant.

Durante viduitate. During widowhood.

Ei incumbit probatio qui dicit, non qui negat. The onus of proving a fact rests upon the man who asserts its truth, not upon the man who denies it.

Ejusdem generis. General words following a list of specific things are construed as relating to things 'of the same kind' as those specifically listed.

Enceinte. Pregnant.

En ventre sa mère. Conceived but not yet born.

Eodem modo quo oritur, eodem modo dissolvitur. What has been created by a certain method may be extinguished by the same method.

Eo instanti. At that instant.

Escrow. A document delivered subject to a condition which must be fulfilled before it becomes a deed.

Estoppel. A rule of evidence which applies in certain circumstances and stops a person from denying the truth of a statement previously made by him.

Et cetera. (Etc) And other things of that sort.

Et seq. (et sequentes). And subsequent pages.

Ex. From; by virtue of.

Ex abundanti cautela. From an abundance of caution.

Ex aequo et bono. According to what is just and equitable.

Ex cathedra. From his seat of office: an authoritative statement made by someone in his official capacity.

Ex concessis. In view of what has already been accepted.

Ex contractu. Arising out of contract.

Ex converso. Conversely.

Ex debito justitiae. That which is due as of right; which the court has no discretion to refuse.

Ex delicto. Arising out of a wrongful act or tort.

Ex dolo malo non oritur actio. No right of action arises out of a fraud.

Ex facie. On the face of it; ostensibly.

Ex gratia. Out of the kindness. Gratuitous; voluntary.

Ex hypothesi. In view of what has already been assumed.

Ex improviso. Unexpectedly, without forethought.

Ex officio. By virtue of one's official position.

Ex pacto illicito non oritur actio. No action can be brought on an unlawful contract.

Ex parte. Proceedings brought on behalf of one interested party without notice to, and in the absence of, the other.

Ex post facto. By reason of a subsequent act; acting retrospectively.

Ex relatione. An action instituted by the Attorney-General on behalf of the Crown on the information of a member of the public who is interested in the matter (the relator).

Expressio unius est exclusio alterius. When one thing is expressly specified, then it prevents anything else being implied.

Expressum facit cessare tacitum. Where terms are expressed, no other terms can be implied.

Ex turpi causa non oritur actio. No action can be brought where the parties are guilty of illegal or immoral conduct.

Faciendum. Something which is to be done.

Factum. Deed; that which has been done; statement of facts or points in issue.

Fait accompli. An accomplished fact.

Falsa demonstratio non nocet cum de corpore constat. Where the substance of the property in question is clearly identified, the addition of an incorrect description of the property does no harm.

Falsus in ono, falsus in omnibus. False in one, false in all.

Fecundatio ab extra. Conception from outside, ie where there has been no penetration.

Feme covert. A married woman.

Feme sole. An unmarried woman.

Ferae naturae. Animals which are by nature dangerous to man.

Fieri facias. A writ addressed to the sheriff: 'that you cause to be made' from the defendant's goods the sum due to the plaintiff under the judgment.

Force majeure. Irresistible compulsion.

Fructus industriales. Cultivated crops.

Fructus naturales. Vegetation which grows naturally without cultivation.

Functus officio. Having discharged his duty; having exhausted its powers.

Genus numquam perit. Particular goods which have been identified may be destroyed, but 'a category or type of article can never perish'.

Habeas corpus (ad subjiciendum). A writ addressed to one who detains another in custody, requiring him 'that you produce the prisoner's body to answer' to the court.

Habitue. A frequent visitor to a place.

Ibid. (ibidem). In the same place, book, or source.

Id certum est quod certum reddi potest. That which is capable of being reduced to a certainty is already a certainty.

Idem. The same thing, or person.

Ideo consideratum est per. Therefore it is considered by the court.

Ignorantia juris haud (neminem) (non) excusat, ignorantia facti excusat. A man may be excused for mistaking facts, but not for mistaking the law.

Ignorantia juris non excusat. Ignorance of the law is no excuse.

Imperitia culpae adnumeratur. Lack of skill is accounted a fault.

In aequali jure melior est conditio possidentis. Where the legal rights of the parties are equal, the party with possession is in the stronger position.

In articulo mortis. On the point of death.

In bonis. In the goods (or estate) of a deceased person.

In capite. In chief; holding as tenant directly under the Crown.

In consimili casu. In a similar case.

In custodia legis. In the keeping of the law.

Indebitatus assumpsit. A form of action in which the plaintiff alleges the defendant 'being already indebted to the plaintiff undertook' to do something.

In delicto. At fault.

Indicia. Signs; marks.

Indicium. Indication; sign; mark.

In esse. In existence.

In expeditione. On actual military service.

In extenso. At full length.

In fieri. In the course of being performed or established.

In flagrante delicto. In the act of committing the offence.

In forma pauperis. In the character of a poor person.

Infra. Below; lower down on a page; later in a book. In futuro. In the future.

In futuro. In the future.

In hac re. In this matter; in this particular aspect.

In jure non remota causa sed proxima spectatur. In law it is the immediate and not the remote cause which is considered.

Injuria. A wrongful act for which the law provides a remedy.

Injuria sine damno. A wrongful act unaccompanied by any damage yet actionable at law.

In lieu of. In place of.

In limine. On the threshold; at the outset.

In loco parentis. In the place of a parent.

In minore delicto. A person who is 'less at fault'.

In omnibus. In every respect.

Inops consilii. Lacking facilities for legal advice.

In pari delicto, potior est conditio defendentis (or possidentis). Where both parties are equally at fault, the defendant (or the party in possession) is in the stronger position.

In pari materia. In an analogous case or position.

In personam. *See* JUS IN PERSONAM.

In pleno. In full.

In praesenti. At the present time.

In propria persona. In his own capacity. In re. In the matter of. In rem. *See* JUS IN REM.

In re. In the matter of.

In rem. *See* JUS IN REM.

In situ. In its place.

In specie. In its own form; not converted into anything else.

In statu quo ante. In the condition in which it, or a person, was before.

Inter alia. Amongst other things.

Inter alios. Amongst other persons.

Interest reipublicae ut sit finis litium. It is in the interests of the community that every law suit should reach a final conclusion (and not be reopened later).

Interim. In the meanwhile; temporary.

Inter partes. Between (the) parties.

In terrorem. As a warning; as a deterrent.

Inter se. Between themselves.

Inter vivos. Between persons who are alive.

In toto. In its entirety; completely.

In transitu. In passage from one place to another.

Intra vires. Within the powers recognised by law as belonging to the person or body in question.

In utero. In the womb.

In vacuo. In the abstract; without considering the circumstances.

In vitro. In glass; in a test tube.

Ipsissima verba. 'The very words' of a speaker.

Ipso facto. By that very fact.

Jura. Rights.

Jura mariti. By virtue of the right of a husband to the goods of his wife.

Jus. A right which is recognised in law.

Jus accrescendi. The right of survivorship; the right of joint tenants to have their interests in the joint property increased by inheriting the interests of the deceased joint tenants until the last survivor inherits the entire property.

Jus in personam. A right which can be enforced against a particular person only.

Jus in rem. A right which can be enforced over the property in question against all other persons.

Jus naturale. Natural justice.

Jus neque in re neque ad rem. A right which is enforceable neither over the property in question against all the world nor against specific persons only.

Jus quaesitum tertio. A right vested in a third party (who is not a party to the contract).

Jus tertii. *See* JUS QUAESITUM TERTIO

Laches. Slackness or delay in pursuing a legal remedy which disentitles a person from action at a later date.

Laesio fidei. Breach of faith.

Laissez faire. 'Let him do what he likes'; permissive.

Lapsus linguae. Slip of the tongue.

Lex domicilii. The law of domicile.

Lex fori. The law of the court in which the case is being heard.

Lex loci celebrationis. The law of the place where the marriage was celebrated.

Lex loci contractus. The law of the place where the contract was made.

Lex loci delicti. The law of the place where the wrong was committed.

Lex loci situs. *See* LEX SITUS.

Lex loci solutionis. The law of the place where the contract is to be performed.

Lex situs. The law of the place where the thing in question is situated.

Lien. The rights to retain possession of goods, deeds or other property belonging to another as security for payment of money.

Lis pendens. Pending action.

Loc. cit. (loco citato). In the passage previously mentioned.

Locus classicus. Authoritative passage in a book or judgment; the principal authority or source for the subject.

Locus in quo. Scene of the event.

Locus poenitentiae. Scope or opportunity for repentance.

Locus standi. Recognised position or standing; the right to appear in court.

Lucrum cessans. A benefit which is terminated.

Magnum opus. A great work of literature.

Mala fide(s). (In) bad faith.

Malitia supplet aetatem. Malice supplements the age of an infant wrongdoer who would (in the absence of malice) be too young to be responsible for his acts.

Malum in se. An act which in itself is morally wrong, eg murder.

Malum prohibitum. An act which is wrong because it is prohibited by human law but is not morally wrong.

Malus animus. Evil intent.

Mansuetae naturae. Animals which are normally of a domesticated disposition.

Mesne. Intermediate; middle; dividing.

Mesne profits. Profits of land lost by the plaintiff while the defendant remained wrongfully in possession.

Mobilia sequuntur personam. The domicile of movable property follows the owner's personal domicile.

Molliter manus imposuit. Gently laid his hand upon the other party.

Mutatis mutandis. With the necessary changes of detail being made.

Natura negotii. The nature of the transaction.

Negotiorum gestio. Handling of other people's affairs.

Nemo dat quod non habet. No one has power to transfer the ownership of that which he does not own.

Nemo debet bis vexari, si constat curiae quod sit pro una et eadem causa. No one ought to be harassed with proceedings twice, if it appears to the court that it is for one and the same cause.

Nemo est haeres viventis. No one can be the heir of a person who is still living.

Nexus. Connection; bond.

Nisi. Unless; (also used of a decree or order which will later be made absolute 'unless' good cause be shown to the contrary); provisional.

Nisi prius. Cases which were directed to be tried at Westminster only if the justices of assize should 'not' have tried them in the country 'previously'.

Nocumenta infinita sunt. There is no limit to the types of situations which constitute nuisances.

Nomen collectivum. A collective name, noun or description; a word descriptive of a class.

Non compos mentis. Not of sound mind and understanding.

Non constat. It is not certain.

Non est factum. That the document in question was not his deed.

Non haec in foedera veni. This is not the agreement which I came to sign.

Non omnibus dormio. I do not turn a blind eye on every instance of misconduct.

Non sequitur. It does not follow; an inconsistent statement.

Noscitur a sociis. The meaning of a word is known from the company it keeps (ie from its context).

Nova causa interveniens. An independent cause which intervenes between the alleged wrong and the damage in question.

Novus actus interveniens. A fresh act of someone other than the defendant which intervenes between the alleged wrong and the damage in question.

Nudum pactum. A bare agreement (unsupported by consideration).

Nullius filius. No man's son; a bastard.

Obiter dictum (dicta). Thing(s) said by the way; opinions expressed by judges in passing, on issues not essential for the decision in the case.

Obligatio quasi ex contractu. An obligation arising out of an act or event, as if from a contract, but independently of the consent of the person bound.

Omnia praesumuntur contra spoliatorem. Every presumption is raised against a wrongdoer.

Omnia praesumuntur rite et solemniter esse acta donec probetur in contrarium. All things are presumed to have been performed with all due formalities until it is proved to the contrary.

Omnis ratihabitio retrotrahitur et mandato priori aequiparatur. Every ratification of a previous act is carried back and made equivalent to a previous command to do it.

Onus probandi. The burden of proving.

Op. cit. (opere citato). In the book referred to previously.

Orse. Otherwise.

Par delictum. Equal fault.

Parens patriae. Parent of the nation.

Pari materia. With equal substance.

Pari passu. On an equal footing; equally; in step with.

Pari ratione. By an equivalent process of reasoning.

Parol. By word of mouth, or unsealed document.

Participes criminis. Accomplices in the crime.

Pater est quem nuptiae demonstrant. He is the father whom the marriage indicates to be so.

Passim. Generally; referred to throughout the book or source in question.

Patrimonium. Beneficial ownership.

Pendente lite. While a law suit is pending.

Per. By; through; in the opinion of a judge.

Per capita. Divided equally between all the persons filling the description.

Per curiam. In the opinion of the court.

Per formam doni. Through the form of wording of the gift or deed.

Per incuriam. Through carelessness or oversight.

Per quod. By reason of which.

Per quod consortium et servitium amisit. By reason of which he has lost the benefit of her company and services.

Per quod servitium amisit. By reason of which he has lost the benefit of his service.

Per se. By itself.

Persona(e) designata(e). A person(s) specified as an individual(s), not identified as a member(s) of a class nor as fulfilling a particular qualification.

Per stirpes. According to the stocks of descent; one share for each line of descendants; where the descendants of a deceased person (however many they may be) inherit between them only the one share which the deceased would have taken if alive.

Per subsequens matrimonium. Legitimation of a child 'by subsequent marriage' of the parents.

Plene administravit. A plea by an executor 'that he has fully administered' all the assets which have come into his hands and that no assets remain out of which the plaintiff's claim could be satisfied.

Plus quam tolerabile. More than can be endured.

Post. After; mentioned in a subsequent passage or page.

Post mortem. After death.

Post nuptial. Made after marriage.

Post obit bond. Agreement or bond by which a borrower agrees to pay the lender a sum larger than the loan on or after the death of a person on whose death he expects to inherit property.

Post obitum. After the death of a specified person.

Pour autrui. On behalf of another.

Prima facie. At first sight.

Primae impressionis. Of first impression.

Pro bono publico. For the public good.

Profit a prendre. The right to enter the land of another and take part of its produce.

Pro hac vice. For this occasion.

Pro privato commodo. For private benefit.

Pro rata. In proportion.

Pro rata itineris. At the same rate per mile as was agreed for the whole journey.

Pro tanto. So far; to that extent.

Pro tempore. For the time being.

Publici juris. Of public right.

Puisne. Inferior; lower in rank; not secured by deposit of deeds; of the High Court.

Punctum temporis. Moment, or point of time.

Pour autre vie. During the life of another person.

q.v. (quod vide). Which see.

Qua. As; in the capacity of.

Quaere. Consider whether it is correct.

Quaeritur. The question is raised.

Quantum. Amount; how much.

Quantum meruit. As much as he has earned.

Quantum valebant. As much as they were worth.

Quare clausum fregit. Because he broke into the plaintiff's enclosure.

Quasi. As if; seemingly.

Quasi ex contractu. *See* OBLIGATIO.

Quatenus. How far; in so far as; since.

Quia timet. Because he fears what he will suffer in the future.

Quicquid plantatur solo solo cedit. Whatever is planted in the soil belongs to the soil.

Quid pro quo. Something for something; consideration.

Qui facit per alium facit per se. He who employs another person to do something does it himself.

Qui prior est tempore potior est jure. He who is earlier in point of time is in the stronger position in law.

Quoad. Until; as far as; as to.

Quoad hoc. As far as this matter is concerned.

Quo animo. With what intention.

Quot judices tot sententiae. There were as many different opinions as there were judges.

Quousque. Until the time when.

Ratio decidendi. The reason for a decision; the principle on which a decision is based.

Ratione domicilii. By reason of a person's domicile.

Re. In the matter of; by the thing or transaction.

Renvoi. Reference to or application of the rules of a foreign legal system in a different country's courts.

Res. Thing; affair; matter; circumstance.

Res extincta. The thing which was intended to be the subject matter of a contract but had previously been destroyed.

Res gestae. Things done; the transaction.

Res integra. A point not covered by the authority of a decided case which must therefore be decided upon principle alone.

Res inter alios acta alteri nocere non debet. A man ought not to be prejudiced by what has taken place between other persons.

Res ipsa loquitur. The thing speaks for itself, ie is evidence of negligence in the absence of an explanation by the defendant.

Res judicata. A matter on which a court has previously reached a binding decision; a matter which cannot be questioned.

Res nova. A matter which has not previously been decided.

Res nullius. Nobody's property.

Respondeat superior. A principal must answer for the acts of his subordinates.

Res sua. Something which a man believes to belong to another when it in fact is 'his own property'.

Restitutio in integrum. Restoration of a party to his original position; full restitution.

Res vendita. The article which was sold.

Rex est procurator fatuorum. The King is the protector of the simple minded.

Rigor aequitatis. The inflexibility of equity.

Sc. *See* SCILICET.

Sciens. Knowing.

Scienter. Knowingly; with knowledge of an animal's dangerous disposition.

Scienti non fit injuria. A man who is aware of the existence of a danger has no remedy if it materialises.

Scilicet. To wit; namely; that is to say.

Scintilla. A spark; trace; or moment.

Scire facias. A writ; that you cause to know.

Scriptum praedictum non est factum suum. A plea that the aforesaid document is not his deed.

Secundum formam doni. In accordance with the form of wording in the gift or deed.

Secus. It is otherwise; the legal position is different.

Sed. But.

Sed quaere. But inquire; look into the matter; consider whether the statement is correct.

Semble. It appears; apparently.

Sentit commodum et periculum rei. He both enjoys the benefit of the thing and bears the risk of its loss.

Seriatim. In series; one by one; point by point.

Serivitium. Service.

Sic. So; in such a manner; (also used to emphasise wording copied or quoted from another source: 'such was the expression used in the original source').

Sic utere tuo ut alienum non laedas. So use your own property as not to injure the property of your neighbour.

Similiter. Similarly; in like manner.

Simplex commendatio non obligat. Mere praise of goods by the seller imposes no liability upon him.

Simpliciter. Simply; merely; alone; without any further action; without qualification.

Sine animo revertendi. Without the intention of returning.

Sine die. Without a day being appointed; indefinitely.

Solatium. Consolation; relief; compensation.

Sotto volce. In an undertone.

Specificatio. The making of a new article out of the chattel of one person by the labour of another.

Spes successionis. The hope of inheriting property on the death of another.

Spondes peritiam artis. If skill is inherent in your profession, you guarantee that you will display it.

Stare decisis. To stand by what has been dedided.

Status quo (ante). The previous position; the position in which things were before; unchanged position.

Stet. Let it stand; do not delete.

Stricto sensu. In the strict sense.

Sub colore officii. Under pretext of someone's official position.

Sub modo. Within limits; to a limited extent.

Sub nom. (sub nomine). Under the name of.

Sub silentio. In silence.

Sub tit. (sub titulo). Under the title of.

Suggestio falsi. The suggestion of something which is untrue.

Sui generis. Of its own special kind; unique.

Sui juris. Of his own right; possessed of full legal capacity.

Sup. *See* SUPRA.

Suppressio veri. The suppression of the truth.

Supra. (Sup.) Above; referred to higher up the page; previously.

Talis qualis. Such as it is.

Tam ... quam. As well ... as.

Toties quoties. As often as occasion shall require; as often as something happens.

Transit in rem judicatam. A right of action merges in the judgment recovered upon it.

Turpis causa. Immoral conduct which constitutes the subject matter of an action.

Uberrima fides. Most abundant good faith.

Ubi jus ibi remedium. Where there is a legally recognised right there is also a remedy.

Ubi supra. In the passage or reference mentioned previously.

Ultimus heres. The ultimate heir who is last in order of priority of those who may be entitled to claim the estate of an intestate.

Ultra vires. Outside the powers recognised by law as belonging to the person or body in question.

Uno flatu. With one breath; at the same moment.

Ut res magis valeat quam pereat. Words must be construed so as to support the validity of the contract rather than to destroy it.

v. (versus). Against.

Verba fortius accipiuntur contra proferentem. Ambiguous wording is construed adversely against the party who introduced it into the document.

Vera copula. True sexual unity.

Verbatim. Word by word; exactly; word for word.

Vice versa. The other way round; in turn.

Vide. See.

Vi et armis (et contra pacem domini regis). By force of arms (and in breach of the King's peace).

Vigilantibus et non dormientibus jura subveniunt (or jus succurrit). The law(s) assist(s) those who are vigilant, not those who doze over their rights.

Vinculum juris. Legal tie; that which binds the parties with mutual obligations.

Virgo intacta. A virgin with hymen intact.

Virtute officii. By virtue of a person's official position.

Vis-a-vis. Face to face; opposite to.

Vis major. Irresistible force.

Viva voce. Orally; oral examination.

Viz. (videlicet). Namely; that is to say.

Voir dire. Examination of a witness before he gives evidence, to ascertain whether he is competent to tell the truth on oath; trial within a trial.

Volens. Willing.

Volenti non fit injuria. In law no wrong is done to a man who consents to undergo it.

Index

Law Update 2000

Law Update 2001 edition – due March 2001

n annual review of the most recent developments in specific legal subject eas, useful for law students at degree and professional levels, others with law ements in their courses and also practitioners seeking a quick update.

ublished around March every year, the Law Update summarises the major gal developments during the course of the previous year. In conjunction with ld Bailey Press textbooks it gives the student a significant advantage when vising for examinations.

ontents

dministrative Law • Civil and Criminal Procedure • Company Law • Conflict Laws • Constitutional Law • Contract Law • Conveyancing • Criminal Law Criminology • English Legal System • Equity and Trusts • European Union aw • Evidence • Family Law • Jurisprudence • Land Law • Law of ternational Trade • Public International Law • Revenue Law • Succession • ort

or further information on contents, please contact:

ail Order
ld Bailey Press
)0 Greyhound Road
ondon
14 9RY
nited Kingdom

elephone No: 00 44 (0) 20 7385 3377
ax No: 00 44 (0) 20 7381 3377

BN 1 85836 347 0
oft cover 246 x 175 mm
)2 pages £9.95
ublished March 2000

Old Bailey Press

The Old Bailey Press integrated student library is planned and written to help you at every stage of your studies. Each of our range of Textbooks, Casebooks, Revision WorkBooks and Statutes are all designed to work together and are regularly revised and updated.

We are also able to offer you Suggested Solutions which provide you with past examination questions and solutions for most of the subject areas listed below.

You can buy Old Bailey Press books from your University Bookshop or your local Bookshop, or in case of difficulty, order direct using this form.

Here is the selection of modules covered by our series:

Administrative Law; Commercial Law; Company Law (no Single Paper 1997); Conflict of Laws (no Suggested Solutions Pack); Constitutional Law: The Machinery of Government; Obligations: Contract Law; Conveyancing (no Revision Workbook); Criminology (Sourcebook in place of a Casebook or Revision WorkBook); Criminal Law; English Legal System; Equity and Trusts; Law of The European Union; Evidence; Family Law; Jurisprudence: The Philosophy of Law (Sourcebook in place of a Casebook); Land: The Law of Real Property; Law of International Trade; Legal Skills and System (Textbook only); Public International Law; Revenue Law (no Casebook); Succession: The Law of Wills and Estates; Obligations: The Law of Tort.

Mail order prices:

Textbook £11.95

Casebook £9.95

Revision WorkBook £7.95

Statutes £9.95

Suggested Solutions Pack (1991–1995) £6.95

Single Paper 1996 £3.00

Single Paper 1997 £3.00

To complete your order, please fill in the form below:

Module	Books required	Quantity	Price	Cost
		Postage		
		TOTAL		

For Europe, add 15% postage and packing (£20 maximum).
For the rest of the world, add 40% for airmail.

ORDERING

By telephone to Mail Order at 020 7385 3377, with your credit card to hand.

By fax to 020 7381 3377 (giving your credit card details).

By post to:

Old Bailey Press, 200 Greyhound Road, London W14 9RY.

When ordering by post, please enclose full payment by cheque or banker's draft, or complete the credit card details below.

We aim to despatch your books within 3 working days of receiving your order.

Name

Address

Postcode   Telephone

Total value of order, including postage: £

I enclose a cheque/banker's draft for the above sum, or

charge my   ☐ Access/Mastercard   ☐ Visa   ☐ American Express
Card number

☐☐☐☐ ☐☐☐☐ ☐☐☐☐ ☐☐☐☐

Expiry date   ☐☐☐☐

Signature: ....Date: ....